AF251131

THE
BERNWARD
GOSPELS

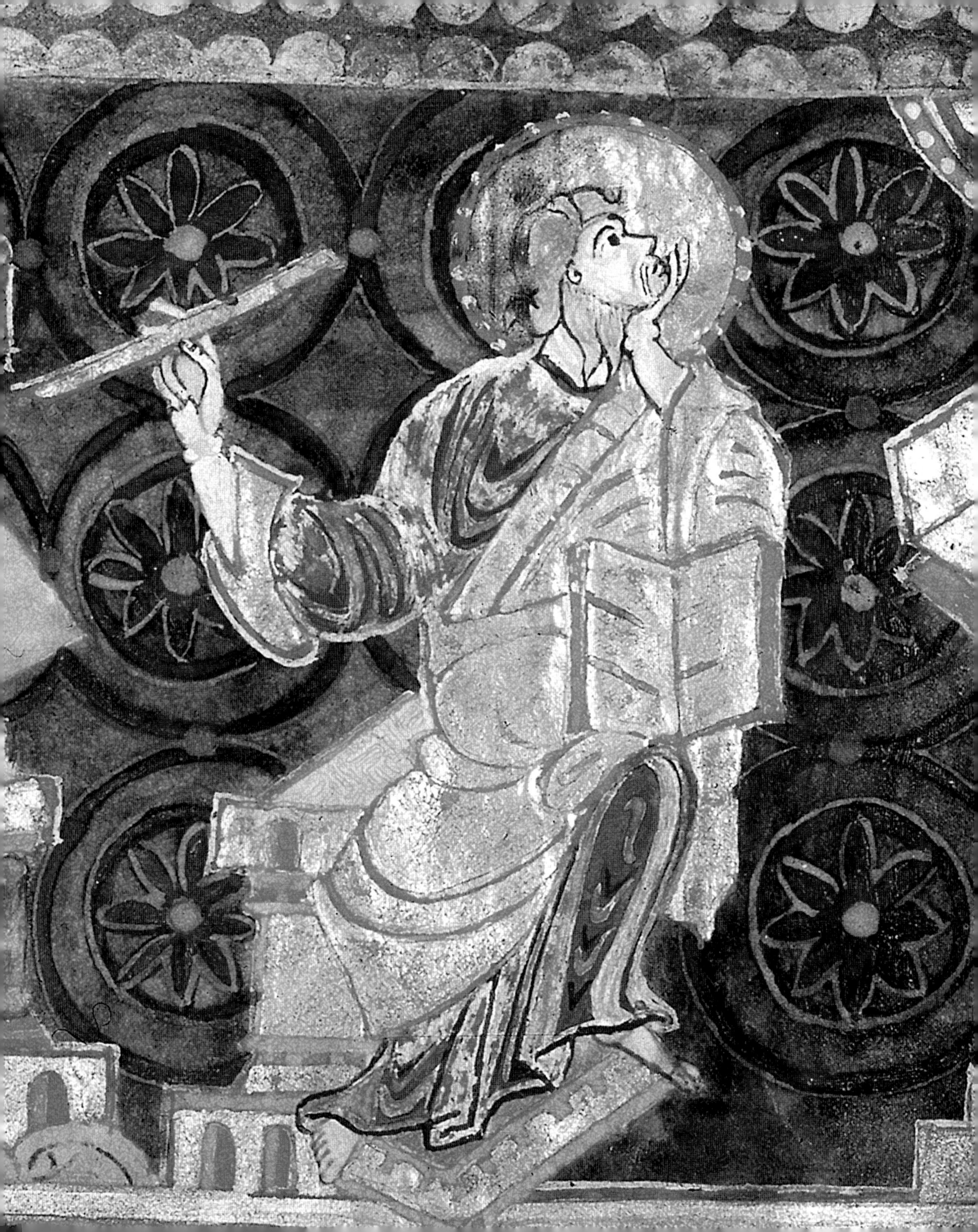

JENNIFER P. KINGSLEY

THE BERNWARD GOSPELS

ART, MEMORY, AND THE EPISCOPATE
IN MEDIEVAL GERMANY

THE PENNSYLVANIA STATE UNIVERSITY PRESS

UNIVERSITY PARK, PENNSYLVANIA

Publication of this book has been supported by the International Center of
Medieval Art and the Samuel H. Kress Foundation. This book was also
published with the generous assistance of a Book Subvention Award
from the Medieval Academy of America.

Library of Congress Cataloging-in-Publication Data

Kingsley, Jennifer P., 1978– , author.
The Bernward Gospels : art, memory, and the episcopate
in medieval Germany / Jennifer P. Kingsley.
p.   cm
Summary: "An interpretive study of the pictorial program of the
Ottonian Bernward Gospels. Examines how the manuscript conditioned
contemporary and future viewers to remember early medieval
Bishop Bernward of Hildesheim"—Provided by publisher.
Includes bibliographical references and index.
ISBN 978-0-271-06079-8 (cloth : alk. paper)
1. Bernward Gospels—Illustrations. 2. Bernward, Bishop of Hildesheim,
approximately 960–1022. 3. Illumination of books and manuscripts,
Medieval—Germany—Hildesheim. 4. Illumination of books and manuscripts,
Ottonian—Germany—Hildesheim. 5. Evangeliaries—Germany—Hildesheim—
Illustrations. 6. Bible. Gospels—Illustrations. 7. Catholic Church—
Liturgy—Texts—Illustrations. 8. Christian art and symbolism—Germany—
Hildesheim—Medieval, 500–1500. 9. Diözesan-Museum Hildesheim. I. Title.

ND3359.B47K56 2014
745.6'70943595—dc23
2013026637

The Pennsylvania State University Press is a member of the
Association of American University Presses.

It is the policy of The Pennsylvania State University Press to use acid-free
paper. Publications on uncoated stock satisfy the minimum requirements
of American National Standard for Information Sciences—Permanence of
Paper for Printed Library Material, ANSI Z39.48–1992.

Frontispiece: Hildesheim, Dom- und Diözesanmuseum,
Domschatz 18 (Bernward Gospels), fol. 175v (detail), *Portrait of
John*. Courtesy Dom- und Diözesanmuseum, Hildesheim.

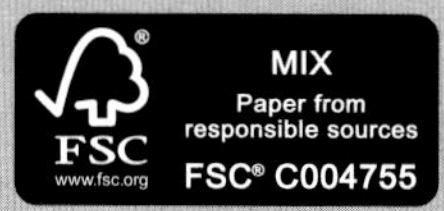

CONTENTS

ILLUSTRATIONS

All images courtesy Dom- und Diözesanmuseum, Hildesheim, unless otherwise noted.

COLOR PLATES
(following page 64)

1. Hildesheim, Dom- und Diözesanmuseum, Domschatz [DS] 18 (Bernward Gospels), front cover
2. DS 18 (Bernward Gospels), fol. 16v, dedication: Bishop Bernward
3. DS 18 (Bernward Gospels), fol. 17r, dedication: Mary and Christ
4. DS 18 (Bernward Gospels), fol. 18r, *Nativity/ Adoration*
5. DS 18 (Bernward Gospels), fol. 18v, *Calling of the Evangelist Matthew* and *Dinner at the House of Levi*
6. DS 18 (Bernward Gospels), fol. 19r, *Portrait of Matthew*
7. DS 18 (Bernward Gospels), fol. 75r, *John the Baptist Preaching* and *Christ Calling the Apostles*
8. DS 18 (Bernward Gospels), fol. 75v, *Noli me tangere* and *Peter Charging Mark to Write the Gospels*
9. DS 18 (Bernward Gospels), fol. 76r, *Portrait of Mark*
10. DS 18 (Bernward Gospels), fol. 111r, *Annunciation to Zacharias* and *Zacharias Leaving the Temple*
11. DS 18 (Bernward Gospels), fol. 111v, *Visitation* and *Naming of John the Baptist*
12. DS 18 (Bernward Gospels), fol. 118r, *Last Supper* and *Judas with the High Priests*
13. DS 18 (Bernward Gospels), fol. 118v, *Heavenly Crucifixion* and *Portrait of Luke*
14. DS 18 (Bernward Gospels), fol. 174r, *Christ in Majesty*
15. DS 18 (Bernward Gospels), fol. 174v, *Baptism of Christ* and *Raising of Lazarus*
16. DS 18 (Bernward Gospels), fol. 175r, *Entry into Jerusalem* and *Crucifixion*
17. DS 18 (Bernward Gospels), fol. 175v, *Ascension* and *Portrait of John*
18. DS 18 (Bernward Gospels), back cover

FIGURES

1. DS 61 (Bernward Bible), early eleventh century, fol. 1r   *2*
2. Codicology of illustrated quires in the Bernward Gospels. Image: author   *5*
3. DS 18 (Bernward Gospels), fol. 15r, Matthew's angel as the Evangelist   *8*
4. DS 18 (Bernward Gospels), fols. 16v–17r, dedication   *16*
5. Baltimore, The Walters Art Museum, W7, mid–eleventh century, fol. 9v. Photo © 2014 The Walters Art Museum, used under a Creative Commons

ACKNOWLEDGMENTS

My interest in the Bernward Gospels began at The Johns Hopkins University and my foremost thanks are due to that institution and its History of Art Department, which provided support throughout my doctoral studies. I owe Herbert Kessler a particularly deep debt of gratitude for his mentorship, continued insight, and ongoing encouragement. I must also thank Henry Maguire for offering necessary advice and support at every stage of this project. At Penn State Press, I am most grateful to Eleanor Goodman for guiding me through the publication process. I also wish to thank the Press as a whole for its concerted effort to produce this book and am delighted to acknowledge the two readers engaged by the Press, Adam Cohen and Lawrence Nees, for their careful review of my study and thoughtful comments.

This project would not have been possible without the financial support of many institutions along the way and the help of those who worked there. In Germany, I continue to rely heavily on the good will of Michael Brandt, Claudia Höhl, and especially Gerhard Lutz of the Dom and Diözesanmuseum in Hildesheim. They have permitted me to consult Bernward's manuscripts, provided beautiful reproductions, and facilitated every stage of my research in Hildesheim. I am also grateful to the Medieval Academy of America, the International Center for Medieval Art, and the Andrew W. Mellon Foundation for their support at various stages.

Over the years that I have been studying and researching Ottonian art, I have benefitted from contact with a wide range of colleagues. Unfortunately, space does not permit me to detail their individual contributions here, but they know who they are, and I thank them for their generous engagement with my work and for our fruitful discussions.

I dedicate this work to my family.

INTRODUCTION

An early eleventh-century painting assimilates Bishop Bernward of Hildesheim to John the Evangelist, Moses, and Jerome (DS 61, fol. 1r; fig. 1).[1] The miniature introduces the only known illustrated Bible made for an Ottonian patron and layers traditional motifs in ways that produce a startling image. A large golden cross dominates the painting; it is flanked by two individuals, a man on the left, and a woman on the right. The cross's monumental size and the picture's composition invite comparison with Crucifixion imagery and suggest that the two figures are to be identified as the Virgin Mary and John the Evangelist. Yet the cross appears inside a church, and its form is that of a work of art, an elaborately wrought processional cross. The placement of the two figures, John on the left and Mary on the right, reverses the usual arrangement, while their pose draws on donation imagery. John presents a book into which he writes the opening words of Genesis: "in principio creavit Deus coelum et terram." Mary stands behind a curtain and gestures her acceptance of that gift. These details suggest that John serves as a stand-in for the episcopal patron, Bernward, who offers his Bible to the saint, making the image a kind of donor portrait. The inscribed text adds a further complication. While the first two words of the inscription echo the beginning of John's gospel, "in principio erat verbum," the complete phrase assimilates John and the patron either to a strangely youthful Moses, the author of Genesis, or to Jerome, the translator of the Bible.[2]

It is probable that a patron as well versed in the conventions of pictorial imagery as Bernward would have considered the male figure to represent his own image and all three models—John, Moses, and Jerome—simultaneously. There are many medieval precedents for comparing

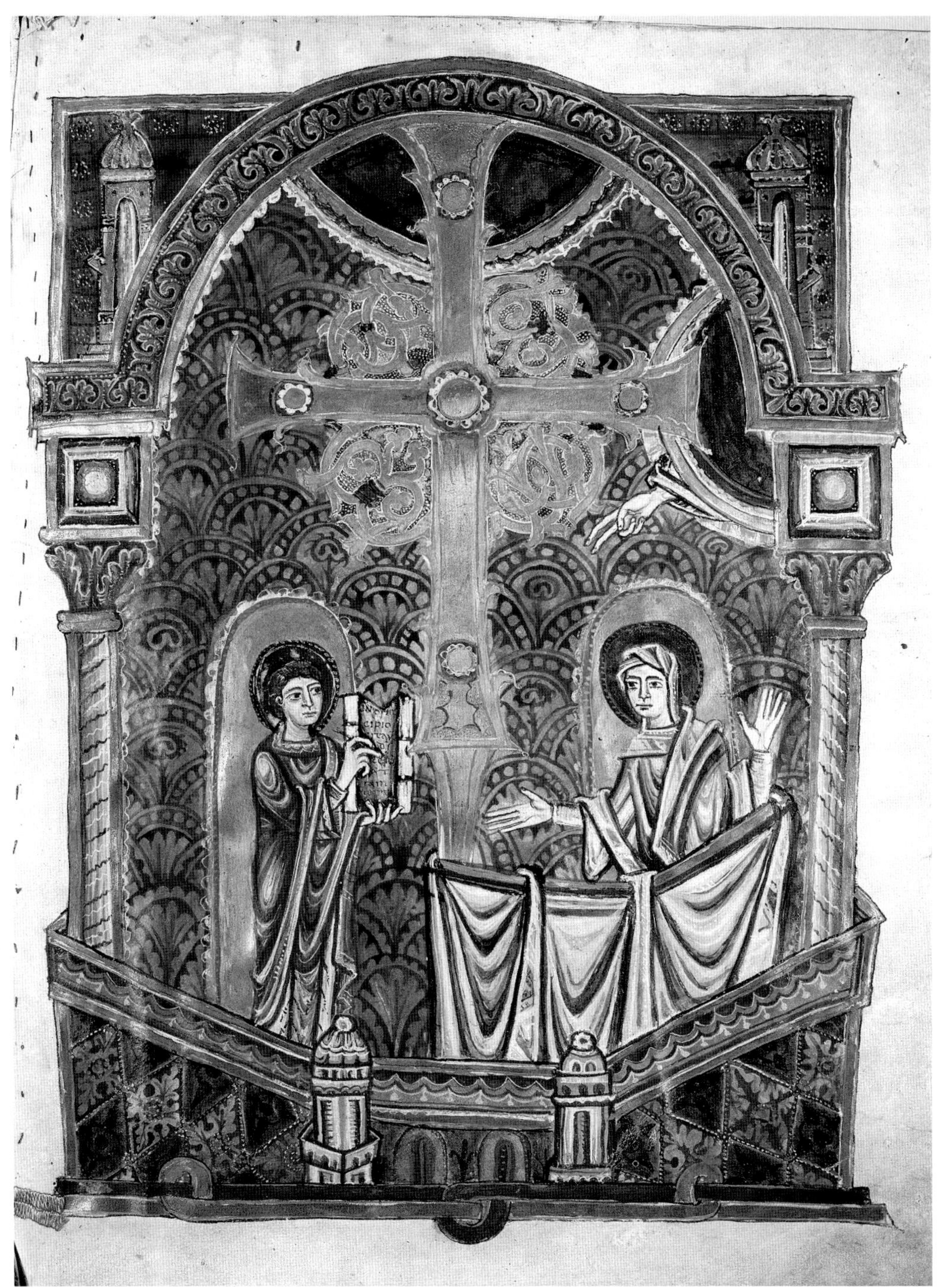

FIGURE 1 Hildesheim, Dom- und Diözesanmuseum, Domschatz 61 (Bernward Bible), early eleventh
century, fol. 1r

an individual patron to a series of exemplars of Christian virtue.[3] What is unusual in this painting, however, is both the degree to which the miniature conflates multiple types of scenes and the specific combination of models it selects. These scenes (the Crucifixion and a donation) and these models (John, Moses, and Jerome) are not commonly associated in medieval culture. Such complicated layering typifies Bernward's artistic commissions, from the manuscripts to the monumental works for which he is still best known: doors and a column that represent the most complex bronze-casting project since antiquity. Although these first gained fame as examples of the medieval response to classical art and of Bernward's interest in ancient Rome (in connection with the notion of an Ottonian imperial *renovatio* focused on continuing the Roman Empire), more recent research has drawn attention to the theological ideas that inform Bernward's choice of medium.[4]

The painting's content similarly underscores the extent to which the bishop's artistic patronage engaged sophisticated theological questions; it also makes somewhat problematic the picture of Bernward as a prelate whose career primarily exemplifies the administrative, jurisdictional, or secular features of the early medieval episcopate.[5] Certainly Bernward was the grandson of a count palatine in Saxony who began his service in the imperial chapel as a notary.[6] Quickly winning favor at court, Bernward became tutor to the future Emperor Otto III before being awarded, in 993, what was in essence a family bishopric.[7] He proved an able administrator, asserting episcopal control over both diocesan property and tithes, building defensive walls around the town, and exercising a rare privilege to mint coins.[8]

Complicating the portrait of a bishop largely engaged by what we might term secular affairs, however, is evidence of Bernward's interest in the monastic reforms that had been emanating from Gorze and Trier since the early tenth century.[9] Bernward's medieval biographers revise our image even further. In a text compiled in the twelfth century, they render the bishop as a man absorbed by the *artes mechanicae*, the "mechanical arts" of the medieval craftsman:

> And although he embraced ardently all liberal sciences with the fire of his vivacious genius, he also found time for the study of those less serious arts that are called mechanical. His handwriting was excellent, his painting accomplished. He excelled also in the art of casting metal and of setting precious stones, and in architecture, as afterward became evident in the many structures he built and adorned sumptuously. . . . Painting and sculpture and casting and goldsmith work and whatever fine craft he was able to think of, he never suffered to be neglected. His interest went so far that he did not let pass by unnoticed whatever rare and beautiful piece he could find among those vessels from overseas and from Scotland, which were being brought as gifts to the royal majesty. . . . He attracted gifted boys to him and to the court and spent much time with them urging them to acquire by practice whatever was most needful in any art. . . . He also taught himself the art of laying mosaic floors and how to make bricks and tiles. . . .[10]

Only the still more mythical stature of Abbot Suger of Saint Denis (1081–1151) rivals this image of a courtier bishop acting as a major patron, collector, and skilled artisan.[11]

Such varied pictures of Bernward illustrate the extent to which bishops of the early Middle Ages were pulled continuously in manifold directions.[12] Bernward's painted portrait suggests, however, that even the broad range of activities and responsibilities presented by the textual record fails to capture the full extent of how individual prelates themselves constructed their roles in early medieval society, how they manifested their presence, expressed their authority, and depicted their person.[13] By manipulating pictorial conventions of representation, the portrait in Bernward's Bible aims at conveying something of the bishop as both an individual and an office.[14] Its layering of highly varied personas—Moses, the prophet and leader who brought God's Law to the people of Israel; Jerome, the ascetic scholar who translated the Bible; and John the Evangelist, the deified theologian venerated in the Middle Ages for his visionary insight—develops a striking image of Bernward as a leader, scholar, and theologian. The painting consequently raises critical questions about the image of the Ottonian episcopacy. How did the early medieval bishop frame his varied responsibilities and actions? How did he portray himself and his office to the court, to his peers, to his flock, to God? What are the implications of Bernward's self-fashioning— by visual means—for our understanding of the early medieval episcopate?[15]

Forming one of the most important networks for cultural production and exchange during the tenth and eleventh centuries, Ottonian prelates seem especially preoccupied with projecting themselves into contemporary visual culture.[16] Bernward himself has left such a clear personal stamp on the (mainly) liturgical objects produced under his direction that these have been grouped under the term "Bernwardian art."[17] Among these celebrated works, one stands out in particular: the manuscript known to German scholars as the "most precious Gospels" of Bernward of Hildesheim (DS 18). Although the codex has been the subject of art-historical inquiry since the nineteenth century, many questions remain about its illustrations, including the meaning of its miniatures both individually and as parts of a program.[18] This study argues that the Bernward Gospels pictorial cycle aimed to condition how contemporary and future viewers would understand the bishop's role in Hildesheim. It thereby offers a unique witness to the self-presentation of this prominent representative of the Ottonian episcopacy.

THE CODEX

The Bernward Gospels measures approximately 280 × 200 mm and consists of 234 folios of vellum bound into thirty-three quires.[19] Consistent peculiarities in the script help attribute the book's writing to a single scribe working in Hildesheim from about 990 to 1020.[20] The text consists of the gospels of Matthew, Mark, Luke, and John, with the preliminary matter proper to each (prefaces and chapter lists).[21] At the beginning of the book (fols. 3v–9r) appear three out of the four standard Jerome prefaces, excluding the letter to Eusebius that starts "Ammonius quidem." The number and order of these prefaces are shared by several Saxon manuscripts, of which some are attributed to Hildesheim and others to the imperial abbey of Corvey.[22] A list of pericopes for the use of

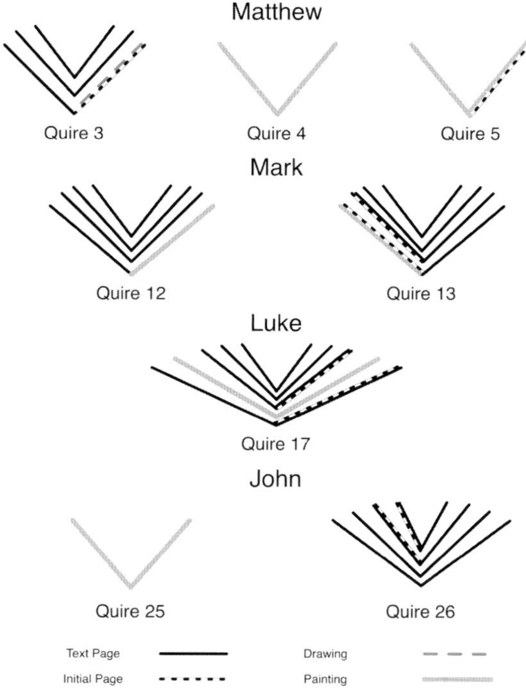

FIGURE 2 Codicology of illustrated quires in the Bernward Gospels

Saint Michael's monks concludes the work (fols. 218v–231r); it notes the readings for the main feasts of the liturgical year. The pericopes' inclusion suggests the manuscript's potential function as a service book.[23]

With its peculiar combination of visual sophistication and naïveté, full of dramatically gesturing figures and covered in the saturated colors of densely ornamented surfaces, the Bernward Gospels is the most extensively decorated of the manuscripts produced for Bernward. Its decoration begins with a minium drawing that depicts Matthew as his symbol, the angel; a dedicatory painting follows. The codex also includes four author portraits of the evangelists, four title pages featuring elegant lines of Roman capitals, and one to two densely ornamented incipit pages per gospel—relatively standard fare for gospel books. More idiosyncratic are the twenty-four miniatures inserted into the codex that illustrate scenes from the New Testament.[24] The pictures are organized into four groups, each designed to introduce one of the gospels, yet their presence frequently disrupts the physical structure of the codex.

An analysis of the manuscript's codicology indicates the following collation: 1^2, 2^8, 3^6, 4–5^2, 6–15^8, 16–17^{10}, 18–20^8, 21^6, 22–24^8, 25^2, 26–32^8, 33^2 (see fig. 2 and appendix). Irregularities occur in all of the quires that contain paintings. The miniatures disturb the organization of the text throughout the manuscript and clearly created a challenge for the manuscript's binder. Particularly infelicitous is the arrangement of the seventeenth, twenty-fifth, and twenty-sixth quires, which contain illustrations for the gospels of Luke and John, respectively.

The New Testament scenes in Luke form part of the seventeenth quire; these appear on the recto and verso of the second bifolium, marked today with the numbers 111 and 118. The first illuminated folio (fol. 111) interrupts the gospel's chapter list (fols. 110 and 112–116), while a second group of pictures (on fol. 118, the other half of the bifolium) appears between the gospel's incipit page and illuminated initial (fols. 117 and 119, respectively). The paintings' location thus leaves the two sets of pictures separate from each other even though they are painted on the same piece of vellum. It also means that the gospel text is interrupted. The problem stems from the attempt to add a painted bifolium into the gospel of Luke at a relatively logical point in the text— somewhere between the prefatory material and the main text—where the scribe had not allowed for it with any quire break.

The binder faced similar difficulties with the gospel of John. He responded by inserting the bifolium of figural scenes as an independent codicological unit that now forms the twenty-fifth quire (fols. 174–175). Consequently, all these miniatures appear in uninterrupted sequence. Yet they mark the shift from the gospel of Luke to that of John, appearing where we would expect to find the gospel's prologue; this prologue actually starts on the following, twenty-sixth, quire (fol. 176r–v). The title page (fol. 178v) and illuminated incipit (fol. 179r) also form part of that quire. They follow the prologue to John and are thus separate from the rest of the gospel's decoration. Again the binder seems to have worked unsuccessfully to organize a sequence as close as possible to a decorative scheme found in many Saxon gospel books, one that consists of an evangelist's portrait followed by a title page and illuminated incipit. This sequence is disrupted because of the need to accommodate the additional historiated bifolia.

Writing about the Bernward Gospels in 1909, Hans Heinz Josten assumed its codicological irregularities occurred during a later rebinding, while more recently Rainer Kahsnitz has attributed them to the first binding, citing the Hildesheim scriptorium's inexperience with elaborate picture cycles as their cause.[25] Indeed there is evidence from the book covers of a twelfth-century intervention in the binding of the Bernward Gospels.[26] Yet several aspects of the codex's physical appearance suggest that the plans for the Bernward Gospels changed during the course of its production, allowing it to expand from a modestly decorated work into a more ambitious and eclectically illustrated codex filled with unusual iconography.

Codicological irregularities, likely already present in the first binding of the leaves, are due to a decision to expand the pictorial program at some point during production. If we remove the inserted painted bifolia from consideration and examine only the quires that include both decorated pages and plain text, the layout would allow for two to three sides of paintings between each gospel's prefatory material and main text. This arrangement would have accommodated at least an author portrait and one to two title pages, which is consistent with the arrangement in other manuscripts produced at Hildesheim, such as the Guntbald Gospels (Hildesheim, DS 33), ca. 1011, and the Hezilo Codex (DS 34), variously dated to the late tenth or early eleventh centuries; it would also agree with the design of a group of closely related gospels produced in Corvey.[27] In this hypothetical layout, the decoration for Matthew, Mark, and Luke would start in each case at the end of a quire (quires 3, 12, and 17; fols. 15, 75, and 117), while the paintings for Luke would still appear within quire 17 (fol. 117v). Quire 17 would have the more usual (for the Bernward Gospels) eight leaves, or four bifolia, instead of the current ten.

Because of the organization of the textual quires, adding the painted bifolia to the codex allows for only two possible binding schemes. The first option involves gathering the narrative scenes into a single quire, which would, however, separate these paintings from the author portraits and decorated text pages. The second option requires the bifolia to be inserted as close as possible to the prefatory material of each gospel, even where it means interrupting the text. The placement of the illustrations for the gospel of Mark suggests that the scriptorium chose the second solution and adopted it before completing the miniatures but after laying out the text. The miniatures in Mark appear not on independent bifolia but as an integral part of quires 12 and 13; each painted leaf therein is one part of a bifolium that has text on its other part and, as with the bifolia inserts, the paintings appear in the following sequence: first narrative scenes, then an author portrait, and finally, decorated title pages.

What of the possibility that the codicological irregularities stem from the scriptorium's inexperience working with narrative picture cycles? The scribe may have been using a model that had only limited decoration, and, tasked with incorporating a full pictorial program into the Bernward Gospels, may not have known how to modify the codex's layout to accommodate more paintings. Yet before making the Bernward Gospels, the Hildesheim scriptorium had already produced the Guntbald Gospels in a very regular layout of quires of eight leaves that allowed five sides to illustrate each gospel; in its present irregular arrangement, the Bernward Gospels also has five to six sides available to illuminate each gospel. If the Bernward Gospels had been intended to carry an extensive pictorial cycle, a suitable model for its current appearance already existed in Hildesheim.

The strongest evidence that the plans for the pictorial program evolved during the manuscript's production is the full-page drawing that currently opens the pictorial cycle in Matthew (fol. 15r; fig. 3). The picture conflates the evangelist Matthew with his symbol and occupies a shorter but wider pictorial field than the other illustrations of the manuscript; unlike those, it also lacks a frame. The drawing's composition differs substantially from the painted portraits

of the evangelists (fols. 19r, 76r, 118v, and 178v; plates 6, 9, 13, and 17). Each of these is portrayed in the lower half of a divided pictorial field. The drawing's style is both looser and more three-dimensional than that of the paintings, particularly in the modeling of drapery and the depiction of objects that recede in space. It clearly belongs to a different decorative scheme than the one ultimately chosen for the Bernward Gospels.[28]

If the design of the Bernward Gospels changed during its making, it evolved from a modest and somewhat conventional plan, modeled in large part on manuscripts produced in the imperial abbey of Corvey, into a fully illustrated New Testament cycle drawing on a wide variety of sources.[29] The designer at that stage incorporated contemporary iconography and ornament that originated in diverse places ranging from medieval Wessex to Constantinople. To date, the account of the sources for the miniatures has tended to treat examples of copying in the manuscript as the passive transmission of models.[30] Yet the Bernward Gospels displays several examples of unique iconography, some of which, such as the theologically complex depiction of the Ascension that shows Christ literally disappearing from view (fol. 175v; plate 17), first appear in the tenth century and/or constitute the earliest example of that particular iconography in Ottonian art.[31] This suggests the presence of an active interest in contemporary developments in both art and theology. The most probable impetus for that interest is the patron, Bernward. He is the one historical person securely connected to the manuscript who was demonstrably familiar with the Roman, Anglo-Saxon, and Byzantine art that so profoundly influenced the Bernward Gospels pictures.[32]

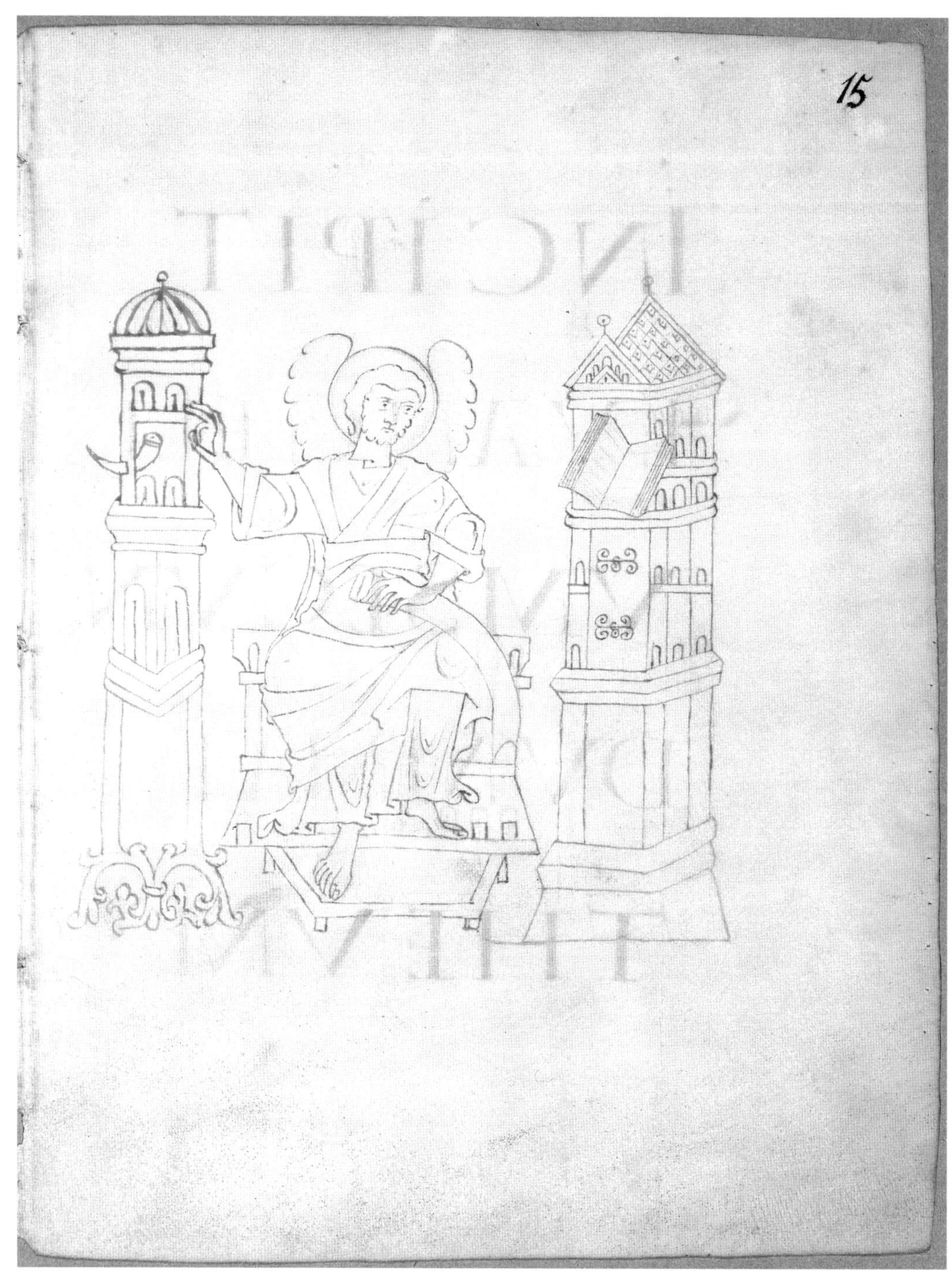

FIGURE 3   Hildesheim, Dom- und Diözesanmuseum,
Domschatz 18 (Bernward Gospels), fol. 15r, Matthew's
angel as the Evangelist

The patron undoubtedly played a formative role in the book's design.[33] From the disappearing Christ inside the manuscript to the standing Virgin carrying a palm on the back cover, a number of iconographic motifs in the manuscript stem from sources to which a painter in Hildesheim was unlikely to have had access. Iconography is something that would be relatively easy for a patron to communicate to an artist. In contrast, the ornament and style of the Bernward Gospels derive primarily from Carolingian manuscripts that the weight of the evidence suggests were physically present in Hildesheim, from codices produced in Corvey that seem to have passed through Hildesheim, and from Byzantine silks that were at that time part of the cathedral's treasury. All of these would have been locally available to the artist(s) as models.[34]

Moreover, the manuscript's pictorial program offers no one-to-one relationship between the manuscript's illuminations, the gospel text, or specific exegetical commentary on the gospels. For example, although Mark describes Christ's Ascension in detail, it is depicted as the concluding picture in the book of John (fol. 175v; plate 17), and although John is the singular source for the so-called Noli me tangere, that scene illustrates the gospel of Mark (fol. 75v; plate 8). The Crucifixion appears twice in the manuscript, both in the gospel of John (fol. 175r; plate 16) and above the portrait of the evangelist Luke (fol. 118v; plate 13). The cycle also presents scenes out of their narrative sequence. Together, these elements suggest idiosyncratic choices made to develop particular themes, themes that over and over again engage complicated theological questions, especially about the nature of Christ and man's perception of that nature. What are the themes of the pictorial program, and what may have prompted their introduction into the Bernward Gospels?

The manuscript was produced for the community of Saint Michael's Abbey, located just outside the town walls of Hildesheim, about five hundred meters north of the cathedral.[35] Verses in Bernward's own hand record the donation (fol. 231v):

> I, Bernward, had this codex written
> and, ordering that my wealth be added
> above, as you see
> I had surrendered [it] to Saint Michael,
> beloved of the Lord
> Let there be a curse of God on anyone who
> takes it from him.[36]

Although the complex would be completed under the bishop's successor, Godehard, Bernward consecrated the monastic church's crypt altar in September 1015; he designated the same area as the site for his burial. Bernward also dedicated the unfinished building shortly before his death in 1022. The Bernward Gospels may have been presented to the monks at the occasion of one of these consecrations, and its expanded program was probably conceived around 1015.[37]

Indeed, the book served as one of the bishop's founding gifts to the monastery, a project and bequest Bernward remembers in a document from November 1019 as a vivid struggle against time.

> The succoring mercy of God finds its expression in the human longing for grace, and adapts itself to the individual person. If we

look for examples of this we immediately find a divine answer: after Adam's fall and the long age of exile Abraham believed the Lord, and precisely that was counted to him for righteousness. By contrast, Moses, who gave the Law, became a leader and teacher of the people of Israel both by God's outreaching grace and through his own merits. And Elijah, worker of miracles, gave evidence of a similar holiness. . . . Clear as daylight is the evidence of the holy Solomon, who after building the temple of God, cleansed himself in accordance with the laws of his religion and brought himself closer to God by participating in cultic mysteries, he who was found to be without equal as a penitent. To all of them God revealed the special nature of their merits through their respective manner of deeds, so that in time they will remain different from all others, always, by virtue of merit and deed, and in eternity they will be equal to the angels.

In view of this I, Bernward, appointed bishop by God's election and not of my own merit, have long given thought to how I, learned court clerk, tutor and keeper of documents for Emperor Otto III of blessed memory, might be deserving of heaven, by what architecture of merit, by what achievement[. . . .]

Then, having ascended the throne of the church of Bennopolis, I wanted to carry out in deed that which I had long been planning in my heart, that is, I wanted to prepare a felicitous memorial to my name as someone who had built churches, instituted the service of God in them and donated all his possessions to the Lord. Now God's decrees

are hidden but always just. I therefore began, with the joyous consent of the faithful, to construct a new house of God, and in so doing both fulfilled my own promise and served the best interests of Christendom, to the praise and glory of the name of the Lord, by settling monks there who were beloved of God. However, when the foundations of the building had been laid, and the outlines of the individual rooms were already visible, I was stricken with fever and was ill for five years[. . . .] But since nothing on earth occurs without a reason, I believe and trust that the Lord was correcting me with his chastisements, yet he did not deliver me unto death, and thus prevented the work of my hope from being interrupted by my absence. I caused monks to occupy this place, which was dedicated to God, the holy cross, the ever pure Virgin Mary and the holy archangel Michael. I united them here according to the principle that, being removed from the activity of this world as laid down in the rule of monks, they might be free of all hindrances of worldly duties. Therefore, with the consent of the Lord and Emperor Henry and of my superior, the archbishop, I gave away everything I had inherited or acquired by my private means in worldly goods, estates, farms, lands, fields, pastures, waters, forests, meadows, churches, relics, books, gold, and silver, and whatever else there might be. Aside from what I bequeathed to the altar of the blessed Mary in the cathedral in the form of golden crowns, chalices, candlesticks, vestments and other ornaments, I made over everything by the hand of my testamentary guardian to God and his saints for the use and benefit of the brothers. I have bequeathed it for the salvation of my aforementioned Lords and Emperors, of myself and my successors, as well as of all those from whom I have acquired inheritances, so that the servants of Christ, free of all earthly duties, secure in the protection of my successors, may enjoy peaceful times and devote themselves to the life of pious contemplation for the salvation of all men.[38]

It is tempting to read in this text something personal about Bernward's artistic projects during the period from the laying of the abbey's foundation in 1010 through the probable duration of his illness (1013–18).[39] The bishop's account suggests a patron suffering for years from an inexplicable and recurrent disease who is anticipating his own death, worrying about his sins and driven to show himself worthy of salvation.

Whether or not Bernward's illness directly influenced the decoration of the Bernward Gospels, his testament goes further than those of other founders in its religious aspirations, and many of its themes—especially the evocation of models who have realized divine election as saints by means of their own merit—are reflected in the codex's program. The document also evokes medieval ideas about gift-giving *pro anima* (for the soul) with its related expectations for intercessory prayers and liturgical commemoration.[40] That process was structured around the idea that mankind might gain eternal rewards by making offerings to the divine. The gift *pro anima* is thus fundamentally preoccupied with the donor's salvation, and it is surely no accident that the only Christological miracle depicted in the Bernward Gospels is the Raising of Lazarus

(fol. 174v; plate 15), a story that functioned in medieval commentary as a *topos* for Christ's Resurrection and therefore an eschatological promise that the dead would rise again in their flesh to be judged by God at the end of time.[41]

The success of the medieval gift *pro anima* and its salvific power depended on the earthly recipients' commemoration of the donor and the capacity of the object to carry his memory even after death.[42] To that purpose, the Bernward Gospels engages the praxis of *memoria*, the multivalent medieval term for memory that suggests equally the cognitive processes of mnemotechnics and the ritual habits of commemorative practices.[43] The codex draws on the cognitive and ritual processes of both in order to decorate an object of particular symbolic power: the gospels, displayed on the altar in order to be venerated as the Word of God made flesh, namely, the incarnate Christ.[44]

The dedicatory bifolium in the Bernward Gospels starts at the point where gift-giving *pro anima*, salvation, and *memoria* intersect. Placed after the codex's prefatory material (fols. 16v–17r; plates 2 and 3), the painting serves as frontispiece and key to the manuscript's pictorial program.[45] It is the starting point for this study and the subject of the first chapter. The painting translates a well-known medieval textual formula, the treasury list, into pictorial form. The resulting display of accumulated wealth underscores the actual and symbolic value of the pictured treasury, adding to the book's efficacy as a gift *pro anima*. The painting simultaneously emphasizes the role of artworks as portals and material hosts in a process modeled on the entry of spirit into matter that takes place during the consecration of the Eucharist. The painting's capacity to project the donor's image into memory depends on the capacity of objects to bridge the distance between earth and heaven.

While the dedicatory painting argues for the power of objects, and thus of the manuscript itself, to prove the donor's merits and carry his memory, the succeeding illuminations in the Bernward Gospels help shape how he is to be remembered. Their study is at the heart of this project's examination of the bishop's self-presentation, and they are the subject of the second through fourth chapters. These develop two main and interconnected themes. The second chapter considers the presentation of varied forms of service. While one aspect of this theme involves the dissemination of the Word more generally, a series of paintings that illustrate the life of John the Baptist develops an argument more specific to episcopal concerns; these emphasize the merits of the *vita activa* that characterizes the priesthood.

A second important theme of the Bernward Gospels is the spiritual perception of God and the desire to unite with Him, which the pictorial program develops in two related groups of miniatures that each focus on a different sense, sight and touch. Chapter 3 investigates a series of pictures in the Bernward Gospels characterized by a representational tendency that is static, frontal, hieratic, and symmetrical; these miniatures treat the nature of corporeal and spiritual sight both by representing vision and by directing the visual experience of the paintings. Chapter 4 focuses on a group of miniatures that present figures engaged in narrative action involving the tactile experience of Christ. These explore connections between the saints' handling of Christ as a human body and the haptic experience of art itself as a Christological body.

In the exploration of these two sensory modes, the paintings again use John the Baptist to link the patron to models of spiritual perception. Among the many roles ascribed to John the Baptist in the Middle Ages was that of visionary witness, and he appears in the Bernward Gospels as one of the group of saints who share a particular power to penetrate the mystery of Christ's dual nature with their spiritual sight. The Bernward Gospels also presents him, highly unusually, as one of the series of figures privileged to come into direct, tactile contact with Christ. As an exemplar for both senses, the optic and the haptic, the model of the Baptist shapes Bernward's portrait as a figure both inspired and worthy of salvation. By means of his sight and touch, the bishop approaches his hoped-for eternal reward.

Despite its often unusual imagery, the Bernward Gospels shares some affinities with contemporary representations of both historical bishops and bishop-saints. At a time (before the Gregorian reform) when they were still relatively independent actors in both ecclesiastical and secular hierarchies, bishops pursued agendas determined by their particular historical circumstances. Yet they also shared concerns stemming from the nature of their office, their role in the Church, and their administrative responsibilities. These concerns shaped not only how bishops presented themselves but also how hagiographers constructed the memory of episcopal saints. By examining both the idiosyncratic and more conventional aspects of the episcopal image in the Bernward Gospels, this study considers how a prominent representative of the Ottonian episcopate understood and presented both himself and his office in the early Middle Ages.

1

MEMORY

The presentation of the Bernward Gospels as a founder's gift to Saint Michael's Abbey in Hildesheim underlies the commemorative nature of its program and is the apparent subject of the painted bifolium inserted between the incipit and text of Matthew's gospel (fols. 16v–17r; plates 2–3 and fig. 4).[1] The miniature depicts Bishop Bernward on the left folio. He raises a closed book in both hands in a gesture of donation, but he does so before an altar set with a portable altar, chalice, and paten, instruments for the celebration of the Eucharist—making his gesture an act of liturgical performance. Bernward faces Mary and Christ; they appear on the right, enthroned between the archangels Michael and Gabriel, whose open arms frame the Virgin and her child like a mandorla. These four are the patron saints of the abbey church's crypt, which Bernward consecrated in September 1015 (and where he would be buried in 1022).

The tituli in the painting's frames verbalize Bernward's act primarily as one of donation, identifying Mary and Christ as the recipients of Bernward's codex. Composed, for the most part, in leonine hexameter, the text reads, on the left folio,

> This small book of the Gospels, with a
>   devoted mind
> the admirer of Virginity hands over to you,
>   Holy Mary,
> Bishop Bernward, only scarcely worthy of
>   this name,
> and of the adornment of such great episcopal
>   vestment.

A further dedicatory line appears in silver letters on the right folio, in the arch above the saints' heads. It completes Bernward's offertory statement.

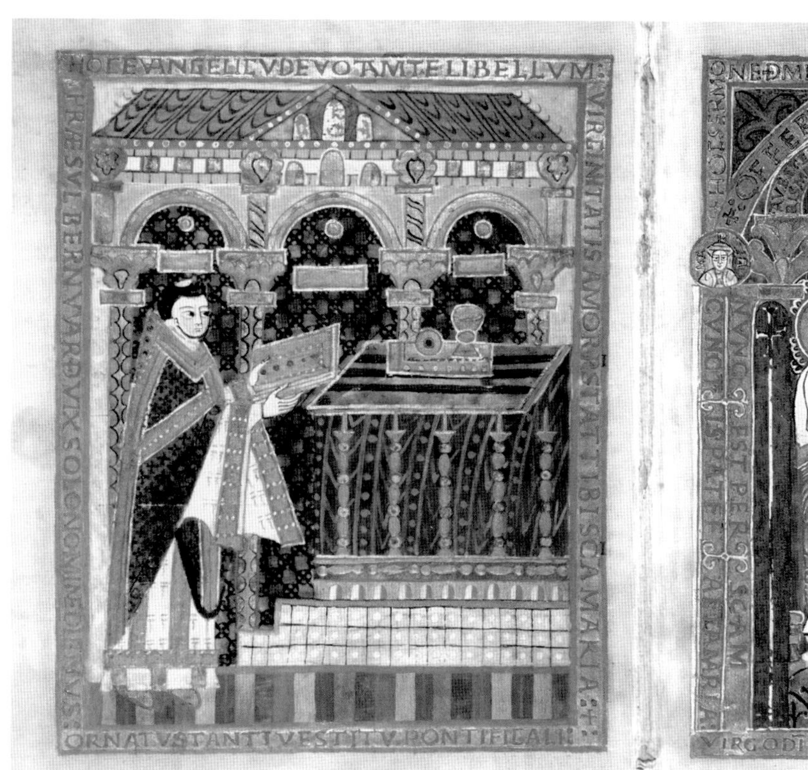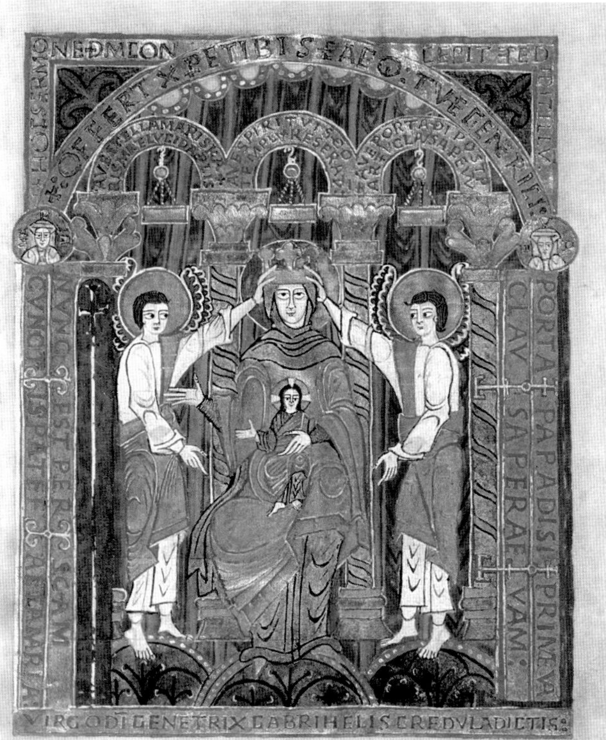

FIGURE 4   Hildesheim, Dom- und Diözesanmuseum, Domschatz 18 (Bernward Gospels), fols. 16v–17r, dedication

He presents [it], Christ, to you and to your holy mother.[2]

The miniature's composition adheres in many respects to the conventional characteristics of early medieval donation pictures. Mary and Christ respond to Bernward's gift with a gesture of blessing that places Bernward in the guise of a Magus at the Adoration, the prototypical medieval donor.[3] Unusually, however, Bernward's act of gift-giving is directed across an altar set with liturgical objects for the celebration of the Eucharist and he wears vestments for the Mass: the amice, alb, dalmatic, and stole.[4] There exists no exact parallel for this in medieval donor imagery, although a number of Ottonian donation scenes use the format of a bifolium, and in the Middle Ages offerings for the saints were generally presented to their altars.[5] A painting in an Ottonian manuscript produced in Reichenau that is now in the Walters Art Museum alludes to such a practice (Baltimore, Walters Art Museum, W7, fol. 9v; fig. 5). The picture portrays a church setting in which an abbot hands a codex to Saint Peter. The saint, in turn, opens a door (note the small hinges), revealing an altar. There, the book already appears with a new cover; from above, the hand of God gestures a blessing. Both details

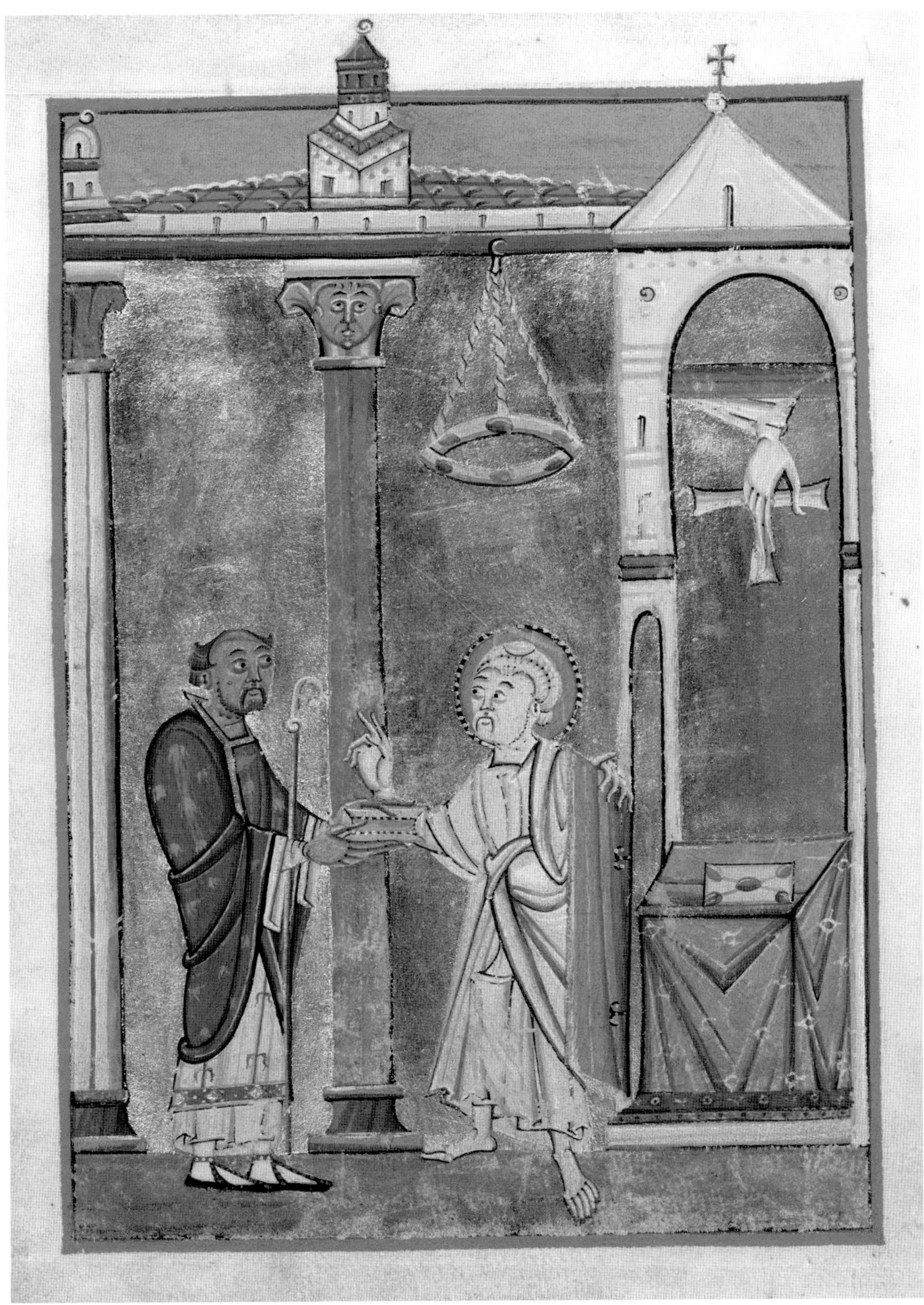

FIGURE 5   Baltimore, The Walters Art Museum, W7,
mid–eleventh century, fol. 9v

suggest that the abbot's gift has been transformed at the altar, giving proof of the donor's merit and signaling that his offering has been accepted by God.[6]

Yet comparing the Reichenau dedication picture to the Bernward Gospels underscores the important differences between the two rather than their similarities. In the former, the donor stands before the recipient to offer the codex directly to the saint, as is usual in donation scenes.[7] The altar appears on the other side of the saint and of a door; each adds to the distance between the donor and the altar. Furthermore, while the altar is covered in textiles, nothing appears on it other than the book. In the Bernward Gospels, however, the altar has been made ready for the Mass. It is covered with textiles, and in front of it are five candlesticks, while above are the chalice and paten, which stand on a portable altar. In these details, the painting draws on the iconography of the Mass. On the late tenth-century ivory panel now in the Liebieghaus Museum in Frankfurt-am-Main, the celebrant similarly stands inside the church, before an altar covered with textiles and set with a chalice, paten, two candlesticks, and two books, one open and one closed (fig. 6). He is garbed in sacerdotal vestments and holds both hands to his chest with palms facing outward. Five clerics stand in a semicircle behind him; they hold closed books. On the other side of the altar, five monks raise their arms in prayer and appear to be singing the Sanctus. The ivory offers an accurate evocation of the Mass. In comparison, the miniature in the Bernward Gospels is less specific; the scene does not correspond to any particular moment in the Mass.[8] Nonetheless, by presenting Bernward in a pose of offering and before an altar prepared

for the Eucharist, the painting suggests that both donor imagery and liturgical ideas inform the picture's design.[9]

The composition relates Bernward's space to the setting of the saints in a way that draws further on liturgical ideas associated with gift-giving. The architecture on the left folio mimics that of the right. Both buildings consist of three arched bays. On the left, the depiction of Bernward's church combines a view of the interior with one of the exterior, resulting in two levels. On the right is a more continuous space unified by the deep purple curtain in the background. Its patterning relates it both to the roof of Bernward's edifice and to the altar covering there. An orange border patterned with white dots lines the edges of the curtain, delimiting the Virgin's space. It echoes the pattern of the cornice line of Bernward's church. On both pages appear gold and silver spiraling columns. One set frames the Virgin, while the other, on the left folio, appears at the clerestory level of the building. Together the curtain, orange bands, and columns relate the Virgin's setting specifically to two areas of Bernward's church: its exterior level and the ritual space of the altar. Such framing devices locate the Virgin outside the boundaries of Bernward's church but link her to the altar, helping present the Virgin's setting as a heavenly reformulation of the bishop's earthly edifice.[10]

Between the two depicted spaces, earthly and heavenly, stands the altar, which serves pictorially as the connection between Bernward and Mary. Taking up more than a quarter of the left folio and placed on an elevated platform accessed by two steps, the altar dominates the painting. It also crosses over the external edges of the building. By projecting beyond the structure, the altar

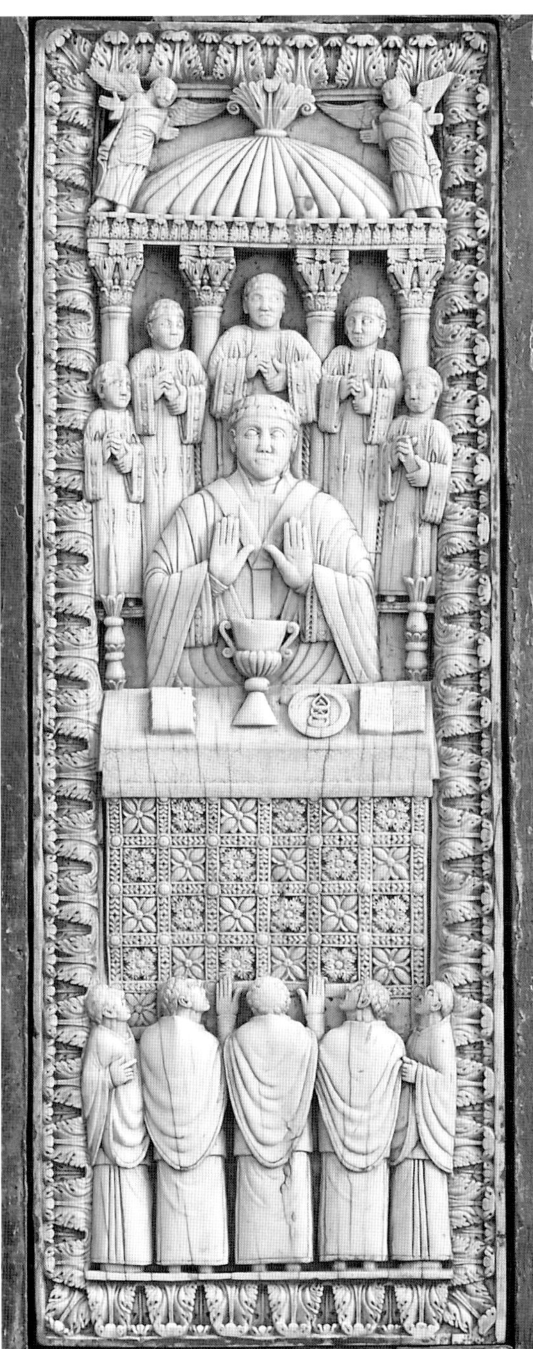

stands ambiguously both inside and outside the church, moving toward the heavenly setting on the opposite page. On that folio the frame's edge is an open door, one of the pair labeled "door of paradise."[11] Whereas the door on the right is marked closed (*clausa*), the one facing the page's inner margin, and thus Bernward's altar, is open (*patefacta*), giving access to the saints.

The painting's careful rendering of the relationship between Bernward's earthly church and the Virgin's heavenly edifice resonates with Eucharistic theology. Mass commentaries of the early Middle Ages point to the concordance between the earthly and heavenly altars, the communion of the faithful and the heavenly communion of the angels. After all, no less an authority than Gregory the Great had proclaimed that at the consecration of the host the angels were present, the earthly was joined to the heavenly, and the visible and invisible became one.[12] The idea that the consecration of the Eucharist opened the heavens laid groundwork that would have particular importance for eleventh-century ideas about gift-giving, a point to which I shall return later in this chapter.

A second set of inscriptions in the painting offers a series of metaphors for the Virgin that emphasize her role in Christ's Incarnation, a theme not only appropriate for a portrait of the Virgin but one that also relates to the Mass, wherein the transformation of the bread and wine into Christ's sacramental body is linked to Christ's Incarnation.[13] Painted above the dedicatory words on the upper corners of the picture frame appears the phrase "By this speech she conceived God and gave birth to him."[14] An inscription in the lower frame completes the verse: "Virgin Mother of God trustful of the words of Gabriel."[15] Additional tituli run over the three arches of the colonnaded arcade painted behind the Virgin; they record epithets for Mary cast in the formula of Gabriel's greeting at the Annunciation.

> Hail Star of the Sea, shining through the
> grace of the Son
> Hail Temple unlocked by the Holy Spirit
> Hail Door of God closed after the birth
> through the ages[16]

Two final inscriptions appear on the doors at each side of the frame. They repeat the metaphor that describes Mary as a door: "The door of Paradise closed through the first Eve, now is through Holy Mary thrown open to all."

The designations "star of the sea," "temple," and "door" refer to titles for Mary common in the West since at least the Carolingian period.[17] However, a tenth-century poem by Hrotsvit, a nun at the convent of Gandersheim in the Hildesheim diocese, uses these metaphors in a way that clarifies their specific meaning for the Bernward Gospels.[18] In her verse narrative of the Virgin's life, Hrotsvit explained that Mary received her name because she was a bright star shining from Christ's diadem.[19] The painting provides a visual echo of this statement. The angels Gabriel and Michael seem to be crowning the Virgin; the way they hold her diadem results in their index fingers' pointing to its central decorative element, the shining "star" of Hrotsvit's text, although Mary rather than Christ wears the crown here.[20]

Labeling Mary "the temple" echoes an epithet Hrotsvit used to describe the Virgin in a later stanza of her poem, where she explains that the title stemmed from the fact that Mary had been

weaving the purple curtain of the Jewish temple at the moment of the Annunciation.[21] The miniature presents a similar relationship between Mary and the temple pictorially by locating the Virgin before an architectural structure that features a purple curtain as well as twisting columns, a further symbolic reference to Solomon's temple.[22]

The third metaphor, that Mary operated as an open door, helps present the Virgin in a typological relationship with Eve. Together with the inscription in the frame of the right half of the painting, this epithet conveys how, by accepting the role Gabriel announced she would play in Christ's Incarnation, Mary reversed Eve's actions, which had caused mankind to be expelled from Paradise. Thus Mary helped open the path to heaven that had been lost by man's original sin. The picture also translates this trope into visual form. Above the two doors labeled *portae paradisi* that flank the central figures of the painting are two roundel portraits of Mary and Eve. Although not used in Hrotsvit's poem, the description of this typological relationship between Mary and Eve was common in contemporary sermons for the feast of the Assumption.[23]

In the Bernward Gospels, these metaphors for Mary are structured as Gabriel's salutation to the annunciate Virgin and thus emphasize her role as the bodily host for Christ's Incarnation. Yet the inscriptions do more than simply reiterate conventional titles for Mary. They also draw attention to the realization of these epithets in material form by means of their representation as a series of pictured things: a crown, textile, building, and doors. Together, the ways in which the composition connects the two halves of the opening to each other, the miniature's combination of donor imagery and Eucharistic content

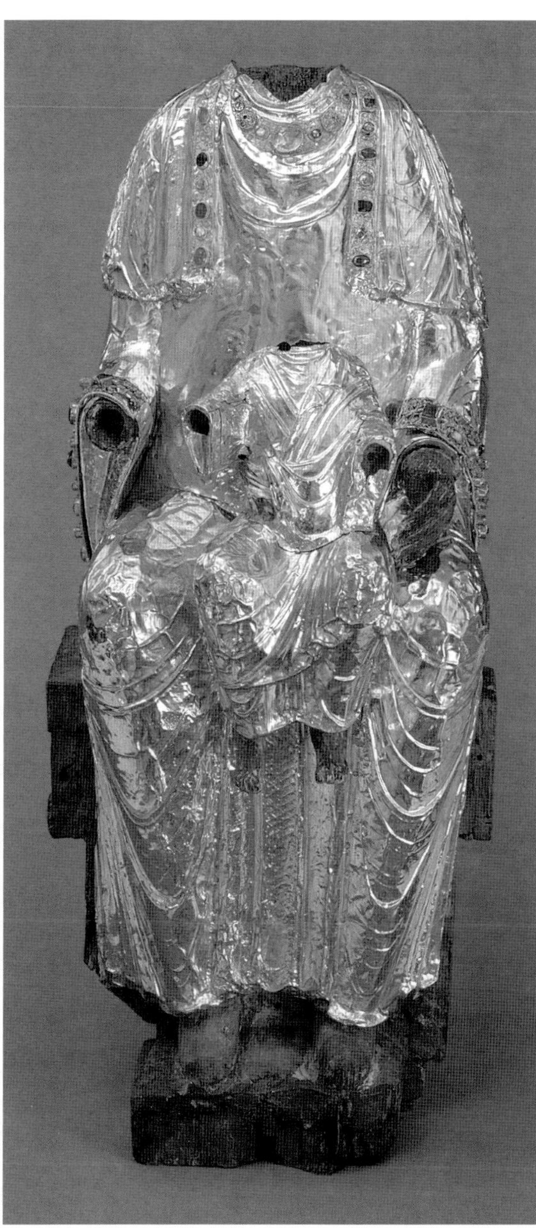

and the right folio's pictorial rendering of the tituli's verbal metaphors, establish a complicated mechanism of dynamic play between word and image, picture and ritual, visible and invisible.

By prompting the viewer to engage with this process, the painting cues a series of cognitive responses in which the crown, curtain, and doors are suddenly revealed as both objects and allegories for Mary, while the representation of Mary herself becomes both a portrait of the saint and an image of a cult statue. In the dedicatory opening the Virgin and Christ are characterized by a frontal pose, speaking gesture, and metallic clothing. A very small Christ floats in an upright posture on the edge of Mary's lap. Both figures have been depicted in a highly symmetrical manner, but certain details add a touch of liveliness. For example, the knees and feet of both figures splay outward rather than mirroring each other exactly. Mary and Christ also both open their right hands, gesturing toward the side. These formal aspects, along with the gold and silver drapery over Mary and Christ's bodies (including the cowl that descends over Mary's shoulders), closely reflect the appearance of a contemporary sculpture that is an early example of the so-called Throne of Wisdom type (fig. 7). Still extant in Hildesheim's cathedral, it is a statue with which the Bernward Gospels artist was likely to be familiar. This sculpture was made under the bishop's direction in the early eleventh century, and in Bernward's time it consisted of a wooden core covered in gilded silver, echoed in the painting by Christ's and Mary's gold and silver vestments.[24] It is probable that the statue, like the Virgin in the miniature, originally wore a crown. According to historical sources in Hildesheim, a "new" crown was made for the statue in 1645, suggesting that it may have already worn one before then, and a crown is already associated in the eleventh century with the oldest extant Marian statue, a tenth-century sculpture from the royal nunnery of Essen.[25]

The materials in which Mary and Christ are rendered are especially significant to considering whether the dedication painting represents a statue. Compared to other depictions of figures in the manuscript, including what is conceptually the closest parallel, a painting of Christ in Majesty (fol. 174r; plate 14), the complete covering of Mary in gold and silver makes her figure read as a metallic object. In the dedication painting, that combination of materials is reserved for the objects around the altar, set pieces of the architecture, and two of the inscriptions. What these elements have in common is their representation as manufactured things.[26] Even the inscriptions, with their carefully delineated silver capitals laid on a gold ground, resemble engraved letters such as those that appear on the back cover of the Bernward Gospels (plate 18).

It is probable that the depiction of Mary does not merely act as a general sign for a cult statue but instead depicts the particular sculpture made under the direction of the manuscript's patron, Bishop Bernward. Artistic copying in the Middle Ages varied in its levels of specificity and verisimilitude, usually indexing what were considered to be significant parts of the model in order to indicate a relationship between model and copy.[27] The picture of a sculpture accompanying its written description in a codex now in Clermont-Ferrand (Clermont-Ferrand, Bibliothèque municipale, MS 145) illustrates this point. Inserted into a book primarily devoted to the works of Gregory of Tours is the description of a Madonna and Child statue commissioned by Bishop Stephen of Clermont-Ferrand in 947. The text includes an account of the statue's history, including the recitation of a vision that had justified its making. In the margin appears an ink drawing of that very sculpture (fol. 130v; fig. 8). Although its iconography follows the description of the statue to some extent, the sketch portrays the Virgin in profile (as if part of an Adoration picture) and includes a halo, which was certainly not a feature of the Clermont-Ferrand sculpture.[28] The drawing in this instance thus reflects only some aspects of the statue's appearance, and it is primarily the text that confirms the relationship between the drawing and an actual object.

Such an approach to copying is broadly consistent with medieval conventions for representing artworks not only in images but also in texts.[29] In the early Middle Ages, descriptions of artworks appear sporadically in narrative sources and frequently in property inventories. An example especially relevant to Hildesheim is an Ottonian account of a series of reliquaries that may have been written either at a monastery in Lamspringe, near Hildesheim, or in Hildesheim's cathedral (Wolfenbüttel, HAB, 427 Helmstedt, fol. 2r).[30] The text provides a useful case study of early medieval descriptive conventions for artworks: "This [relic] is contained in a glass case. . . . This is contained in a case, the cover of which is carved with the lamb of God. . . . These are contained in a case that is painted with a green color. . . . These are contained in an oblong case with red paint without so much viredine. . . . These are contained in a case that on the cover presents the likeness of the throne of the Lord."[31] This laconic inventory describes the reliquaries only sparsely, yet identifies select distinctive

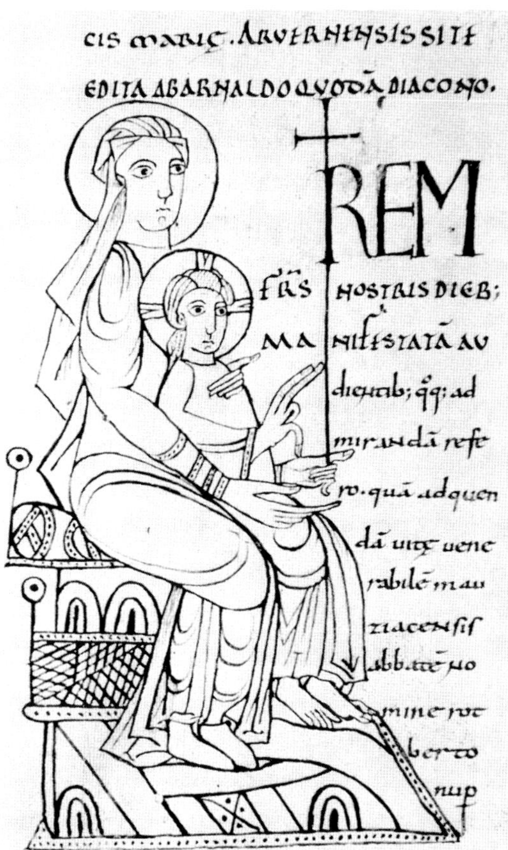

FIGURE 8   Clermont Communauté, Bibliothèque du Patrimoine, MS 145, tenth century, fol. 130v (detail), drawing of a reliquary

details to help distinguish individual examples within a single corpus. In the first instance, the list mentions the case's material. In two separate examples, the text cites the color of the object and provides a brief explanation of the picture visible on the casket's lid.

Such lack of specificity suggests that the writer of the inventory assumed his readers would have independent knowledge of the treasury.[32] In this circumstance, the description would serve essentially as a mnemonic cue for something already familiar. Indeed, the text's careful delineation of distinguishing characteristics within a more generic description relates directly to how medieval audiences learned to remember things.[33] Rhetorical and meditative treatises that lay the basis for how medieval authors described mnemonic processes emphasize the forming of mental pictures as an aid to memory.[34] In these texts, images are considered effective for remembering if they evoke something known by fixing minimal distinctive details in the mind—such as, in the descriptions discussed above, the material or color of an object, or, in the Bernward Gospels painting, the figures' pose together with their gold and silver robes. To make the visualization even more memorable, the image could be elaborated by invention.[35] That is, medieval systems of memory relied not on mimesis but rather on creative mental indexing. Read against such practices, the painted statue in the Bernward Gospels reproduces the appearance of Bernward's sculpture with surprising fidelity. In this connection, the high level of verisimilitude in the reproduction of the Marian statue in the Bernward Gospels is significant.[36]

Why engage the memory of a golden cult object donated by the bishop to the Cathedral of Hildesheim in the representation of Mary and Christ in the Bernward Gospels, a manuscript intended for the monastery of Saint Michael's? While reproducing a gift in a medieval donor image is to be expected and the sketch of the Clermont-Ferrand statue logically accompanies a text about the object, the painting in the Bernward Gospels follows from neither principle. Moreover, although the merging of the reproduction of an object with the image of the Virgin and Child is consistent with the painting's tendency to play with varied and related referents, it comes dangerously close to what medieval theologians defined as idolatry, the conflation of a manufactured object with the saint to which it refers. To parse what was at stake in painting an image of the golden Marian statue in the Bernward Gospels requires an analysis of the characteristics of this object and its eleventh-century context.

The statue is a sculpture that seems always to have been part of the treasury of the cathedral, whose main altar was dedicated to Mary. In 1840 Johann Michael Kratz wrote that the figures were "mit Heiligtümern angefüllt" (filled with holy things), and during a restoration in the 1950s, conservators opened the large cavity closed by a wooden panel in the statue's back to find small bits of wood there.[37] The nineteenth-century description together with the hidden opening and wooden pieces raised the possibility that the statue functioned as a reliquary and was perhaps designed as such.[38] Since no contemporary records pertaining to Bernward's golden statue exist, the object's exact use in Hildesheim remains difficult to reconstruct. Yet it can partly be extrapolated from liturgical conventions attested to at other Ottonian churches. By the eleventh century, statues of the Virgin and Child actuated the presence of the saints during the rites and processions of high feast days dedicated particularly to Mary, such as the Assumption, and on certain feasts of the Christmas and Easter seasons.[39] As an image of the patron saint of the cathedral, the Hildesheim sculpture might also have been processed through Hildesheim to commemorate important anniversaries in diocesan history, such as the cathedral's dedication. A sixteenth-century source records that just such a reliquary procession was the custom in the later Middle Ages; the extent to which this reflects earlier practices is, however, difficult to ascertain.[40]

What Bernward may have anticipated the statue would mean to the Benedictine community dedicated to Saint Michael that he founded (and for which he constructed a walled complex just outside the town limits) is even less certain. However, the altar of the monastic church's crypt was dedicated primarily to Mary, and late medieval sources indicate a stational processional took place on Palm Sunday and included Saint Michael's.[41] Regardless of whether Bernward's sculpture was ever carried to Saint Michael's on these occasions, the monks may also have had occasion to see it displayed in the cathedral on high feast days.[42]

A sense of the significance such statues had for medieval communities can be derived from Bernard of Angers' tenth-century chronicle of the miracles of Sainte Foy in Conques. It offers a window into contemporary ideas about statues of saints, which were becoming increasingly popular in the tenth and eleventh centuries: "For it is a deeply rooted practice and firmly established custom that, if land given to Saint Foy is unjustly appropriated by an usurper for any reason, the reliquary of the holy Virgin is carried out to that land as a witness in regaining the right to her property."[43] In other passages, Bernard describes such statues holding councils and appearing in visions.[44] Bernard's account reveals the extent to which these objects served to authorize, support, and advocate for communities' spiritual and legal claims, thus acting not only as liturgical objects but also, potentially, as public carriers of memory.[45] The painting of the Virgin and Child thus reproduces a type of object that the patron and recipients of the codex would have understood to bear a high degree of symbolic power in rituals of a liturgical as well as a commemorative nature. It also, significantly, represents a contemporary work of art associated with Bishop Bernward.[46]

Related observations can be made about other objects depicted in the dedicatory bifolium. As mentioned above, the two rectangles depicted to each side of the saints on the right folio are topped by roundels containing portraits of Mary and Eve; these painted doors present a typological relationship between the two women. The verses together with the portraits echo the iconography of monumental bronze doors commissioned by Bernward for Saint Michael's Abbey that were completed by 1015, contemporary with the Bernward Gospels.[47] These depict, on one panel, narratives from Genesis centered on Eve, and on the other, corresponding moments in the life of Mary and Christ. Both the painting and bronze door present Eve as responsible for closing the doors of Paradise when she gave in to the serpent's temptation, and they make Mary's acceptance of God's message the reason for the gates' reopening. Both also interpret Mary as the new Eve, arguing that salvation is made possible by Christ's and Mary's reversal of Adam's and Eve's actions.[48] The doors are now displayed in the cathedral but were probably designed for Saint Michael's.[49]

Although the reconstitution of their original location remains somewhat disputed, as doors, the bronze panels operated as thresholds between spaces and in that way served as liminal zones in a manner similar to Bernward's golden statue, which mediated the presence of the saints for the faithful. The miniature argues through pictorial means that the painted doors function as much as portals as their bronze referent. As already described, an inscription proclaims that the door

on the Virgin's left, the one bearing Eve's portrait, is *clausa* (closed), and it is pictorially highlighted as such by the prominence of the hinges which jut into the adjacent column. In contrast, the door on Bernward's side is marked "cunctis patefacta" (thrown open to all), and its location at the edge of the picture frame presents it as a passageway to the saints.

Like the Marian statue, the bronze doors may have played a public role in constructing the memory of a specific moment or event at Hildesheim. In a study of the doors, Adam Cohen and Anne Derbes suggest that the panels depict Eve as a sexually provocative woman as part of a project to identify a local nun (and sister to the emperor), Sophia of Gandersheim, as malevolent and dissolute. In historical texts produced in Hildesheim, Sophia was held responsible for prompting the efforts of the archbishop of Mainz to lay claim to the wealthy nunnery of Gandersheim that the bishops of Hildesheim considered to be under their aegis.[50] By offering a polemical argument against the dangers posed by seductive and insolent women, the doors may have served to assert Bernward's legal and spiritual claim to this nunnery. Completed shortly after the initial settlement of the dispute in Bernward's favor, the doors thus potentially directed the diocese's memory of a specific conflict in a public statement of Bernward's authority. The memorial association between the doors and the patron is especially significant; within the inscription on the panels appears the phrase *B[ernwardus] ep[iscopus] dive mem[oriae]* (Bishop Bernward, blessed of memory). Reproduced in the dedicatory painting, the depiction of the doors may help reiterate and extend that commemorative message.[51]

In the painting, a white cross appears within the blue opening of the left door, marking the passage as the way of Christ. It consists of two parts: a crucifix and a long handle that extends to the bottom frame of the picture. The latter detail indicates that the object is a processional cross. The representation here is particularly generic. Nevertheless, processional crosses were important objects for the liturgy and Bernward did commission several in Hildesheim. For example, a gilded silver cross now in the diocese's museum dates to the eleventh century.[52] It bears the inscription "Bishop Bernward made this" (meaning "had this made") on its verso, together with a list of saints, including Dionysius, whose relics were purportedly presented to the bishop by the king of France in 1007.[53] This cross was at Saint Michael's until the nineteenth century and, like the golden statue and bronze doors, served to commemorate both the bishop and the community, as it bears the patron's name on its back together with a list of relics to which the monks would add in the later Middle Ages.[54]

An important ritual object, the cross would not only have been carried in processions but also, detached from its base, would have stood at the altar to represent the presence of Christ during the Eucharistic celebration. Thus like both the statue and doors it played the role of a mediator between man and God, earth and heaven, which the picture in the Bernward Gospels underscores by the cross's placement in the passageway to Paradise. A parallel in the Bible Bernward gave to Saint Michael's emphasizes this point. As discussed in the introduction, the Bible's dedicatory painting is a complex and layered image (DS 61, fol. 1r; fig. 1). A processional cross dominates the picture and its embellishments of gold medallions, incised lines, and punch marks, together with the entwined vines and punch marks between the cross's arms, are carefully rendered details that mimic contemporary metalwork.[55] The low curtain that wraps around the cross's base can be understood as an altar covering. The painting thus represents, on the one hand, a golden processional cross standing at the altar inside a church.[56] On the other hand, the picture draws on Crucifixion iconography, and the golden cross is shown to reach the heavenly opening at the top and right side of the painting, where the blessing Hand of God reaches into the church. Like the painting in the Bernward Gospels, the Bible's miniature thus conflates the representation of a work of art with the evocation of the Crucifixion, adding an extra charge to the sign's theological and liturgical importance in denoting the presence of the divine.

In the Bernward Gospels, the prominent purple curtain hanging behind the Virgin adds to the objects on the page that are identifiable as works of art mediating access to the divine. A silk pasted into the back cover of the Bernward Gospels and another found covering relics sealed by Bernward's predecessor indicate the presence of Byzantine textiles in Hildesheim.[57] Although, like the processional cross, its depiction is generic enough that tying it to a specific work at Saint Michael's is impossible, it is another reference to a valued category of object commonly found in churches of the period. The composer of the dedication inscription on the left folio indeed highlights the importance of liturgical textiles in Hildesheim when he notes Bernward's ceremonial vestments, whose repeating weave pattern marks them as silk: *ornatus tanti vestitu pontificali.*

While there is no evidence that any specific textile in Hildesheim served to shape local memory, the pictured curtain behind the Virgin does resemble the other objects just analyzed in that it acts as a portal. It does so not only pictorially, by means of its similarity to the altar curtain and roof depicted on the left folio, but also metaphorically. The association of a curtain with Mary plays into a complicated semiotic system within which medieval theologians understood curtains to operate. Compared to the concealing temple curtain of the Old Testament, the curtain in the New Testament was said to mark the path to the secrets of the heavens revealed by Christ's Incarnation: "Having therefore, brethren, a confidence in the entering into the holies by the blood of Christ; A new and living way which he hath dedicated for us through the veil, that is to say, his flesh" (Hebrews 10:19–20). In this passage, Christ's flesh is linked to the veil of the tabernacle that Christians penetrated when they consumed Christ's body during the sacrament of the Eucharist. From this idea developed figurative language that associated the temple curtain with the flesh of Christ, resulting in the increased pictorial presentation, in early medieval art, of the curtain motif in depictions of the Incarnation and of the Virgin. The metaphorical fusion of the curtain and Christ's body crystallized in Western thought during the eleventh century.

Indeed, the curtain-flesh trope appeared frequently in the Ottonian period, even outside exegetical commentary. In her poem on Mary, the nun Hrotsvit, for example, referred to Christ's Incarnation as the covering of his divine nature with a veil of human form. The picture of the Baptism in the Bernward Gospels (fol. 174v; plate 15) presents the same idea in a painting.

Standing to each side of Christ, two angels hold open a white curtain with a gold border. Its color and V-pattern closely resemble the shading of Christ's body, thus visually linking the two. By means of this association, the curtain becomes not only the portal and conduit to the sacred but also, and at the same time, a metaphorical membrane in which the divine manifests its presence.

A peculiar detail emphasizes the extent to which their nature—as both portals and membranes in the mode of Christ's incarnate and sacramental body—informs the selection of the objects reproduced in the dedicatory painting, the manner of these works' depiction, and their resulting symbolic power. On the left folio, the church in which Bernward stands includes two central rows of windows. The lower one, at the clerestory level, is painted gold and silver; it reads as part of the metallic patterning that repeats over the surface of the page. These windows appear impermeable to the eye.

In contrast, the representation of the three windows in the gable suggest a sense of transparency. Lines around the central window frame its arch. These begin at the top of the window and split along a vertical part into two groups of parallel lines that curl around the window, creating a pattern that resembles hair and suggestively conjures the impression of a face in the window (fig. 9).[58] There is only scattered evidence for the presence of historiated windows in Germany in the Carolingian and Ottonian period.[59] Although archeological research indicates the presence of fragments of colored glass in Europe since at least the sixth century, it remains difficult to reconstruct what such fragments originally depicted.[60] Extant eleventh-century glass panels that may have portrayed a figure offer only inconclusive

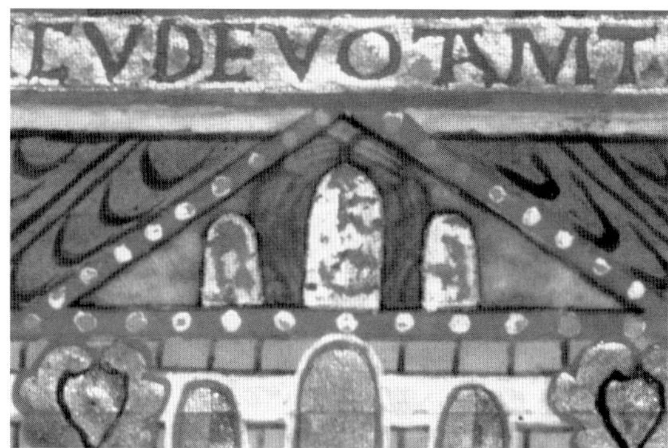

FIGURE 9   Hildesheim, Dom- und Diözesanmuseum, Domschatz 18 (Bernward Gospels), fol. 16v, window (detail)

evidence.[61] In Germany, two late eleventh-century roundels from Lorsch and Wissenbourg have been restored. Each portrays a bearded man, but other reconstructed details in the windows are disputed, so that identifying the subjects of these panels remains a contentious issue.[62]

Despite the lack of material evidence, however, numerous medieval texts associate Christ with glass and suggest that the hair around the painted window may be intended to visualize metaphors that compare the passage of light through a window to the Incarnation. Two sermons that were attributed to Augustine in the Middle Ages popularized this trope.[63] The concept's importance in fashioning eleventh-century discourse about the Incarnation is attested to by its appearance in a German vernacular poem by the end of that century. A verse addressed to the Virgin summarizes the metaphor: "Since you gave birth to the Child, you were wholly stronger and virgin from the companionship of man. If this seems impossible, consider glass, to which you are similar. The sunlight appears through the glass; it is twinkling and stronger than it was before; through the blinking glass it enters the

house dispelling darkness. You are the blinking glass through which comes the light, which takes the darkness from the world. From you shines the light of God in all lands."[64] In this passage, the poet associates the window with the Virgin's body, while the light that shines through the glass is Christ. When these lines are considered against all the other textual and pictorial references to the Incarnation in the bifolium, it becomes highly probable that the window framed by hair pictorially renders Christ's Incarnation in matter.

On the one hand, to the extent that the glass serves as the material support that gives visible shape to the divine light, the window, like both the curtain and reliquary statue of the Virgin, contains and transmits the sacred. On the other hand, the glass acts also in the reverse direction, like doors, as a mediating portal between Bernward's church and the divine. The two rows of windows—one a transparent membrane that models the Incarnation, and the other reflective, and blocking—in effect resemble the works reproduced on the right folio (doors, curtain, statue) in their capacity to be either active/ open/revealing or still/closed/concealing. These both evoke actual works of art from Hildesheim and share the same symbolic power to mediate the sacred via a process allegorically related to Christ's Incarnation.

A series of objects with similar characteristics appears on the left folio, primarily around the altar. The most easily identifiable works are the five golden candleholders with a triangular base and silver knobs that surround the altar. They reflect the shape and material of a pair of candlesticks that were discovered in Bernward's tomb in the twelfth century and bear an inscription naming the bishop.[65] Drawn more generically, as types,

the chalice, paten, portable altar, and various
textiles on the left folio offer more conventional
depictions of common ecclesiastical objects.
Yet these too may index products of Bernward's
patronage. According to his biographers, Bernward donated several chalices and patens to Saint
Michael's.[66] Additionally, a portable altar from
the cathedral treasury is connected by figural
style and iconography to the Bernward Gospels.[67]
Where the golden object displayed on the main
altar in the painting includes a series of silver
arches on the front face, however, the extant portable altar in Hildesheim features niello engrav-
ings on gold-plated silver. Two additional objects
decorated in a manner similar to the painted
portable altar appear in other miniatures of the
Bernward Gospels: an Adoration scene that follows the dedication painting (fol. 18r; plate 4) and
the first illustration to the gospel of John (fol. 174r;
plate 14). These further examples underscore that,
just as for the objects of the right folio, the artworks on the left folio are reproduced to varying
degrees of verisimilitude and specificity.

The works depicted on the left folio are
centered around a particular category of objects,
the *vasa sacra*, which form part of the material
instruments of the Mass; this made them sites
of mediating power. During the Mass the *vasa
sacra* served symbolically to mark God's presence in the church. Among these the chalice and
paten were particularly significant for coming
into direct contact with the sacramental body
of Christ. As such, the *vasa sacra* stood at the
threshold between the visible and invisible, the
material and the immaterial. In the painting
they key the multidirectional communication
with God in which the reproduced artworks
participate. That linking of sacrament with *vasa*

sacra and other objects in the church developed
essentially from medieval liturgical habits.

Similar ideas underlay the offertory procession, which, until the middle of the eleventh
century, took place at the beginning of the Mass.
During this procession, the congregation presented gifts to the altar. Subsequently, before the
recitation of the Canon, which contained prayers
specific to the host, the priest would perform the
secreta, where he asked God to accept and sanc-
tify the congregation's offerings.[68] Then, during
the Canon, the celebrant would pray that the consecrated host be raised to heaven and blessed by
God, thus ritually connecting the gifts to an act of
transformation. Contemporary monastic pream-
bles to donation records draw on this liturgical
association between the offering and the Eucharist in order to explain that the effectiveness of
a gift depended on its being transformed at the
altar.[69] By this process the object was converted
from an earthly good to something accepted
by God, giving proof of the donor's merit. That
potential for transformation and divine acceptance invested the offerings with the capacity to
bridge the gap between earth and heaven. When
such gifts were then employed in ecclesiastical
rituals—whether because they were themselves
liturgical objects, such as, for example, chalices,
reliquaries, textiles, and certain types of books,
or because they were to be added to a liturgical
object, such as a gem placed on a reliquary—that
power was amplified.[70] By merging the representation of a dedicatory act with references to
the Eucharistic ritual, the painting reinforces the
place of objects at the nexus of Bernward's communication with God.

A painting in the contemporary Uta Codex
(Munich, Bayerische Staatsbibliothek, Codex

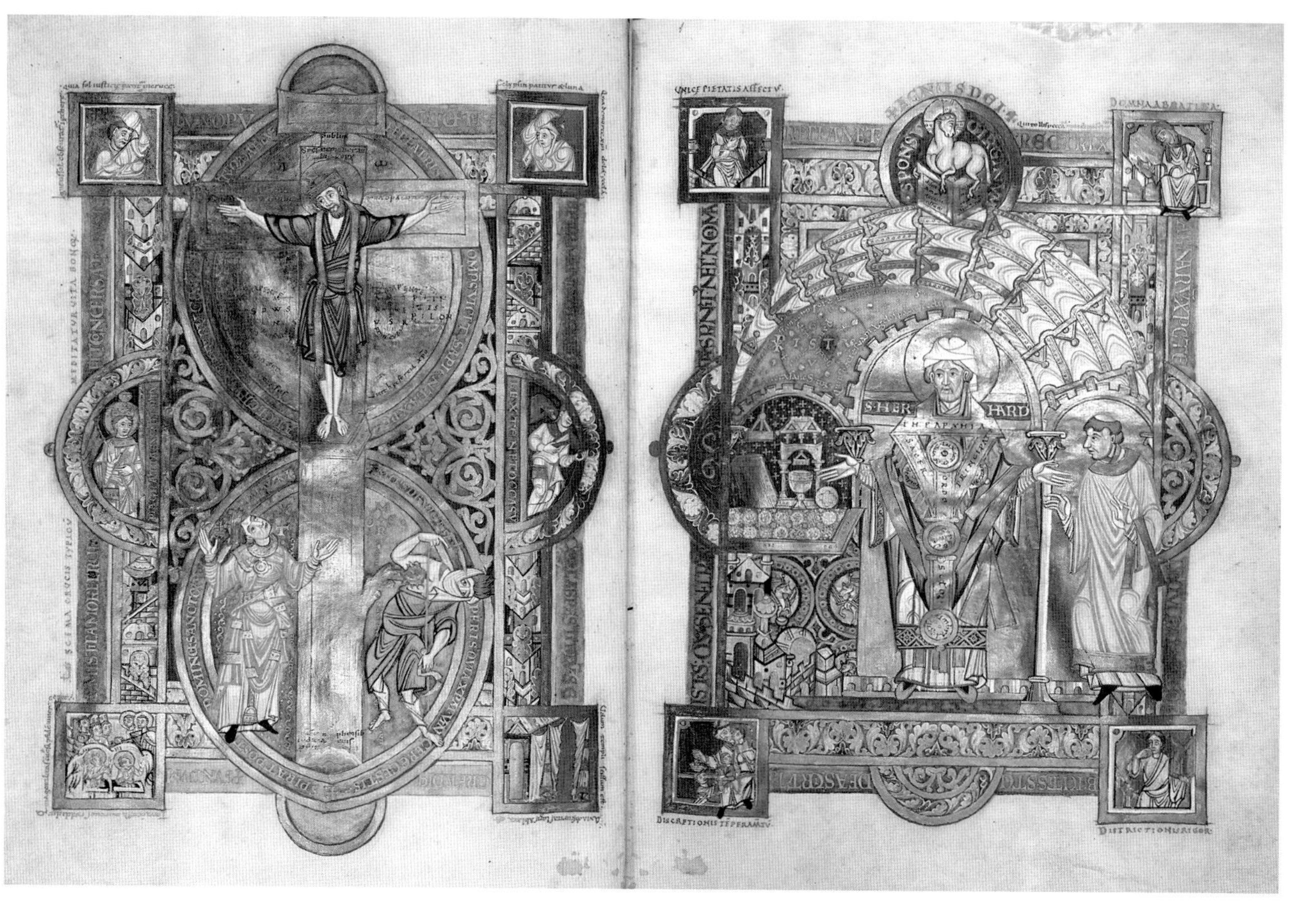

FIGURE 10   Munich, Bayerische Staatsbibliothek, Codex Latinus Monacensis 13601 (Uta Codex), fols. 3v–4r, *Symbolic Crucifixion* (left); *Bishop Erhard Celebrating the Mass* (right)

Latinus Monacensis 13601) elaborates themes similar to the Bernward Gospels; it offers a useful comparison that clarifies what is at stake in the depiction of objects in the Bernward Gospels. Made for the nunnery of Niedermünster in the 1020s, the Uta Codex contains painted reproductions of objects from the treasury of a neighboring male monastery dedicated to Saint Emmeram.[71] These appear in a bifolium showing, on the left, a symbolic crucifixion, and on the right, the bishop-saint Erhard celebrating the

Mass (fols. 3v–4r; fig. 10). As Adam Cohen has analyzed this miniature extensively in his monograph on the Uta Codex, I will here only summarize those aspects of the painting most relevant to the dedication of the Bernward Gospels.[72]

First, the miniature in the Uta Codex portrays a liturgical act. Erhard wears the vestments of a priestly celebrant—in this case, the Jewish high priest of the Old Testament. Both bishops direct their gaze forward across an altar to the opposite folio. By raising the book in both hands,

Bernward both offers the codex to the saints and raises the book before the altar as if to perform a ritual; Erhard is depicted frontally, in an orans posture, and the presence of the deacon beside him frames the scene primarily as a liturgical event.

Second, the altar stands at the center of Erhard's ritual and intercessory actions directed toward Christ, who appears in a symbolic Crucifixion on the opposite folio. The paintings' geometric structure and the architectural patterns in the inner border of each half of the opening link the pictures to each other. The gaze of both the deacon and Saint Erhard create a movement from right to left that directs attention to the Crucifixion. There, at the level of the altar on Erhard's page, the personification of Synagoga moves away from Christ, contrasting sharply with the direction of Erhard and the deacon's attention. Tituli in the opening address the targeted audience of the work, the nuns of Niedermünster, ordering them to learn and strive after the virtues represented by the paintings, presupposing the audience's contemplation of the page and Erhard's role as a mediator between them and Christ.[73]

The Erhard miniature also incorporates a group of golden objects that can be identified with works from the treasury of the monastery of Saint Emmeram in Regensburg. These were gifts from the ninth-century emperor Arnulf of Carinthia and they are described in a life of Saint Emmeram written within ten years of the Uta Codex.[74] The most recognizable of the reproduced objects is a portable altar known as the Arnulf ciborium; it is the two-level structure surmounted by a crossing triangular roof that appears in the middle of the altar.[75] Beside the painted ciborium is a book, drawn quite conventionally, perhaps a reference to the renowned Codex Aureus of Saint Emmeram (Munich, Bayerische Staatsbibliothek, Clm 14000). A chalice and paten appear just before the ciborium and are also quite generic in their appearance—they correspond to donations cited in the slightly later text. A walled complex depicted below the altar probably represents Arnulf's royal palace, one of the monastery's properties, while the object that hangs above the altar may be Arnulf's royal crown. In front of the altar is a Sassanian or Byzantine silk decorated with medallions that show facing winged horses. Although no such textile survives at Saint Emmeram today, the biographical text notes that Arnulf gave the community colored cloths and, as Cohen has pointed out, dotted medallions are a common ninth-century textile motif.[76] Moreover, because precious patterned silks were frequently used for burial or to cover relics, they rarely survive intact to the present day.[77]

These objects bridge the space between the bishop-celebrant and God not only formally, because they appear between the bishop-celebrant and the Crucifixion, but also symbolically. Cohen argues that a complex pseudo-Dionysian process underlies the page's design, in which the golden objects serve to transport the viewer anagogically from the material world to the immaterial contemplation of the divine.[78] By doing so, the miniature positions the objects of the treasury on the threshold between the earthly and heavenly, and they thus become sites of communication and presence. Such a focus on material objects as mediating membranes duplicates the ideas developed in the Bernward Gospels dedication painting, which, however, draws on metaphors for the Incarnation and liturgical habits rather than on philosophical concepts in order to convey the objects' power.

Further similarities include the fact that the painting reproduces known works of art to varying degrees of verisimilitude. Although the Arnulf ciborium is readily identifiable because of its shape and material, the chalice, paten, book, and crown are quite generic. In contrast, the silk by the altar is reproduced in large format as if to ensure that it would be recognized by its specific pattern, although the textual descriptions of Arnulf's colored cloths offer no indication of the textiles' decoration. Moreover, the artworks selected to be reproduced in both manuscripts played an active role in the shaping of communal memory, both individually and as a group. This has already been established for the dedicatory bifolium in the Bernward Gospels, and Cohen explains how the citation of these objects in Saint Emmeram's slightly later biography served as part of that text's larger project to resist the episcopal authority being exerted over the monastery by the local bishops.[79] The careful attention paid to Arnulf's gifts in this document suggest that they were particularly important carriers of memory in that project.

Why reproduce treasury objects from a neighboring male monastery in a book made for the nuns of Niedermünster? Cohen offers a variety of possible explanations, but most important for our understanding of the Bernward Gospels is his suggestion that the miniature can be read as a recapitulation of Abbess Uta's reform of Niedermünster, which had earlier been a house of canonesses.[80] By gazing at the miniature, the future abbesses and nuns of Niedermünster, who are addressed directly by the tituli, remember the institution's new, reformed identity.[81] Did the objects play a role in that process? Since they originated in the monastery of Saint Emmeram, which charged Uta with reforming the nunnery, they were works of art that, like the figure of Saint Erhard himself, represented a past better suited to the community's reformed present. Perhaps in that way were the nuns to forget that they had ever been a house for canonesses.[82]

Underscoring that the simulated objects play a commemorative function is that they are treasury objects, and what the parallels between the Bernward Gospels and Uta Codex further make clear is that by displaying a group of simulated objects, each highlighted for their precious and symbolic materials but only sparsely identified, these Ottonian miniatures deliberately translate a construct that would have been very familiar to medieval audiences: the treasury list. One such inventory from the Hitda Codex (Darmstadt, Universitäts- und Landesbibliothek, HS1640), dating to the first third of the eleventh century, provides a useful comparative example. The document (fol. 1v) lists objects added to the treasury of Meschede, in the Cologne diocese, by a certain Abbess Hitda.[83]

The wandering Hitda, guardian of this place, gave these offerings to God and Saint Walburga on behalf of herself and her own in accordance with a vow. Crosses: III, decorated with gold and precious stones and one out of gold and ivory. A statue of holy Mary made with gold and precious stones and wearing a small cloak. Book: I with gold and gems, and two golden. Golden censer: I. Banners: IV. Ampullas: III, one onyx, II crystal. Napkins: III. Chasuble: I with silk and a gold stole. III icons. Three caskets.

Hangings: II. Curtains: III. One leather. Small vessels: II for the use of the sacrifice, one of precious stones and the other of ivory. Pillows: III scarlet ones for the purpose of carrying books. If anyone should remove or reduce any part from the holy use, let them be cursed.[84]

Hitda's portrait follows just a few folia after this text (fol. 6r). There the abbess stands directly before Saint Walburga, supporting a proffered codex with both hands.[85] The saint responds by grasping the book at its top edge with her right hand. The miniature portrays the two unusually close, standing in the same space and not only linked through their hold on the book but also through their gaze.

As in the Bernward Gospels and Uta Codex, the object that serves as the site of Hitda's inventory also mediates her communication with the saint. In one of the better known miniatures of this codex, the painting of Christ in Majesty,[86] the power of the manuscript to serve as material host in a reciprocal process of communication between earth and heaven is established by a titulus on the facing page: "this visible product of the imagination represents the invisible truth whose splendor penetrates the world through the two-times-two lights of the new doctrine." The term "imagination" here (*imaginatum* in the Latin) implies a dynamic process in which the viewer moves from the image to the contemplation of the divine and back again.[87]

Hitda's treasury list also illustrates a characteristic feature of such documents—the way in which their format serves to emphasize the treasury's accrued value. Medieval inventories repetitively enumerate the number and type of objects along with their luxurious materials (in Hitda's inventory: gold, gems, ivory, and silk). In so doing the texts convey the treasury's formal qualities as a subtly varied group of related objects whose dominant characteristics are preciousness and material similarity. The dedicatory painting in the Bernward Gospels shares these formal features with Hitda's text. Textile patterns decorate the painting's background, serving to create flat surfaces of delicately varying colors that present the illusion of silken parchment.[88] The effort to produce that effect is especially apparent on the left folio, where the choice of color and pattern in Bernward's green chasuble causes the figure to blend somewhat into the green patterned ground. Over the opening's silken surface accrues gold and silver, which create a shimmering and subtly varying effect. Together, these real and simulated materials contribute to the thesaurization of the page.[89] By means of this display of accumulated wealth, the painting underscores the actual and symbolic value of the treasury, both of which informed how medieval donors and recipients understood the gift-giving process through which medieval treasuries were constituted.[90]

As a depository of both monetary and symbolic capital, the medieval treasury had the capacity to carry *memoria*. Yet the early medieval treasury was essentially a mass of miscellaneous gifts.[91] Consequently, its commemorative associations depended on how the gifts' recipients shaped the meaning of that mass. In 1967, Bernhard Bischoff edited 151 documents from the ninth to the thirteenth centuries that pertain to the treasuries of diverse religious communities.[92] For the most part, the texts drafted for that purpose state that they record the treasury in its contemporary form, using variations of *hic est thesaurus* (this is the treasury) or, quite commonly, *commemoratio*, literally "commemoration" of the treasury. A few rare cases emphasize that the documents act as the testimony of a witness by using verbs for "to see," *videbatur* (for example, no. 46), or "to discover/find" (no. 96). Some include formulas such as *augmentabantur* (augmented), indicating a subgroup of the treasury added under the most recent abbacy or episcopacy (nos. 17, 25, 44, 76).

All these documents also follow the conventions described earlier. They index objects in an abbreviated format that emphasizes the number and material for each category of object, underscores the treasury's value, and only occasionally includes contextual information such as an object's function or the name of a donor. Moreover, despite their claims to the contrary, these documents do not serve as unproblematic records. Rather, they are attempts to construct memory, especially by the Ottonian period, when treasury inventories were more commonly written by the treasury's owners than in earlier times.[93] These owners selectively list works from the treasury, in effect collecting them, and narrate the resulting group of objects in ways that serve the community's contemporary purposes.[94]

Constantly in flux as communities received goods and then recirculated them, treasuries offered donors and recipients numerous opportunities not only for making but also for changing memory—a process that required the creation of a "record" of some kind. Although such records depended to some extent on objects' actual preexisting commemorative associations, they also worked to structure those associations' meaning, readily eliding, shifting emphasis, perhaps deliberately confusing, and even sometimes entirely inventing them.[95] Donors had to understand that in that process, their commemoration hinged on the capacity of their gifts to project, fix, and stabilize their image and presence in the recipients' memory not only in the present, but also in the future.

Such manipulations of the treasury record to shape memory relate closely both to medieval mnemotechnic and commemorative practices, the mental picturing of the *thesaurus* as an organizational system being a fundamental process in the creation of both types of memory and composition, *inventio* being memory's most vital tool.[96] Medieval records of the treasury and its donors thus employ a cognitive structure that, because it is reused, continuously performed, and linked to sacred objects, has the potential to fix communal memory. Yet that memory remains something that is inherently disorganized and unstable.[97] Against that background, each new instance of creating a treasury list must be understood in two ways: first, as an attempt to establish and fix memory at a particular moment in time, and second, as a practice meant to maintain this memory in concrete things, objects that existed outside of the record itself. By picturing the treasury, the Bernward Gospels aimed both to create the memory of a moment of great personal significance to the bishop—the foundation of Saint Michael's Abbey together with the offering of the gospels—and to prompt a commemorative response from the monks which might stabilize that memory.

In sum, the dedication painting explores multiple themes: from the praxis of *memoria* to the exegetical treatment of Christ's Incarnation; from expectations about gift-giving to ideas about the Eucharist; and from views of the relationship between the earthly and the heavenly church to notions about the power of cult objects as sites for the entry of spirit into matter. In so doing, the painting displays three main characteristics. It combines the picture of a donation scene with Mass imagery; it represents signs for Christ's incarnate body as manufactured objects that operate in the mode of the Eucharist; and it translates the treasury list into painted form.

Each of these iconographic choices relate to ideas about gift-giving *pro anima*. While gift exchange took many forms in the Middle Ages, the medieval offering *pro anima* specifically served to negotiate social and spiritual bonds between donors and at least two recipients: the earthly religious communities that took ownership of the gift and the heavenly community of saints to whom the gift was dedicated. The goal was to set into motion mechanisms and actors that would guarantee the donor a place in heaven. That process was structured around the idea that mankind might gain eternal rewards by making offerings to the divine. The gift *pro anima* is thus fundamentally preoccupied with the donor's salvation and draws particular charge from the early medieval liturgical habit of linking offerings to the consecration of the Eucharist and from the praxis of *memoria*.[98] The painting depicts Bernward as both the Mass celebrant and the founder of Saint Michael's, surrounded by the products of his artistic patronage; it memorializes the bishop's exceptional patronage, placing him simultaneously before the altar of the monastic foundation where he would be buried and at the threshold of the heavenly church, the bishop's hoped-for eternal reward. Achieving that reward requires the commemorative and intercessory prayers of the monks of Saint Michael's. The dedicatory painting effects the symbolic transformation of the Bernward Gospels itself into treasure, both to fix a personal moment and to stabilize the bishop's image and presence in the monks' memory for present and succeeding generations.

2

SERVICE

While the dedication opening of the Bernward Gospels sets into motion mechanisms for fixing the bishop's image in the monks' memory, the manuscript's succeeding illuminations shape that picture in ways specific to episcopal concerns. A significant theme develops from the related content of paintings that appear in each of the four gospels. These portray episodes from the lives of the saints Matthew, Mark, and John the Baptist. In the case of the two evangelists, the paintings show the key moments in which Matthew and Mark entered Christ's ministry (fols. 18v and 75v, plates 5 and 8). A more extensive cycle is devoted to the Baptist.[1] Six scenes present stories about John, more than are devoted to any other figure in the manuscript except Christ. Two of these episodes appear frequently in medieval art because they involve Christ: the Visitation (fol. 111v; plate 11) and the Baptism (fol. 174v;

plate 15). The remaining four scenes, however, are rarely represented. One shows the naming of John the Baptist (fol. 111v; plate 11) and another the Baptist preaching (fol. 75r; plate 7), while two vignettes serve to narrate how Zacharias learned, and doubted, the prophecy of John's miraculous conception (fol. 111r; plate 10).

Matthew's gospel is illustrated with four main scenes that run across three sequential sides of vellum (fols. 18r–19r; plates 4–6). While the first painting depicts Christ's Nativity (fol. 18r), the next picture portrays two consecutive gospel episodes from Matthew's life (fol. 18v; fig. 11). Above, Christ calls Matthew to his service, and below, Christ dines with Matthew at the house of Levi. Directly across from these paintings is Matthew's author portrait; it is paired with the evangelist's symbol, the man, which appears in an independently framed space above, depicted within a medallion and inside a garden framed

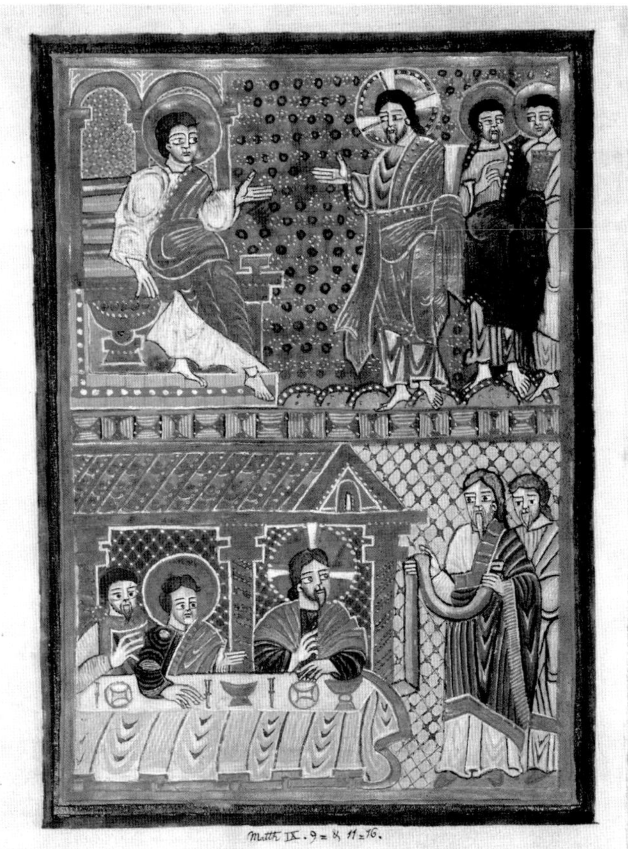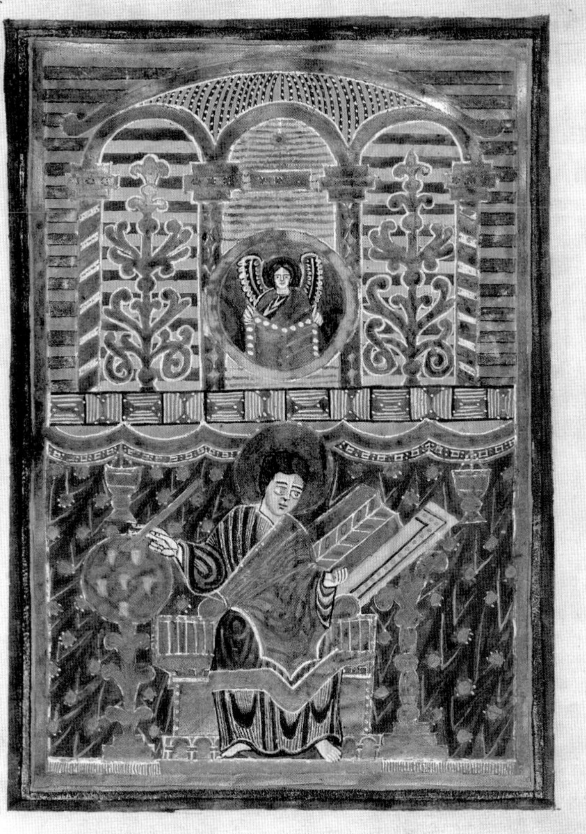

FIGURE 11   Hildesheim, Dom- und Diözesanmuseum, Domschatz 18 (Bernward Gospels), fols. 18v–19r, *Calling of the Evangelist Matthew* (above left) and *Dinner at the House of Levi* (below left); *Portrait of Matthew* (right)

by a ciborium-shaped structure (fol. 19r; fig. 11). Matthew is depicted as a youth, with unbearded face and full, wavy brown hair. The heavily ornamented background takes the form of a curtain.

The illustrations in Mark's gospel consist of five scenes presented in sequence. The first page (fol. 75r; plate 7) depicts John the Baptist preaching (above) and Christ calling his first four disciples (below). On the second page appears the gospel episode known as the Noli me tangere (above), which will be discussed in chapter 4, and

a single scene from the life of Mark (below) in which an older man hands Mark a book (fol. 75v; plate 8 and fig. 12). The scene relates to the gospel's prologue, which explains how Mark entered Christ's service by becoming a student of the apostle Peter.[2] The picture shows Peter charging Mark to write (or perhaps dictating to Mark) his gospel. Directly across from this painting is the evangelist's portrait and symbol, the lion, which, like Matthew's, appears in a separate scene within a garden setting and is framed by architecture

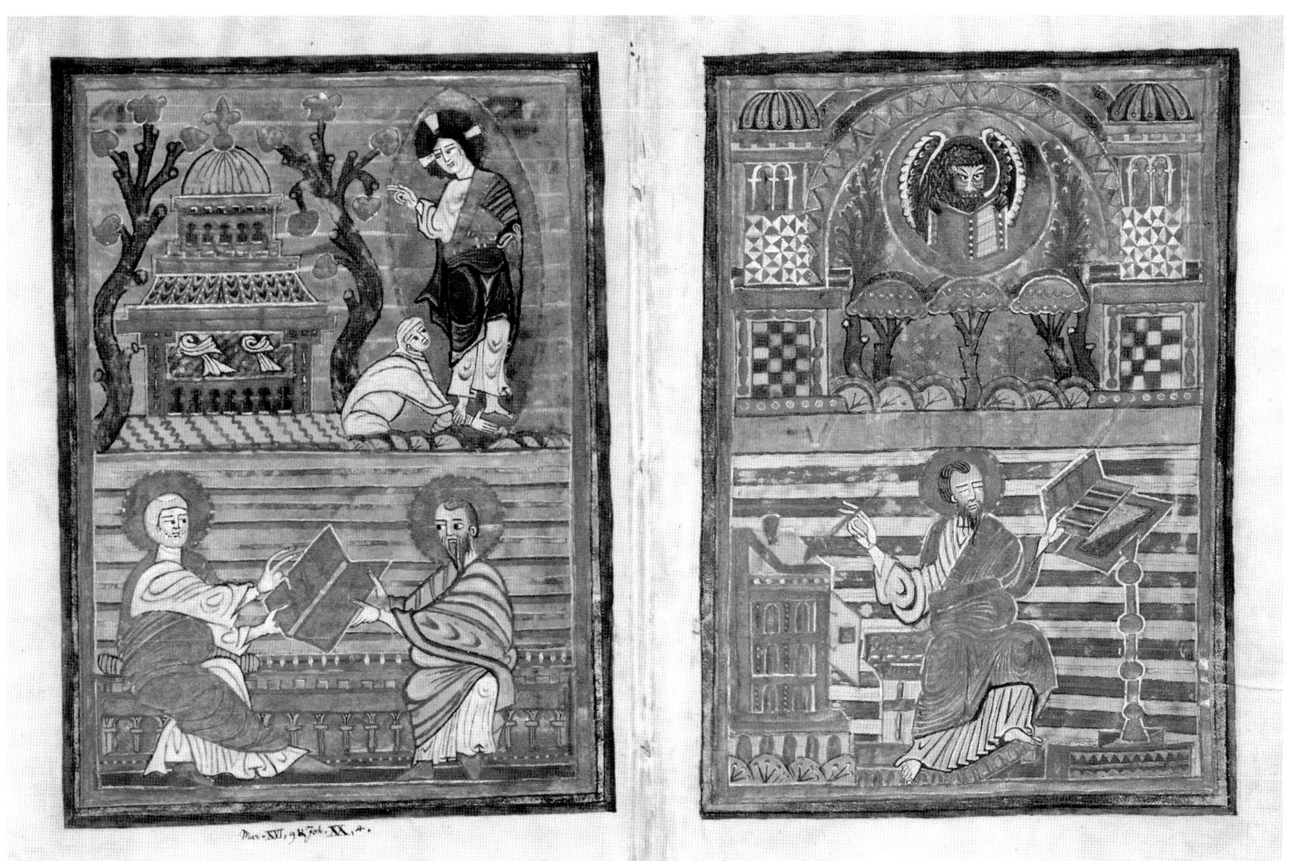

FIGURE 12   Hildesheim, Dom- und Diözesanmu-
seum, Domschatz 18 (Bernward Gospels), fols. 75v–76r,
Noli me tangere (above left) and *Peter Charging Mark to
Write the Gospels* (below left); *Portrait of Mark* (right)

(fol. 76r; plate 9 and fig. 12). Mark's author portrait shares some characteristics with Matthew's,
most notably in the evangelists' poses. Yet there
are also important differences, such as the fact
that Mark is portrayed as a mature man with
long beard and widow's peak and the fact that the
background consists of a simple flat pattern of
multicolored stripes rather than a curtain.

   Neither the illustrations for the gospel of
Luke nor those for the gospel of John include
episodes from their lives. Instead, the portraits of

Luke and John are paired with pictures of Christ;
he appears in the space above the evangelists in
conjunction with their symbols, the ox and the
eagle (fols. 118v and 175v; plates 13 and 17, and
see figs. 25 and 26). In contrast to the portraits
of Matthew and Mark, the portraits of Luke and
John each appear on the verso rather than recto of
a bifolium, and they face text rather than narrative scenes. While there are certain compositional
similarities between the paintings of these last
two evangelists, most notably the tilted footstools

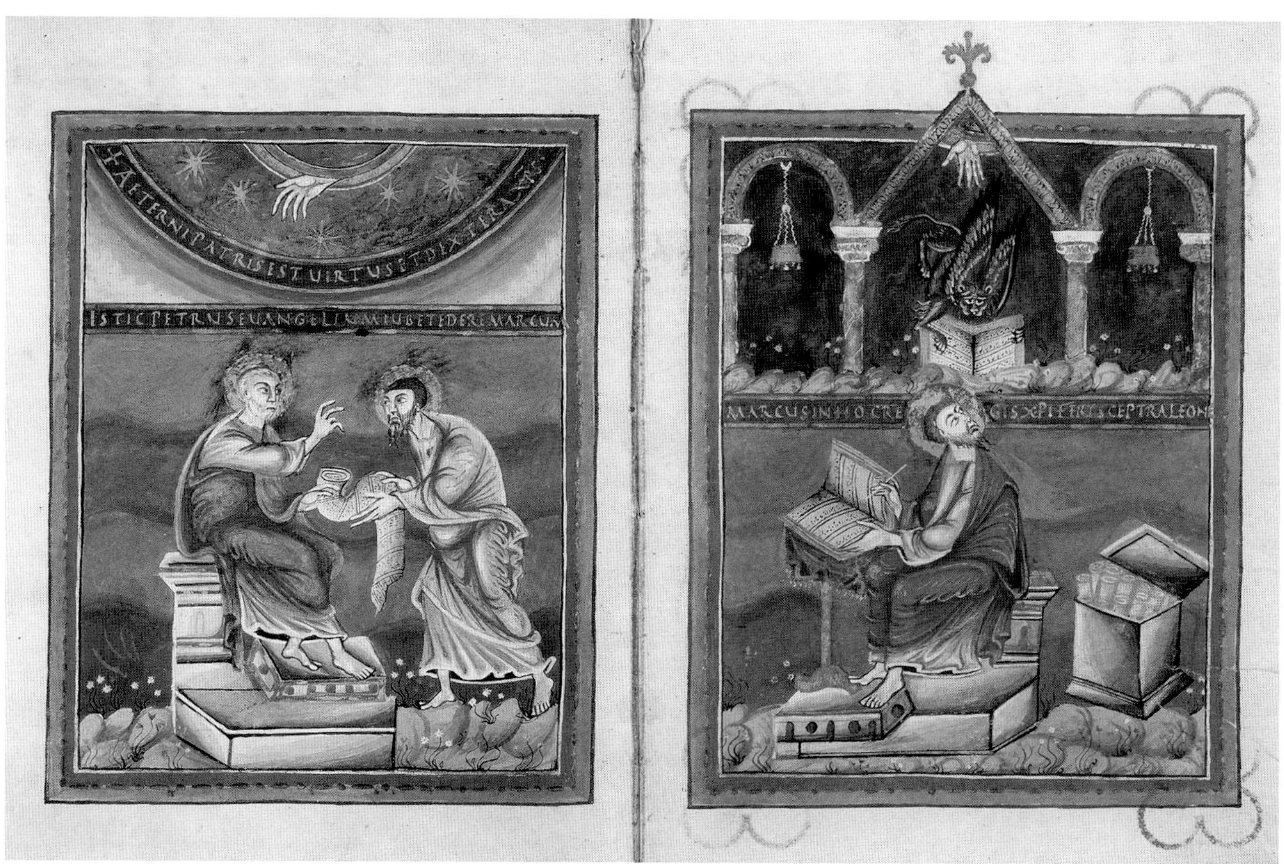

FIGURE 13   Prague, Knihovna metropolitní kapituly, Cim. 2 (Prague Gospels), ninth century, fols. 82v–83r, *Mark with Peter* (left); *Portrait of Mark* (right)

and the combined scroll case and inkstand to the figures' right, the pictures differ from each other in significant ways. Like Matthew, Luke appears as an unbearded youth with long brown hair and sits in front of a curtain. In contrast, John is portrayed as the visionary author of Revelation. He is an older man with a flowing grayish tan beard and hair and adopts a contemplative pose. As in the portrait of Mark, the painting's background is a flat repeating pattern of ornament.

Medieval exegetes and illuminators often treated the evangelists in pairs, and it is also not unusual for theologians to single John out from the other evangelists for having a particularly penetrating spiritual insight.[3] Yet the usual grouping links Matthew to John because both were contemporaries of Christ, while Mark and Luke belonged to the following generation, being disciples, respectively, of the apostles Peter and Paul.[4] Instead, the Bernward Gospels employs compositional devices that relate Matthew to Mark and Luke to John; simultaneously, youthful portrait types and the motif of a curtain connect the portraits of Matthew and Luke, while older

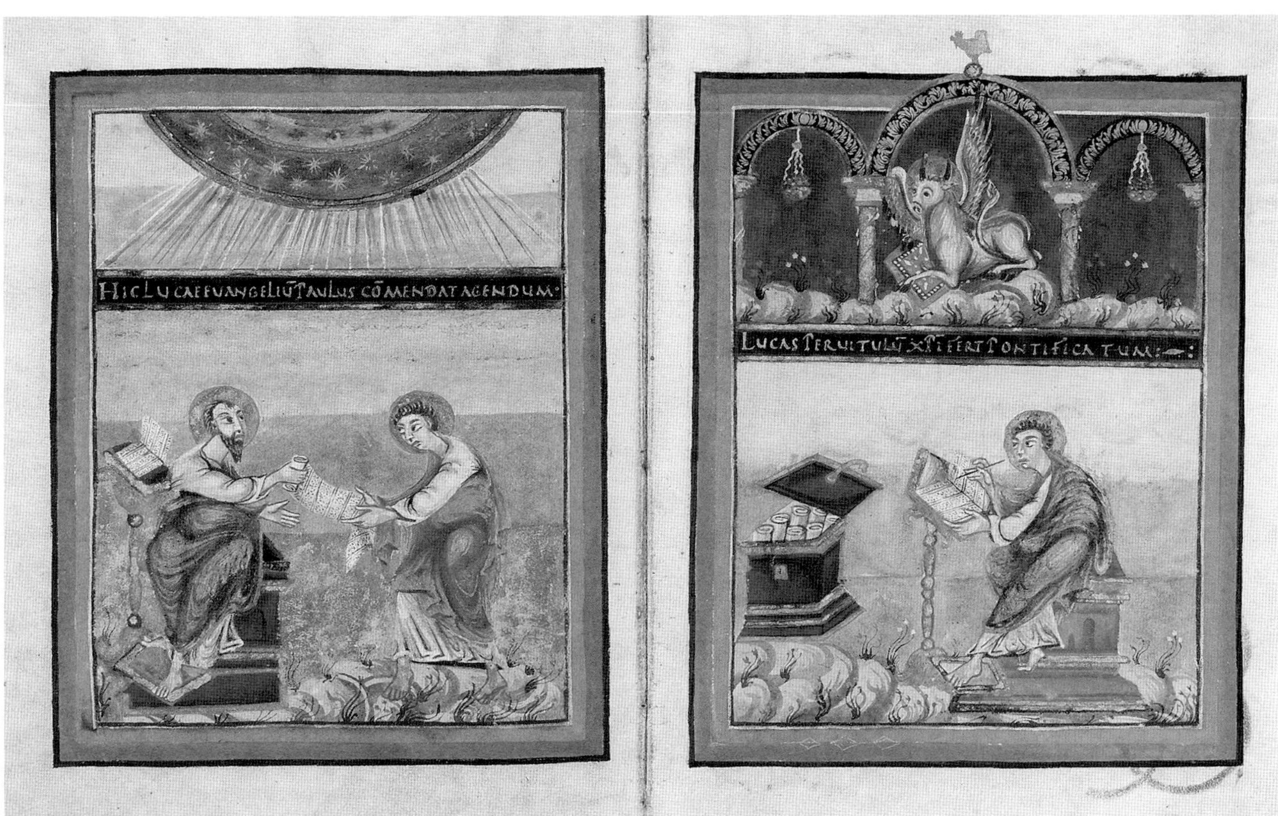

FIGURE 14   Prague, Knihovna metropolitní kapituly, Cim. 2 (Prague Gospels), fols. 125v–126r, *Luke with Paul* (left); *Portrait of Luke* (right)

portrait types and a flatly patterned background link the portraits of Mark and John.

These choices mark a departure from the manuscripts that served as models for the Bernward Gospels.[5] A Carolingian gospel book to which the Bernward Gospels bears a close relationship (Prague, Kapitulní Knihovna, Cim. 2) pairs Mark's portrait with a painting of Mark accompanied by Peter (fols. 82v–83r; fig. 13) and Luke's portrait with a picture of Luke accompanied by Paul (fols. 125v–126r; fig. 14). Mark and Luke each appear, then, with the apostle who taught him. The equivalent arrangement in Matthew pairs the evangelist's portrait with the scene of Christ calling Matthew to his service (fols. 23v–24r; fig. 15), and in John, the evangelist is presented alongside a painting of the Last Supper, where John appears as Christ's most beloved apostle, resting his head against Christ's breast (fol. 185v–186r; fig. 16). Byzantine manuscripts that have also been proposed as possible models for the Bernward Gospels follow a related pattern. Greek codices that include a painting of Mark accompanied by Peter usually substitute it for Mark's portrait and do the same thing with the picture of Luke with his teacher, Paul.[6] In those instances Matthew

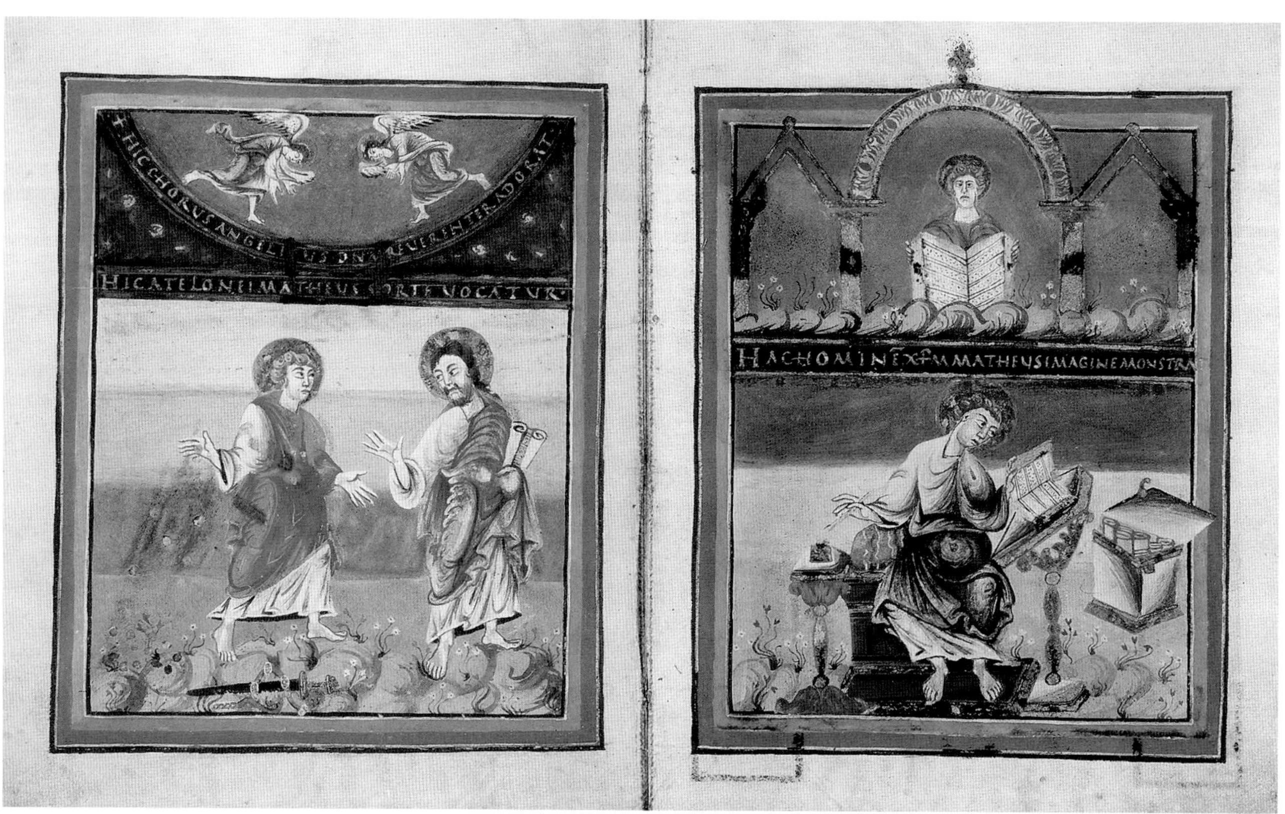

FIGURE 15   Prague, Knihovna metropolitni kapituly, Cim. 2 (Prague Gospels), fols. 23v–24r, *Christ Calls Matthew* (left); *Portrait of Matthew* (right)

and John generally appear alone, each portrayed as an author. The Bernward Gospels varies from each of these Carolingian and Byzantine strategies. Why?

One possibility is that the shift in the codex's decorative scheme discussed in the introduction occurred as a series of progressive modifications in the program. An alternative is that the differences among the gospels' illustrations are the result of amalgamating independent models. Indeed, the biographical scenes depend heavily on the Prague gospels, while the Ascension that is paired with the portrait of John draws on Anglo-Saxon iconography.[7] Neither of these

explanations is entirely satisfactory, however, especially because each portrait combines a limited set of varying details—the background, portrait type, and composition—in ways that, in effect, link the paintings each to the others. For example, the portrait of Mark echoes some characteristics of Matthew's portrait, and other aspects of Luke's and John's. It is worth noting that a fundamental tenet of the medieval understanding of the New Testament is the harmony of the gospels, a principle that more or less explicitly informs the decoration of most gospel books from the period.[8] While not a main focus of the pictorial program in the Bernward Gospels, the

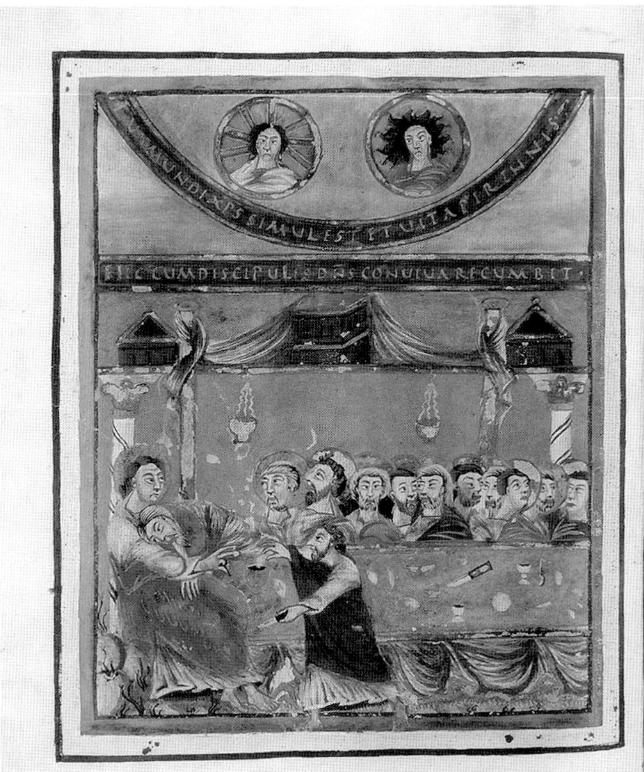 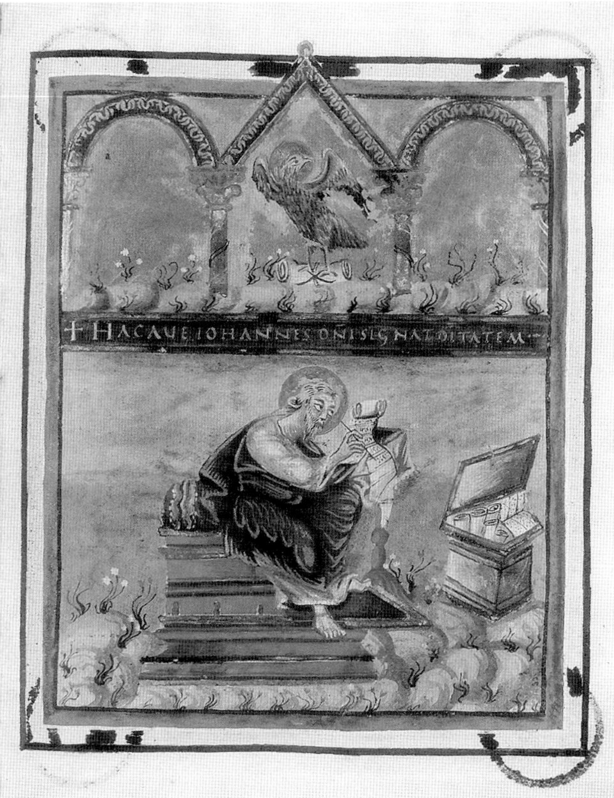

FIGURE 16   Prague, Knihovna metropolitní kapituly, Cim. 2 (Prague Gospels), fols. 185v–186r, *Last Supper* (left); *Portrait of John* (right)

alternating details of the miniatures do allow for this harmony while developing different themes in the portraits of Matthew and Mark versus those of Luke and John.

Of the evidence that these two sets of portraits (one paired with images of Christ, the other not) should be treated independently, the most important to consider is the inclusion in the manuscript of additional pictures of Christ that share the same iconic pictorial mode. These will be the subject of the next chapter. At the same time, the codex physically connects the paintings of the Crucifixion and Ascension, respectively, to

the portraits of Luke and John just as the placement and content of the biographical episodes link the pictures of the Calling of Matthew to the portrait of Matthew, and the depiction of Peter charging Mark to write the gospels to the portrait of Mark. It is therefore important to consider how these two types of pictures might relate to each other.

Since the studies of George Galavaris and Robert Nelson on the relationship between textual prefaces and the illustrations of Byzantine gospel books, representations of Mark with the apostle Peter have been connected to a particular evangelist portrait type in which an accompanying figure is introduced. Galavaris and Nelson have argued that this genre derived from the gospels' prefatory commentary and served generally as a motif of witness, authority, or inspiration.[9] Rainer Kahsnitz has made similar arguments about the Calling of Matthew in Byzantine and Western art.[10] Kahsnitz's conclusions point to the possibility that both biographical episodes in the Bernward Gospels function as authentication or inspiration motifs. However, as Kahsnitz also recognizes, outside of the Bernward Gospels and one manuscript from Corvey (a center closely connected to Hildesheim), there are no Ottonian paintings of Mark with Peter (or Luke with Paul, for that matter), and the programmatic linking of the Calling of Matthew to the "accompanied evangelist" picture is found only in the Prague Gospels and the Bernward Gospels. Kahsnitz's argument also depends on interpreting the depictions of all four evangelists in the Prague Gospels, including the connections the manuscript draws between John's portrait and John's image at the Last Supper, which is not a feature of the Bernward Gospels.

Except for the Bernward Gospels, the rare Ottonian examples of the Calling of Matthew appear without any connection to an evangelist's portrait. In Archbishop Egbert of Trier's tenth-century lectionary, the scene, together with a depiction of Christ dining at the house of Levi, illustrates the pericope for the sixth week after Epiphany (Trier, Stadtbibliothek, cod. 24, fols. 28v–29r). The placement of both miniatures in the manuscript follows the liturgical calendar. The evangelist portraits, in contrast, appear together at the beginning of Egbert's lectionary (fols. 3v–6r).[11] In a later manuscript that may have been influenced by Egbert's manuscripts, the Codex Aureus from Echternach (ca. 1030), the same scenes do directly precede Matthew's portrait (Nürnberg, Germanisches Nationalmuseum, MS 156142, fols. 19r–20v). However, they form part of a larger group of seventeen narrative miniatures laid out on two bifolia.[12] A final parallel may be the now-lost frescoes that once decorated the Cathedral of Mainz.[13] According to extant verses that may have served as tituli for Mainz's pictorial cycle, a scene involving a tax collector appeared among a series of healing miracles, a placement that logically derives from the order of events narrated in the gospel.[14] There are no Ottonian examples to compare to the painting of Mark with Peter in the Bernward Gospels.

The evidence suggests that although not unknown in the West, these biographical episodes featuring the evangelists were far from popular. The only scene for which other Ottonian examples exist, the Calling of Matthew, did not bear the specificity of associations for Ottonian patrons and viewers that it held for Byzantine ones or for the Carolingians who commissioned the Prague Gospels. Moreover, the representation of the Calling of Matthew in the Bernward Gospels differs from the other depictions cited thus far in two main ways (fol. 18v; plate 5 and fig. 11). The first is that the Bernward Gospels portrays Matthew with a halo even in the narrative scenes. The second is that it offers a more dramatic presentation of both this and the gospel story depicted below (Christ dining in the house of Levi) than other Ottonian or Carolingian and Byzantine examples. In the painting of Christ calling Matthew to his service, Christ faces Matthew directly, but at a certain distance. Traces of the outline of a figure appear between Matthew and Christ, partly overlapped by Christ's right hand. These remains suggest that the painting's design was changed to show Matthew seated and to create more distance between Matthew and Christ. Indeed, in the Carolingian model for this scene, Matthew walks behind Christ, already following him (Prague, Kapitulni Knihovna, Cim. 2, fols. 23v–24r; fig. 15). In contrast, the Bernward Gospels composition places the energy of Christ's command at the center of the painting. The focal point of the scene becomes the empty space between Christ and Matthew, which is charged with the force of Christ's call. Behind Jesus, two disciples turn their bodies and gaze toward each other, absorbed not by the event before them but by their own conversation.

The miniature below depicts Christ dining at the house of Levi (fol. 18v; plate 5 and fig. 11). The scene centers on the moment when the Pharisees express reservations about Christ's decision to keep company with publicans, tax collectors, and other sinners (Matthew 9:10–14; Mark 2:15–18; Luke 5:29–33). The men who stand for the Pharisees appear in the same place as Christ's two disciples in the miniature above; this helps link the two groups and underscores that both doubted Christ. Although the two paintings show consecutive episodes in the gospels, the scene of Christ dining at the House of Levi is not necessary for narrating Matthew's entry into Christ's ministry. Together, however, they emphasize that Matthew was a sinner who proved himself worthy by accepting Christ's call to serve.

It follows from the fact that the Bernward Gospels includes a painting showing Mark with Peter, but not the equivalent picture of Luke with Paul, that this scene has meaning beyond the mere tracing of Mark's religious lineage to Peter in order to authenticate his writings. The portrayal of Peter with Mark takes as its primary subject the circumstances under which the evangelist entered Christ's service, which he performs by writing his gospel. The representation dramatizes the communication between the scene's protagonists. Set at a distance from one another, but sharing the same long bench that spans the entire miniature, Peter and Mark turn to each other. Peter extends the book with his left hand and makes a speaking gesture with his right hand. Mark turns both palms up in order to receive both the codex and Peter's words. In contrast to equivalent paintings in Byzantine art and the Carolingian model (Prague, Kapitulni Knihovna, Cim. 2, fol. 82v; fig. 13), where both the titulus and picture show Mark to be subservient to Peter, in the Bernward Gospels painting, Peter and Mark have equal weight.[15] That difference underscores the point that the Ottonian painting is less about Mark's inspiration or about lending authority to his gospel than it is about Mark's participation in Christ's ministry. What the Calling of Matthew and Peter's charging Mark to write about Christ have in common is that both present the key moment when the evangelists began to serve Christ. Matthew is an apostle chosen by Christ, and Saint Peter, one of Christ's foremost disciples, prompted Mark to write his text. Their service includes bearing witness to Christ, and through that witness, the evangelists enter into a privileged relationship with Him.

It is probable that at least the latter two themes also inform the decision to pair the portraits of John and Luke with visions of Christ, a point to which I shall return at the end. The portrait of John appears in conjunction with a painting of the Ascension that follows an iconographic type first developed in Anglo-Saxon England during the tenth century. In his study of this so-called disappearing Christ imagery, Robert Deshman offered one explanation for John's vision, suggesting that it, together with John's contemplative pose, demonstrated this evangelist's superior spiritual understanding.[16] While this observation helps illuminate the Bernward Gospels program, on the surface it does not immediately explain why a second vision would be depicted above the portrait of Luke, who is not generally considered a visionary, nor how these two miniatures relate to the episodes drawn from Matthew's and Mark's lives.

The two visionary miniatures may best be understood through the scenes illustrating the life of John the Baptist. Of twenty narrative pictures in the gospel book, six present John in different guises that articulate linked themes. These scenes are half-page miniatures that open the painting cycles of the last three gospels. The gospel of Mark depicts John addressing Jewish priests (fol. 75r, above; plate 7); the gospel of Luke illustrates John's infancy (fols. 111r and 111v; plates 10–11); and the gospel of John presents the Baptist in his best-known act from the gospels, baptizing Christ (fol. 174v, above; plate 15).

A significant focus of these paintings is the typological relationship between the Baptist and Christ. The first picture is a rarely illustrated scene of the Baptist preaching (fol. 75r, above; fig. 17). John stands before a group of men whose pointed caps, along with the foremost figure's staff and costume, mark them as Jewish priests.[17] He wears a tunic girded with a golden sash that drapes over his left shoulder and wraps around his waist in the manner required of medieval deacons when they participated in the Mass.[18]

These details echo aspects of the painting below, which shows Christ calling the first disciples (fol. 75r, below; fig. 17).[19] In these paired scenes, Christ and the Baptist stand one above the other, each proselytizing to a group of exactly four men. Both adopt the same pose—head tilted and holding a book in the left hand while gesturing with the right—and have the same halo, which, in contrast to those of the other figures, incorporates white dots in its borders. In addition, the two plants that flank John are prominent framing elements that appear throughout the manuscript primarily in association with Christ. For example, in the manuscript's Noli me tangere (fol. 75v, above; plate 8), this motif frames Christ's empty grave. In two paintings of the Crucifixion, as well as the pictures of the Raising of Lazarus and Ascension (fols. 118v, 174v, 175r, and 175v; plates 13 and 15–17), the same motif accompanies Christ himself.

Ornament both associates and differentiates the two scenes, visually presenting a similarity of form that simultaneously highlights difference (fol. 75r; plate 7). Broad horizontal bands of color articulate both pictures' backgrounds; a gold and purple palette sets off Christ, while slightly paler hues appear behind John the Baptist. The water under the Baptist flows from the mouth of a personification of the river Jordan, whose head is aligned with Christ below, evoking a trope discussed by numerous medieval writers, including Hrabanus Maurus, that identified the flow of water from Paradise as the image of Christ flowing from God's fountain and hence also as the Word of God irrigating the Church.[20] The typological relationship established between the Baptist and Christ, together with this latter detail, places John between the Old Law, to which he

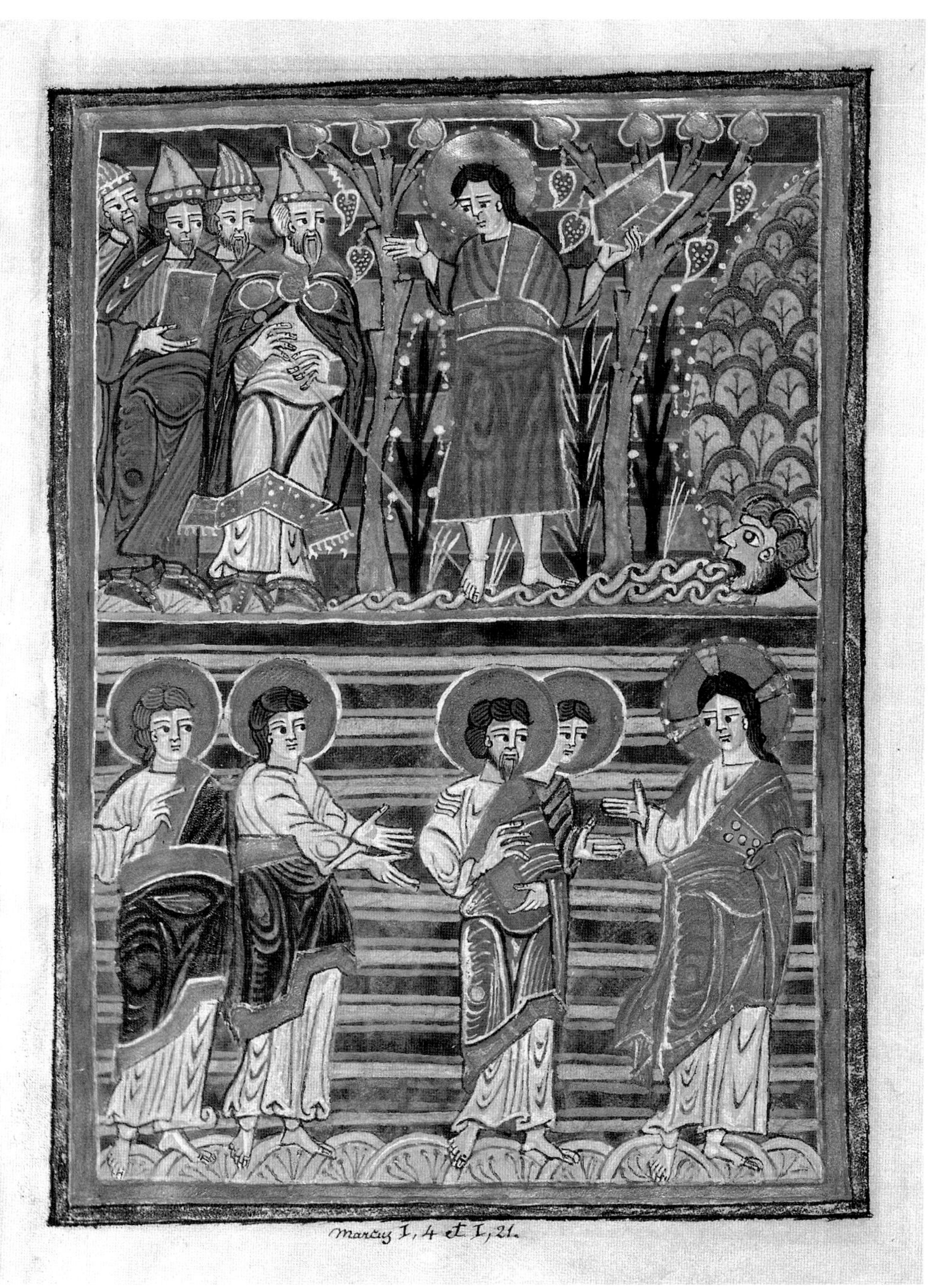

FIGURE 17   Hildesheim, Dom- und Diözesanmuseum, Domschatz 18 (Bernward Gospels), fol. 75r, *John the Baptist Preaching* (above) and *Christ Calling the Apostles* (below)

preaches, and the New Law of Christ, for whom he "prepares the way" (Mark 1:1–8). It also places the Baptist in the company of Christ's followers, the first of the Christian priesthood. Indeed, John is linked in this painting not only to Christ but also to his disciples, who wear variations on the Baptist's costume; the strips of gold that border their tunics echo the shape and material of John's sash.

The illustrations in Luke's gospel continue to present the Baptist as a type for Christ and for the Christian priesthood. Four scenes illustrate the Baptist's infancy as it is described in the text's opening verses.[21] The first page shows two consecutive moments from the prophecy of John's miraculous conception, which parallels Christ's (fol. 111r; plate 10 and fig. 18). In the painting above, John's father, the priest Zacharias, enters the inner sanctum of the Jewish temple to perform the incense offering. There the archangel Gabriel announces to him the coming of the Baptist. Zacharias expresses his skepticism and, because of this doubt, loses his voice. That event appears below.

The second page presents two scenes: the Visitation and John's naming (fol. 111v; plate 11 and fig. 19). In contrast to the usual pictorial convention for the Visitation, in which Mary and Elizabeth embrace, the codex emphasizes Mary's spoken response to Elizabeth's greeting: the Magnificat (Luke 1:40–56), whose lines culminate in the interpretation of Mary's conception as the fulfillment of the divine plan foretold in the Old Testament. To the right is a throne from which hangs a votive crown; these are conventional motifs drawn from Annunciation imagery. Below, standing next to his wife, Elizabeth, Zacharias displays a vertical scroll marked "Iohann[nes]

e[st] nom[en] eius," indicating with these words that his son will be named John. In another instance of the idiosyncratic iconography of the Bernward Gospels, Zacharias is depicted holding a tablet engraved with the word "Benedictus," a reference to his canticle (Luke 1:68), which begins by emphasizing Christ's Incarnation as the Redeemer and concludes with a description of John's service to prepare the way for Christ.

The infancy cycle articulates the ways in which the Baptist's birth is a sign of Christ's impending advent and shows John to be a type for Christ. It also refers to the liturgy of the hours. The Magnificat and Benedictus were important hymns recited daily as part of the Divine Office. The Benedictus was generally chanted during morning prayers, at lauds, and the Magnificat in the evening, at vespers. Familiar to both the patron and recipients of the codex, these liturgical canticles formed the basis for understanding John as the forerunner and type for Christ. The picture reinforces the prayers' message. The alignment of Mary's Magnificat, acknowledging Christ's presence inside her body, with Zacharias's Benedictus, acknowledging God's message about his son, evokes the typological relationship between John and Christ that exegetes traced to their very birth.[22] The depiction of Mary's throne in the Visitation, because it acts as a reference to the Annunciation, also creates a parallel between the miraculous nature of both her and Elizabeth's conceptions.

The emphasis on the Baptist's typological relationship to Christ developed alongside the growth of his cult in the fourth century. Augustine is the first witness to a feast commemorating the birth of John the Baptist on 24 June. His significant remarks on the Baptist—in the dozen or

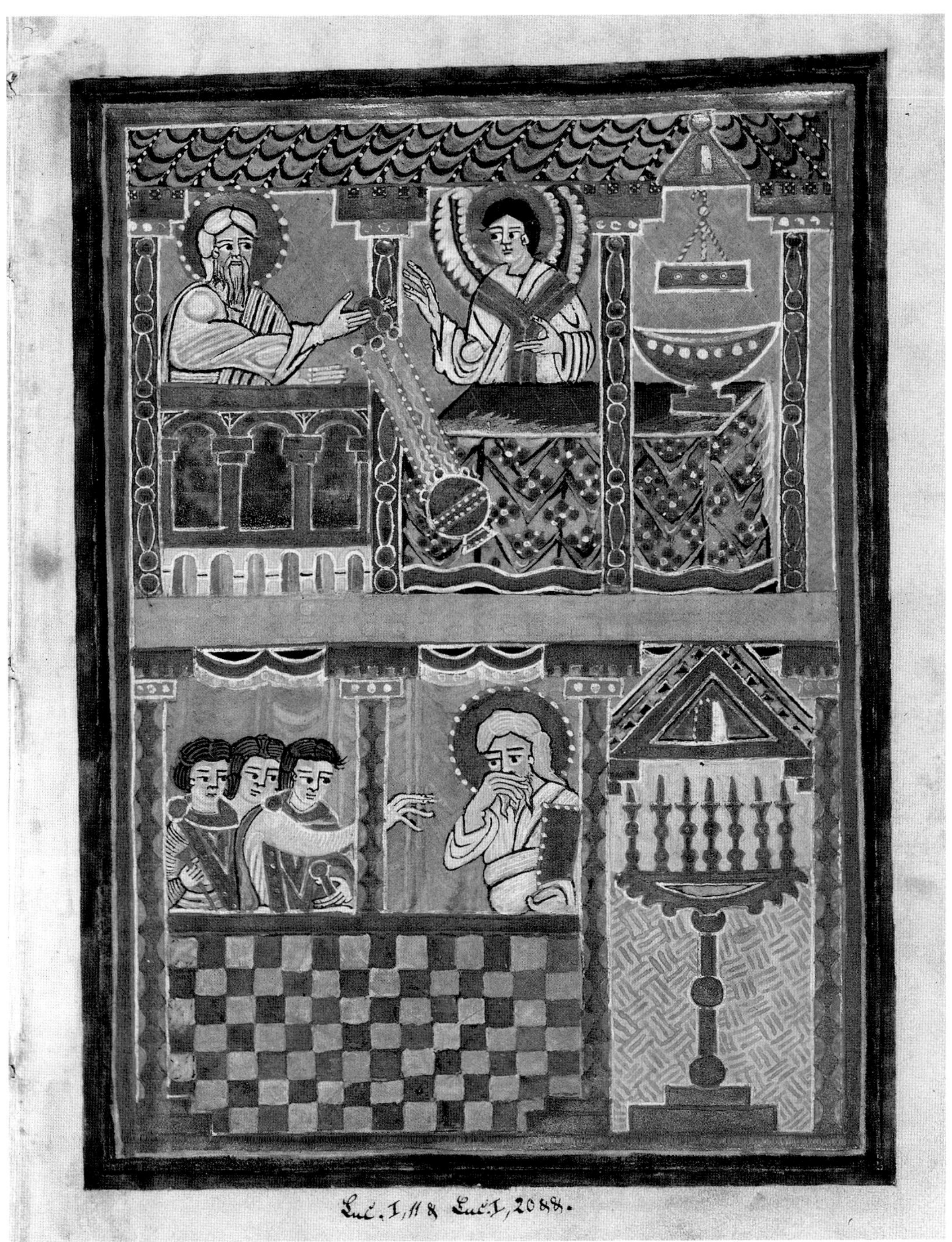

FIGURE 18   Hildesheim, Dom- und Diözesanmu-
seum, Domschatz 18 (Bernward Gospels), fol. 111r,
Annunciation to Zacharias (above) and *Zacharias
Leaving the Temple* (below)

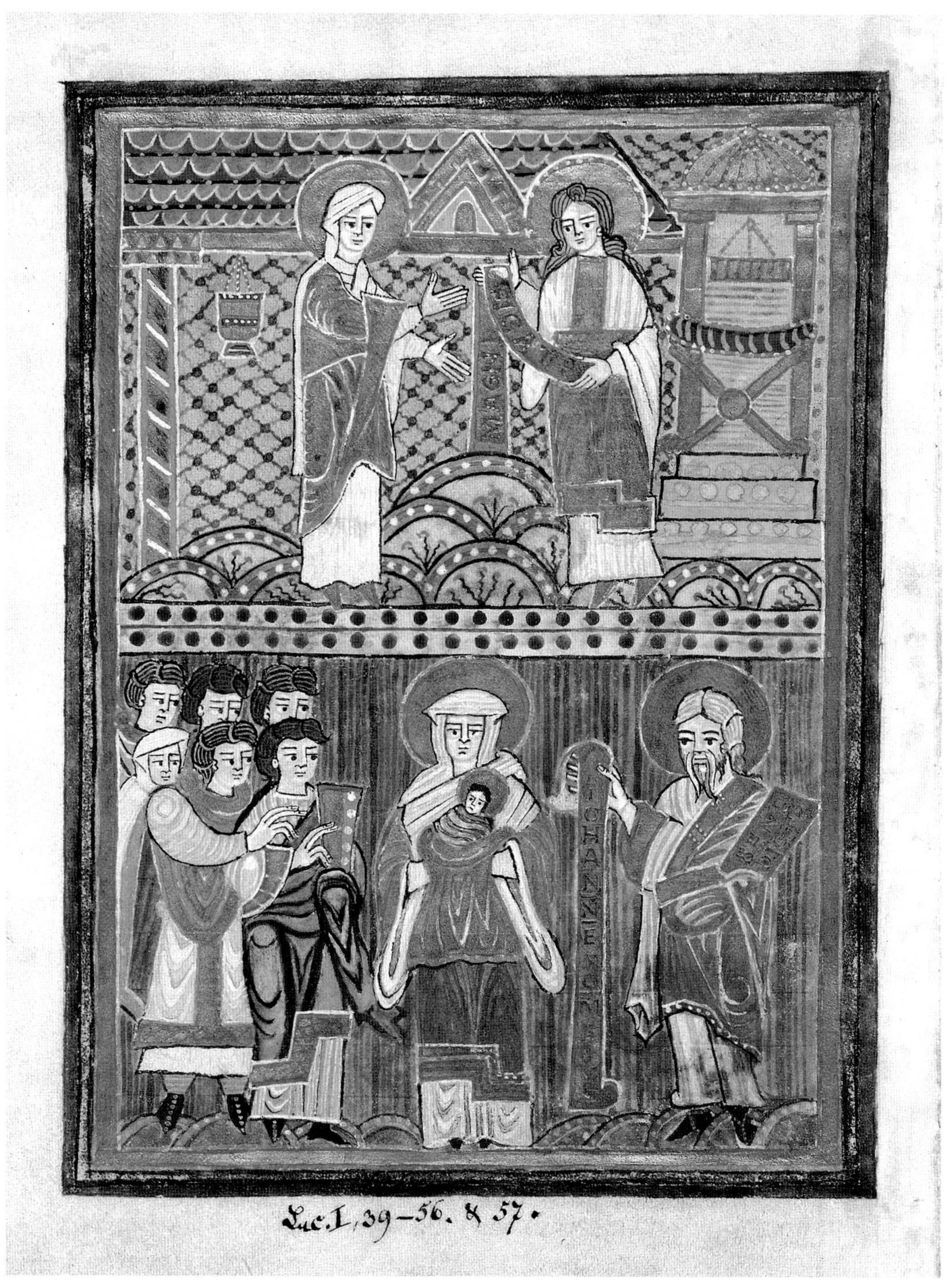

FIGURE 19   Hildesheim, Dom- und Diözesanmuseum, Domschatz 18 (Bernward Gospels), fol. 111v, *Visitation* (above) and *Naming of John the Baptist* (below)

so surviving sermons he preached on the Nativity of the Baptist, in three of his tracts commenting on the gospel of John the Evangelist, and in one of the *De diversis quaestionibus*—lay the basis for the medieval understanding of the Baptist. Augustine's commentary is primarily concerned with analyzing the parallels between the Baptist and Christ, both of whose births the gospels presented as miraculous events announced by the angel Gabriel. John was born above hope, to a sterile woman, while Christ was born above nature, to a virgin. For Augustine, John the Baptist, the forerunner and herald of Christ, is the voice to Christ's word and the lamp to Christ's light. He is the boundary stone between the two testaments, the Old and the New.[23]

Following Augustine, early medieval exegetes continued to underscore the similarities between Christ and John the Baptist, but beginning with Bede, they particularly highlighted John's priestly lineage. While Bede follows Augustine in describing the Baptist as the line between law and gospel, Bede adds to Augustine's discussion that John came from a priestly lineage in order to proclaim a change in the priesthood. In a homily for the Vigil of the Nativity of John the Baptist, Bede deliberately narrates John's bloodline through his father back to Abijah, the descendant of the high priest Aaron, who was the eighth priest David had selected to serve as chief to one of the twenty-four orders into which David divided the priesthood (1 Chronicles 24).[24] Carolingian exegesis on the Continent, such as the sermons of Haimo of Auxerre and Hrabanus Maurus, continues in the same vein.[25]

The Bernward Gospels infancy cycle includes significant liturgical content that suggests an attempt to draw particular attention to the fact that John was born of priests. In the Annunciation to Zacharias, there is a special emphasis on ritual implements. Zacharias holds a censer, featured prominently as it crosses over the column that appears between Zacharias and the angel. The area between the chains that carry the censer is activated by squiggly lines on a blue band that contrasts with the predominantly pink tones of the painting; the implement thus stands out starkly from the page. On the far right appears a series of liturgical objects—a hanging lamp, bowl, and candelabra, whose strict alignment emphasizes the importance of these works to the painting's meaning. Finally, as already described, the paintings of the Visitation and of John's naming include allusions to canticles recited daily as part of the Divine Office. Although by no means a direct sign of John's priesthood, it is worth noting that the references to these prayers are uncommon additions that add one more liturgical reference to the infancy cycle. Finally, in the last representation of the Baptist, which illustrates the gospel of John (fol. 174v above; plate 15 and fig. 20), the Baptist performs a paradigmatic priestly act, the sacrament of baptism.

The Bernward Gospels presents the Baptist not only as a type for Christ and the priesthood in general, but also as a surrogate for the manuscript's episcopal patron, a point the codex makes explicit in certain unusual aspects of the iconography of the Baptist. The choice to vest John in the contemporary liturgical garb of a deacon in the scene that shows him preaching (fol. 75r above; plate 7 and fig. 17) relates to the emphasis that the dedication painting places on the fact that Bernward wears Mass vestments (fol. 16v; plate 2). Bernward is clothed in the alb, cope, stole, and dalmatic required by the liturgy.

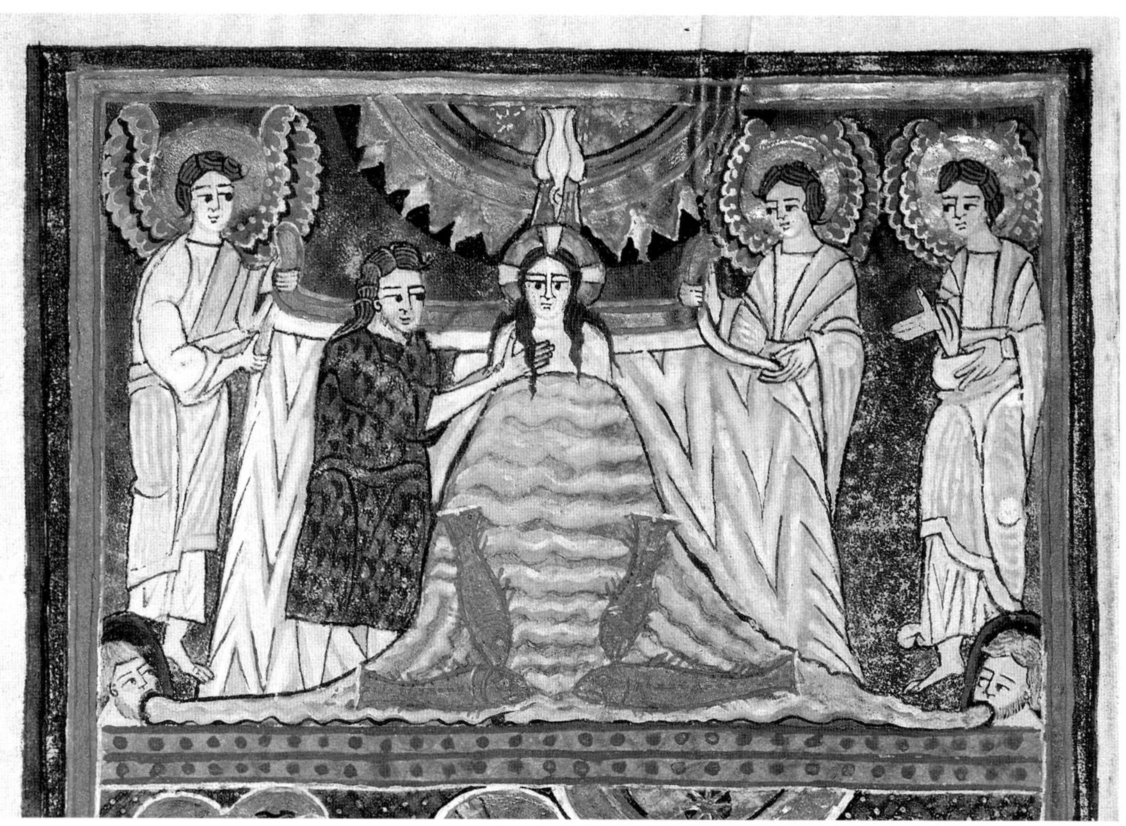

FIGURE 20   Hildesheim, Dom- und Diözesanmuseum, Domschatz 18 (Bernward Gospels), fol. 174v,
Baptism of Christ (detail)

His garments are highlighted by an inscription in the lower frame that reads "Bernwardus ornatus tanti vestitu pontificali" (Bernward adorned with such great episcopal vestments). Like John's father, Zacharias (fol. 111r above; plate 10 and fig. 18), Bernward stands before an altar set for the celebration of a ritual—the Eucharistic sacrament, with the chalice, paten, and portable altar. Bernward's book helps move him into the space of the altar toward the saints. Similarly, Zacharias's censer crosses into the innermost sanctuary of the Jewish temple toward the angel. Finally, Bernward's two-handed grip on the gospel book

during a moment that the dedicatory picture constructs as both gift-giving and sacramental performance imitates the Baptist's unusual touch of Christ's shoulder in the Baptism, which was for the Church the sacramental act through which Christians became part of the community of the saved (fol. 174v above; plate 15 and fig. 20).[26]

Baptismal rites played a significant role in developing John as a model more specific to the episcopate; they involved the priest's authority of incorporation, an authority to which Western bishops sought to maintain a privileged relationship throughout the Middle Ages.[27] The Baptism is John's most celebrated act from the gospels and the earliest to be represented in art. Yet where the gospels use the event primarily to develop John's identity as a witness to Christ's divinity, the liturgy offered a way to understand John typologically in relation to the baptizing priest. Already in the fourth century, monuments used images of the Baptism to develop connections between the biblical narrative and contemporary baptismal rituals. In the baptisteries of Ravenna, for example, a mosaic rendering of the Baptism appears at the center of each dome directly above the baptismal font. This placement establishes a visual link between the Baptist above and the living bishop below.[28] When Christian artists first started representing John the Baptist as an isolated figure in the sixth century, they continued to relate him to the episcopacy. The ivory cathedra made for Archbishop Maximian of Ravenna in the middle of that century may be the earliest direct comparison between the Baptist and a historical bishop, while the ivory book covers of the Carolingian Drogo Sacramentary (Paris, Bibliothèque nationale, MS lat. 9428) use the Baptist to present Bishop Drogo, the patron and user of the manuscript, as part of the sacramental priesthood.[29]

In light of such liturgical and pictorial associations, it is not surprising to find that eighth- and ninth-century hagiographers often compared historical bishops to the Baptist when establishing claims for their subjects' sanctity. Much of the point of the textual comparison's focus in this early period is on the fact that the Baptist's saintliness was indicated even before his birth. The early anonymous life of Saint Cuthbert, a bishop and monk from Northumbria, for example, explains how Cuthbert was like Samuel, David, Jeremiah, and John the Baptist, all having been "a vulva matris sanctificati leguntur" (sanctified for the work of the Lord in their mothers' wombs).[30] Alcuin's life of Archbishop Willibrord and Hincmar of Rheims's biography of Bishop Remigius compare their episcopal subjects to the Baptist on the same grounds.[31]

Among these, Hincmar offers the most extensive presentation of his subject's Baptist-like attributes, arguing two main points. First, Hincmar suggests—conventionally—that Remigius's sanctity was indicated even before his birth.[32] With his second point, however, he offers a fresh comparison for which the Baptist serves specifically as a model of pastoral action. Hincmar explains that Remigius converted the Franks to the light of the gospels, just as John had brought his people to Christ.[33] The Baptist serves in these Carolingian texts to establish the hagiographic subject's holiness as an intrinsic quality, one with which the saint is born, although the comparison might be extended to characterize a bishop's engagement in the world as a saintly pursuit, a theme that would become increasingly important during the course of the tenth and eleventh centuries.

References to the Baptist continue to appear in tenth- and eleventh-century biographies, but as part of a subtle shift of focus compared to earlier examples.[34] Although rarely treating officially canonized subjects, these texts use the formulas of hagiographic writing, wherein comparisons to biblical models serve to prove the sanctity of their subjects. In several instances, for which the life of the monk John of Gorze is illustrative, authors justify their treatment of their subjects as saints by citing the example of the Baptist. The preface to the Life explains, "And now we may pass over the rest in silence, for John himself, compared to whom, according to the gospel witness, no one was greater among those born from woman, made no miracle [*signa*]. It has been put to sleep for perpetuity in the silence of all of Scripture whether while he was struck by the sword in prison, he was distinguished by some last miracle [*signa*] from any type of murderers or thieves."[35] Here the author reveals his purpose: he cannot or will not prove John of Gorze's holiness by establishing that he performed miracles. Rather, as with much of the hagiography written under the influence of the tenth-century reforms emerging from Gorze and Cluny, the biography constructs John of Gorze's sanctity primarily by means of cataloguing the monk's virtues and good deeds.[36] The Baptist, like John of Gorze, did not perform miracles but was nonetheless among those saints whom exegetes acknowledged to be most like Christ.

Cluniac hagiography follows the same trend. In the early tenth century, Odo of Cluny wrote a biography that specifically evoked the comparison to the Baptist to explain why he treats his subject as a saint, even though—as with John of Gorze—no miracles can be or will be ascribed to him.[37] This is especially significant because the biography centers on a noble, Count Gerard, and with this text Odo is establishing a novel type of saint—the Christian knight, who, although he never took monastic vows, was nonetheless considered worthy of sainthood because he led a virtuous life.[38] The text's central message, like that of the biography of John of Gorze, is that sanctity stems primarily from leading a life pleasing to Christ, even when it is a life engaged in worldly affairs. A century later, the reformer Peter Damian would use the Baptist for the

same purpose, but in the biography of an Italian monk, Saint Romuald.[39] What these examples suggest is that under the impetus of the tenth- and eleventh-century Benedictine reforms, the persona of the Baptist was adapted to a variety of subjects in ways that reconciled their activities in the world with more traditional and monastically inspired spiritual ideals.

In Ottonian accounts, the model of the Baptist often refers specifically to the active life of the priesthood. For example, the mid-eleventh-century biography of Archbishop Heribert of Cologne, an important member of the Ottonian episcopate who, like Bernward, served in the imperial chapel, names the archbishop another Elijah or John the Baptist on the grounds that he corrected the behavior of both clerics and laymen: "because of a drought the crop was entirely perishing, and another Elijah, like the saving John the Baptist, taking refuge with the known protections from God, admonished both the clergy and people."[40] The author here selects John the Baptist as a model in the specific instance of describing Bishop Heribert's pastoral care, which involved actions that in this period were essentially reserved to the priesthood: the responsibility and authority of preaching.

Throughout the eleventh century, the comparison between hagiographic subject and the Baptist continues to present John as a type for the Christian priesthood. In the *Vita Theodorici* (written before 1091), for example, the author reports that during her pregnancy, Theodoric's mother had a vision in which a nun told her that her son would be a priest "through whom will be provided salvation for many."[41] These same words were spoken by the angel that prophesied John the Baptist's conception. Here the comparison suggests not only the pastoral responsibility of the protagonist—in this instance, a future abbot—but also more specifically the spiritual leadership exercised by his actions as a priest, as opposed to an ideal based on the more purely contemplative life generally associated with monks. This is significant because the responsibilities of the medieval priesthood were theoretically incompatible with the virtues of the monastic life. Indeed, in the Rule of Saint Benedict priests appear as a disruptive presence in the monastery. Chapters concerning priests emphasize how the *ordine sacerdotum*, meaning bishops, priests, and deacons, should not be too readily granted permission to reside in the monastery.[42] In contrast, tenth- and eleventh-century biographies use the comparison to the Baptist to present as exemplary the active life of the priesthood, even for monks and abbots like John of Gorze and Theodoric.

The Baptist was in general a saint of burgeoning importance in the tenth and eleventh centuries, one whom Bishop Bernward seems to have particularly esteemed.[43] An altar had been consecrated to the Baptist in the crypt of the cathedral by the eleventh century, and another altar dedicated to the Baptist is described at Saint Michael's monastic church in the context of the burial of an abbot in the east choir around 1141; the altar itself undoubtedly predates that mention.[44] Bernward's artistic commissions for Saint Michael's give special emphasis to the Baptist. For example, a sacramentary from 1014 uses a gold and silver initial to mark the Baptist's feast and records, over three folios, a long vigil and Mass to celebrate the saint.[45] The decoration of the bronze column Bernward presented to Saint Michael's Abbey features a number of scenes showing the Baptist's imprisonment and death at the hands of

Herod. Along with the story of Lazarus and the rich man, these representations are the only ones that do not feature Christ. While the logic behind the selection of scenes on the column has yet to be entirely elucidated, its carvings highlight the figure of the Baptist and do so in the context of reliefs that narrate Christ's ministry, including Jesus's paradigmatic parable about the virtuous life. In this way the column evokes themes analogous to the Bernward Gospels.[46]

The deployment of the Baptist to present as exemplary the active life of the priesthood—often for bishops, but even for monks and abbots like John of Gorze and Theodoric—together with Bernward's particular interest in the saint provides a context in which to understand the significance of the Baptist for the manuscript's episcopal patron. John offers a multivalent guise for the bishop that was gaining prominence during the reform movements of the tenth and eleventh centuries as a model with the potential to reconcile activities more typical of the secular clergy with the traditions of the monastic life.[47] It is a commonplace to observe that in the performance of their duties, early medieval bishops were required to move between what contemporary texts considered to be spiritual versus worldly concerns. Against that background, the model of the Baptist accommodates the ideals of the religious life with bishops' broad exercise of authority in the world, both in spiritual matters and in what modern observers might characterize as their more "secular" administrative tasks. Using the Baptist in this way is consistent with contemporary trends; Ottonian bishops frequently framed their political, jurisdictional, and even military leadership as aspects of their liturgical or pastoral responsibilities.[48]

The Baptist is a significant figure in the Bernward Gospels who serves to link Bernward to various biblical *exempla* and thus to shape how the bishop is to be remembered at Saint Michael's. His deployment as a surrogate for the bishop also offers one way to approach the question posed earlier in this chapter concerning the relationship between the scenes from the lives of Matthew and Mark and the visions of Christ that appear above the portraits of Luke and John. An important focus of both the Baptist paintings and the biographical episodes is participation in Christ's ministry. As it is depicted in the codex, the nature of the Baptist's and evangelists' service ranges from disseminating the Word by writing and preaching to performing the Baptism, the rite wherein, not incidentally, catechumens are initiated into the mysteries of the gospels.

The paintings paired with the portraits of Luke and John develop a different emphasis involving contemplation of the Godhead. Yet here, too, the symbolic role of the Baptist offers a starting point for understanding the significance of these evangelists.[49] The Baptist is not only a witness but also a herald of Christ's advent, which places him in the company of Old Testament prophets like Isaiah and Elijah and connects him to the visionary John of Revelation, the Evangelist.[50] Like these, John the Baptist is a figure of penetrating spiritual insight.[51] In these ways, the Baptist serves as a point of intersection between the themes of service and of witness and spiritual understanding in the Bernward Gospels. Admittedly, the pairing of Luke with what is essentially a vision of the Crucifixion is more unexpected than the depiction of John having a vision.[52] Moreover, both the representation of the cross and the painting of the Ascension are part of a sequence of images of visions that invite consideration of the visual perception of the divine. Yet, as will be treated more fully in the next chapter, these two visions can also be understood in part as signs of Christ's second coming and as representations of his dual nature, to which the authors of the gospels attest.

By using models of service and witness as symbolic surrogates for the patron, the New Testament pictorial cycle develops further the ideas presented in the dedication scene. The models of the evangelists and especially the Baptist present Bernward as a virtuous and even Christo-mimetic bishop.[53] These *exempla* argue for the patron's worthiness, adding weight to the gift-giving process (described in chapter 1) wherein it is hoped the codex will offer proof of the donor's merit.

3

———

SIGHT

Among the ideas treated in the Bernward Gospels is the spiritual perception of the divine. The manuscript explores this concept in two related groups of miniatures that adopt contrasting pictorial styles.[1] One mode, considered in this chapter, is characterized by a representational tendency that is static, frontal, hieratic, and symmetrical; it treats the nature of sight.[2] Paintings of this type elaborate themes that intersect with those of the dedication painting, most notably by emphasizing the hoped-for eternal reward intrinsic to the operation of the gift *pro anima* and by placing Christological *imagines* at the heart of that process.[3] The other mode presents figures in either profile or three-quarter view performing narrative actions. Among these is a series depicting haptic experiences, which will be discussed in chapter 4.

Six miniatures in the Bernward Gospels emphasize axial symmetry and order as a means of marking their focus on visual processes. Four of these iconic pictures appear in conjunction with portraits of the evangelists (fols. 19r, 76r, 118v, and 175v; plates 6, 9, 13, and 17), while two others serve as the first miniature of the set of paintings that illustrate the gospels of Matthew and John, respectively (fols. 18r and 174r; plates 4 and 14). The paintings are connected not only by their formal similarities but also by their common subject matter. Each scene portrays a heavenly setting, at the edges of which appear different characters who gaze into, upon, or toward it. The representation of a static space, separated by ornament and frames from figures engaged in "seeing," serves to identify these miniatures as visions of the divine.[4]

The first painting illustrates Matthew's gospel (fol. 18r; plate 4 and fig. 21). It follows the dedicatory bifolium and combines iconographic elements common to medieval depictions of the

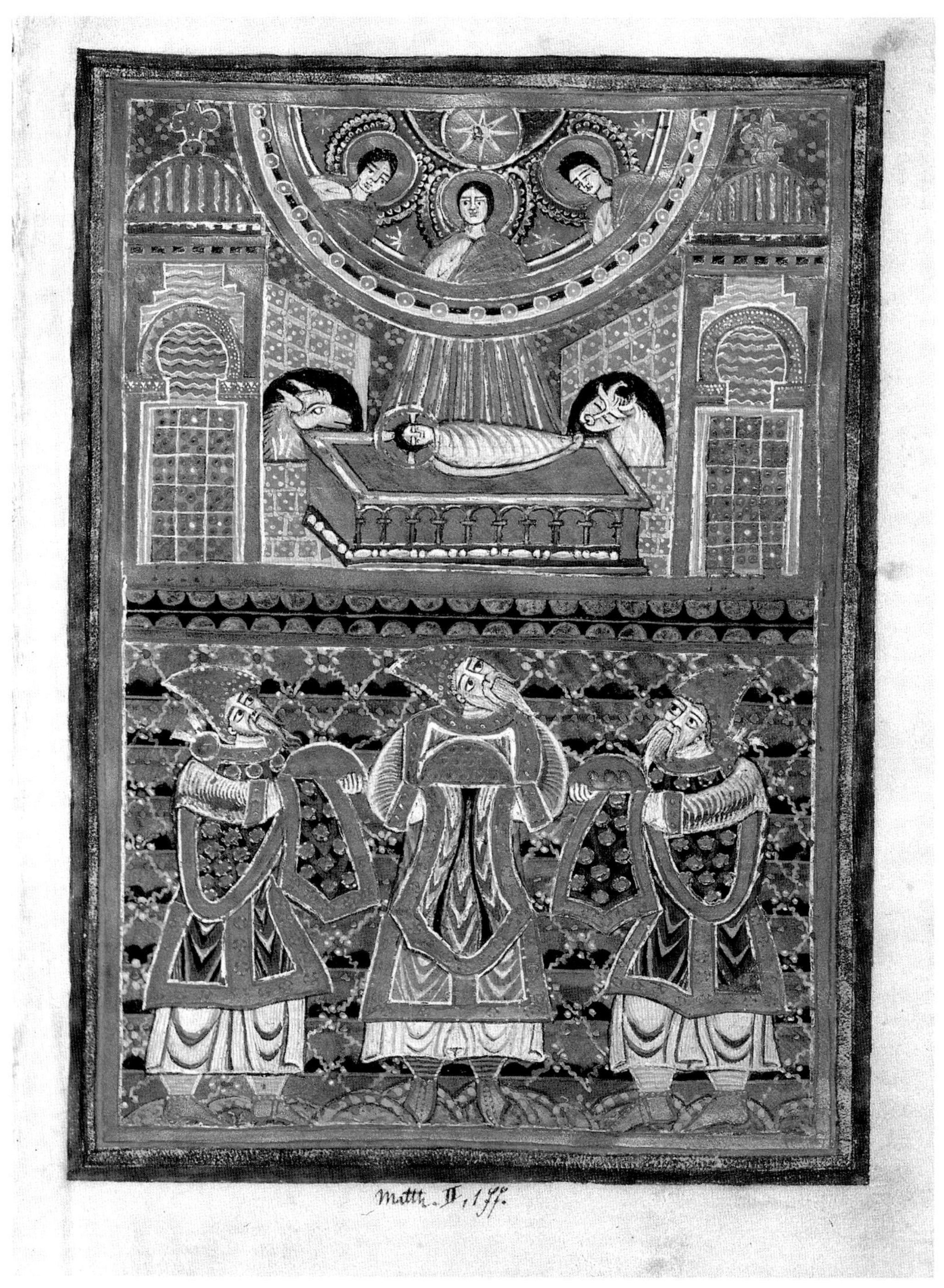

FIGURE 21   Hildesheim, Dom- und Diözesanmuseum, Domschatz 18 (Bernward Gospels), fol. 18r, *Nativity/Adoration*

Nativity and Adoration of the Magi. It is divided in half by a horizontal band featuring gold semicircles on a black ground. Frames further divide the miniature's upper zone into two parts, the top section formed of three concentric semicircles. Three sets of three figures appear, one above the other, along the picture's central vertical axis. The Magi, dressed in pointed caps, richly ornamented cloaks, and short tunics, are depicted in the lower half of the painting, while the busts of three angels are portrayed in the lunette above. In the middle zone appears the Christ child, positioned between the ox and ass of the Nativity story.

The painting differs from standard eleventh-century Adorations, transforming the conventional narrative representation into an iconic display of Christ.[5] Indeed, the figures' placement and pose underscore a static hierarchy rather than the movement and communication characteristic of a more narrative mode of depiction. The Magi stand in the lower half of the painting, in an amorphous space defined by an irregular groundline and a flat, patterned background. The central Magus is depicted frontally, only the turn of his head breaking the symmetry of his form. The two remaining kings are shown to each side, in profile, mirror images of each other down to the ornament of their cloaks. In the upper zone of the painting, the Christ child appears alone, lying on an architectonic crib that tilts up slightly. The manger has been transformed into a symmetrical structure consisting of two domed towers, each with a façade marked by a horseshoe opening and rectangular door, and walls formed by courses of orange rectangles. Although the architectural setting is not unusual in and of itself, the building's form furthers the hieratic focus on Christ because of the way the mirroring

of the architecture across the central axis echoes the pose of the two flanking Magi below.[6] This doubled mirroring underscores the painting's symmetry along its vertical axis, where Christ appears at the center of not only the vertical but also the diagonal and horizontal organization of the setting, the surrounding figures, and the direction of their gazes.

The pattern and ornament that animate the background of the painting serve both to relate and differentiate the two halves of the miniature. In the upper zone of the picture, the background is a diaper pattern of blue flowers over a mass of purplish pink. The same motif appears below, but instead of a solid ground color, the diaper overlays stripes of black semicircles and purplish-pink bands. This repetition of color and pattern with subtle variations links and yet distinguishes the upper section of the painting from the lower one. The Magi stand in a zone that the prominent groundline and heavier mass of ornament marks as earthly, while the angels float among stars. Between both is the incarnate Christ, whom the heavens irradiate with light.

The picture's iconography highlights different types of visual perception that take place both within and across each framed space. Both the angels and Magi gaze at Christ. Whereas the angels look from a heavenly opening that penetrates into Christ's space, the Magi gaze from below, their seeing initially obscured by the horizontal band that divides the miniature and by the altar upon which the child lies. This play of unobstructed seeing versus either not seeing or partial seeing occurs again in the two animals that flank Christ. The eyes of the ass are open; those of the ox, closed. The contrast may evoke the popular medieval trope that opposed the blindness of the Jews, or Synagoga, to the ability of the gentiles (i.e., Ecclesia) to see and recognize Christ as the Son of God.[7] The light, which takes the form of colored rays of white, blue, gold, and orange, indicates symbolically the invisible spirit made visible through Christ's humanity.[8]

The painting's ornament not only organizes the composition but also frames and directs the operation of these differentiated modes of seeing. A repeating motif of semicircles animates the otherwise static picture, setting into motion a visual process that complements the painting's iconography.[9] Dark lines of semicircles run as bands across the background of the lower half of the painting. Their arcing form echoes the shape of the gifts held by the Magi, replicates a golden line in the central band that divides the picture, and, in a more regular pattern, repeats the shape of the groundline on which the Magi stand. Arches also appear prominently in the upper half of the painting, both below Christ on the crib and in modified form in the doorways of the two towers, while the lunettes at the top of the picture concentrate the motif into one large set of concentric semicircles that reverses the pattern's direction. An echo of these reversed forms appears in the horizontal band that separates the two halves of the painting.

The repetition and reversal of this motif establishes a mechanism in which sight moves between earthly and heavenly spaces and oscillates at the junctures between them. The visual movement first ascends, following the direction of the Magi's gaze, to hit a formal resistance in the center. There the arcing ornament mirrors itself, concentrating the gaze before it pushes through to Christ and then the angels. At the top of the painting the shape of the lunette and direction of the angels' gaze move the eye down again to the level of the Christ child, where the crib's colonnaded arcade turns the eye back once more. Thus the gaze hovers first between the two halves of the painting, and then over the image of Christ. Since both the architecture and presence of the ass and ox in the upper half of the painting compress its pictorial field horizontally, the vertical motion produced by the ornament takes place in a condensed area, adding to the visual tension centered on Christ.

What is the object of these varied and dynamic modes of seeing? On the one hand, the object of the gaze is Christ incarnate, the *imago Dei*. Christ appears to the Magi after his birth, when he becomes perceptible to bodily sight by taking on human form. On the other hand, the Christ child lies not in an ordinary crib but on a rectangular metal box that has a stepped base and overhanging lid. These details, along with the colonnaded arcade that decorates the object's front, recall contemporary examples of portable altars, as well as the representation of one in the dedication painting in the Bernward Gospels (fol. 16v; plate 2).[10] Although the depiction of Christ's crib with architectonic details is not unusual in medieval art, the specificity of its portrayal as a portable altar raises points important to characterizing the representation of Christ in this picture.

Christ serves in the painting not only as the incarnate *imago Dei* at the time of his birth, but also as the sacramental *imago* of the Mass, the Eucharist.[11] The infant Christ lies on a portable altar, just as the instruments of the Eucharist do in the dedication painting (fols. 16v–17r; plates 2 and 3), while above the heavens open to reveal the choir of angels. Both motifs emphasize the identity of Christ's incarnate body with the sacramental species, a realist interpretation of the Eucharist that was increasingly accepted as orthodoxy during the course of the tenth century.[12] This is significant to the picture's meaning in two main ways. First, it underscores the fact that the miniature invokes ritual experiences specific to the Mass and thus invites comparison with the dedication painting. Second, it indicates that these same liturgical experiences are the starting point for the optical process the picture directs.

The Matthew frontispiece echoes several aspects of the dedication painting. Both paintings position the altar between earthly and heavenly spaces to communicate a significant exegetical understanding of the Mass, that the moment of Eucharistic consecration opened a conduit between the earthly and heavenly altars.[13] Both paintings also emphasize gift-giving in ways that relate the Magi to the patron and donor of the manuscript, Bishop Bernward. The dedication opening depicts the bishop in the conventional pose of a Magus at the Adoration—striding toward the Virgin and child and presenting his gift with extended arms. Moreover, while the Magi serve as prototypical donors in medieval art, liturgical commentators commonly compared them to the faithful who present gifts to the altar during the offertory rite of the Mass.[14]

The complex design of the Matthew frontispiece thus combines iconography drawn from donor imagery and from the liturgy of the Mass. It is also informed by contemporary ideas about how *imagines* work to elevate the devout toward the spiritual perception of God. As is well known, these developed out of Carolingian debates about pictures which first emerged in connection with Byzantine clashes between iconoclasts and iconodules.[15] Early medieval art engages this discourse with a variety of pictorial strategies that tend, on the one hand, to argue that material images cannot fully represent God while, on the other hand, instituting sensible relationships between devotional objects and the Deity that engage cognitive or affective mechanisms analogous to those needed to contemplate the invisible Divine.[16] By employing frames and ornament that alternately block and allow vision, the Bernward Gospels picture demonstrates the limits of sight for perceiving God. At the same time, the miniature models an optical process in which the faithful aim to see material things, specifically the sacramental species, with a higher level of spiritual understanding, thereby engaging the second level of perception in Augustine's well-known tripartite system of vision.[17] As the picture communicates through both its ornament and iconography, such an optical process involves different stages of seeing and not seeing. Through its ornament, the Matthew frontispiece directs the eye toward heaven and then back to hover over the consecrated host on the altar. While the angels see Christ there directly, the animals in the manger both see and do not see, and what the Magi perceive from below can only be the earthly altar, unless they understand that the consecration of the bread opens a conduit to heaven and that the host is, at that moment, the incarnate Christ.

Learning to see the Eucharist spiritually as Christ requires a mental action similar to penetrating the central mystery of the Christian faith, Christ's fully human and fully divine nature, which brings the faithful closer to achieving Augustine's third and highest level of sight, the intellectual. The mechanism at work here is conditioned by and enacted in the Mass prayers. The use of the Magi as stand-ins for the donor demonstrates that their visual experience is a model of particular relevance for the bishop. The identity of the consecrated host and the Christ child is the precondition for the transformation of the gift *pro anima*, a process which, as described in chapter 1, gives proof of the donor's merit, bringing the bishop closer to his hoped-for eternal reward—to unite with his Savior. The dedication painting enacts that desire, showing a vision of the patron saints of Saint Michael's crypt altar in the heavenly church. The bishop's offering uses the mechanisms of the Mass to attain that vision, processes that he, as the presider over the Mass, directs and that enable him to communicate with these saints.

Three more paintings in the manuscript that portray visions of Christ underscore the extent to which donor expectations of the gift *pro anima* inform how the manuscript depicts sight. The first painting in the gospel of John (fol. 174r; plate 14 and fig. 22) is closely related to the Matthew frontispiece (fol. 18r; plate 4 and fig. 23)[18] and should be considered a pendant to it; it shares the latter's format and repeats many of its motifs. A horizontal band ornamented with semicircles similarly divides the picture in half, but it differs from that in the Nativity/Adoration picture in one small detail: the absence of a central line—a point to which I shall return. Groups of three figures appear along the central vertical axis in the resulting two sections of the painting. Above, two seraphs flank an enthroned figure whose cruciform halo identifies him as Christ. Below, the head of a sea monster appears between personifications of Ocean and Earth. At the center of the painting's bottom half is the infant Christ. As in the Matthew frontispiece, Christ lies on a portable altar, a golden rectangular box with a protruding base, overhanging lid, and decorative arcade.

Formal contrasts both separate and relate the two halves of the painting to each other. The upper zone is built of spherical shapes. Christ sits on a globe, a mandorla appears behind him, and a golden sphere encloses him with the flanking seraphs. A series of concentric half-circles fills the rest of the upper zone's pictorial field, marking it as a heavenly space. In contrast to the spheres that shape the top half of the painting, rectangular bands ornament the lower zone. Its background consists of a blue lozenge pattern laid over wide horizontal pink and green stripes. Both the band of water at the bottom of the painting and the box-like shape of Christ's crib highlight the rectangularity of the lower field and help identify this space as an earthly zone.[19]

As in the Matthew frontispiece, the act of looking is a critical component of the painting in John. Earth, Ocean, and the sea serpent look up toward the enthroned Christ above. Between them and the object of their gaze are frames, rays of light, and the Christ child, presented on a crib shaped like a portable altar. These motifs suggest, on the one hand, that the personifications' gaze is blocked, and on the other, that the spiritual perception of the sacramental species as the incarnate Christ will actuate the full vision of the invisible Deity. Such mediated sight contrasts with the capacity of the seraphim, whose eyes also focus on Christ. These angels appear as part of the enthroned Christ's enclosed space; they see Him directly. This play of different types of seeing, with its attendant indications of a

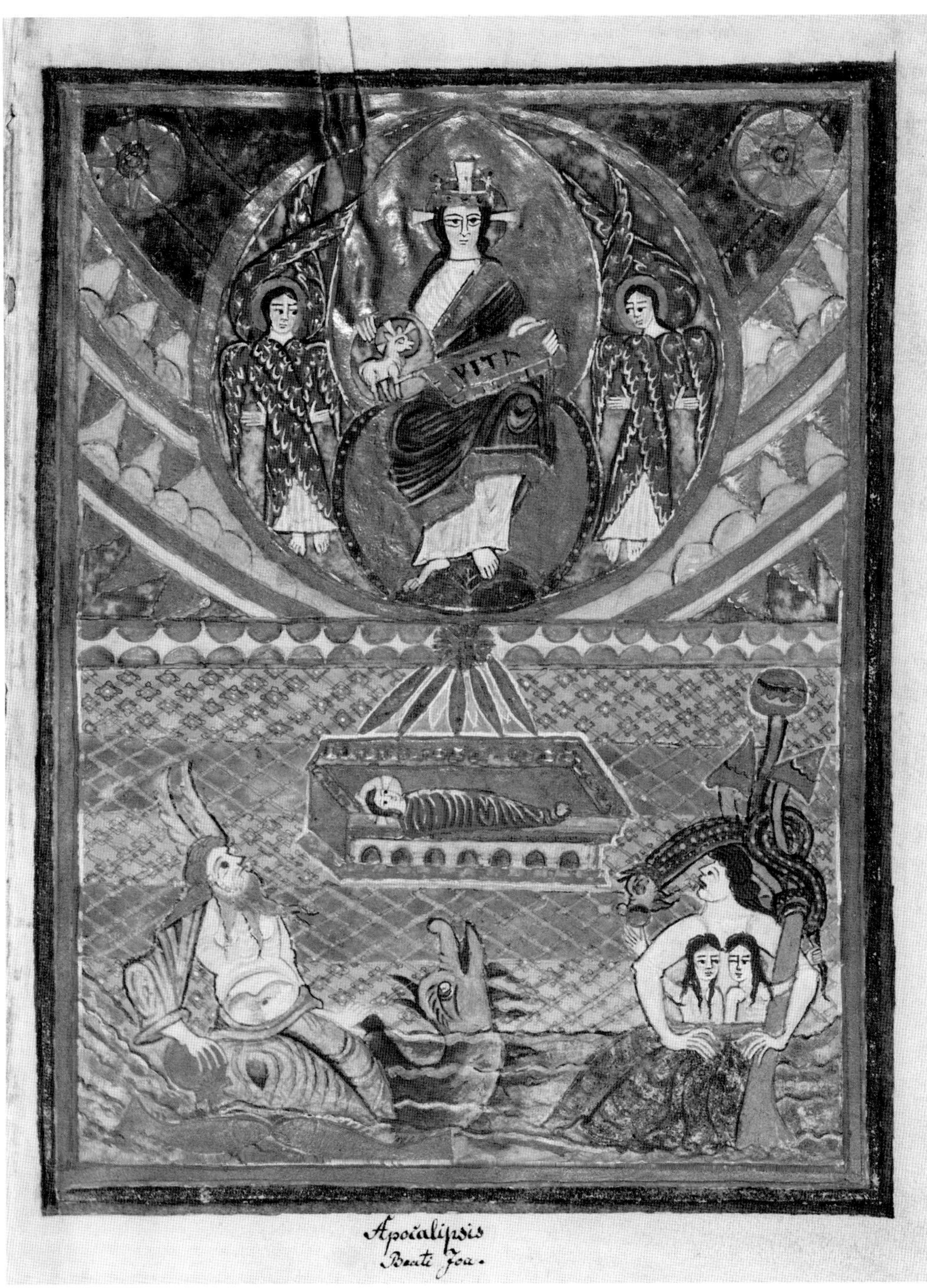

FIGURE 22   Hildesheim, Dom- und Diözesanmuseum, Domschatz 18 (Bernward Gospels), fol. 174r, *Christ in Majesty*

varying capacity to perceive the invisible divine, is reinforced by one additional detail. On Earth's lap, two small figures gaze at each other instead of Christ. Their portrayal as the children of Earth, along with their gestures, identifies them as Adam and Eve. Both reach up to a serpent coiled around the branches of a tree above them; it offers them the golden fruit of the tree of knowledge. Man has fallen from grace and lost the ability to see the Godhead.

The picture's iconography stresses that the upper half of the painting depicts the vision of Christ as the *imago Dei* at the Last Judgment. The top section of the miniature includes motifs drawn from prophetic visions of the end of time. The representation of Christ enthroned employs pictorial conventions for the Maestas that derive from a combination of Revelation 4:2 and Isaiah 6:3.[20] Directly echoing Revelation 5, a lamb appears in Christ's right hand, its leg touching a sealed text labeled *vita*, which Christ holds in his left hand. The insertion of a sea creature in the lower half of the painting also draws on the text of John's visions. Appearing in a few medieval pictures of Christ enthroned, the motif of Oceanus riding the sea monster stems from Revelation 13:1–2, where John the Evangelist describes a beast emerging from the sea that uses his mouth to blaspheme God.[21] The light and clouds that appear in bands around the enthroned Christ evoke yet another biblical description of a future vision, Matthew's account of the Second Coming: "For as lightning comes from the east, and flashes as far as the west, so will be the coming of the Son of Man. . . . And they will see the Son of Man coming on the clouds of heaven with power and great glory" (Matthew 24:27–31).[22]

The John frontispiece is also closely related to two other eleventh-century paintings, and a comparison to these is useful for clarifying its content. The first is the portrait of the evangelist John in the Uta Codex, made in Regensburg around 1025 (Munich, Clm 13601, fol. 89v [detail]; fig. 23). The second is from a gospel book produced in Cologne ca. 1050 (Bamberg, Msc. Bibl. 94, fols. 154v–155r; fig. 24).[23] All three illustrate aspects of the first fourteen lines of John's gospel, which appear in the frames of the paintings of both the Uta Codex and Cologne manuscript. The verses are worth quoting in full for that reason.

In the beginning was the Word, and the Word was with God, and the Word was God. He was in the beginning with God. All things came into being through him and without him not one thing came into being. What has come into being in him was life, and the life was the light of all people. The light shines in the darkness, and the darkness did not overcome it. There was a man sent from God whose name was John [the Baptist]. He came as a witness to testify to the light, so that all might believe through him. He himself was not the light, but he came to testify to the light. The true light, which enlightens everyone, was coming into the world. He was in the world, and the world came into being through him; yet the world did not know him. He came to what was his own and his own people did not accept him. But to all who received him, who believed in his name, he gave power to become children of God, who were born, not of blood or of the will of the flesh or of the will of man, but of God. And the Word became flesh and

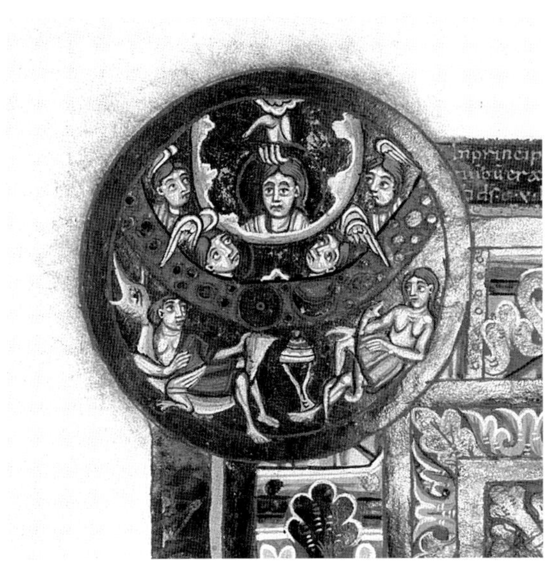

FIGURE 23   Munich, Bayerische Staatsbibliothek, Codex Latinus Monacensis 13601 (Uta Codex), fol. 89v, *Christ in Majesty* (detail)

lived among us, and we have seen his glory, the glory as of a father's only son, full of grace and truth. (John 1:1–14)

The three miniatures illustrate the symbolic content of these verses, a theological exposition about the nature of God and his incarnation in Christ. Each shares certain commonalities with the Bernward Gospels. All three portray the Word-made-flesh of verse fourteen as the child of the Nativity story—in the lower zone of the Bernward Gospels painting, the lower right medallion in the frame of the Uta Codex illustration, and in the top left corner of the right page of the Cologne bifolio painting. Unique to the Bernward Gospels, however, is the representation of Christ's crib as an altar and the resulting emphasis on the sacramental *imago*.

All three paintings also include personifications of Ocean and Earth—in the lowest band in the left folio of the Cologne miniature, and at the bottom of the top left medallion in the frame of the Uta Codex frontispiece. In the Cologne manuscript they are clearly labeled *mare* and *terra* and accompany two further personifications, labeled *ignis* and *aer*. These titles indicate that the personifications relate to Platonic ideas about the four elements from which was formed the universe.[24] Only the Bernward Gospels, however, portrays Earth's children as Adam and Eve engaged in the temptation that prompted the Fall.

The Uta Codex and Bernward Gospels also share the representation of semicircular bands that frame Christ. The upper left corner medallion in the Uta Codex frontispiece shows the hand of God pulling Christ by his halo. Below him are two bands, one with four small winged figures, probably personifying the four winds,[25] and the other containing stars, the sun, and the moon. In the Bernward Gospels, the motif is more elaborate, featuring five carefully delineated bands. From lowest to highest the bands shift in color and content. The first presents golden rays of light on a blue ground. The next level includes both light and clouds on a pale green ground. Above it, a whitish gray band features another segment of light and clouds. Finally, the last two semicircles are dark green; the first layer presents two star-shaped orbs, while the second stands empty. Such references to clouds, wind, light, stars, sun, and moon mark these zones in both paintings as sky—that upper region of the earth whose outermost edge, the firmament, is the veil between earth and heaven. What is more apparent in the elaboration of this motif in the Bernward Gospels, however, is its debt to medieval scientific diagrams that divide the universe into temperature bands.[26]

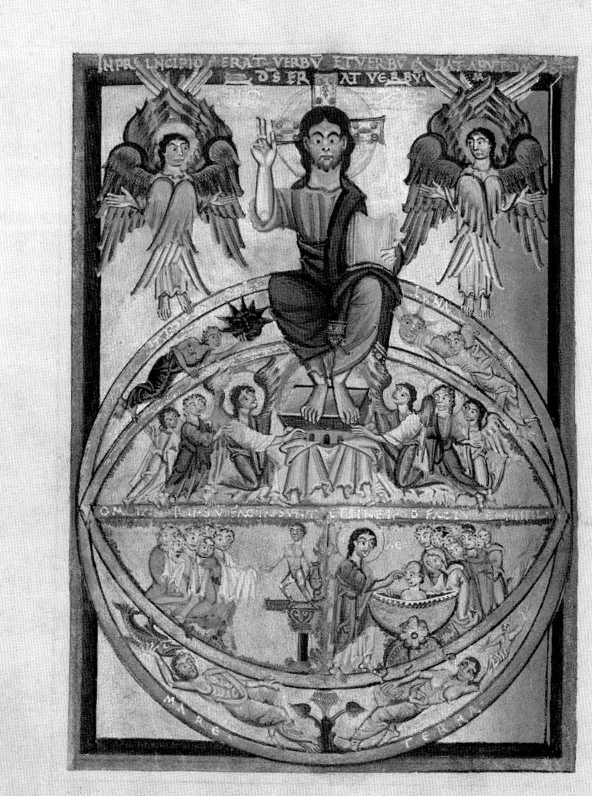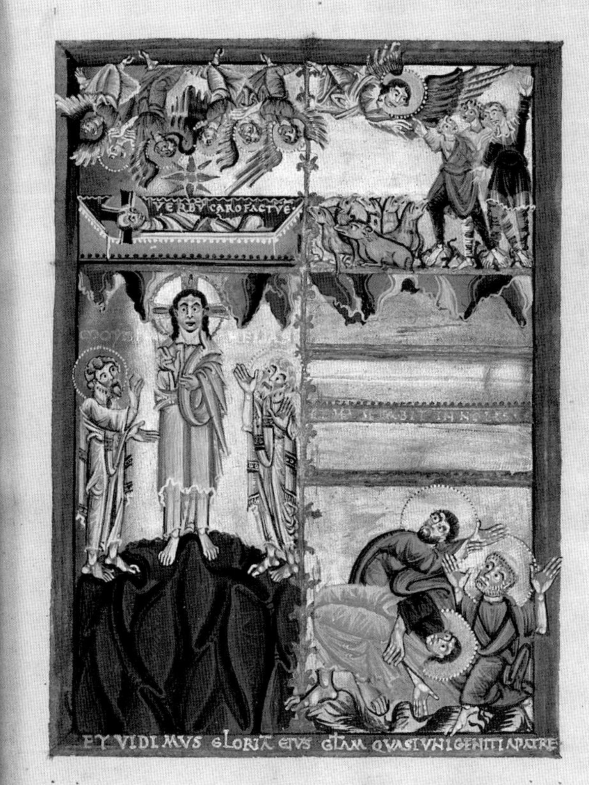

FIGURE 24 Bamberg, Staatsbibliothek, Msc. Bibl. 94 (Gospels from Cologne), fols. 154v–155r, prefatory page to John

Like the Cologne manuscript, the Bernward Gospels painting represents Christ as a full-length enthroned figure who carries a book in his left hand and is accompanied by seraphs. Both derive from conventions for the Maestas. However, the painting in the Bernward Gospels presents the book explicitly as the book of life and differs from the Cologne manuscript by the inclusion of the lamb touching the book's first seal. Along with the representation of the Christ child, these two motifs relate to medieval commentary that interpreted Christ's Incarnation as

the rupturing of the first seal of the book of life. In their well-known discussions, the Carolingian authors Haimo of Auxerre, Ambrosius Autpertus, and Pseudo-Alcuin highlighted the relationship between Christ's first and second advent, his birth and his return at the end of time, by arguing that this first seal signified the Incarnation.[27]

The three paintings' shared elements invoke specific lines from John's gospel and emphasize the cosmic significance of Christ's Incarnation by linking it to a depiction of the created universe. In doing so, the miniatures illustrate the general medieval understanding of the typological relationship between John's *In principio*, which narrates the Incarnation, and the opening of Genesis, "In principio creavit Deus caelum et terram," which describes the Creation of the cosmos.[28] The depiction of personifications of Ocean and Earth was sometimes used in Carolingian painting to refer to the third day of Creation.[29] The additional representation in the Bernward Gospels of Earth's children as Adam and Eve further invokes Genesis by alluding to the Fall. Such motifs tighten the visual conflation of Christ enthroned and God the sovereign Creator.

These detailed comparisons of the three miniatures underscore the many similarities among them. They also illuminate elements unique to the Bernward Gospels and thus highlight its painting's particular focus. The picture represents three significant Christological *imagines*. Christ enthroned is the *imago* of the sovereign God, Creator of the universe and judge. The lamb of God, with its cruciform halo, is Christ the sacrifice who "takes away the sin of the world" (John 1:29) as well as the risen lamb of Revelation. The child lying on the portable altar is both incarnate Christ and sacramental host. Together with the inclusion of Adam and Eve, these aspects of the painting's iconography—the Eucharist foremost among them—emphasize both the approaching Judgment and the redemptive power of Christ's image. In comparison to the Matthew frontispiece, the sacramental *imago* here appears entirely in the earthly realm, below the ornamented border that separates the two halves of the painting. Yet the altar and its sacrifice serve equally as the Christological image that marks the transition from earth to heaven and from bodily to spiritual sight.

Viewed as a pair, the Nativity/Adoration pictures in the gospel of Matthew and the John frontispiece present the eternal reward as the direct vision of God, presently unavailable to mankind. In a sermon on Christ's Ascension, Augustine discusses the opening lines of John's gospel as part of an analysis that presents salvation in just this way—as the recovery of the lost *imago Dei*. He explains that the visibility of the Godhead is compromised by the Fall of man, while Christ's Incarnation makes possible the restitution of God's lost image and hence man's salvation: "If there had been an eye that had seen that *In the beginning was the Word*, which had seen, which had grasped, which had embraced, which had rejoiced, there would have been no need that the Word should take Flesh and dwell among us. But because the inner eye that could grasp and take delight in Him had been blinded by the dust of sin, there was no way whereby men could come to know the Word; and that He might be sent Whom men before could not see, then afterwards could see, He deigned to become Flesh."[30] Christ serves as the visible image of the invisible Father in order that man may regain the original image of God and return to the full vision man enjoyed in Paradise.[31] An inscription from Bernward's tomb (from about 1022) repeats the idea that uniting with God in the last days is signified by a visual experience. The tomb's cover adapts a text from Job 19:25–27 and articulates the bishop's desired reward: "Then I know that my Redeemer lives and that on the youngest day I will rise from the earth and I will again be surrounded with my skin and I will see God, my Savior, in my flesh. I, and not another, will see Him myself and my eyes will perceive Him. This hope has been placed in my breast."[32] What the Bernward

Gospels paintings add to both the Carolingian commentary on the Apocalypse cited above, the Augustinian account, and the quote from Job is the central place they accord the sacramental species in the process of recovering the *imago Dei*.

The portraits of the four evangelists, discussed in the previous chapter in connection with the theme of service, also play a role in this visionary program (fols. 19r, 76r, 118v, and 175v; plates 6, 9, 13, and 17), and two of these develop eschatological themes. All four paintings are divided in half horizontally and portray, in an upper segment, the particular evangelist's symbol.[33] That symbol always appears in a golden medallion and with an open book. In two cases, the portrait of Matthew and the portrait of Mark, this medallion is framed by architecture. In the other two cases, the portrait of Luke and the portrait of John, the medallion is part of the representation of a vision of Christ. Although I will briefly address the pictorial devices used in the former to locate the evangelist's symbol somewhere between the earthly and heavenly church, I will focus primarily on the latter miniatures, which depict Christ and engage ideas related to the content of the Matthew and John frontispieces.

The architectural setting for Matthew's symbol is symmetrical and recalls a baldachin or ciborium, an honorific canopy placed over a sacred area of the church. Traditionally, ciboria appear near altars or tabernacles. In buildings the structure can be found above ambos, where the gospel would be read, and baptismal fonts, where catechumens would become part of the Christian community. Consequently, already in late antiquity the four columns of the ciborium were conventionally interpreted as the four gospels, while the vault provided a reference to the heavenly

firmament—which medieval theologians understood as a permeable membrane between the faithful and God.[34] The same motif sometimes appears in pictures of the enthroned Christ, again serving to mark a transitory space between visible earth and invisible heaven. The miniature also depicts two elaborate gold foliate objects flanking the evangelical symbol. They evoke the appearance of candelabra, which were frequently placed near the altar in the medieval church, as is illustrated in the manuscript's dedication painting (fols. 16v–17r; plates 2–3). The plantlike shape of these candlesticks may also echo the idea of Paradise as a garden setting. Together the presence of the honorific canopy and candlestick-plant motifs suggest that Matthew's symbol, like Christ in the Nativity/Adoration miniature, appears in the heavenly church.[35] The portrait of Mark also explicitly depicts the evangelical symbol in a heavenly setting. The ox floats above a garden between two domed towers connected to each other by arcing stripes of green and blue paired with golden rays of light. The architecture framing Mark's lion repeats the two domed towers of the Nativity, complete with checker-patterned entryways. The setting for both symbols thus evokes an imagined realm that exists between earth and heaven. There, the creatures display the Word of God and inspire the evangelists who write the gospels, that is, who present a visible and material manifestation of the Word, namely, the Word-made-flesh or incarnate Christ.

Above the portraits of Luke and John appear, along with their symbols, two different types of representations of Christ (fols. 118v and 175v; plates 13 and 17; figs. 25 and 26). The first shows Christ on the cross; the second portrays him at the Ascension. Similar to the full-page Matthew

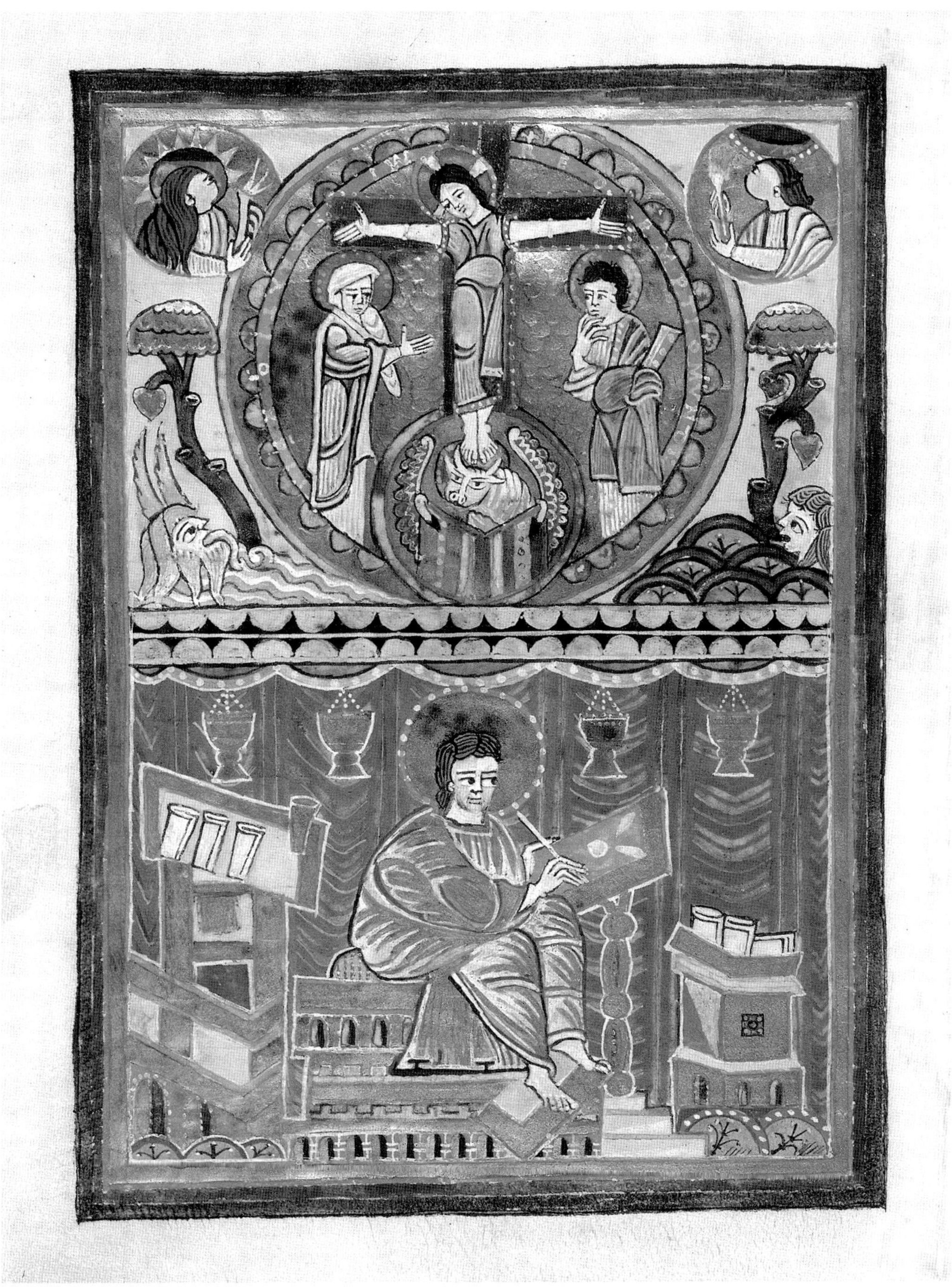

FIGURE 25   Hildesheim, Dom- und Diözesanmuseum, Domschatz 18 (Bernward Gospels), fol. 118v,
Heavenly Crucifixion (above) and *Portrait of Luke*
(below)

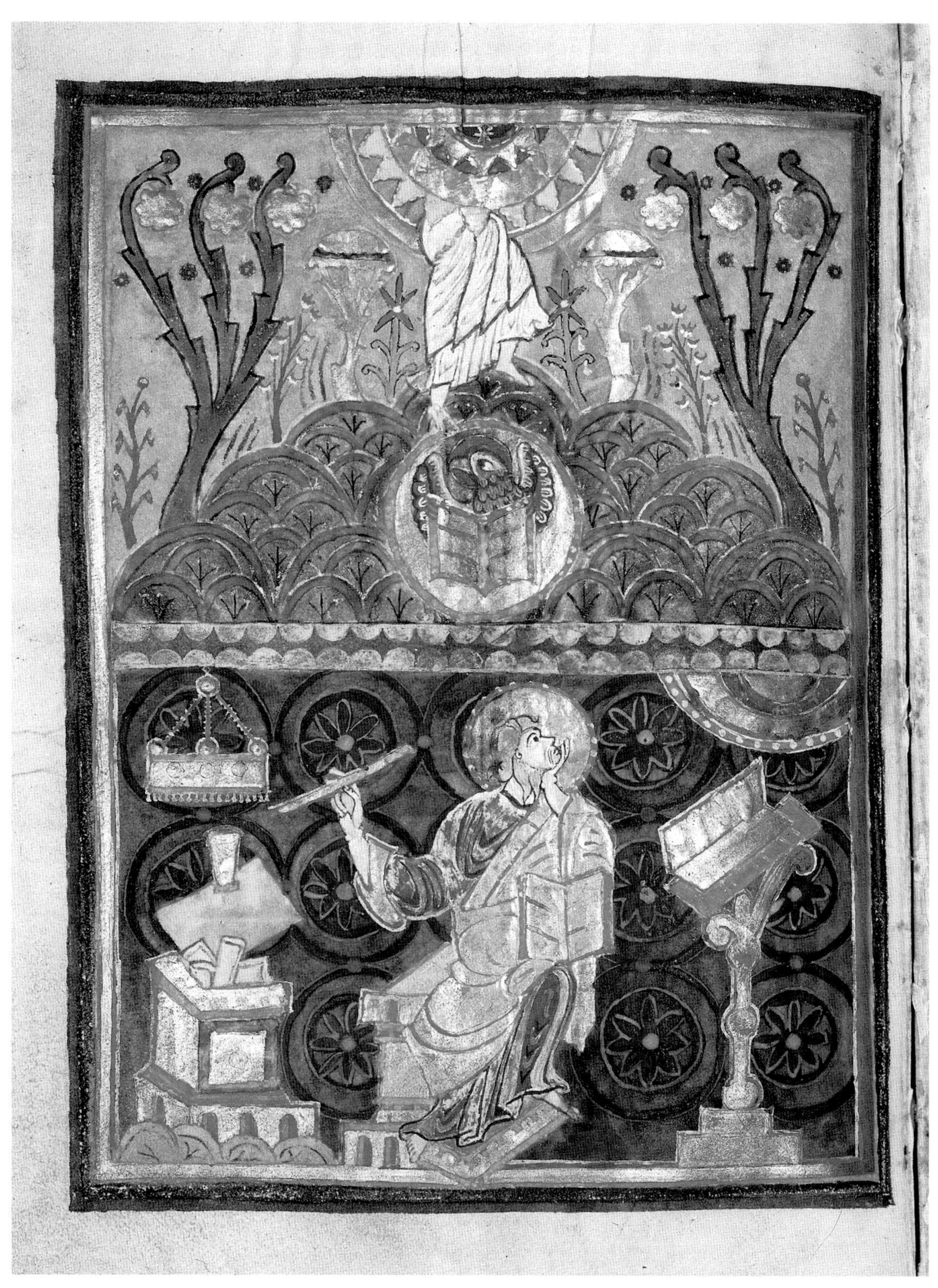

FIGURE 26   Hildesheim, Dom- und Diözesanmuseum, Domschatz 18 (Bernward Gospels), fol. 175v, *Ascension* (above) and *Portrait of John* (below)

and John frontispieces, these half-page depictions of Christ are highly symmetrical in form and portray acts of seeing. In the case of the painting paired with Luke's portrait, the Christological image above operates independently from the evangelist's image below. The ornamented band of semicircles that appears at the center of the folio, although it resembles those in the Matthew and John frontispieces and is a motif that accompanies the visions of Christ exclusively, seems here to separate rather than mediate between the two pictorial spaces—a point to which I will return.

The upper painting depicts a Heavenly Crucifixion. Christ on the cross appears in a golden roundel, just outside of which are personifications of Ocean, with water spilling from his mouth, and Earth, with a tree growing from her mouth. Flanking him are the grieving Mary and John the Evangelist. Christ wears a purple colobium, an imperial symbol that alludes to the relationship between Christ's death and his victorious exaltation as the King of Kings.[36] Christ's feet touch the halo of the winged ox, Luke's symbol, and the cross that carries his body is painted in two shades of green. The color suggests the idea, popular in the Middle Ages, that the cross carrying Christ was formed of the wood of the tree of life, the antithesis to the tree of knowledge whose fruit led to Adam and Eve's expulsion from Paradise.[37] Thus, like the frontispiece illustrating John's gospel, the miniature presents a Christological vision that underscores its salvific power. A titulus in the miniature makes that point explicitly. In the golden roundel an inner band contains the inscription in white letters on an orange ground: to the left of the cross, "the compassion of Christ," and to the right, "the redemption of the world."[38]

Concentric frames help locate the redemptive cross in heaven. The outermost zone of the picture features four personifications. Busts of the Sun and Moon that, as narrated in the gospel account, hide their faces from the sight of Christ's death appear in golden roundels in the top corners of the frame. The heads of Ocean and Earth, who look up toward Christ, are in the lower corners. These four figures mark the space outside the roundel featuring the Crucifixion as the created world, presenting, in condensed form, the same distinction between earthly and heavenly zones that exists in the John frontispiece. Frames mark the transitions between connected and successive areas inside the golden roundel. The outermost blue band separates the inside of the medallion from the external space occupied by the four personifications. The next concentric band is composed of blue semicircles. These indicate the firmament that medieval theologians understood to be the permeable barrier between sky and heaven.

The ornament also marks the shift between an earthly space visible to bodily eyes and the symbolic and spiritual message of the heavenly cross. The scalloped edge touches the inscription that expresses the salvific power of the Crucifixion, and the same pattern activates the gold surface of the innermost section of the medallion. By making the light fragment as it touches the page, the ornament produces a shimmer that creates the impression of light shining from Christ out of the page. Consequently, to see Christ fully, the eye must also penetrate the ornament, moving through light. A related pattern of repeating semicircles also marks the transition from earthly to heavenly church in both the Matthew and John frontispieces.

Further links between the pictures are found in their diagrammatic formats, which draw a particular connection between the visions of the Heavenly Crucifixion in Luke and of Christ in Majesty in the John frontispiece (fols. 118v and 175v; figs. 25 and 26). In the miniature from the gospel of Luke, the format helps portray the Heavenly Crucifixion as a sign of the Second Coming. The medieval association of a heavenly cross with the end of days derives from Matthew's prophecy that at the end of time, along with the Son of Man in glory, "the sign of the Son of Man will appear in heaven"—namely, the cross (Matthew 24:30).[39] As Bianca Kühnel has pointed out, this thematic connection appears particularly frequently in pictures produced at and following the turn of the millennium. It may reflect a heightened eschatological concern in the early eleventh century.[40] More importantly, here it helps emphasize the role of Christ's image in salvation history.

By placing the cross above a gold sphere framed by sky and earth, the miniature in the Bernward Gospels emphasizes that the salvific cross reaches beyond the boundaries of time and space. In its schematic form, the painting, like that illustrating the opening to John, also recalls Carolingian and Ottonian quincunx diagrams that expressed ideas of harmony and concordance between the microcosm of the created world and the macrocosm of the Christian cosmos. In these schemata, the placement of the cross in the middle of the picture underscores the theological point that the cross supports the architecture of the world. The same diagrammatic structure was crucial in early medieval art to help visualize the dual nature of Christ.[41] Here, by superimposing the representation of

the Crucifixion on successive spheres that do not, ultimately, contain it, the picture performs a similar task, signaling that the vision of Christ exists beyond the circumscription of the painting.[42] Thus the painting repeats the lesson about the complex relationship between seeing and spiritual understanding developed in the other visionary miniatures in the Bernward Gospels.

The final visionary miniature of the Bernward Gospels is also the last figurative painting in the manuscript (fol. 175v; plate 17 and fig. 26). A representation of the Ascension is paired with the portrait of John the Evangelist, and (unlike the portrait of Luke) the two scenes are both formally and iconographically connected. The rosette motifs that form the background to John's portrait create rounded shapes that relate to the pattern of semicircles representing the groundline in the Ascension. Both also include a motif composed of concentric bands of gold, white, orange, and blue—the same colors used for the light shining on the incarnate Christ in the Matthew and John frontispieces. Moreover, John looks up toward the Christological image rather than down at his gospel.

In the Ascension, despite Christ's diagonal movement up the slope and the depiction of his legs in profile, the mirrored placement of plants and the centered semicircular bands of colored light create a static axial symmetry. The episode's content centers on the act of seeing; it is, in the gospel account, the moment in which the apostles observe Christ departing the earth. Underscoring the visionary aspects of the story, the Bernward Gospels employs the Anglo-Saxon composition studied by Robert Deshman known as the "disappearing Christ." Christ's corporeal being, represented by his feet, remains visible, while his ascending divinity, represented by his upper body, is obscured by concentric rays of light and literally disappears from view.

The iconography for this type of Ascension was prompted by a commentary tradition that emphasized the episode's role in teaching the apostles to abandon their bodily sight of the historical Christ in favor of spiritual contemplation. As Deshman has shown, contemporary Anglo-Saxon sermons demonstrate a particular interest in this theme, and the iconography appears to have developed in England in parallel with these commentaries.[43] Yet in the Bernward Gospels the usual Anglo-Saxon iconography has been modified in two important ways, suggesting that the designer of the codex was familiar with the symbolic meaning of the composition and that he made modifications to suit the manuscript's programmatic focus. Significantly, the apostles have been replaced by the single figure of John, and his expected writing gesture has been changed to indicate an act of contemplation.

John gazes up toward the corner where a light- and cloud-filled semicircle appears, the same motif that hides Christ's divinity from bodily eyes in the Ascension. By means of pairing the portrait of John with an image of the Ascension and changing John's usual pose, the painting presents John the Evangelist as a witness to Christ's Ascension and singles him out for his penetrating spiritual insight.[44] Unlike the other evangelists in the book—even Luke, whose portrait is also paired with a heavenly vision— John actually looks to Christ in heaven, and in contrast to other gazing figures represented in the manuscript, he does so by gazing beyond the material *imago*.[45] Between John and Christ in the picture is the same band of semicircles without the addition of the middle line that appears in the

John frontispiece (fol. 174r; plate 14 and fig. 22)— the content of which is also one of John's visions, as he was identified as the author both of the gospels and the book of Revelation.

It is probable that like the Magi, John the Evangelist serves here in part as a surrogate and model for the patron, Bishop Bernward, although as an *exemplum* of Christian service and spiritual insight rather than in the guise of a donor. Chapter 2 has already shown how the four evangelists participate in the pictorial program's development of models of service and how the figure of John the Baptist helps relate that service specifically to the manuscript's patron. As discussed in the introduction, Bishop Bernward also adopts the guise of John the Evangelist in at least one other instance, in the frontispiece to the Bible he commissioned for Saint Michael's (Hildesheim, DS 61, fol. 1r; fig. 1). This is not unusual: contemporary texts and images describe John the Evangelist as a priest, and at least two bishops, Frithestan and Aethelwold, both of Winchester, were already in the tenth century compared to him in either (or both) text and image.[46] Finally, the pairing of the two Johns relates to the common theological trope that they were joint heirs with Christ.[47] In the Bernward Gospels this pairing is more implied than explicit, but significant to the extent that both the Baptist and the Evangelist are singled out from the other figures of the manuscript, albeit in different ways (the former by the number of scenes devoted to him, the latter by his contemplative pose and the message of the Ascension's unusual iconography).

A second significant difference from the Anglo-Saxon iconography to which the Ascension miniature bears a relationship is that Christ's feet remain in contact with the earth.[48] This may refer to a common medieval trope that Christ's lower limbs represented the members of the Church, who would remain part of the earth until the Day of Judgment.[49] Since the completion of Christ's Ascension required the raising of these "members," among whom bishops were first in the clerical hierarchy, the picture of Christ's partial ascent serves also as a promise of Bernward's hoped-for eternal reward, to come face-to-face with God.

One painting that, owing to its formal qualities, belongs properly to the Bernward Gospels group of narrative miniatures, but is unique in the cycle as the only depiction of a Christological miracle, is the Raising of Lazarus (fol. 174v, below; plate 15). It exhibits some unusual features that connect it to the visionary pictures and reinforce their eschatological themes. In the miniature, Lazarus's wrapped body sits up in its rectangular tomb. He is only lightly sketched and practically dissolves into the walls of his sarcophagus. Although Lazarus faces the miracle worker, Christ's pose is completely unresponsive: both of his arms stretch out; his feet hang together as if weightless; and his head tilts back to look at a semicircular opening of blue and gold centered on a star. Conventionally, Christ should be making some form of a blessing gesture or at least interacting with the subject of his miracle.[50] Christ's pose instead recalls Carolingian and Ottonian compositions of the Transfiguration, where Christ's divinity is revealed to the apostles.[51]

The association of the Raising of Lazarus with Christ's revelation of his divinity is unsurprising. The miracle story functioned in medieval commentary as a type for Christ's Resurrection.[52] Perhaps more important is that in the opening to the Bernward Gospels, Lazarus's resurrection occurs in conjunction with the historical picture of Christ's Crucifixion on the facing folio. According to Matthew's gospel, the bodies of many holy people rose from their tombs at the moment of Christ's death (27:51–53). Reference to this passage appears frequently in both Carolingian and Ottonian pictures of the Crucifixion, usually through the representation of several figures emerging from graves or of a single sarcophagus.[53] Although the pictorial relationships among the Raising of Lazarus, the historical Crucifixion, and allusions to Christ's future Ascension may be relatively conventional, because this scene is the only miracle painted in Bernward's gospel book, the Raising of Lazarus takes on a certain programmatic importance in the gospels. And because the Raising of Lazarus frequently decorated funerary objects, starting with the Early Christian period, the story's subject matter is also fundamentally connected to how early and medieval Christians articulated their hopes for salvation.[54]

The four pictures of the Nativity/Adoration, the Heavenly Crucifixion, Christ in Majesty, and the Ascension are schematic paintings that treat the nature of sight in an eschatological context. Together these miniatures pick up and elaborate several of the themes introduced in the dedication painting, where Bernward not only offers his gift to the saints but also celebrates a combination of rites centered on the altar (offertory, altar dedication, and Mass). By means of a sophisticated pictorial argument, the manuscript shows how Bernward's gift and sacramental performance brings him, or rather more specifically his perception, to the edge of the heavenly church and through the open door to Paradise. In brief, Bernward is shown facing the door marked "opened" (*patefacta*), and the reach of his arms directs his attention through that door toward the heavenly church on the right folio. There, Mary and Christ's gestures, together with the closed door on the far right of the painting, push back in the opposite direction so that ultimately both halves of the miniature focus the bishop's communication with the saints on the altar. By such iconography and framing devices, the dedication painting creates a dynamic visual movement from left to right and back again that comes to be compressed around the altar.

The perceptual mechanism at work in the dedication painting is reproduced in the Matthew frontispiece, but modified in the three other depictions of Christological visions. The Nativity/Adoration miniature compresses the visual movement between lower and upper half of the painting to focus attention on the altar and its Christological sacrifice. The John frontispiece splits its visual emphasis between the altar in the lower half of the painting and Christ enthroned in the upper half. In comparison, the Heavenly Crucifixion works to center the gaze on the cross, but the ornamented gold ground creates a visual movement in and out of the painting, rather than between pictorial zones within the miniature. Finally, the portrait of John the Evangelist with the disappearing Christ at the Ascension directs sight out of the picture entirely to focus on that which is not pictured: the upper half of Christ's body, which signifies his divinity.

A second significant theme of the dedication painting elaborated in the schematic pictures is the presentation of artworks that, like the sacramental species, serve as Christological *imagines*. This grounds the bishop's contemplation of God in the representation of the material world of the church, its sacraments, and its ornaments. The schematic paintings each present visionary images that are also pictures, whose lavishly ornamented surfaces not only add to the paintings' content but also announce their overt materiality and the optical shift that takes place between material *imago* and Christological vision. In each instance, heavily and regularly patterned backgrounds characterize earthly zones such as the place of the Magi and manger, the lower half of the John frontispiece, and both portraits of the evangelists Luke and John, while solid color, often accompanied by light and cloud motifs, marks the heavenly space of the remaining paintings. It is worth noting here that although the pictorial mode of the visionary miniatures differs from all the other paintings in the codex, the more earthly zones within the visionary miniatures do share one feature with the narrative paintings in the Bernward Gospels. In both cases, the backgrounds are decorated with colorful patterns. This contrasts with the heavenly space, where spiritual sight is to be engaged, and singles the visions out even from the rest of the physical fabric of the codex. The visionary miniatures thereby communicate their nature as art while showing the viewer how to see Christ, the *imago Dei*, in and through them. The lesson of the dedication painting is extended to the other illuminations of the book.

The images of seeing in the Bernward Gospels show the patron brought closer to Christ not simply by virtue of his offering and his service, or by celebrating the cultic mysteries, but by exercising spiritual sight. The eschatological content of the visionary images corresponds to the expectations of the donor's gift *pro anima* and would have held particular meaning for the bishop, who aimed

with his gift to assure himself a place in heaven.
Such an emphasis on the Eucharist both as the
prototype of the Christological *imago* and as a
significant prompt for spiritual sight may offer
a particularly episcopal point of view. From the
Carolingian period on, the idea of communion as
a common sacrifice came to be displaced in favor
of consecration by the priest alone; the celebrant
recited the Canon prayers in a low voice away
from the rest of the faithful. Tenth-century texts
on the Eucharist and its consecration suggest
that these shifts prompted discussions about the
privileges of bishops, who considered themselves
to be first among priests and seem in the tenth
and eleventh centuries to have tried to restrict
to themselves something common to the whole
priesthood: the grace of the Holy Spirit, by which
the Eucharist is consecrated.[55] Related themes
permeate the pictures of touch in the Bernward
Gospels, discussed in the following chapter.

4

———

TOUCH

The theme of spiritual perception and the bishop's desire to unite with God continues in a series of narrative pictures that show figures coming into direct physical contact with Christ (fols. 75v, 118r, and 174v; plates 8, 12, and 15).[1] The paintings are a subset of the narrative miniatures in the Bernward Gospels and are distinguished by idiosyncratic iconography that communicates the significance of touch for apprehending Christ's dual corporeal and incorporeal nature.[2] Like the visionary miniatures, these illustrations of haptic experiences depict persons from sacred history, such as John the Baptist, who serve as exempla and surrogates for the bishop. The pictures also engage early medieval theories about images, though they institute not only visual but also tangible relationships with the Deity.

An unusual representation of the Noli me tangere serves as the top scene of the second illustrated folio in the Gospel of Mark (fol. 75v; plate 8 and fig. 27). Departing from every medieval convention for the scene, the painting depicts Mary Magdalene touching Christ. According to the Gospels, after Christ's death Mary Magdalene visits his tomb and is surprised to find it empty. Mary is filled with sorrow, but she suddenly recognizes that the man standing by the tomb in the guise of a gardener is actually the resurrected Christ. Rejoicing that Christ lives, the Magdalene reaches out to embrace him, but her desire to touch is frustrated. Christ commands, "do not touch me, for I have not yet ascended to my father!" (John 20:17). In patristic and medieval commentary, the central point of this Gospel episode is Christ's command not to touch, often dramatically represented in the West. Customarily, Mary stretches her arms toward Christ in longing, while Christ stops her with a gesture. A certain amount of space left between the

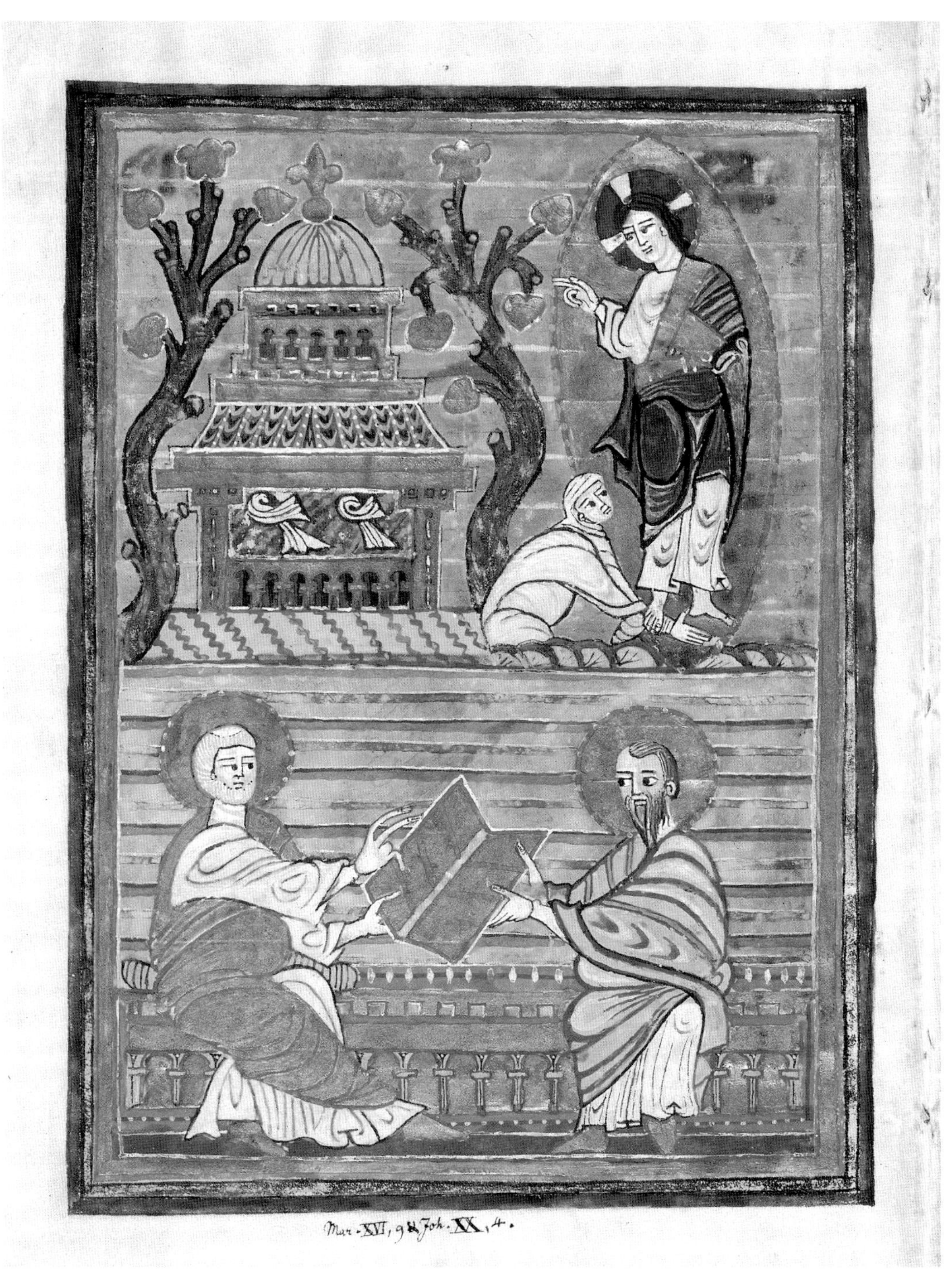

FIGURE 27   Hildesheim, Dom- und Diözesanmuseum, Domschatz 18 (Bernward Gospels), fol. 75v, *Noli me tangere* (above) and *Peter Charging Mark to Write the Gospels* (below)

figures draws attention to the fact that Mary does not in fact touch Christ.[3] In the Bernward Gospels, in flagrant violation of Christ's command, Mary actually comes into contact with Christ's feet.

Based on his interpretation of the disappearing Christ motif that illustrates the Ascension discussed in the previous chapter, Robert Deshman has offered an explanation for the Noli me tangere's puzzling iconography, suggesting that these two strikingly original paintings be treated as a pair and that the same Augustinian exegetical tradition explains both paintings.[4] Certainly, patristic and medieval exegetes interpreted both the Ascension and the Noli me tangere as lessons in understanding Christ's dual nature as fully human and fully divine. Theologians articulated the idea that Christ had to ascend in part to teach the Apostles the truth about Christ's divinity. Similarly, commentators explained that Mary Magdalene was forbidden to touch Christ because she did not yet understand the theological point that Christ is equal to his father in divinity. She, like the apostles, could not perceive his nature as both fully human and fully divine—and would not be able to do so until Christ's Ascension.

If this essentially Augustinian exegetical tradition underlies the iconography of both the Ascension painting and the Noli me tangere, then both might be understood as a lesson about seeing.[5] As Deshman has pointed out, the Anglo-Saxon sermons that developed in parallel with the iconography of the disappearing Christ explained Christ's physical disappearance from the apostles' bodily eyes as an encouragement to abandon corporeal sight in favor of spiritual vision.[6] Moreover, since it was commonplace for medieval writers to follow Augustine in presenting sight as the highest sense, with the greatest capacity for spiritual understanding, it is certainly possible to interpret Mary's touch in visual rather than tactile terms.[7] Mary's dramatic act, in which she reaches for Christ's foot through his mandorla, a symbol of his godhood, would thus not be a touch at all but rather a sign for visionary perception.[8] Following Deshman's argument, this would make both the Noli me tangere and the disappearing Christ mimetic prompts for the viewers of the Bernward Gospels to train their spiritual sight.

Although this is a powerful argument for understanding the new Ascension imagery based on its Anglo-Saxon context, the interpretation that Mary's touch serves as a sign for visionary perception subsumes the sense of touch to that of sight. Such a translation of the depicted tactile experience into a visual one, though it may be consistent with a general privileging of sight over touch in medieval theology, does not take into account the manuscript's pictorial evidence.[9] Not only does the codex place a special emphasis on the sense of touch in several additional miniatures, but it also employs a different and more narrative pictorial mode for these as compared to the visionary paintings.[10]

The painting of the Noli me tangere shows Christ's sepulcher to be a centrally planned, two-story domed building; the structure is on the left, framed by two large plants. Christ appears off-center, on the right, in a golden mandorla. The painting distributes the figures and architecture unevenly, creating a sense of imbalance and thus motion that contrasts with the static symmetry of the visionary miniatures. The figures' poses and gestures subtly underscore this motion, emphasizing the picture's focus on narrative action. Mary kneels in profile beside Christ, stretching out her arms toward his feet. Although Christ's lower body is partially turned away from Mary, his torso twists back toward her and he raises his right arm in a gesture of speech.

Mary transgresses the limits of Christ's mandorla, her entire upper body overlapping the golden oval. Contact occurs, but the Magdalene's touch is the most minimal touch possible. The edge of her thumb barely grazes Christ's left heel. Christ, too, touches Mary, his foot crossing over her arm as he begins to rise off the ground. Their contact thus works in a reciprocal motion and meets at the threshold between earthly and heavenly. While Mary enters the space of Christ's godhood, the mandorla, Christ's ascending feet graze Mary's earthly, human flesh. The posing of Christ's foot over Mary's arm communicates two possible meanings: either it depicts an overlap that creates a minimized contact, or represents an aggressive attempt to prevent Mary's touch. In either case, the touch clearly connects the two figures while at the same time resisting contact. Mary's and Christ's gestures perform a haptic perception that involves either non-touching or denied-touching.

Such a dynamic non-touching touch has, to my knowledge, no parallel in either medieval pictures or exegesis. However, a philosophical text, Calcidius's well-known fourth- or fifth-century Latin translation of Plato's *Timaeus*, includes an extended discussion of what it describes as "sine sensu tangentis tangentur," that is, touching without the sense of touch—in essence, a non-touching form of haptic perception.[11] In his commentary, Calcidius explains the physical process of such an experience:

Yet there is some superficial contact but no real touch, and this with the bodies in it rather than with itself. When these are perceived, the feeling arises that matter itself is perceived because it seems to be formed by the "species" it takes in, whereas, in reality, it is formless. And thus the perception of the forms present in matter is clear but that of matter itself, which underlies these forms, is obscure, and a co-perception rather than a perception. Therefore, since not matter itself is perceived but what is of matter, and since it only seems to be perceived together with the material things, there arises such an uncertain sense. And consequently, it is well said that "matter is touched without being perceived by the man who touches it," for it is not really touched. . . . matter is tangible, because one gets the impression that it is touched, when that which is touched first of all comes within reach of the senses. However, contact with matter is accidental, it is untouchable itself, because it is perceived by neither the sense of touch nor the other senses.[12]

This description of touching without the sense of touch, a touch that involves some superficial contact but no real contact, with something true that is yet untouchable itself, is the verbal equivalent to the haptic process represented in the painting.

Bishop Bernward knew the *Timaeus*. By the late tenth and early eleventh centuries there was a dramatic increase in the production of Calcidius's text throughout Northern Europe, including in the Ottonian territories.[13] Also critical at that time were shifts in the location and form of the glosses that increasingly became interlinear explanations and definitions.[14] This, along with the insertion of explanatory diagrams, suggests that by the eleventh century Calcidius's *Timaeus* had become part of school curricula.[15] Among others, the widely traveled Abbo of Fleury and the future pope Gerbert of Aurillac, also closely connected to the Ottonian imperial court, studied and taught Calcidius's translation and commentary.[16] Although no extant copies can be associated with Bishop Bernward directly, his 1019 charter for Saint Michael's derives its discussion of the relationship between matter and soul from the *Timaeus*, using specific and uncommon vocabulary from Calcidius's translation, and a second painting in the Bernward Gospels owes its cosmological content in part to the *Timaeus*.[17]

That picture is the visionary miniature that illustrates the symbolic content of John's opening verses discussed in chapter 3 (fol. 174r; plate 14). Of the many layers of meaning in this highly complex miniature, several pertain to the Platonic cosmology found in the *Timaeus*. Below the Christ child appear the personifications of two of the four elements from which the artificer of the *Timaeus* (the creator figure) formed the cosmos: water (as Oceanus) and earth (as Terra). In the upper section, the Deity sits above a globular universe, an almond-shaped mandorla behind him. His feet rest on a green semicircle that represents the created earth. Immediately around the earth is a golden sphere bordered with a dotted green band that serves as the outer edge of the cosmos, the place where the stars of the zodiac are affixed.[18] In line with Calcidius's commentary, the earth is thus placed at the center of the celestial bodies. The resulting structure forms a figure eight, which relates to an ancient diagram illustrating the relationship between the moveable

and fixed stars that frequently illustrated Calcidius's commentary on the *Timaeus*.[19] Merged with this figure is another scientific diagram dividing the universe into temperature zones, a schema that had migrated into Calcidius's *Timaeus* by the eleventh century.[20]

This astronomically influenced painting is directly relevant to Calcidius's notion of a non-touching touch, because Calcidius's phrase "sine sensu tangentis tangentur" appears precisely in the section of his text that treats the nature of primordial matter, the so-called matter of the third kind.[21] In the second part of the *Timaeus*, Calcidius confronts Plato's assertion that such matter (*hyle* in the Greek) is neither corporeal nor incorporeal ("neque corpus necque incorporeum"), material nor immaterial.[22] Translating Plato's term for matter as *silva*, Calcidius attempts to explain the paradox of such matter by focusing on the relationship between its incorporeal nature and its ability to take form.[23] Matter is, Calcidius explains—basing his argument on Aristotle's notion of potentiality—"sed tam corpus quam incorporeum possibilitate," potentially both corporeal and incorporeal.[24]

Calcidius continues, following Plato, by explaining that the potentiality of such matter is what makes it perceptible.[25] It is at this moment, when he translates and explains Plato's linking of the potentiality and perceptibility of matter, that Calcidius introduces a change of language that produces the notion of a haptic perception that can be performed without the bodily sense of touch. Whereas in the Greek, Plato described in generic terms that such matter (*hyle*) was apprehensible (*hapton*) with the aid of non-perception (*met'anaisthesias*), in Calcidius's Latin version, matter potentially material and immaterial is touched (*tangitur*) without the sense of touch (*sensus tangentis*).[26] Calcidius thus forges a direct link between tactile experience and the perception of matter that is potentially material and immaterial.

How does Calcidius's non-touching touch of *silva* relate to the tactile perception of Christ in the Bernward Gospels? For medieval Christians reading Calcidius, the potential of such matter to be both corporeal and incorporeal naturally suggested the theological understanding of Christ as both human and divine, perceptible man and imperceptible God. The medieval tradition conventionally interpreted the *Timaeus*, and Calcidius's accompanying commentary, as an equivalent of the Genesis creation story, which was in turn understood typologically in relation to John the Evangelist's account of Christ's Incarnation. The Genesis passage opens with the phrase "In principio creavit Deus caelum et terram" (in the beginning God created heaven and earth). Similarly, John's Gospel begins "In principio erat verbum" (in the beginning was the Word), a phrase that generated the popular medieval metaphor for Christ incarnate as the Word-made-flesh. The textual and conceptual echo of the two *In principio* phrases, and their relationship to Calcidius's description of the cosmos, was lost neither on medieval commentators nor on the designer of the John frontispiece in the Bernward Gospels.[27]

As previously stated, this painting draws on a variety of sources to illustrate the symbolic content of John's opening verse. The multivalent picture portrays the fulfillment of God's scheme of salvation begun by his act of Creation in Genesis, the first *In principio*, continued by Christ's Incarnation, the second *In principio*, and fulfilled in Revelation. The painting's Platonic content

links the matter of Creation (*silva* in Calcidius's terms) to the flesh of Christ's Incarnation as the *imago Dei*. While the John frontispiece focuses on the optic perception of Christ, by reading the Noli me tangere's haptic imagery against the Platonic ideas about matter illustrated in this visionary painting, it becomes clear that Calcidius's ideas about the tangibility of such matter informs the portrayal of Mary's non-touching touch of Christ's resurrected body.

Historical evidence suggests that this question of the tangibility of Christ was especially significant to contemporary discussions about the Resurrection; it was also used within a short time of the making of the Bernward Gospels as the basis for defending the material nature of the sacraments and even art. In the first quarter of the eleventh century, the Ottonian dioceses of upper Lotharingia as well as Frankish regions around Orleans were the sites of a lay movement accused of the so-called Manichean heresy. According to Ademar of Chabannes and Gerard of Arras-Cambrai, this group rejected the materiality of the sacred: relics, the corporeality of the resurrected Christ, and the stuff of church ritual—altar, incense, bells, and pictures. In arguing against these heretics, both men used Gregory the Great's commentary on the book of Job to assert the bodily resurrection of Christ (*in carne*) and to justify church practices involving both bodies and matter.[28]

In book 14 of the *Moralia in Job*, an exegetical treatise that circulated widely in the eleventh century, Gregory had established an influential interpretation of Job's prophecy that he would resurrect in the same body that he wore in life.[29] From this Gregory had concluded that Christ would resurrect in his incarnate body. Proof of this resurrection *in carne* was Doubting Thomas's touch of Christ's wounds, because it showed the palpability (*palpabile*) of Christ's body after the Resurrection.[30] By using Job's prophecy, Ademar and Gerard engaged with Gregory's commentary, reiterating long-standing medieval theories that God's embodiment as Christ justified, and even required, the materialization of the sacred in the church. They thereby also broadened the language that defended the use of art on the basis of Christ's Incarnation as the *imago Dei* in a way that linked the natures of his incarnate and resurrected body. In light of Calcidius's commentary and exegesis that associated the palpability of Christ's body with the proof of the Resurrection *in carne* (in the flesh), it becomes probable that Mary's touch in the Bernward Gospels painting acts not as a sign for sight, but rather as the haptic perception of the divine Christ's fully embodied Resurrection. The Noli me tangere's philosophical and theological content also suggests that the picture models a form of touch in which the physical experience of Christological *imagines* sets into motion mechanisms for apprehending Christ's dual corporeal and incorporeal nature.

Emphasizing that the Noli me tangere argues for the tangibility of the *imago* is suggested by the pictorial echo of Mary's touch in the scene below. In this painting, touch is again portrayed as the sense employed for perceiving Christ *in carne*, in this case made manifest in the form of another sacred body, the Gospels, the Word-made-flesh (fol. 75v, below; plate 8 and fig. 12). The evangelist Mark receives a book from Saint Peter. The book's spine points directly to where Christ's foot crosses over Mary's arm, and the respective contact of Mary to Christ and Mark to the book

helps forge a link between the two objects of their perception—the pictured body of Christ above and the pictured book as body below. The book as Word-made-flesh becomes the Bernward Gospels itself in the portrait of Mark that appears on the opposite folio (fol. 76r, below; plate 9 and fig. 28). There the evangelist writes his Gospel in a codex portrayed as the Bernward Gospels. The ornament of the represented book, purple and light blue stripes on an orange ground, repeats the pattern decorating the Gospels on that page in the background behind Mark.

The theological content of the Noli me tangere also communicates eschatological ideas. When Gregory argued for Christ's resurrection *in carne* he extrapolated that Christians, too, would resurrect in their actual bodies at the end of time, which undoubtedly explains the Job passage's appearance on Bernward's tomb: "Then I know that my Redeemer lives and that on the youngest day I will rise from the earth and I will again be surrounded with my skin and I will see God, my Savior, in my flesh. I, and not another, will see Him myself and my eyes will perceive Him. This hope has been placed in my breast."[31] Among other themes, the text emphasizes resurrection *in carne* and suggests that salvation is an embodied experience in which the perceptual organs of the resurrected body bear a relationship to those of the present, living body.

The Bernward Gospels program explores how to see and grasp Christ with the present senses in anticipation of a more perfect apprehension. Just as the visionary miniatures present varied modes of optic perception, the codex also illustrates different types of haptic perception. In a half-page painting of the Last Supper, Judas is placed apart from the other apostles (fol. 118r; plate 12 and

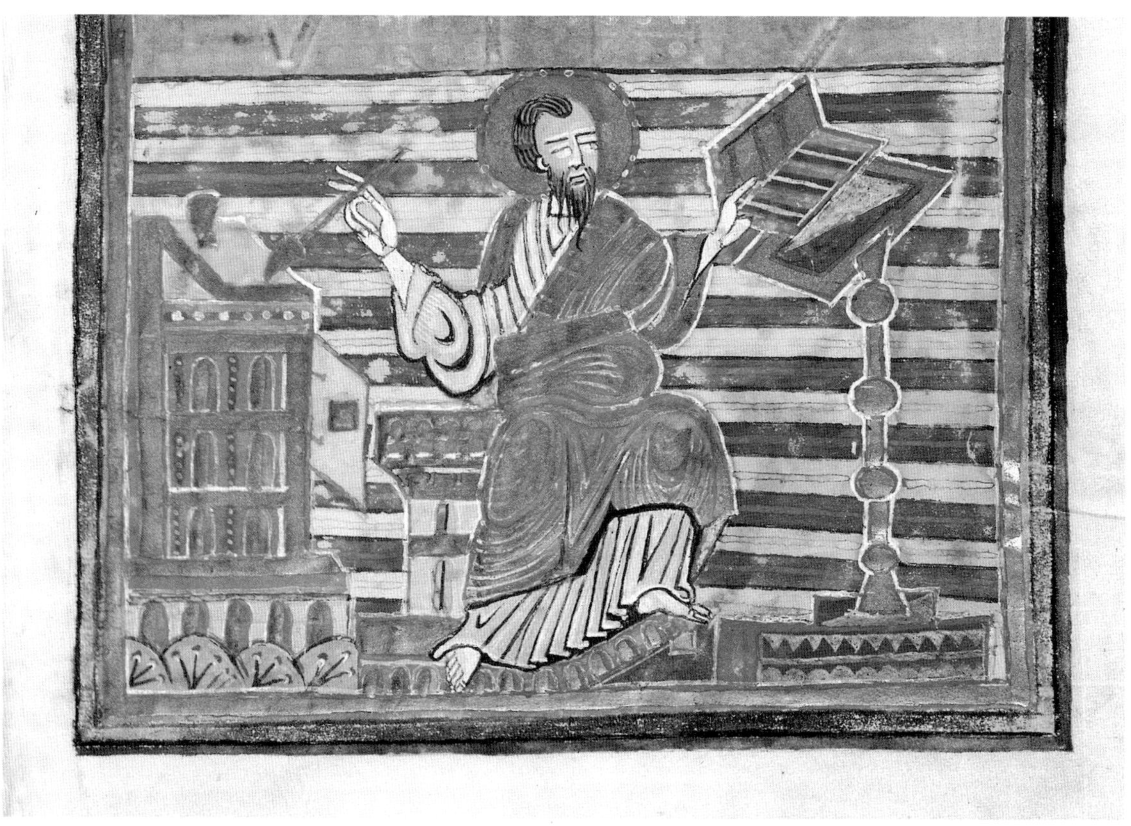

FIGURE 28   Hildesheim, Dom- und Diözesanmuseum, Domschatz 18 (Bernward Gospels), fol. 76r,
Portrait of Mark (detail)

fig. 29). He kneels in front of a table above which appear the other figures of the painting, and his lower body overlaps the picture's architectural frame. Judas's right hand is laid on Christ's wrist, and his mouth opens to receive the bread that Christ proffers. The oblong shape and pinkish color of the bread conflate it with Christ's fingers, making explicit the connection between Christ's flesh and the apostolic meal, and presenting Judas's haptic experience of Christ's body as both a grasping of Christ's incarnate body—the hand—and the embrace of his sacramental body—the Eucharist.

In the scene below, Judas appears inside an enclosed space, cupping his hands to catch a line of gold coins. The pairing of these two episodes highlights contrasts important to the pictures' meaning. The three men who pay for Judas's betrayal are aligned with the crowd of believing disciples above. Judas appears in the same spot in both pictures. Above, he kneels and touches Christ. Below, he stands facing in the opposite direction, turning away from Christ's body. Generically described as a betrayer, Judas served in the Middle Ages as a model of limited perception as well, following an idea put forth

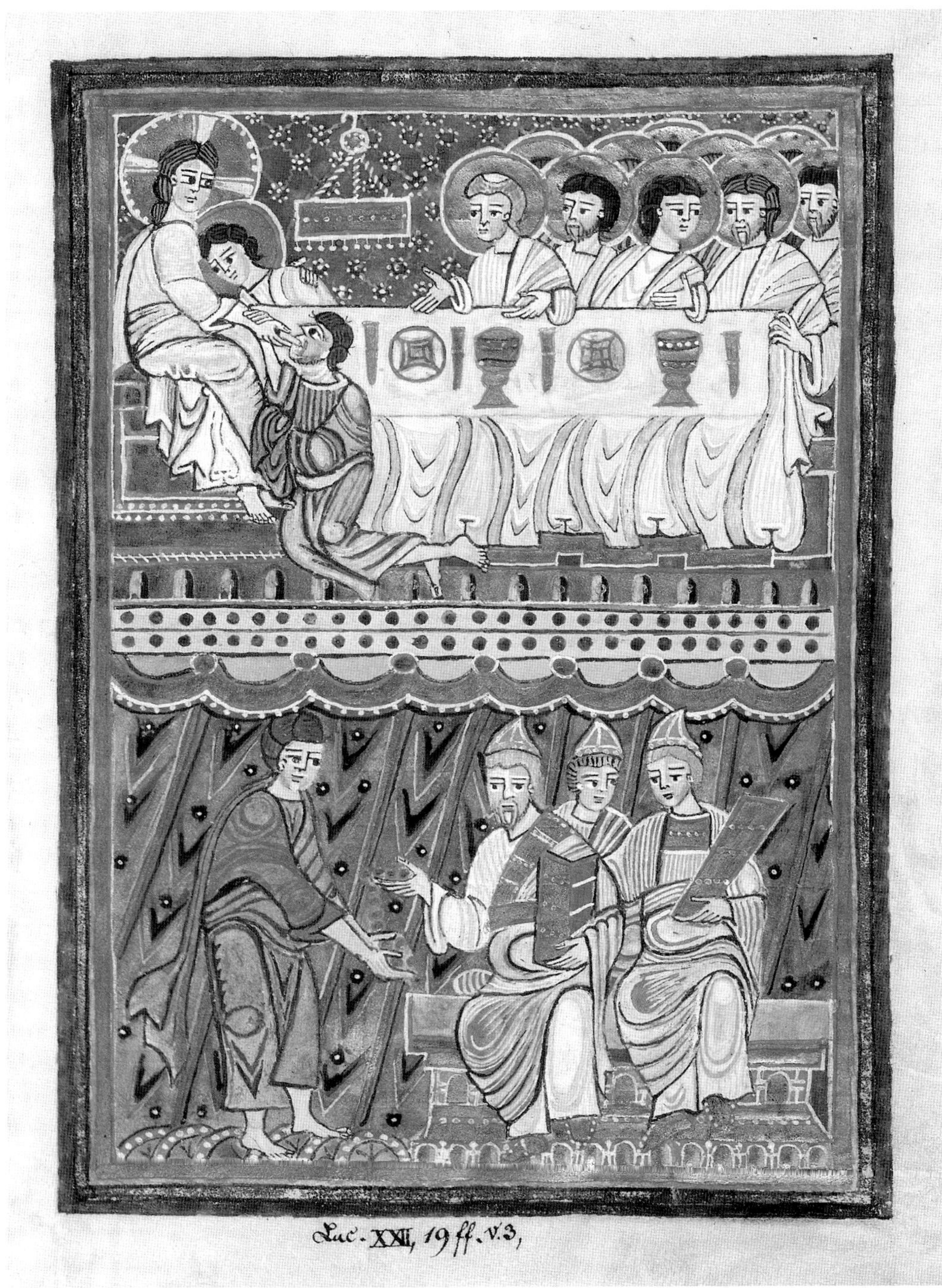

FIGURE 29 Hildesheim, Dom- und Diözesanmu-seum, Domschatz 18 (Bernward Gospels), fol. 118r, *Last Supper* (above) and *Judas with the High Priests* (below)

by Augustine.[32] Augustine contrasted Judas's experience at the Last Supper with that of Peter. Although both partook of the salvific body of Christ, because of his lack of faith, Judas partook unto death, while Peter partook unto life.[33] For Judas consumed the bread, but his perception remained limited to external things. Following 1 Corinthians 2:28–29, the body and blood of Christ are absent from the Eucharist received by unbelievers and sinners because they lack spiritual awareness.[34] In the Bernward Gospels paintings, although Judas opens his mouth to receive the sop and touches Christ, he remains physically separate from the experience. Judas's placement not only in front of the table but also outside of the picture's frame, along with his second appearance below as someone who turns his back on Christ, suggests that Judas remains bound to the earthly realm. He tastes the sop only as bread and touches merely the outside edges of Christ's skin, his human body. Theologically and pictorially, Judas's touch is purely corporeal and therefore limited.

The priests' offering of gold rather than silver coins contrasts with the biblical account of Judas's betrayal, but it creates two parallels within the gospel book's pictorial program that strengthen the identification of Judas as a counter-model to a type of haptic perception that includes spiritual understanding. At the beginning of the manuscript (fol. 18r; plate 4), the Magi, coiffed like these three priests of the Old Testament, present gold coins to the Christ child as pious offerings. Gold coins also appear in the scene of Christ calling Matthew to his service (fol. 18v; plate 5), in which Matthew abandons the coins that signify his work as a tax collector. Both scenes portray a response to material treasures in which

spiritual understanding—that is, the realization of Christ's divine nature as the Messiah, the son of God—motivates the giving away of gold. The first involves a votive offering, and the second, the abandonment of secular work in favor of spiritual service. Judas, in contrast, betrays Christ, having fallen into the trap of being captivated by the surface of things.[35]

The last miniature involving haptic perception is the Baptism of Christ. In this painting, John (unusually) grasps Christ's shoulder in both hands (fol. 174v; see plate 15 and fig. 20).[36] A lock of Christ's hair falls over the Baptist's fingers, underscoring that their touch involves a close physical contact that, like the Magdalene's, overlaps their two bodies. Conventionally understood as a theophany, the Baptism represents the moment when John realizes and proclaims Christ's divinity. However, a detail underscores the fact that at the moment he perceives Christ's godhood, John is handling Christ's *human* body.[37] The angels who flank Christ open a large curtain between them, quite different in its prominence and gold border from the small indistinct towels that angels sometimes hold in medieval renderings of the Baptism.[38] Christ's flesh has been painted in the same shade and pattern as this cloth, seeming, in this way, partly to dissolve into the broader expanse of the textile. Such a conflation of Christ's body and the curtain evokes the conventional metaphor that first appeared in Paul's letter to the Hebrews and crystallized in Western thought during the eleventh century, wherein the curtain serves as a marker for Christ's human flesh.[39]

Like the manuscript's presentation of visionary perception, the tactile experience of the Magdalene and the Baptist is focused on Christ, and its perceptual activity shifts back and forth between earthly and heavenly realms, between the corporeal and the spiritual senses. On the one hand, when John touches Christ's body he establishes its fleshly limits, grasping Christ's humanity. On the other hand, Christ's flesh dissolves into the curtain, and because the moment of baptism is also a theophany, at the moment of touch, John also perceives Christ's divinity. This reverses Mary's experience in the Noli me tangere to the extent that instead of penetrating a symbol of his godhood to touch his humanity, John the Baptist handles Christ's incarnate human flesh and perceives his divinity. The Baptist thus mimics with his touch what John the Evangelist most directly models for sight in the manuscript. Both perceive beyond but through the boundaries of earthly matter.[40] That perception contrasts with Judas's limited experience.

These models of haptic perception serve as exempla for Bernward himself. Among them, John the Baptist stands out as a particular case. As discussed in chapter 2, of the twenty narrative pictures in the gospel book, six illustrate episodes from John the Baptist's life, and each portrays him as a model for the manuscript's patron, Bernward. As not only a model but also a stand-in for the bishop, the Baptist's ritual touch of Christ keys Bernward's experience of the liturgical objects pictured in the dedicatory painting.

It is the nature of the book as a body, and specifically a Christological body, that underlies the process by which the Bernward Gospels links the bishop's perception in the earthly church to the saints' perception of Christ. That perception stems not only from the commonplace that the Gospels were the Christ Logos, or Word-made-flesh,[41] but also from the process of making

and using manuscripts. Medieval manuscript production was an intense physical activity that required the stretching and scraping of animal flesh followed by the cutting, pricking, and scoring of the parchment—that is, the penetration of a tool into the skin to mark the layout of the text and pictures.[42] Once the body was prepared, scribes and artists painstakingly applied the ink, pigment, and precious metals, an act of creation sometimes rendered metaphorically as the process by which Christ's divinity overshadowed Mary's flesh, becoming incarnate.[43]

Using manuscripts also involved the somatic engagement of the paired senses of touch and sight. Opening the book and turning its pages allowed the eye to read the text and contemplate the illustrations while the hand felt the pages' shifting surface texture. That shifting texture results from a peculiarity of making manuscripts from animal skin, the palpable difference between parchment's hair and flesh sides. Medieval makers and users were keenly aware of this physical quality. Manuscripts, including the Bernward Gospels, tend to be organized codicologically so that one hair side faces another, and each flesh side, with its smoother surface, touches another flesh side, thus maintaining an even tactile and visual sensation across the opening.

A further quality particular to illuminated manuscripts is the perceptible variation in the mass of certain parchment folios. Scribes and artists often reserved a thicker and thus slightly stiffer piece of vellum for painted illustrations; these absorbed the quantity of pigments used better. Thus, users could identify painted pages by both touch and sight—quickly finding these within the larger book by looking for them with the eyes, or by running fingers across the book's cut edge—and the book also became something that varied in both surface *and* mass, just as a body did.

In the dedication painting (fols. 16v–17r; see plates 2–3 and fig. 4), Bernward holds the still closed book/body in two hands, touching the manuscript's outside edges, its cover—just as, upon first glance, the Baptist appears to touch the surface of Christ's skin. Although he has not yet penetrated the book, Bernward grasps it in the context of a liturgical performance that includes allusions to the Eucharistic rite. Christ's Incarnation is actively in process, and the work of the bishop's offering as a support for opening the passageway to the heavenly church is amplified by the depiction on the page of numerous other gifted objects that serve also as Christological *imagines.*

The early medieval discourse about art associated it with consecrated matter, relics, and the sacraments. The pictorial references in the Bernward Gospels to the Eucharist and offertory rites of the Mass underscore these connections and key the processes by which the material *imago* and the inherent properties of its medium are to be apprehended and their meaning understood. By means of his gift and the Eucharistic consecration, Bernward comes to the edge of the heavenly church. Similar to the Magi's shifting sight and the Magdalene's non-touching touch, his perception oscillates between the earthly and heavenly altars. The perceptual process is somewhat different from the Baptist's penetrating touch, which rather resembles the operation of John the Evangelist's gaze. Both the work of John the Baptist's touch in the depiction of Christ's Baptism and the object of John the Evangelist's contemplation in the picture of Christ's Ascension direct attention

away from the *imago.* This is more obvious in the iconography of the Ascension because it literally conceals Christ's upper body (his divinity) from physical sight. The iconography of the Baptism makes a similar argument, however, when it dissolves Christ's body under John's hands, a signal that Christ disappears from the Baptist's physical grasp. The relationship between the Baptist's touch and the Evangelist's sight, together with the similarities between the Magdalene's touch and the Magi's sight, suggests that the manuscript presents a series of visual/tactile pairs comprising the two Johns, Mary with the Magi, and Judas with the unseeing figures of the visionary paintings.

The parallels between how the Bernward Gospels depicts the sensory mechanism of sight and that of touch are significant. Like the visionary miniatures discussed in the previous chapter, the representations of touch engage medieval theories about art that justify images in relation to Christ's dual nature. More than merely visible, however, the early medieval *imago*, because it foregrounds its own materiality, is particularly palpable.[44] That tangibility creates an especially acute tension for the use of images in devotional practice. Because the haptic sense is traditionally understood as the most corporeal, it runs the danger of being captivated by the material surfaces of art. Failing to penetrate that surface to the spiritual truth of Christ's nature could result in idolatry.[45] Consequently, it is exceedingly difficult to find traces of contemporary ideas about the haptic qualities of devotional objects in Carolingian and Ottonian sources. Early medieval texts that justify the use of religious images focus for the most part on the visual means by which they engage mechanisms for apprehending God, while medieval theology is usually consistent with Augustine's interpretation of haptic perception as a sign for sight.

Indeed, the series of haptic paintings in the Bernward Gospels is entirely novel, and its elements appear to have been invented for the manuscript. Whereas there are several precedents for the various details of the visionary miniatures, from individual iconographic motifs to their iconic pictorial mode, the scenes of touch have few if any parallels in medieval art. Although Augustine's commentary and its clever pictorialization in the disappearing Christ offered a solution to the problem of seeing, the issue of corporeal touch clearly required the driving force behind the codex's design, most probably Bernward himself, to find another approach. In neo-Platonic philosophy, the bishop found an analysis of touch and matter of the third kind that suggested parallels with Augustinian ideas about spiritual sight. By elaborating on this concept in ways that echo Augustine's visual system, the Bernward Gospels pictures adapt to the haptic sense what was a long-standing discourse about vision in the medieval understanding of art. But why consider touch at all?

A number of Ottonian objects and texts tantalizingly hint that in this period, art's materiality and resulting tangibility was especially important to contemporary ideas about how art might prompt the spiritual understanding of the Godhead.[46] An altar originally commissioned by Bruno of Cologne that is now only preserved in a drawing (Xanten, Stiftsarchiv, StiX H 19, 1734, p. 395) explains in a titulus the importance of matter for conveying Christ's dual nature: "The material and this image show things doubly, / The image renders the form of man, the gold

signifies his divinity."[47] The same principle was at stake in the sermon Bishop Gerard of Arras-Cambrai delivered, not long after the making of this antependium, at the Council of Arras in 1025 as part of his counter to local heretical movements.[48] In his defense of Church practices, Gerard not only emphasized the real presence of Christ in the Eucharist and articulated a position on Christ's Resurrection but he also discussed extensively the biblical example of the bronze serpent Moses raised in the desert (Numbers 21:9), a figure usually interpreted as a type for the crucified Christ. In the biblical account, God tells Moses that looking at the bronze sculpture will heal the Israelites of the snakebites afflicting them as punishment for having doubted Him. Gerard uses the story to argue for the salvific power of images of the Crucifixion. Yet in building the typological association between brazen serpent and Crucifixion, Gerard explains how the bronze sculpture expresses the complicated message that the Crucifixion signifies both death and triumph over death. The snake, namely the image, symbolizes death and humility, while the durable metal, namely the medium, stands for eternity.[49]

Gerard allegorizes not only the serpent but also its bronze substance. By doing so he implies that both matter and image must be fully apprehended in order to understand the significance of the typology he presents. Slightly earlier in the eleventh century, Thietmar of Merseburg goes even further than Gerard when he recounts how a bishop "healed" (*curavit*) a wooden crucifix—the term *curavit* suggesting that the author was presenting the sculpture itself as a type of living body. The process of healing the sculpture involved inserting pieces of the Eucharist and true cross into a fissure, which disappeared once the sculpture was healed. In this story the two bodies of art and Christ—the sculpture together with the Eucharist and relic—become one.[50]

Several of Bishop Bernward's artistic commissions similarly draw attention to their own medium for rendering Christ's dual nature. A pair of candlesticks cast in gilded silver, for example, calls on the viewer to discern its technique and material: "Bishop Bernward ordered his servant to cast these candlesticks in the first flower of this art, not out of gold, not out of silver, and nevertheless as you discern [it here]."[51] The phrase "not out of gold, not out of silver" (*non auro non argento*) draws on widely circulating discussions of the metal electrum in medieval encyclopedias as well as theological exegesis from Gregory the Great to Bruno of Segni (1047–1123) that used electrum as a metaphor for the two natures of Christ—gold signifying his divinity, and silver, his humanity.[52] The negative turn of phrase in the reference to electrum evokes the biblical axiom that man would be saved neither through gold nor silver but through the blood of Christ (1 Peter 18–21), and perhaps a popular distich in medieval representations of Christ: *nec Deus, nec homo*. Together with the candlesticks' iconography, which presents the salvific movement of the virtuous toward the light of Christ, the inscription directs the faithful to puzzle out (*ut cernis*) the significance of the medium for rendering the Savior's human and divine natures.[53]

Such emphasis on the materiality of art intersected with ongoing tactile practices in the Church. Various liturgical and devotional behavior involved the touching of artworks. A tenth-century monk from Reichenau describes that the brothers regularly touched a painting

of the Virgin and Child during prayer, while an eleventh-century miracle described in the Life of Dominic of Sora requires other haptic behaviors: the kissing and embracing of a saint's image.[54] Certain acts of touch were required by the conventions of the Mass and helped link the body of Christ to particular objects. It was usual, for example, for the medieval celebrant to kiss the gospels to honor Christ as the Word-made-flesh. Liturgical *ordines* also directed the devout to touch the cross as part of the celebration of Good Friday. Conventionally, the priest, followed by local religious communities and finally the laity, remembered Christ's death by kissing the crucifix at a predetermined point in the rites.

Such habits seem to have stimulated or related to haptic desire toward the sacred. In the fourth century Bishop Paulinus of Nola had described a sailor whose ear had been touched by God. Paulinus recounted that he fingered this man's ear incessantly, explaining, "Valgius is the living earth on which we see impressed the traces of the Lord's body, if with the eye of faith and spiritual sight we scrutinize what Christ's bosom and Christ's hand have touched in him, if we frequently stroke with our hands the gray hair which often reclined on the Lord's knee and grew warm in the Lord's embrace, if we repeatedly touch that tender ear which heavenly fingers pulled."[55] Here Paulinus links spiritual sight and touch together in experiencing Valgius as a kind of relic, and in the same letter he relates his desire to connect with God through these paired sensations to the sentiment that draws pilgrims to Jerusalem, to see and touch the places where Christ was physically present. Later, in the eighth century, the author of a treatise rather hostile to art's effects, Theodulf of Orleans, cautions Carolingian priests not to allow the laity to touch any of the instruments of the Mass, the *vasa sacra*, and especially to keep women away from the altar in order to avoid their contaminating touch.[56] By 1100, the theologian Rupert of Deutz could describe a tactile vision of the crucifix in which the sculpture comes to life. Christ on the cross opens his mouth so that Rupert may kiss him more deeply.[57]

Extant objects, too, show evidence of having been touched, rubbed, or embraced. The ivory cover of Bernward's Franco-Saxon Gospels (DS 13; fig. 30) includes signs of wear that suggest that in this carving of the Crucifixion, the representations of Mary and Christ, patron saints of Saint Michael's, were more frequently touched than that of John the Evangelist. The Virgin's face is particularly worn, and Christ's slightly less so, while John appears to be in good condition and the carved lines of all three figures' garments remain quite crisp. This may be the result of the celebrant's kissing the gospels, and since Mary and Christ were more important than John to the monks of Saint Michael's (who owned this book), it makes sense to find that those two had been kissed more frequently. It is, however, very interesting because it suggests that devotional touching was more than merely rote behavior but was rather consciously directed—just as sight has often been argued to be.[58]

More than merely reflecting these practices, the nature of the Baptist's touch explains the significance of touch for Bernward; it expresses his sacramental power. It is surely not coincidental that the key exemplar for the bishop's touch occurs in a scene of Baptism, the ceremony that establishes the community and sanctity of the church and symbolizes the sacramental nature of the episcopal office. Baptism is a characteristic feature of episcopal hagiography, both in texts and in the illustrated Lives of bishop-saints.[59] It is also prominent in the representation of historical bishops. For example, as Robert Deshman has pointed out, the benedictional of the Anglo-Saxon bishop Aethelwold of Winchester (London, British Library, MS Additional 49598) links John's Baptism of Christ (fol. 25r) to a representation of the bishop blessing his congregation (fol. 118v), a picture that prefaces the blessing for the dedication of the Church, which was understood liturgically as a type of baptism.[60] Similarly, in the Bernward Gospels, the Baptist's baptismal gesture, that unusual two-handed grasp, is echoed in Bernward's portrait, which combines liturgical content from the Eucharistic rite, Mass offertory, and an altar dedication in a picture that commemorates the bishop.

Touch held particular meaning for the medieval episcopate. A bishop's touch admitted the saved into the Church, expelled the damned, and defined the holy. Bishops were the limbs (and often more specifically the arms) of the body of the Church. Their power and sanctity worked through their hands. Arm-shaped reliquaries are predominantly those of saints associated with the institutional church, and especially bishops, whose hands are sacralized by the liturgical rituals they perform. Cynthia Hahn has shown how such reliquaries might even substitute for episcopal hands during liturgical performances. In this period, the Roman rite for the Mass concluded with an episcopal blessing, the sign of the cross, which was expressly forbidden to other priests. Eventually priests came to use relics, pieces of the true cross, or the paten or corporal to transmit this blessing, and Hahn suggests how the arm reliquary could be used in analogous ways.[61]

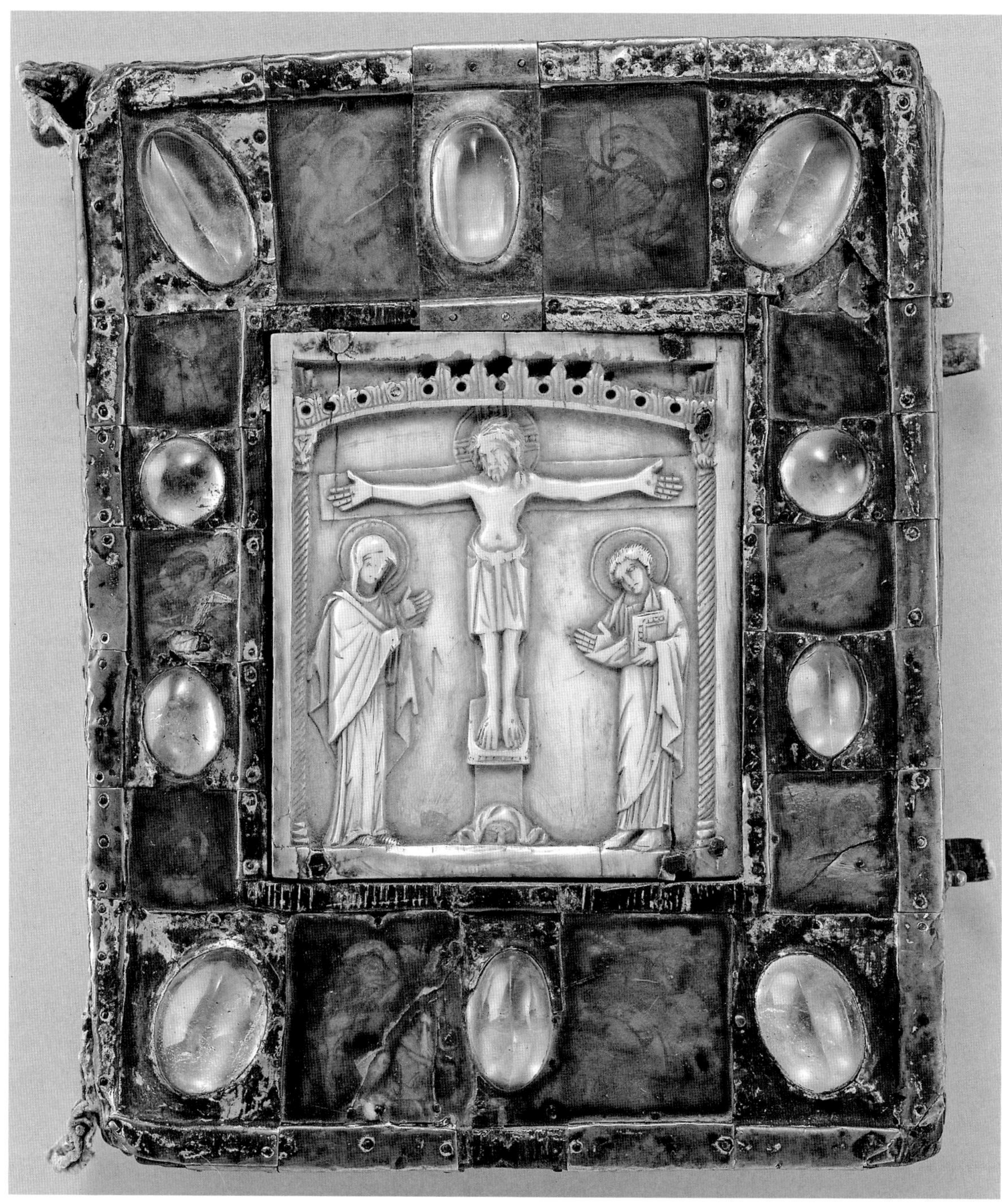

FIGURE 30   Hildesheim, Dom- und Diözesanmuseum, Domschatz 13 (Franco-Saxon Gospels), front cover

The Bernward Gospels pictures treat both sight and touch and are closely related by a number of shared themes, including eschatological ones. These express something of the patron's personal concerns for his own salvation. To restate the salvific mechanisms of the gift *pro anima* using Calcidius's terminology, the Mass constructs the offering as a site of potentiality, where matter (body) rises to the level of the immaterial (spirit), and the immaterial (spirit) overshadows matter (body). Through this process Bernward's gift makes the sacred realm both visible and tangible, giving proof of the donor's merit. The bishop, however, is to be remembered to the saints not only as a donor but also as the founder of Saint Michael's—dedicating the first altar of the new building—and as Mass celebrant. Significant to the codex's treatment of the senses are references to the liturgy, with a special emphasis on the sacraments of the Eucharist and Baptism. This links models from sacred history to Bernward and expresses the sacramental power of his episcopal office. The bishop is, in this way, embedded in the institutional hierarchy of the Church and shown to act as the full instrument of the divine, becoming himself, in turn, a model for how to see and grasp Christ.

CONCLUSION

One of the better-known bishops of the early eleventh century, Bernward of Hildesheim led the type of life long considered typical for the episcopate of the period. He was the younger son of a comital family from the Saxon heartland of Ottonian Germany; he trained in the liberal arts at the cathedral school of Hildesheim; and he began his career in the imperial chapel.[1] Bernward was also deeply embedded in the cultural mores and politics of the court.[2] He served as tutor to Otto III, and though he was predominantly preoccupied with local diocesan matters after his episcopal appointment—particularly border raids by Vikings and Slavs and the so-called Gandersheim conflict—he continued to maintain advantageous relationships with the emperor.[3] In early 1001, Bernward joined Otto III in Rome to petition Pope Sylvester II (another former tutor to the emperor) for confirmation of his claim to the royal nunnery of Gandersheim. While there, the bishop witnessed and participated in the strife between the allied imperial-papal power and local Roman nobles that marked the early months of the year. After Otto's death, Bernward remained implicated in politics. He supported the Saxon candidate Ekkehart I of Meissen over Henry II's ultimately successful bid for the German throne, honoring Ekkehart as royalty during a visit to Hildesheim in 1002. This does not seem to have brought any obvious negative consequences, however, and in 1007, Bernward participated in Henry II's military campaign against Baldwin IV of Flanders. Afterward, the two traveled together to the court of the Frankish king Robert II.

Throughout his episcopacy Bernward sought to secure the privileges of the church in matters large and small. A letter from 1003 concerns parish tithes that had passed into lay hands, and in 1020, Bernward decreed that four synods a year be held in different locations in Hildesheim to discuss grievances, disputes, forgotten statutes concerning rights, and other legal matters important to the church.[4] Bernward also exercised his pastoral responsibilities with care, endowing not only Saint Michael's but also the cathedral with great wealth and supporting local nunneries such as Ringelheim, where his sister Judith was the abbess. Moreover, he seems to have been an ongoing actor in clerical reform. In 1019 he presided over the Synod of Goslar, one of several councils that sought to curtail clerical marriage and concubinage.[5]

Bernward's decision to build Saint Michael's as a memorial foundation parallels the actions of many of his peers as well as the efforts of Emperor Henry II at Bamberg. Several Bernwardian objects also share visual traits with products of both episcopal and royal artistic patronage. Bernward's manuscripts, including the Bernward Gospels, use an ornamental vocabulary inspired by silk patterns, a vocabulary that appears in manuscripts produced (often for royalty) at Corvey in the tenth century and Echternach in the later eleventh century.[6] Two of Bernward's codices include Byzantine ivories on their covers, a feature common to a number of manuscripts commissioned by the imperial family and ecclesiastical elite, especially bishops.[7] References to Rome in the iconography of the Virgin in the Bernward Gospels and in the type of monumental bronzes cast in Hildesheim not only reflect an interest shared by Otto III, but also may respond to works made for Archbishop Willigis of Mainz, Bernward's rival in the Gandersheim conflict and a man who served as imperial chancellor, a major political power and significant spiritual leader.[8]

Anthony Cutler and William North have offered the provocative suggestion that the turn of the millennium marked the emergence of a new element in Ottonian episcopal self-identity: the self-conscious and public assertion by bishops of their roles as cultural impresarios and arbiters of taste. This may also have motivated the form of Bernward's commissions. Certainly the bishop had his name recorded on an unusual number of the works produced during his episcopacy, and these sometimes also include inscriptions that draw attention to their artistic merit.[9] As C. Stephen Jaeger has shown, critical to bishops' expression of their social education was an awareness of correct gesture and comportment, and Cutler and North's study raises the possibility that art served as part of that display.[10]

Artistic patronage played an important role in constructing medieval bishops' identity and power, not only socially and politically but also spiritually. It thus offers an important body of evidence for examining episcopal activity. As part of evaluating how Ottonian bishops perceived and shaped their own image, it is especially critical to consider the Ottonian heartland—namely, the region of Saxony, the seat of the Liudolfing family that began to rule East Frankish lands in the tenth century.[11] The weight of the evidence suggests that Bernward, a Saxon bishop, not only commissioned the Bernward Gospels but also played a significant part in its design, and this study has argued that the codex aims to shape the bishop's own reception—that is, both to ensure that the community of Saint Michael's to whom he gave the book would remember him and to direct *how* it would remember him. Bishop Bernward is both representative and idiosyncratic in how he constructs that image. The pictorial program of the Bernward Gospels presents a complex picture of a bishop who cares for his diocese through a life of service that imitates Christ and through his exceptional patronage, who exercises the sacerdotal authority of his office, and who is fundamentally preoccupied with his own salvation and desire to unite with God.

Although expressing the patron's personal concerns, the themes developed in the Bernward Gospels also share characteristics with hagiographic narratives, with contemporary episcopal contemporary portraiture, and with imagery in the lives of bishop-saints, suggesting that the book's pictures fashion an image not only of the individual but also of his office. That representation offers insight into how a prominent representative of the episcopate, which ideally pursued the contemplative life but also had important administrative responsibilities, understood, or at least presented, his role to the saints and to the earthly communities called upon to remember him.

PICTURING THE EPISCOPATE

As Éric Palazzo has pointed out in his study of the pontifical, a liturgical book designed specifically for bishops that first appears in the eleventh century, bishops' patronage operated on multiple levels. It might help constitute a personal and an ecclesiastical memory, glorify and remember the sovereign, and fortify and define the status of the bishop in politics, liturgy, and society.[12] Pierre-Alain Mariaux and Robert Deshman, in separate case studies of contemporary liturgical manuscripts produced, respectively, for the northern Italian bishop Warmund of Ivrea and the Anglo-Saxon bishop Aethelwold of Winchester,

have shown the ways in which these episcopal commissions communicated and even negotiated relationships between the imperial/royal and episcopal offices while expressing content specific to the patron's historical concerns. Mariaux places Warmund's sacramentary in the context of contemporary regional politics and argues that it presents an episcopal point of view that celebrates the authorities and privileges of the local bishop based on the "good defense" of the emperor, on the bishop's relationship to Christ, and on his devotion to the Virgin Mary.[13] Deshman's analysis emphasizes the dual royal and monastic program of Aethelwold's benedictional, which, among other things, points to that bishop's key role in the English Benedictine reform of the episcopacy.[14] More recently, Evan Gatti has shown how contemporary episcopal portraits in these and other manuscripts, including the sacramentary of Sigebert of Minden and the benedictional of Engilmar of Parenzo, highlight the performance of the liturgy and are part of a genre of liturgical portraiture that emphasizes bishops' power, especially their sacramental authority.[15] Gatti explains how Warmund's sacramentary, like the liturgy, thus mediates the sacred and the secular, the imperial and the episcopal, and even the Italian and the Ottonian.[16]

In the period around 1015, the Gandersheim conflict appeared to have finally been resolved in Hildesheim's favor. Adam Cohen and Anne Derbes have suggested that Bishop Bernward's bronze doors allude to that triumph, and they have shown certain similarities between the themes of the doors and the dedication painting in the Bernward Gospels. Regardless of whether the codex also subtly celebrates Bernward's political victory, the book was produced during the

same period, a time of intense artistic production, of relative political confidence, and also,
it seems, of physical illness. Unlike the works
studied by Palazzo, Mariaux, and Deshman,
the Bernward Gospels pictorial program does
not seem directly concerned with royal themes,
political matters, or reform. This is not especially
surprising. The bishop maintained good relations
with the imperial court; he was a member of the
local ruling comital family; and, as far as he was
concerned, he faced no more opposition about
Gandersheim, the only real political conflict that
marked his episcopacy. Although preoccupied
by spiritual matters and participating in the
era's general push for clerical celibacy, Bernward
did not undertake any historically noteworthy
reforms. In fact, if Bernward's 1019 testament
is any indication, the achievement by which he
considered he might be most deserving of heaven
was the foundation of Saint Michael's.

Where the Bernward Gospels does resemble
other episcopal commissions is in its emphasis on
the bishop's relationship with Christ. It also offers
liturgical references that underscore the sacerdotal nature of the episcopal office, presenting as
ideal the active life of the priesthood, especially
through the model of the Baptist. Indeed the
Baptist offers a complex hagiographic model that
seems to have been especially popular for recon-
ciling the *vita activa* with more traditional ideals
of a spiritual life withdrawn from the world,
a choice the nature of the episcopal office made
untenable for bishops.[17]

Taken altogether, the Bernward Gospels paintings commemorate Bernward and his founding
of Saint Michael's; emphasize his donations and
gifts; cast him as a good servant awaiting his
Lord's final return; present the bishop's hopes

for unity with his Savior; and picture him as
a Christo-mimetic model of the sacramental
priesthood who not only preaches, baptizes and
celebrates Mass, but also sees and grasps the
Godhead. In so doing, the Bernward Gospels
program shares affinities with contemporary
pictorial narratives of the lives of episcopal saints.
Cynthia Hahn has shown how these illustrate
the nature of the episcopacy in three main ways.
The bishop cares for his people with acts of
exceptional charity, and the Bernward Gospels
dedication painting presents Bernward's greatest
legacy as, to quote from his testament, "someone
who had built churches, instituted the service
of God in them and donated all his possessions
to the Lord." Bishops are officers of the Church
who take their place at the head of a heavenly
and earthly hierarchy, which these narratives
communicate by combining apostolic prestige
with liturgical formulations, and Bernward's
manuscript uses the models of the evangelists'
and Baptist's service; it portrays him, as in the
episcopal portraits studied by Evan Gatti, adopt-
ing a liturgical posture. Finally, characteristic
for the pictured lives of bishop-saints are images
of preaching, baptizing and praying, all activities emphasized in the Baptist's modeling of the
sacramental priesthood.[18] More idiosyncratic in
the Bernward Gospels is the emphasis on seeing
and touching in how the pictures formulate the
nature of the relationship between the bishop and
God, the concern in the dedication painting with
setting into motion commemorative mechanisms, and the repeated references to salvation
and judgment. These themes would be repeated
in the design of Bernward's tomb.[19]

Critical to its effectiveness as a gift *pro anima*,
the Bernward Gospels aims to set into motion

mechanisms that evoke specific responses from the patron saints and monks of Saint Michael's. Offered in conjunction with the consecration of Saint Michael's crypt altar, the pictures prompt the book's recipients literally to re-collect Bernward. The book demonstrates the bishop's likeness to the ideals of his office and also communicates related, but more idiosyncratic, spiritual concerns. The dedication bifolium especially, but equally the use of John the Baptist as a model priest, visionary, and toucher of Christ, serves to establish the bishop's privileged relationship to God and places him at the center of a process in which the episcopate serves as the full instrument of the divine.[20]

REMEMBERING THE BISHOP
AT SAINT MICHAEL'S

Although it is difficult to reconstruct from historical sources the exact function of the Bernward Gospels within the community of Saint Michael's, certainly at the moment of its donation, and later as one of its most precious treasures, the manuscript would have played some role in the liturgy. The *Vita Bernwardi,* in a section probably written in the twelfth century, claims that Bernward gave preciously decorated gospel books to be carried during feast processions, indicating the monastery's practice at that time.[21] The good physical condition of the Bernward Gospels underscores that it, unlike other manuscripts given to the monastery by Bernward (such as the sacramentary [DS 19]), was not frequently touched or opened in services. Yet after the bishop's death, the Bernward Gospels served as one of several foci for Bernward's memory, to such an extent

that the monks of Saint Michael's in Hildesheim renovated the manuscript's covers during their twelfth-century campaign to have the bishop canonized as a saint.[22] The restoration involved an important intervention in the work's design, although the current covers reuse parts of a book box that originally housed the Bernward Gospels.[23] Today, the front prominently features a Byzantine ivory spolium on which an early eleventh-century inscription names Bernward (plate 1 and fig. 31). It is probable that the ivory was an original component of the book box.[24] The gold frame around it, however, dates to the twelfth century. On the back appear niello cut-outs that show evidence of having been scaled down, also probably from the eleventh-century book box (plate 18 and fig. 32). There a second inscription names Bernward and serves as a frame for the image of the Virgin and child. The Greek letters MP ΘV that originally identified Mary as the Theotokos, the mother of God, are repositioned in ways that suggest that for the twelfth-century restorer, they may have been essentially decorative motifs; they appear out of legible order.

Further additions to the Bernward Gospels suggest that the book served the community of Saint Michael's as a locus for remembering their founder throughout the Middle Ages, albeit as part of contemporary efforts to shape the bishop's image for their own purposes. A thirteenth-century hand records Bernward's twelfth-century canonization on fol. 232r. This crucial event helped make the monastery the site of a regional cult precisely in those decades that followed the efforts by the cathedral and a rival local monastery to develop the renown of Bishop Godehard, Bernward's successor, who had been canonized in

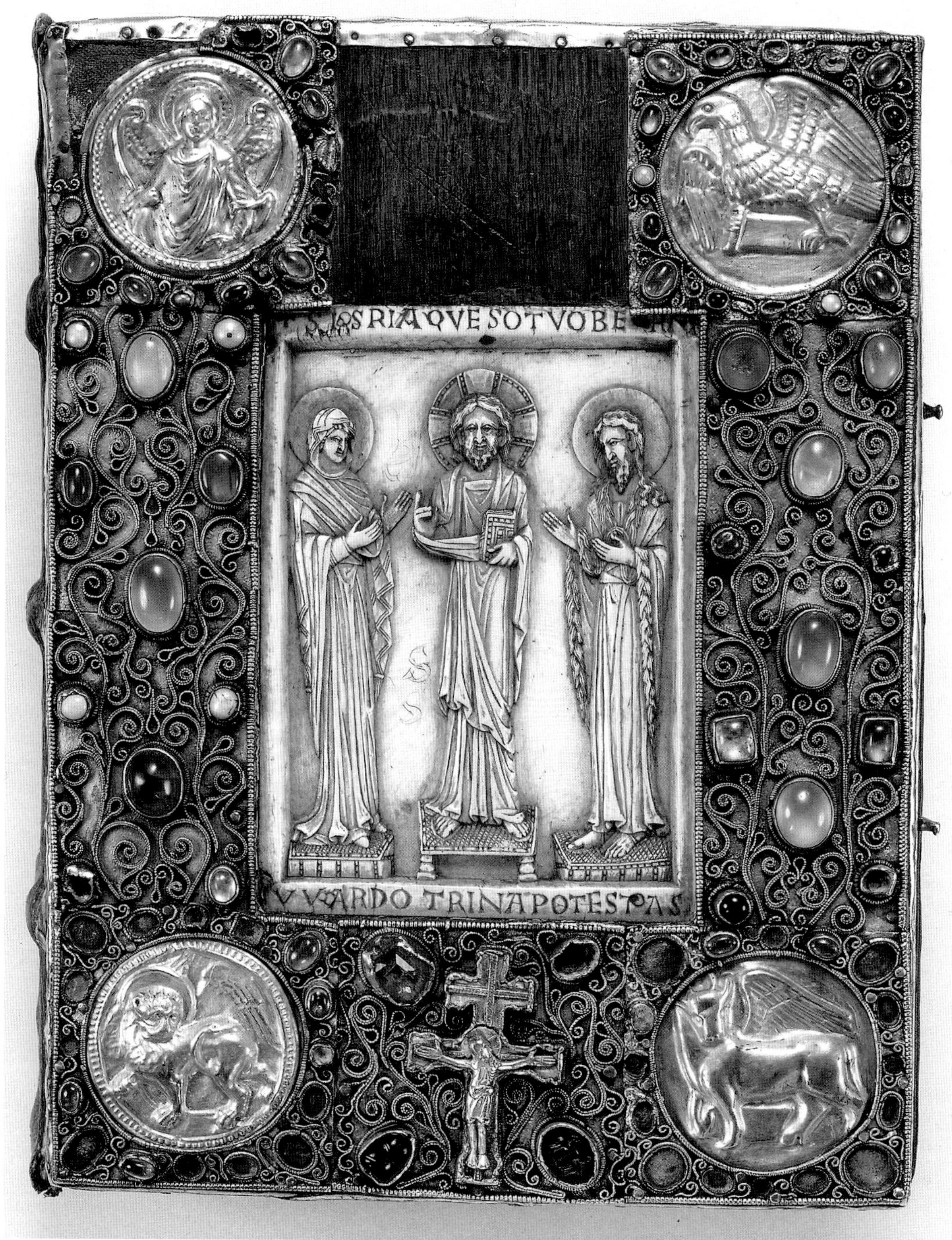

FIGURE 31   Hildesheim, Dom- und Diözesanmuseum, Domschatz 18 (Bernward Gospels), front cover

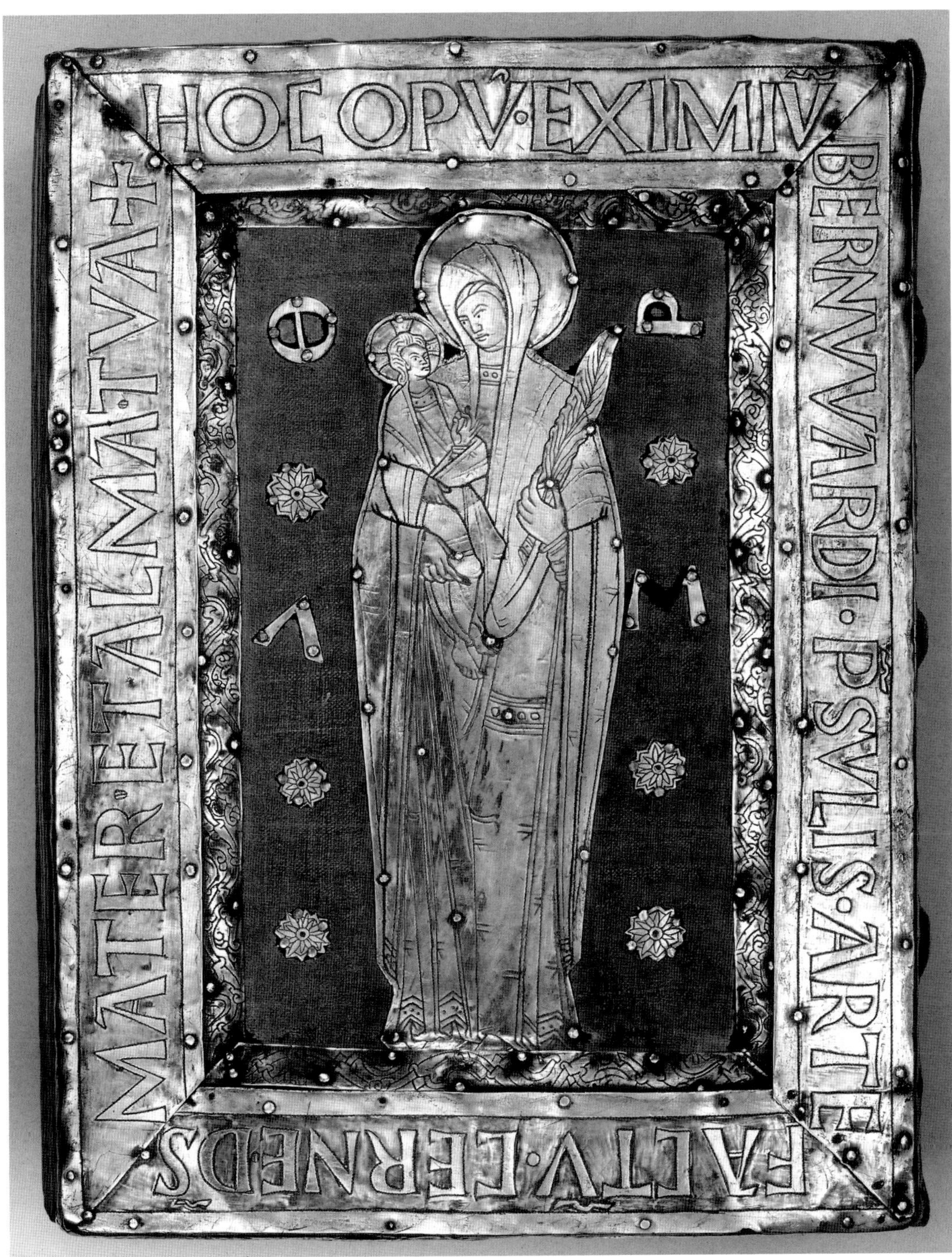

FIGURE 32   Hildesheim, Dom- und Diözesanmuseum, Domschatz 18 (Bernward Gospels), back cover

1131.[25] By the fourteenth century, a monk sought to extend Bernward's presence in Saint Michael's treasury further by inscribing a Byzantinizing ivory with the bishop's name.[26] That act may have been motivated by the presence of Byzantine ivories on two of Bernward's gospel books—not only the Bernward Gospels, but also a Carolingian work that bears the bishop's monogram on the back cover.[27] Then, in the fifteenth century, the abbot of Saint Michael's added a list of the contents of two major reliquary shrines on the same leaf where Bernward himself had recorded his donation of the Bernward Gospels to Saint Michael's (fol. 231v). By then, the Bernward Gospels had been entirely co-opted for the monastic community's self-fashioning as, among other things, a center for important relics. Bernward formed only one part of the resulting portrait of Saint Michael's Abbey.

Such activities illustrate the central importance of artworks in shaping how the bishop was remembered. Indeed the monks' restoration of the Bernward Gospels was part of a broader regional trend, starting about 1150, to use, modify, and create liturgical objects connected to Bernward. Some works from the monastery's treasury underwent only minor modifications, such as when the monks updated a list of relics engraved on the back of Bernward's gilded silver cross (fig. 33).[28] Other works involved more heavy-handed interventions. The monks incorporated only fragments of Bernwardian metalwork into a new *gemma crucis* for the relics of the true cross that Bernward was said to have received as a gift from Emperor Otto III (fig. 34).[29] A legend cited in Bernward's biography ascribes the making of this cross to Bernward himself; it also explains that an angel helped the bishop complete the

work. A contemporaneous painting refers to this legend in the miniature that introduces the feast day of Saint Bernward (Los Angeles, CA, Getty Museum, MS 64, fol. 156r; ca. 1170); shortly thereafter, the monks had a copy of the reliquary cross made.[30]

From the twelfth century until the monastery's secularization, the cross was presented in Saint Michael's as a relic of the bishop, displayed not only on feasts dedicated to the cross but also on the anniversary of Bernward's death. By 1400, the same cross was portrayed in two sculpted portraits of the bishop. One statue may have stood in Saint Michael's crypt (fig. 35). The other now appears in the northwest portal of the cathedral. Both sculptures served to identify the bishop publicly with an object in the Saint Michael's treasury that the bishop, in fact, neither made nor commissioned.[31] The history of this cross and its representation suggests the process by which the monks deployed art and liturgy to add new layers to Bernward's memory; these layers did not always correspond to the bishop's self-presentation in the eleventh century. The emphasis given to identifying Bernward as an artist in his biography, for example, dates to the twelfth-century compilation. Adding to that trend is a paten from the Guelph treasure now at the Cleveland Museum of Art. A twelfth-century work, the paten has been displayed in an ostensorium as a relic of the bishop since the second half of the fourteenth century. The container includes an authenticating inscription that identifies Bernward as the artist, a claim repeated by yet another text, the fifteenth-century vernacular biography of the bishop.[32]

After the bishop's death, the monks of Saint Michael's went to great lengths not only to

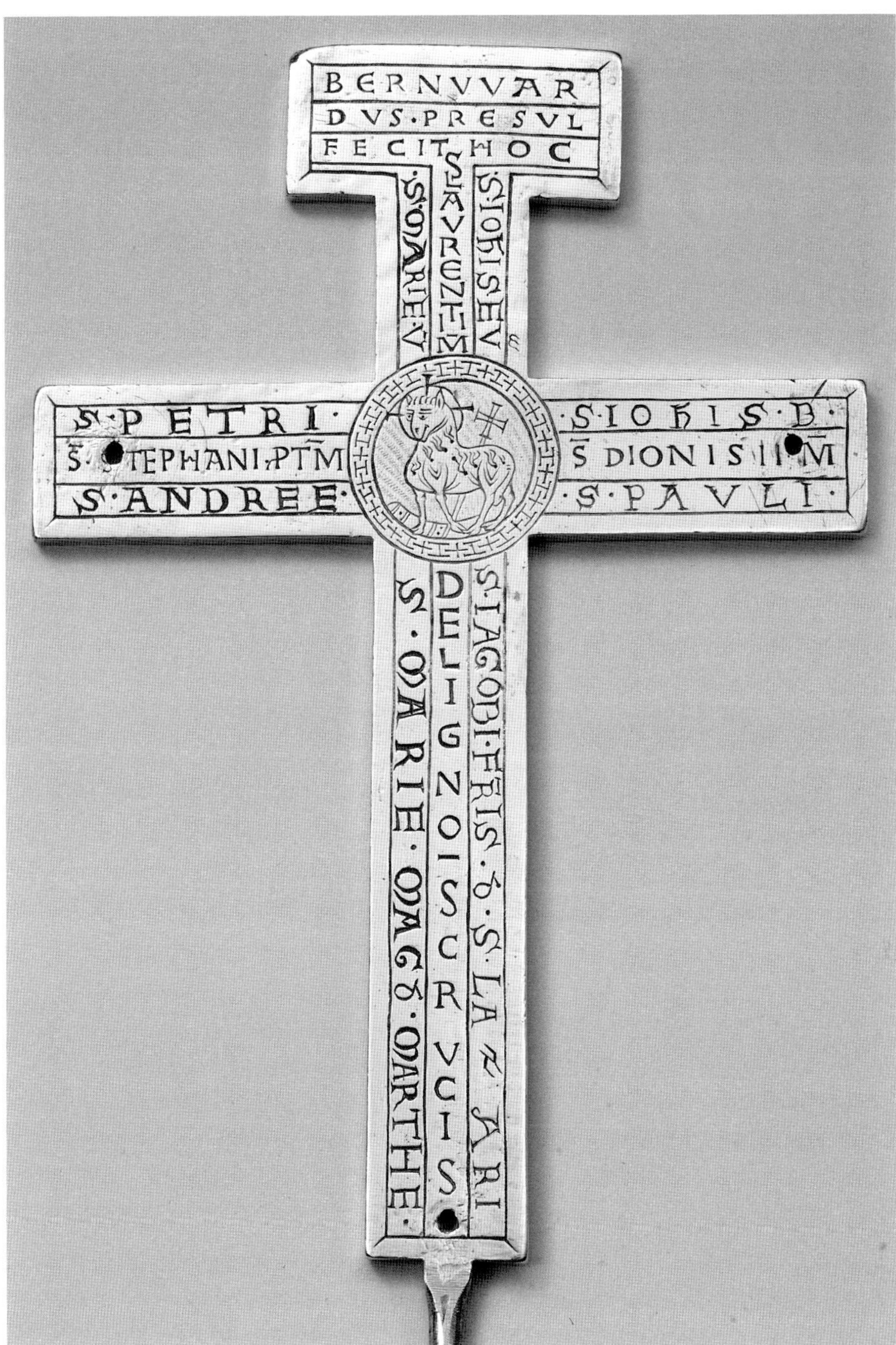

FIGURE 33   Hildesheim, Dom- und Diözesanmuseum, Domschatz 6, crucifix, after 1007 with twelfth-
century additions

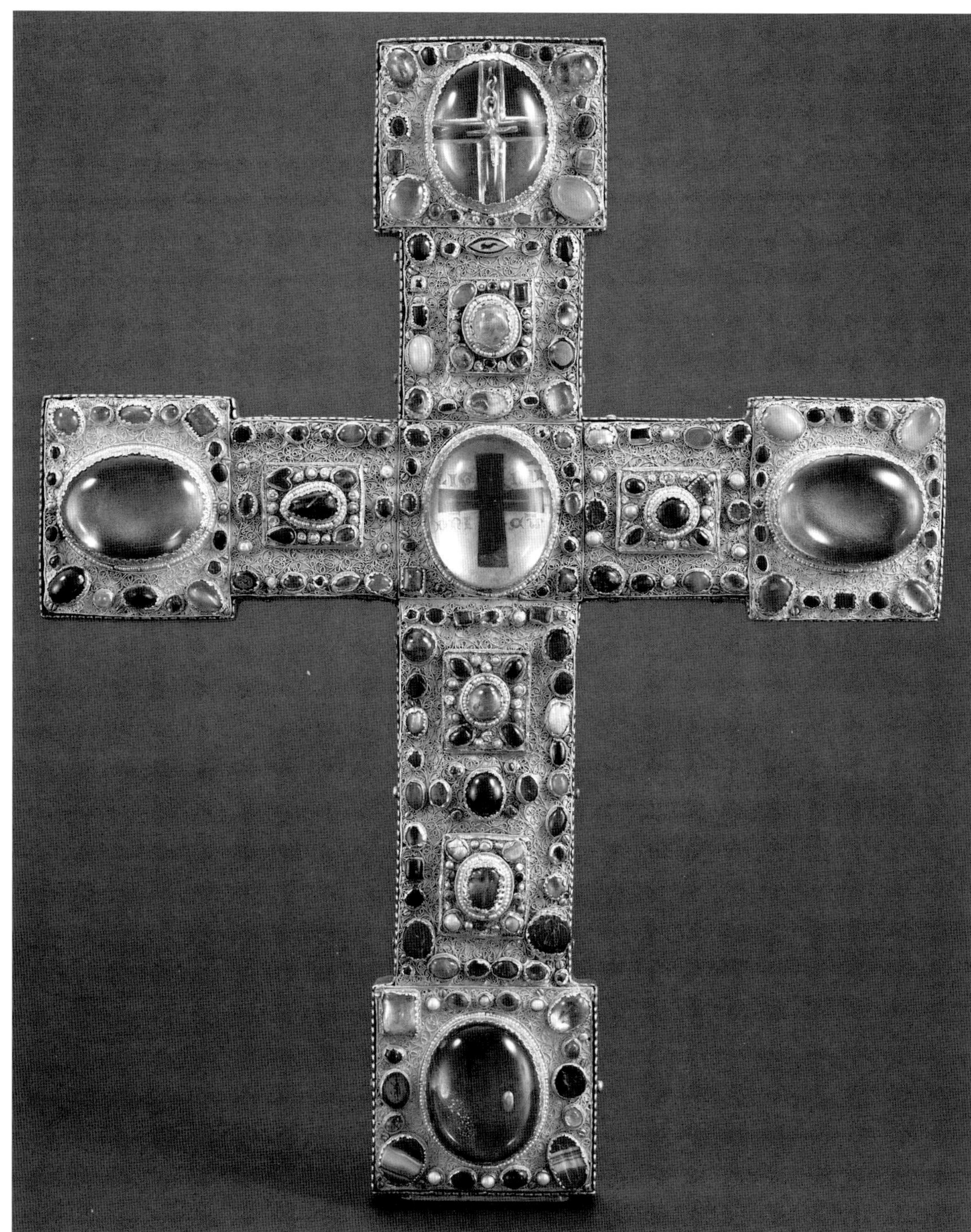

FIGURE 34   Hildesheim, Dom- und Diözesanmuseum, Domschatz L 109, *crux gemmata*, ca. 1150–93, with eleventh-century spolia

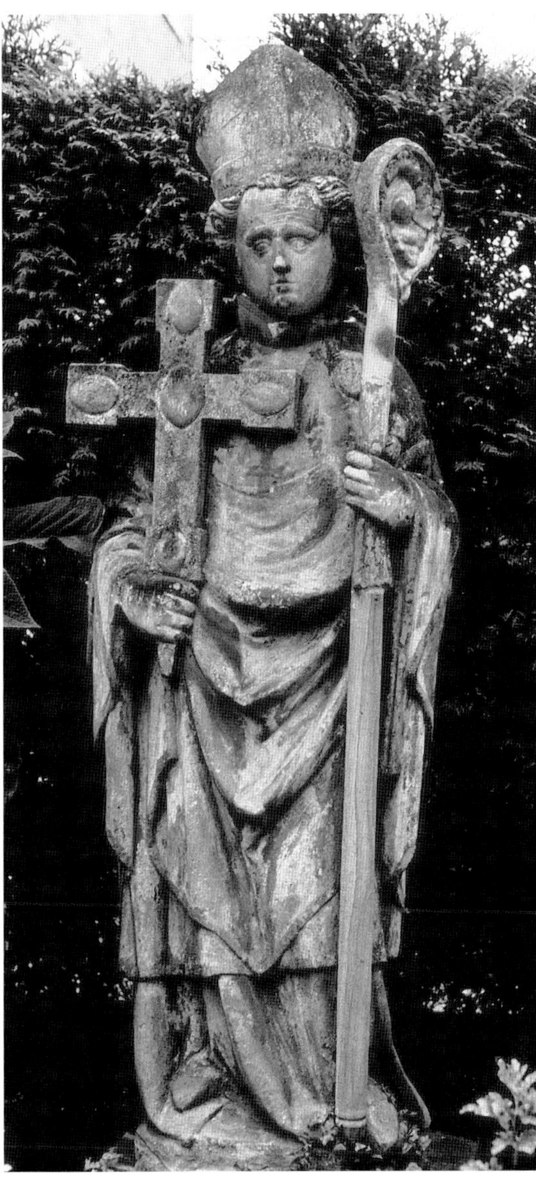

modify and invent objects associated with Bernward, but also, in many cases, to preserve pieces of Bernwardian works. In the same manner, they used Bernward's *memoria* as a springboard for their own, reshaping the bishop's image to suit their needs, yet doing so in a manner that placed the bishop and the monks in active dialogue with each other. This continued shaping of the bishop's image throughout the Middle Ages suggests an ongoing monastic effort to use Bernward in order to fix the memory and identity of their own community. It underscores the extent to which their own and the bishop's *memoria* remained unstable, responsive to contemporary circumstances.[33] The pictorial program developed for the Bernward Gospels in the eleventh century anticipates this instability, aiming to create and fix a particular image of the bishop that proves his merit and thereby secures his salvation.

Hildesheim, Dom- und Diözesanmuseum, Domschatz 18

ca. 1015

2 endleaves + 232 fols.

280 × 200 mm

COLLATION

I² (endleaf–1), II⁸ (fols. 2–9), III⁶ (fols. 10–15), IV–V² (fols. 16–19), VI–XV⁸ (fols. 20–99), XVI–XVII¹⁰ (fols. 100–119), XVIII–XX⁸ (fols. 120–143), XXI⁶ (fols. 144–149), XXII–XXIV⁸ (fols. 150–173), XXV² (fols. 174–175), XXVI–XXXII⁸ (fols. 176–231), XXXIII² (fol. 232–endleaf).

LAYOUT

Prickings are visible along outer edge of leaves. Single lines marked by a stylus run full across each margin. Ruled for three columns of 20 lines (except for pericopes list on fol. 223r, which has 21 lines); the first column records ammonian sections, the second serves for initials, and the third for the main text. Text block is 190 × 125–35 mm.

TEXTUAL AND PICTORIAL CONTENTS

Quire	Number	Folios	Content of leaves
1	2	endleaf–1v	Blank
2	8	2r–3r	Blank
		3v	Begins Prologus quattuor evangeliorum: Plures Fuisse . . . viris canendas
		4r–5v	Continues Plures Fuisse
		6r	Begins Beato papa Damaso: Novum opus . . . papa beatissime
		6v–7v	Continues Beato papa
		8r	Ends Beato papa Damaso

Quire	Number	Folios	Content of leaves
		8v	Begins Sciendum etiam . . . quod solum est
		9r	Ends Sciendum etiam
		9v	Blank
3	6	10r	Begins Preface to Matthew: Matheus ex Judea . . . non tacere
		10v	Ends Preface to Matthew; begins chapter list (28)
		11r–14r	Continues chapter list
		14v	Ends chapter list
		15r	Drawing of Evangelist Matthew as his symbol
		15v	*Incipit to Matthew*
4	2	16r	Blank
		16v	*Painting: Dedication*
		17r	*Painting: Dedication*
		17v	Blank
5	2	18r	*Painting: Nativity/Adoration*
		18v	*Painting: Calling of the Evangelist Matthew / Dinner at the House of Levi*
		19r	*Painting: Portrait of Matthew*
		19v	*Title page: Initium . . . Liber*
6	8	20r	*Title page: Generationis . . . David*
		20v	Begins Gospel of Matthew
		21r–27v	Continues Gospel of Matthew
7	8	28r–35v	Continues Gospel of Matthew
8	8	36r–43v	Continues Gospel of Matthew
9	8	44r–51v	Continues Gospel of Matthew
10	8	52r–59v	Continues Gospel of Matthew
11	8	60r–67v	Continues Gospel of Matthew
12	8	68r–71r	Continues Gospel of Matthew
		71v	Ends Gospel of Matthew; begins Preface to Mark: Marcus evangelista Dei . . . praestat Deus est
		72r	Continues Preface to Mark
		72v	Ends Preface to Mark; begins chapter list (13)
		73r–74r	Continues chapter list
		74v	Ends chapter list
		75r	*Painting: John the Baptist Preaching / Christ Calling the Apostles*
		75v	*Painting: Noli me tangere / Peter Charging Mark to Write the Gospels*
13	8	76r	*Painting: Portrait of Mark*

Quire	Number	Folios	Content of leaves
		76v	*Incipit to Mark*
		77r	*Title page: Initium . . . Evangelii*
		77v–83v	Begins Gospel of Mark
14	8	84r–91v	Continues Gospel of Mark
15	8	92r–99v	Continues Gospel of Mark
16	10	100r–108v	Continues Gospel of Mark
		109r	Ends Gospel of Mark
		109v	Begins Preface to Luke: Lucas Syrus, natione . . . fastidientibus prodidisse
17	10	110r	Continues Preface to Luke
		110v	Ends Preface to Luke; begins chapter list (21)
		111r	*Painting: Annunciation to Zacharias / Zacharias Leaving the Temple*
		111v	*Painting: Visitation / Naming of John the Baptist*
		112r–117r	Continues chapter list
		117v	*Incipit*
		118r	*Painting: Last Supper / Judas with the High Priests*
		118v	*Painting: Heavenly Crucifixion / Portrait of Luke*
		119r	*Title page: Quoniam quidem*
		119v	Begins Gospel of Luke
18	8	120r–127v	Continues Gospel of Luke
19	8	128r–135v	Continues Gospel of Luke
20	8	136r–143v	Continues Gospel of Luke
21	6	144r–149v	Continues Gospel of Luke
22	8	150r–157v	Continues Gospel of Luke
23	8	158r–165v	Continues Gospel of Luke
24	8	166r–173v	Continues Gospel of Luke; ends Gospel of Luke
25	2	174r	*Painting: Christ in Majesty*
		174v	*Painting: Baptism of Christ / Raising of Lazarus*
		175r	*Painting: Entry into Jerusalem / Crucifixion*
		175v	*Painting: Ascension / Portrait of John*
26	8	176r–176v	Preface to John; begins chapter list (14)
		177r–178r	Continues and ends chapter list
		178v	*Incipit*
		179r	*Title page: In Principio erat verbum*
		179v	Begins Gospel of John
		180r–183v	Continues Gospel of John

Quire	Number	Folios	Content of leaves
27	8	184r–191v	Continues Gospel of John
28	8	192r–199v	Continues Gospel of John
29	8	200r–207v	Continues Gospel of John
30	8	208r–215v	Continues Gospel of John
31	8	216r–217v	Continues Gospel of John
		218r	Ends Gospel of John
		218v–223v	Begins pericope list
32	8	224r–231r	Continues and ends pericope list
		231v	Dedicatory inscription; relic list
33	2	232r	Record of Bishop Bernward's canonization on 8 January 1193
		232v–endleaf	Blank

BINDING

Cut-down from a larger book box, especially apparent on the back, where the corner letters of the inscriptions around the edge have been trimmed.

FRONT COVER INSCRIPTION

Cross marks the beginning of the inscription.

Top:	✚SIS RIA QUESO TVO BERN	Be benevolent to your Bern
Bottom:	VVARDO TRINAPOTESTAS	ward, three-fold power

O three-fold power, I beg you to be benevolent towards your Bernward

BACK COVER INSCRIPTION

Dots and crosses part of the inscription; two fastening marks between words on left not included.

Top:	HOC OPV • EXIMIV	this precious work
Right:	BERNVVARDI • PSVLIS • ARTE	by the skill of Bishop Bernward
Bottom:	FACTV • CERNE DS	made. See God
Left:	MATER ET ALMA TVA✚	and your nourishing mother

God, and your nourishing mother, see this precious work made by the skill/craft/knowledge of Bishop Bernward.

FOL. 231V INSCRIPTION

Probably in Bernward's own hand (the same hand records the same inscription in the so-called Gunt-bald Gospels, Hildesheim, Dom- und Diözesanmuseum Domschatz 33, fol. 270r).

Hunc ego Bernwardus codicem conscribere feci	I, Bernward, had this codex written
Atq[ue] meas ut cernis opes super addere iubens	and, ordering that my wealth be added above, as you see
Dilecto d[omi]ni dederam s[an]c[t]o Michaheli	I had surrendered [it] to Saint Michael, beloved of the Lord
Sit anathema d[e]i quisq[ui]s sibi dempserit illum	Let there be a curse of God on anyone who takes it from him

COLOR PLATES

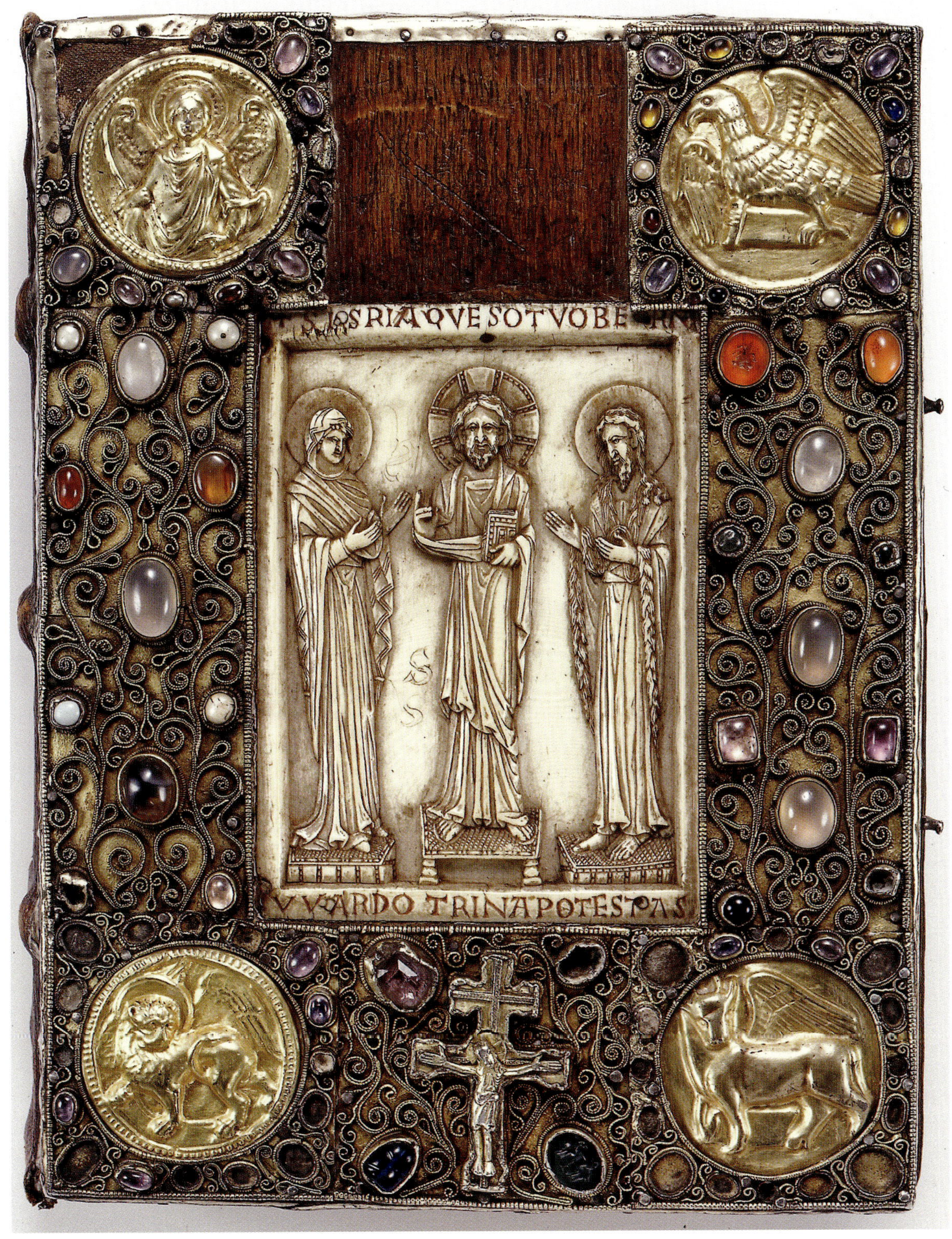

COLOR PLATE 1   Hildesheim, Dom- und Diözesanmuseum, Domschatz 18
(Bernward Gospels), front cover

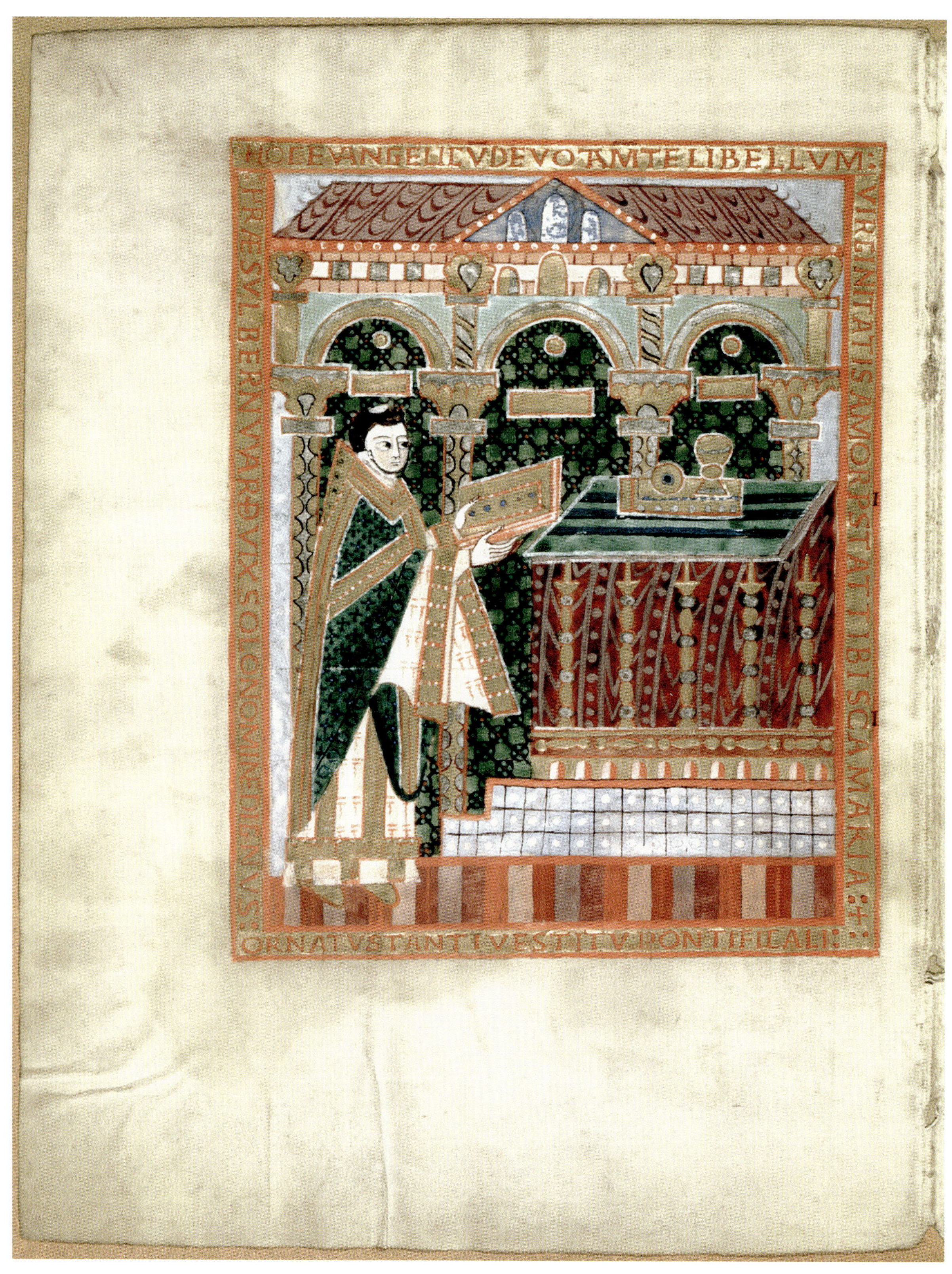

COLOR PLATE 2   Hildesheim, Dom- und Diözesanmuseum, Domschatz 18
(Bernward Gospels), fol. 16v, dedication: Bishop Bernward

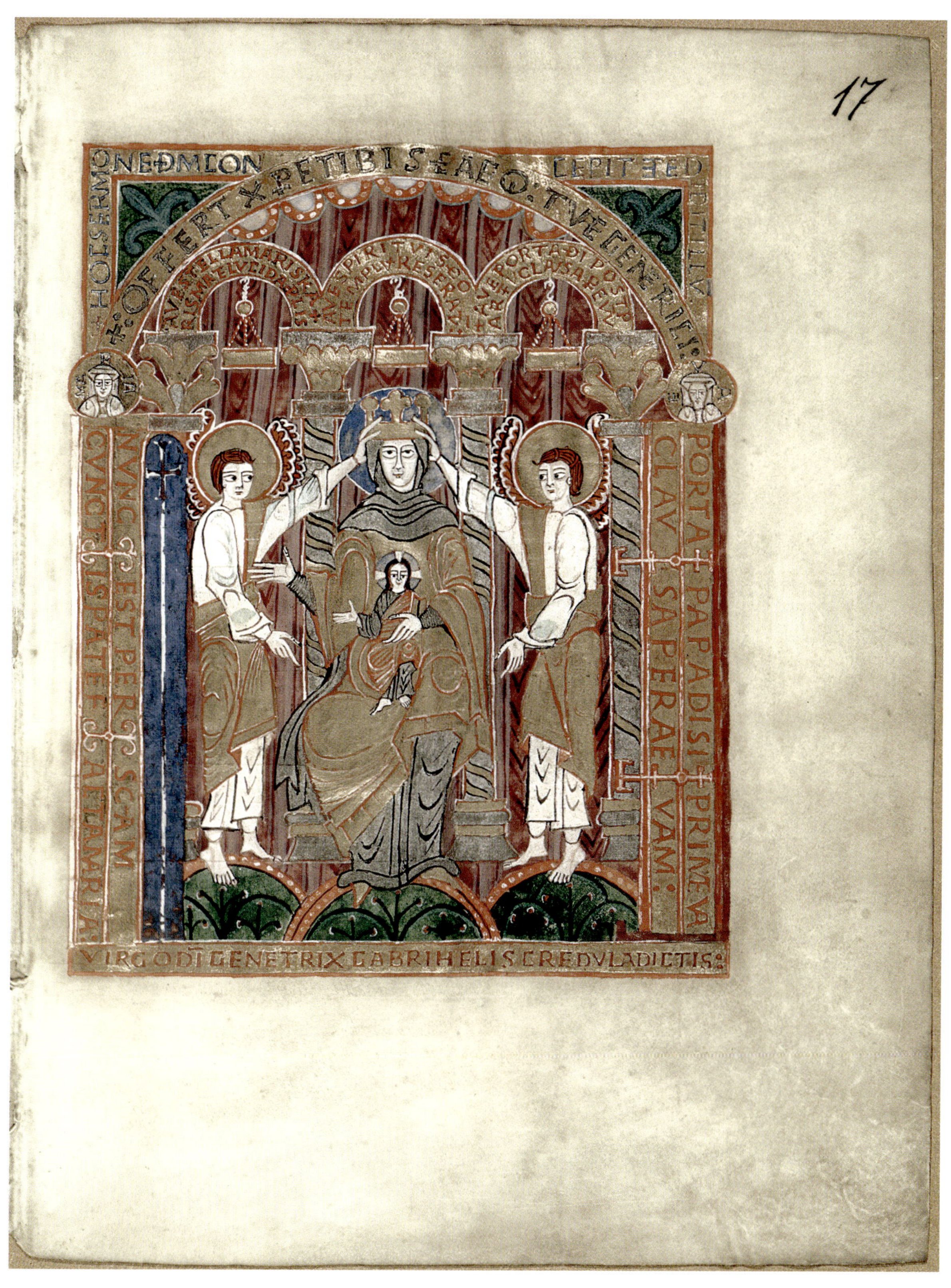

COLOR PLATE 3   Hildesheim, Dom- und Diözesanmuseum, Domschatz 18
(Bernward Gospels), fol. 17r, dedication: Mary and Christ

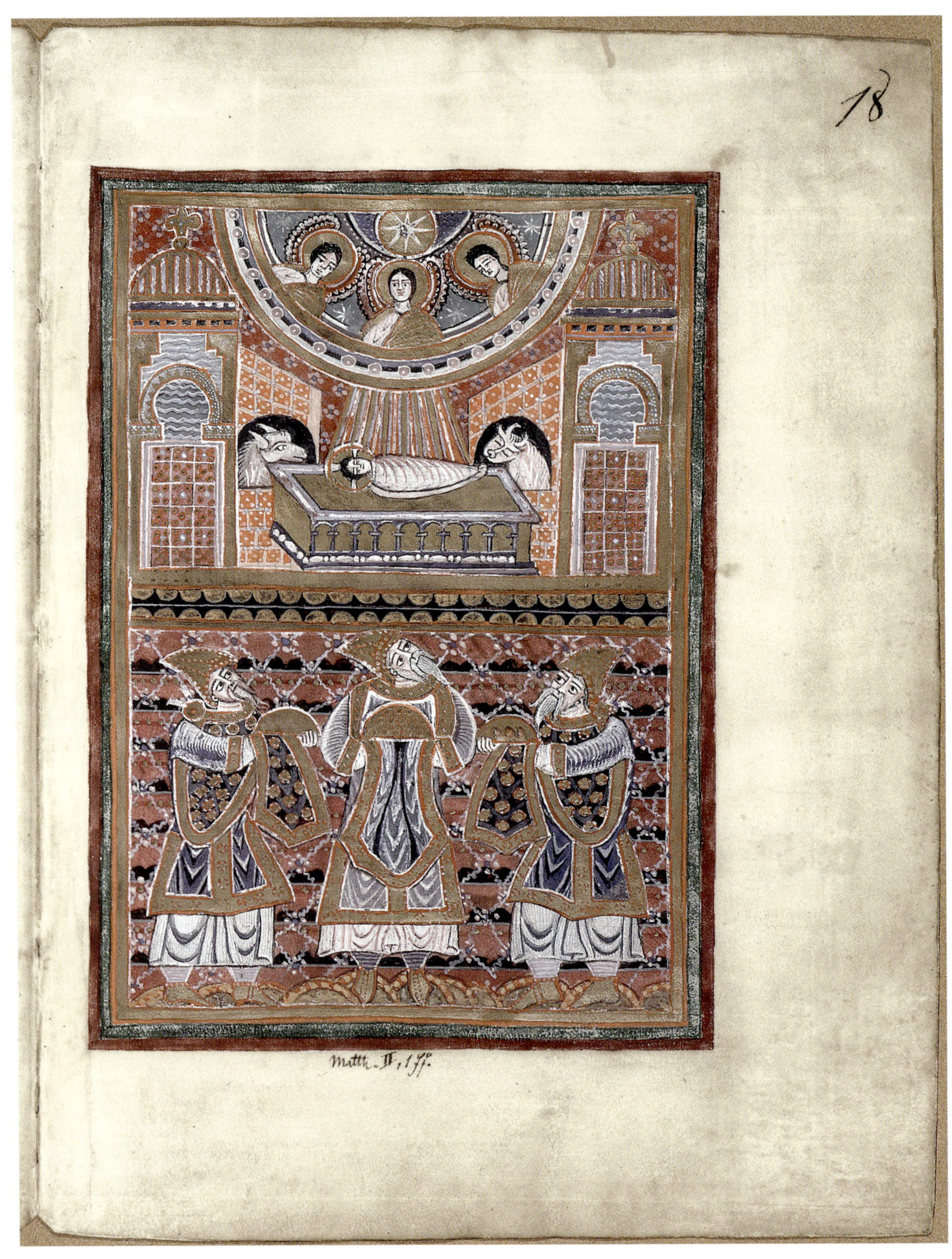

COLOR PLATE 4   Hildesheim, Dom- und Diözesanmuseum, Domschatz 18
(Bernward Gospels), fol. 18r, *Nativity/Adoration*

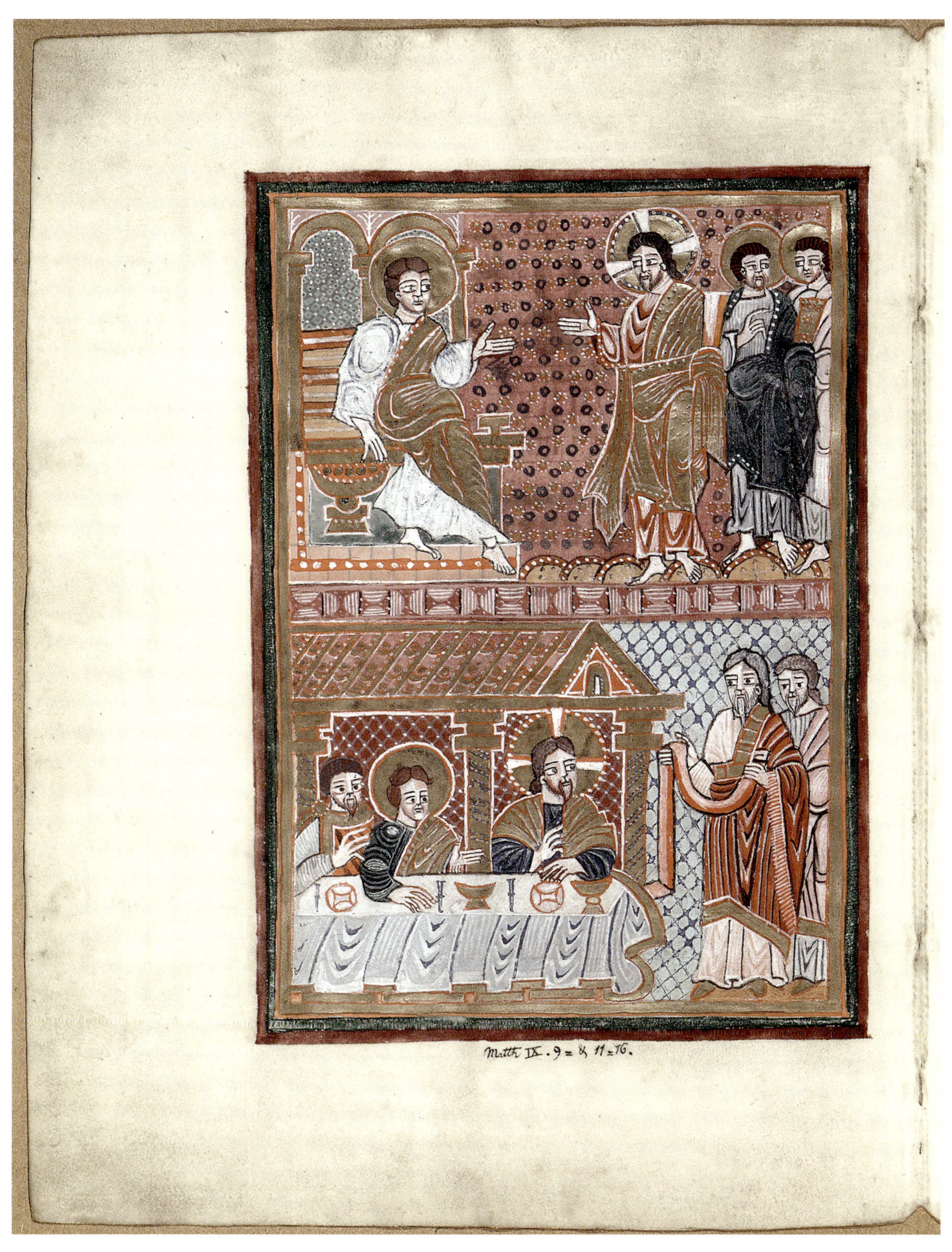

COLOR PLATE 5   Hildesheim, Dom- und Diözesanmuseum, Domschatz 18
(Bernward Gospels), fol. 18v, *Calling of the Evangelist Matthew* (above) and
Dinner at the House of Levi (below)

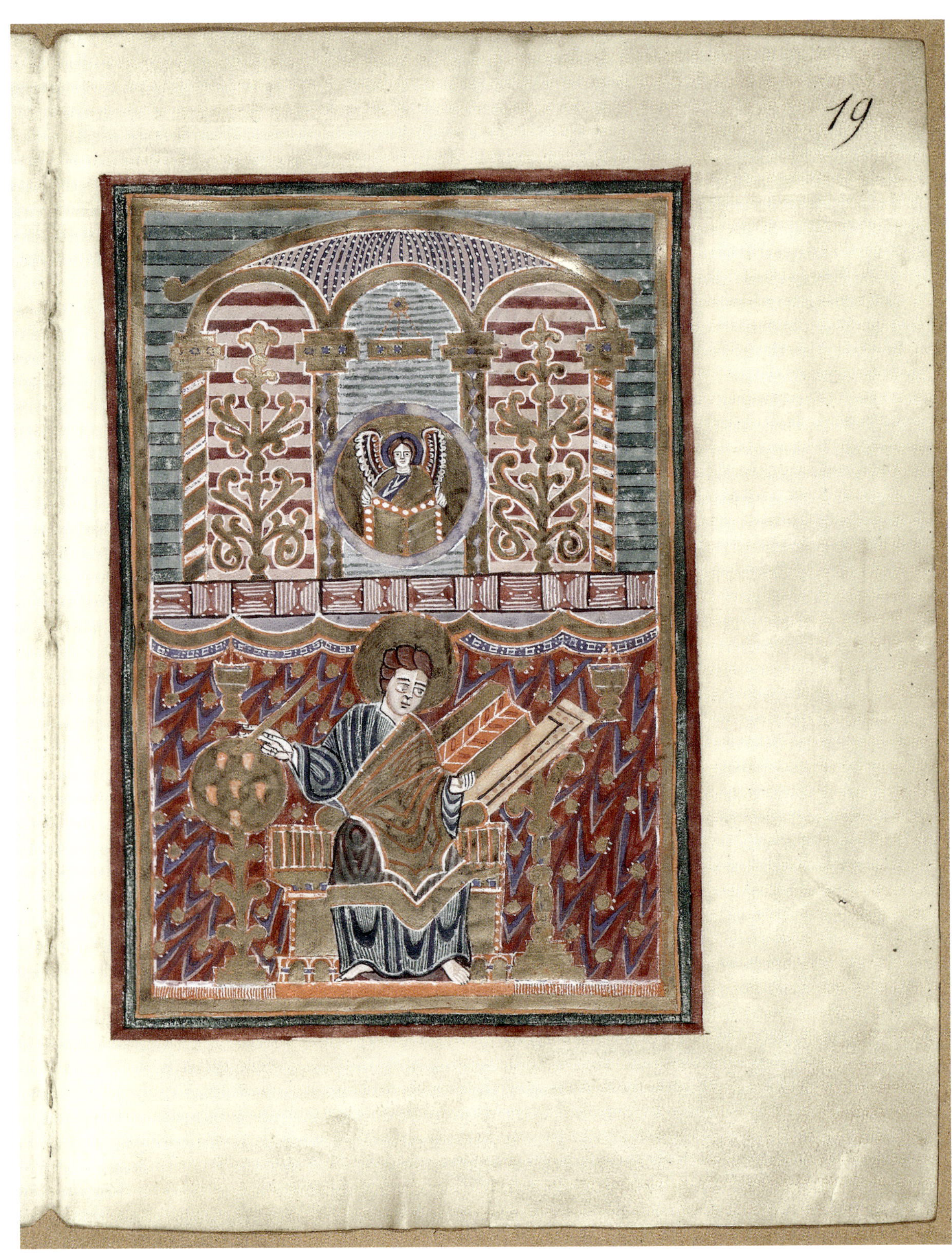

COLOR PLATE 6   Hildesheim, Dom- und Diözesanmuseum, Domschatz 18 (Bernward Gospels), fol. 19r, *Portrait of Matthew*

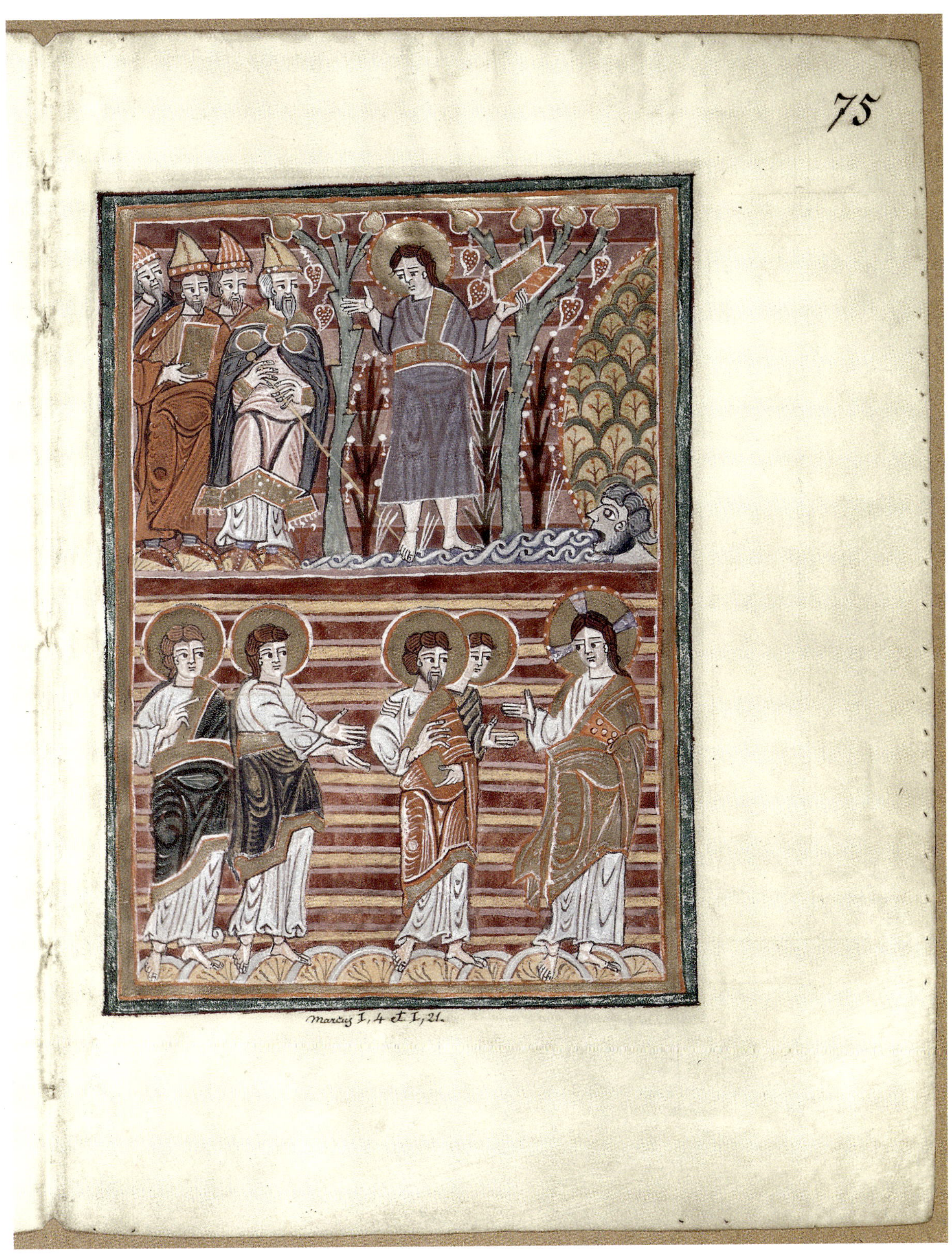

COLOR PLATE 7   Hildesheim, Dom- und Diözesanmuseum, Domschatz 18 (Bernward Gospels), fol. 75r, *John the Baptist Preaching* (above) and *Christ Calling the Apostles* (below)

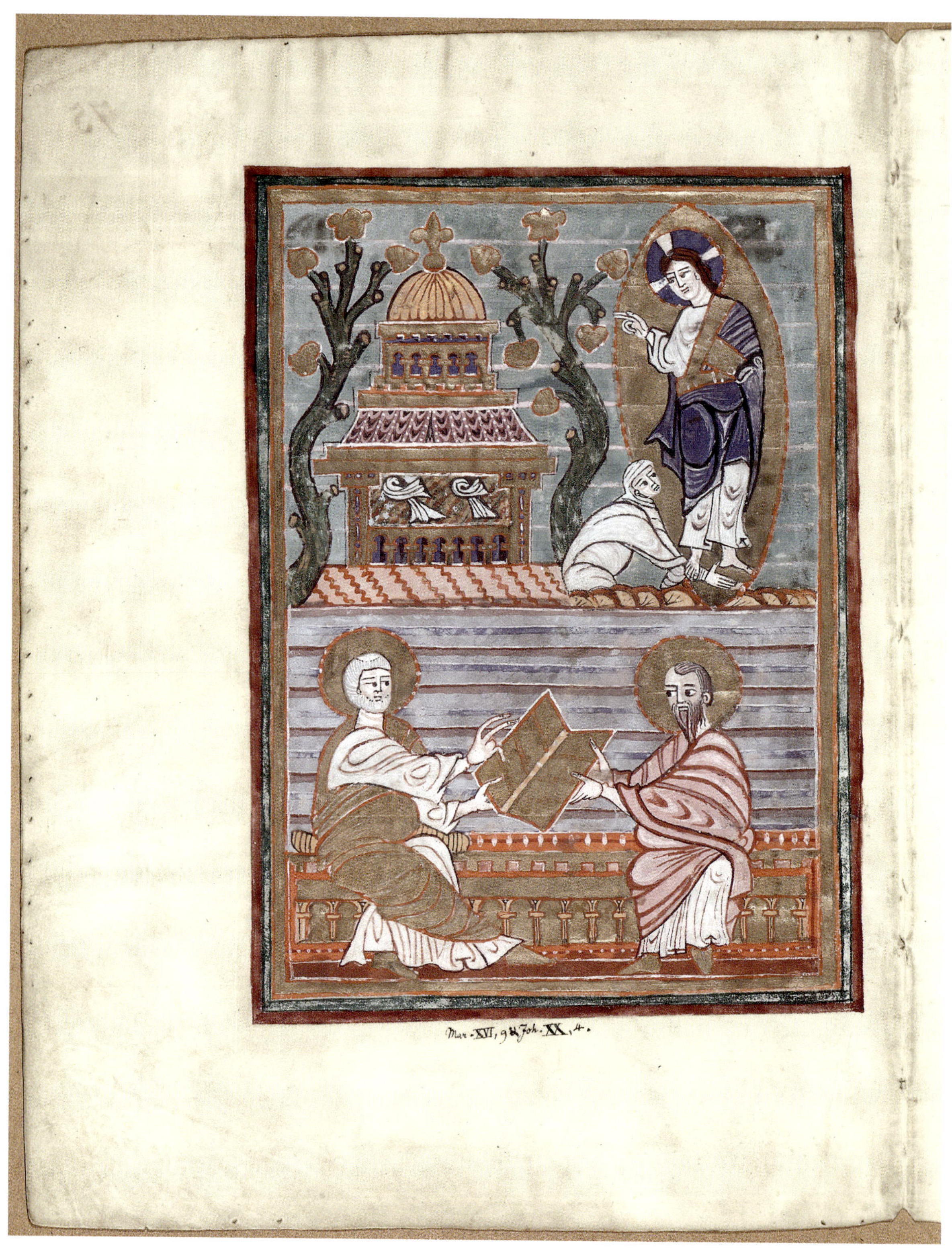

COLOR PLATE 8   Hildesheim, Dom- und Diözesanmuseum, Domschatz
18 (Bernward Gospels), fol. 75v, *Noli me tangere* (above) and *Peter Charging
Mark to Write the Gospels* (below)

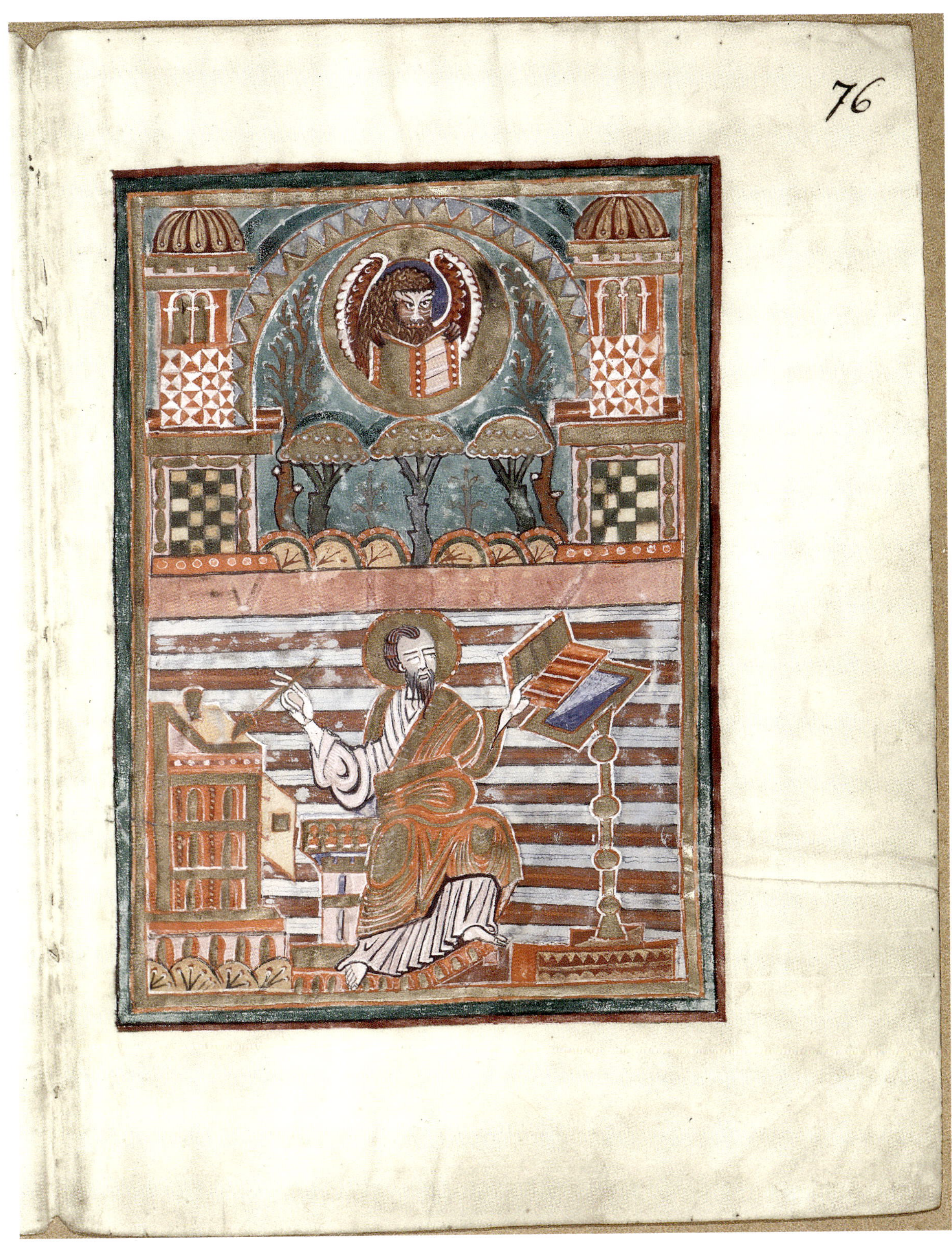

COLOR PLATE 9   Hildesheim, Dom- und Diözesanmuseum, Domschatz 18
(Bernward Gospels), fol. 76r, *Portrait of Mark*

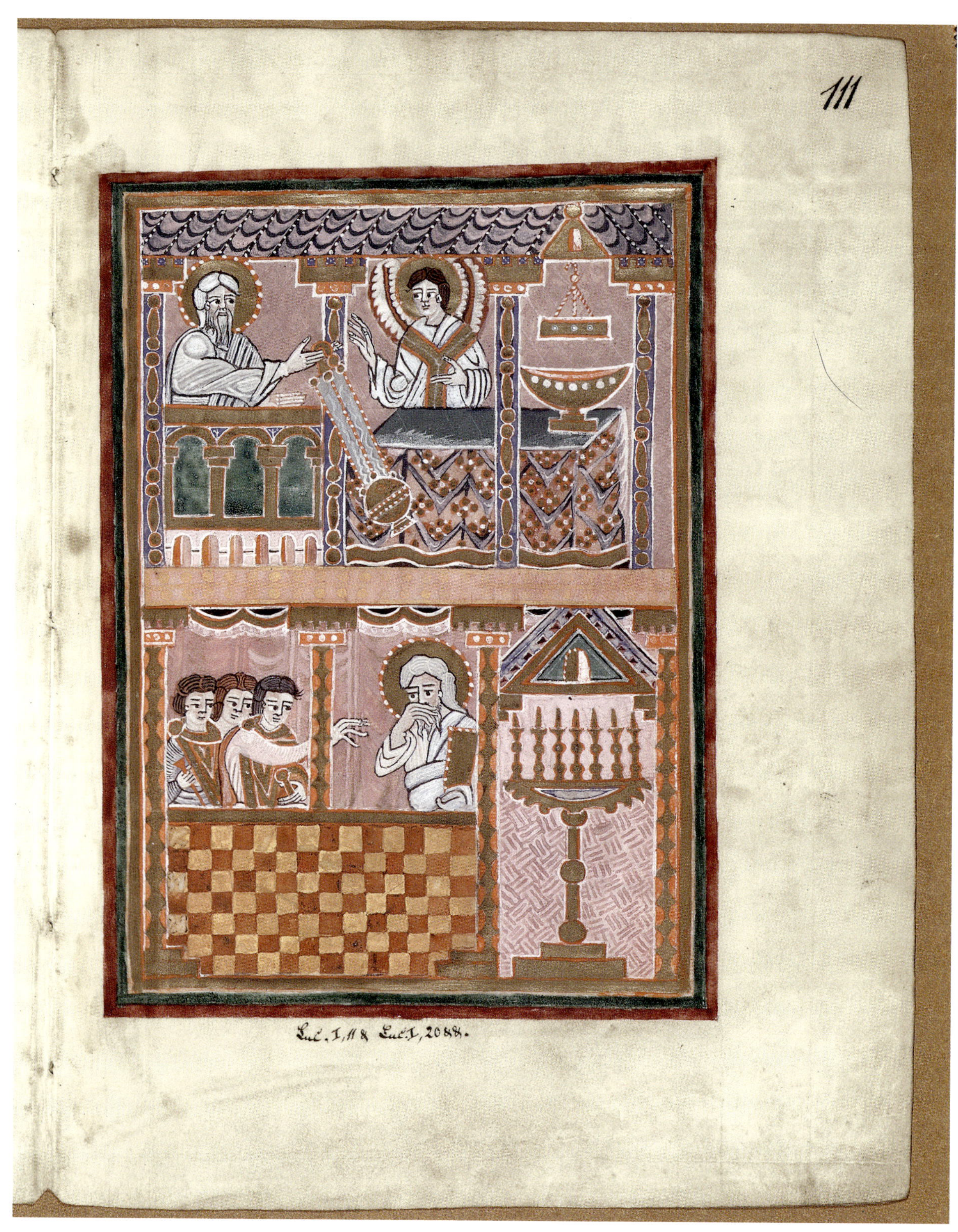

COLOR PLATE 10   Hildesheim, Dom- und Diözesanmuseum, Domschatz 18 (Bernward Gospels), fol. 111r, *Annunciation to Zacharias* (above) and *Zacharias Leaving the Temple* (below)

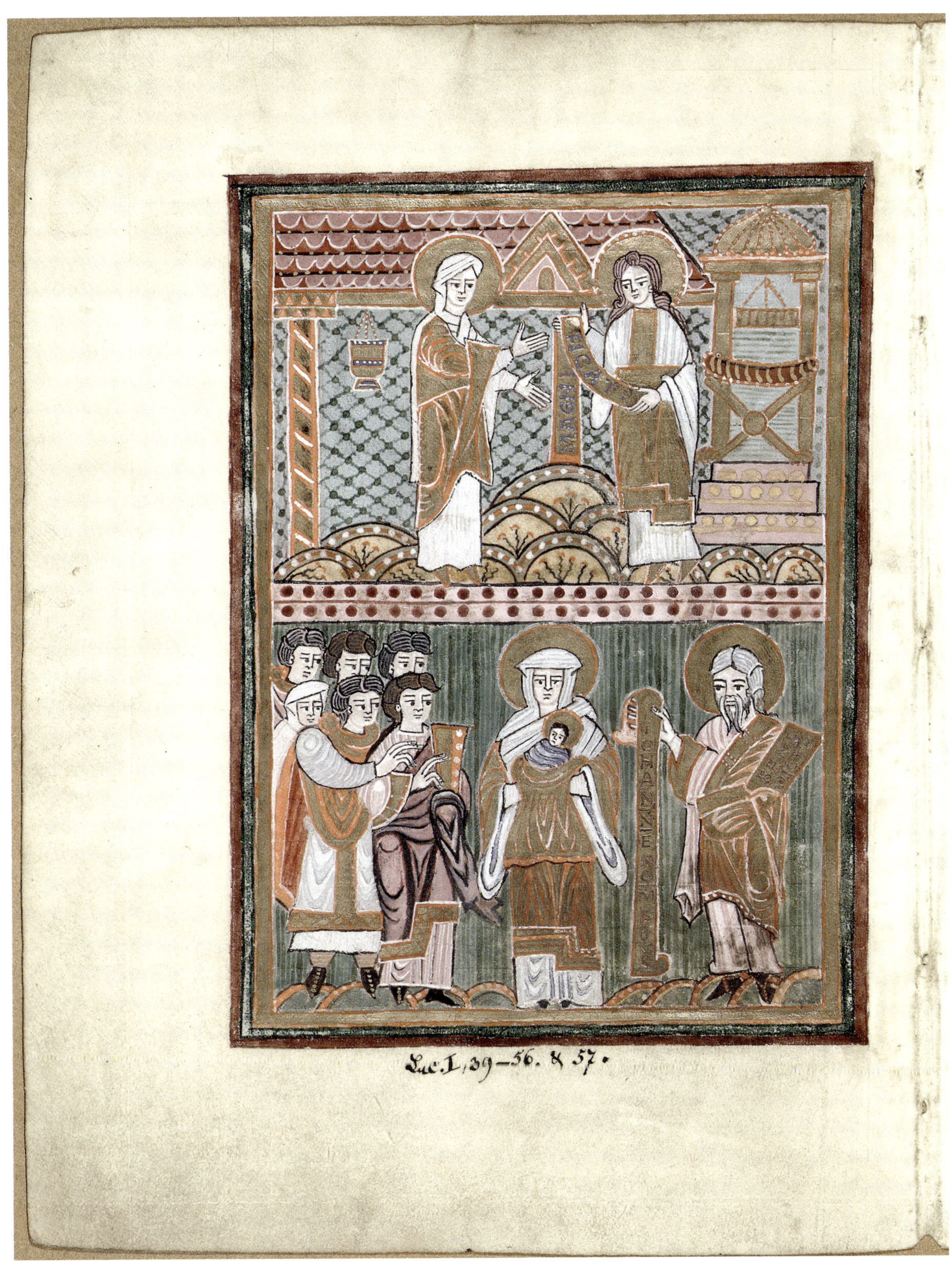

COLOR PLATE 11   Hildesheim, Dom- und Diözesanmuseum, Domschatz 18 (Bernward Gospels), fol. 111v, *Visitation* (above) and *Naming of John the Baptist* (below)

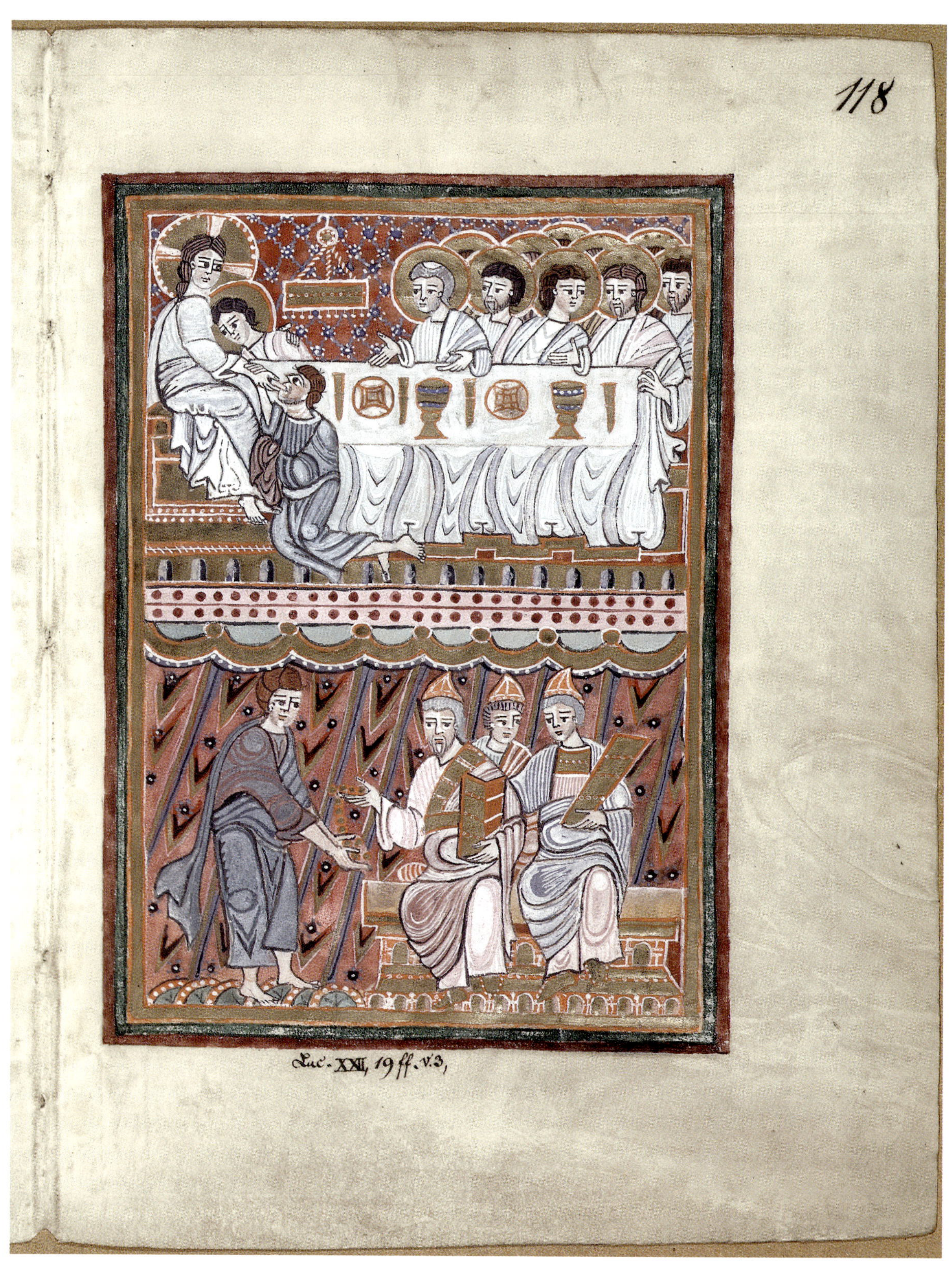

COLOR PLATE 12   Hildesheim, Dom- und Diözesanmuseum, Domschatz 18 (Bernward Gospels), fol. 118r, *Last Supper* (above) and *Judas with the High Priests* (below)

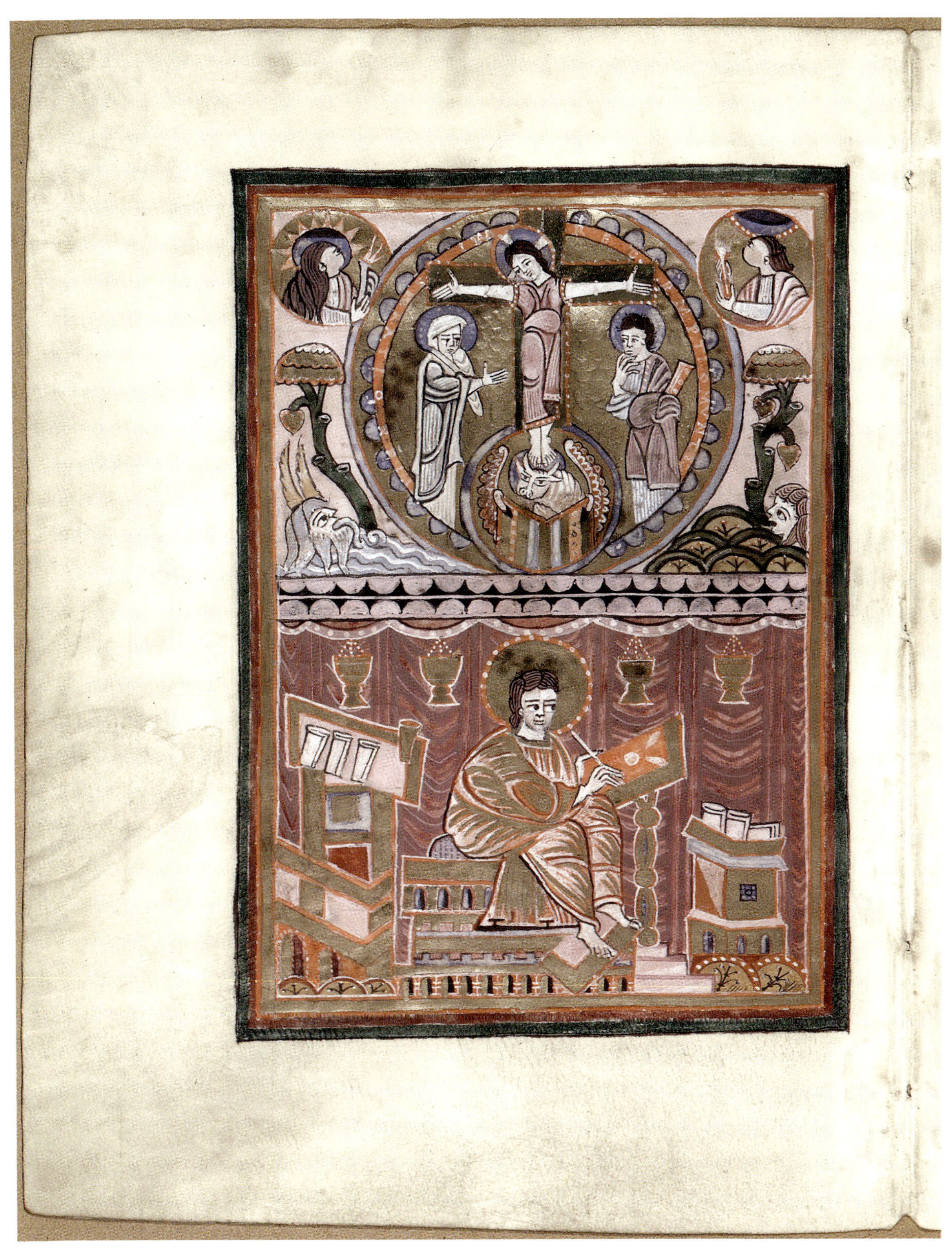

COLOR PLATE 13   Hildesheim, Dom- und Diözesanmuseum, Domschatz 18
(Bernward Gospels), fol. 118v, *Heavenly Crucifixion* (above) and
Portrait of Luke (below)

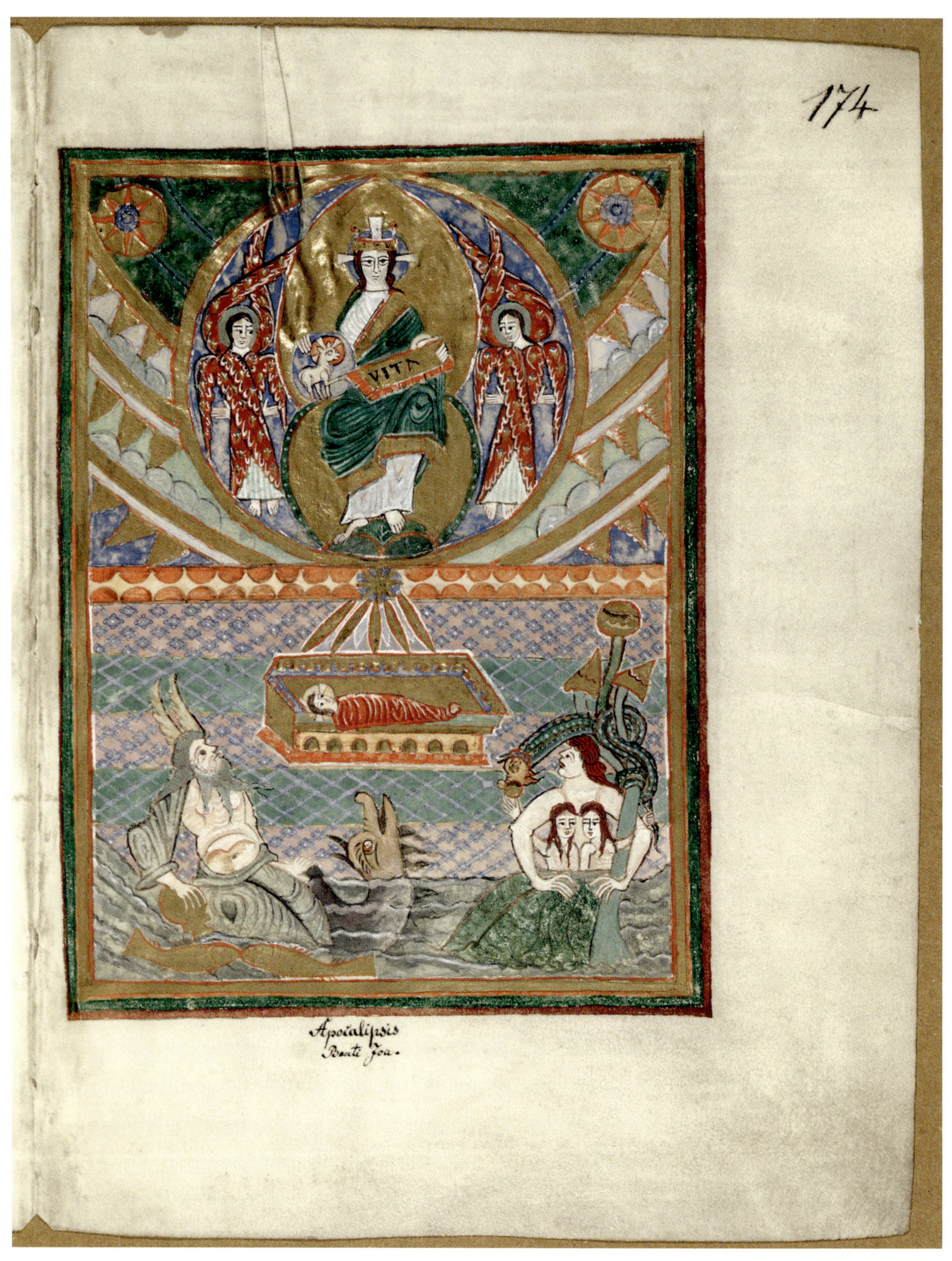

COLOR PLATE 14   Hildesheim, Dom- und Diözesanmuseum, Domschatz 18
(Bernward Gospels), fol. 174r, *Christ in Majesty*

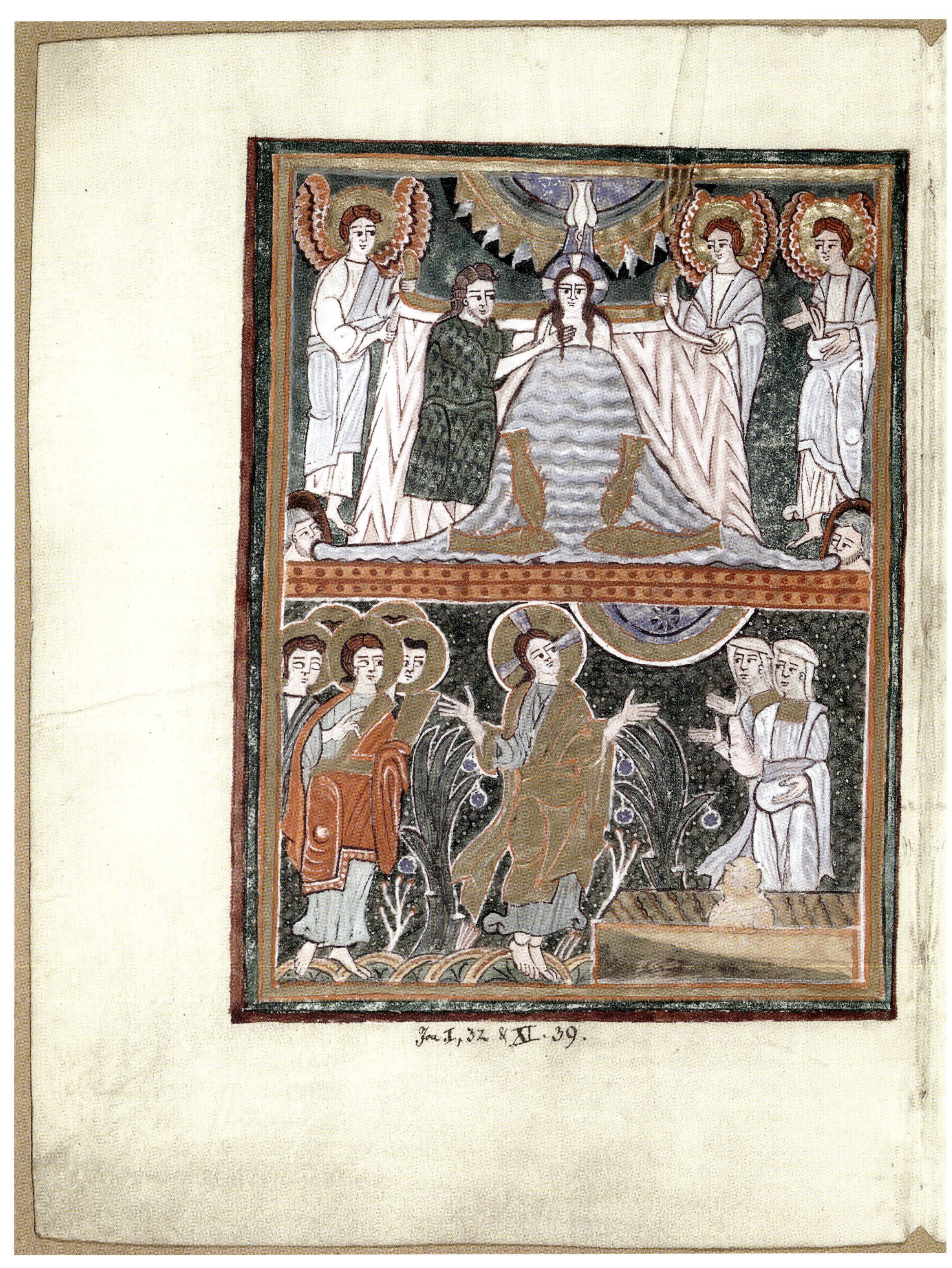

COLOR PLATE 15   Hildesheim, Dom- und Diözesanmuseum, Domschatz 18 (Bernward Gospels), fol. 174v, *Baptism of Christ* (above) and *Raising of Lazarus* (below)

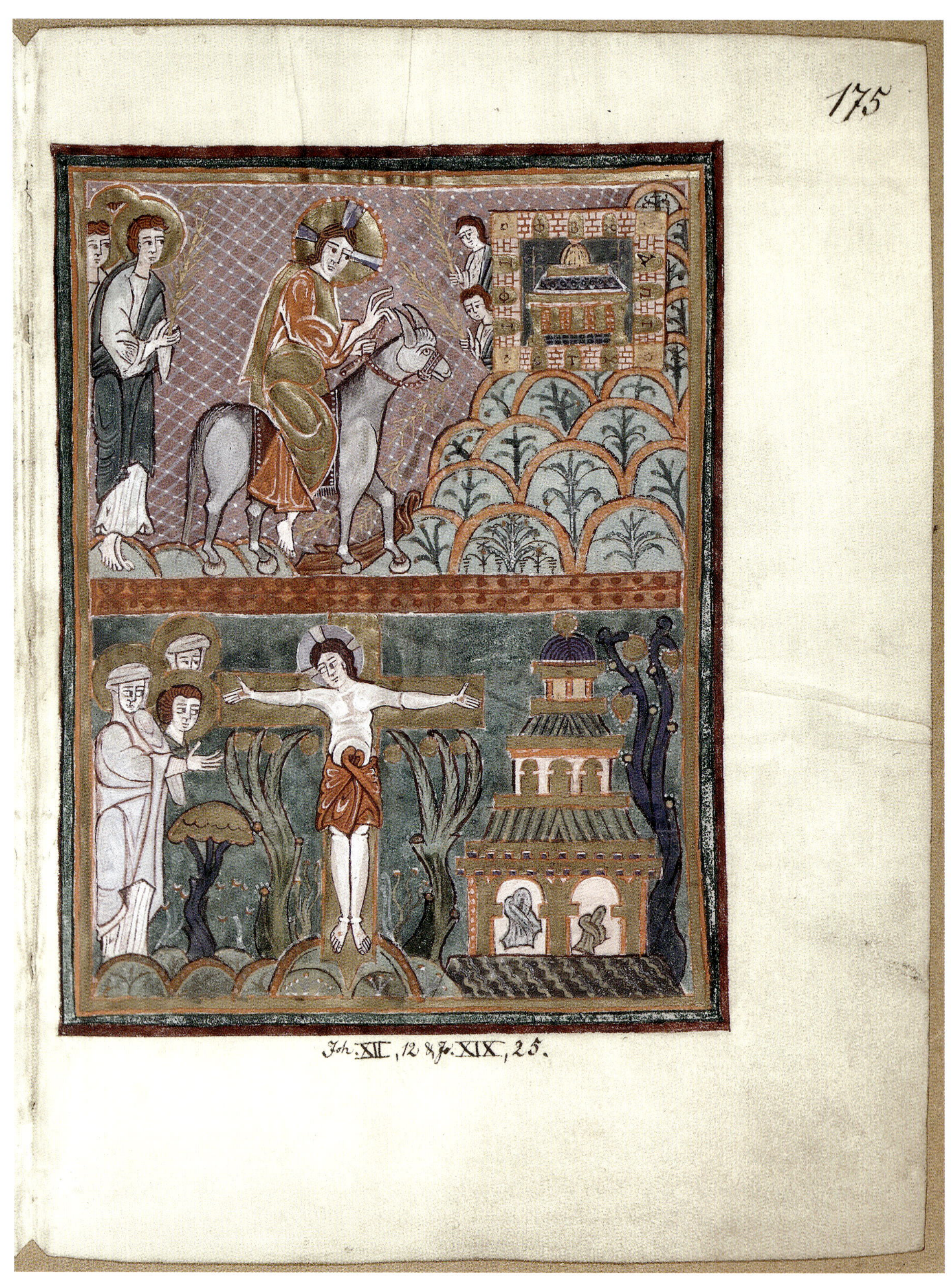

COLOR PLATE 16   Hildesheim, Dom- und Diözesanmuseum, Domschatz
18 (Bernward Gospels), fol. 175r, *Entry into Jerusalem* (above) and *Crucifixion*
(below)

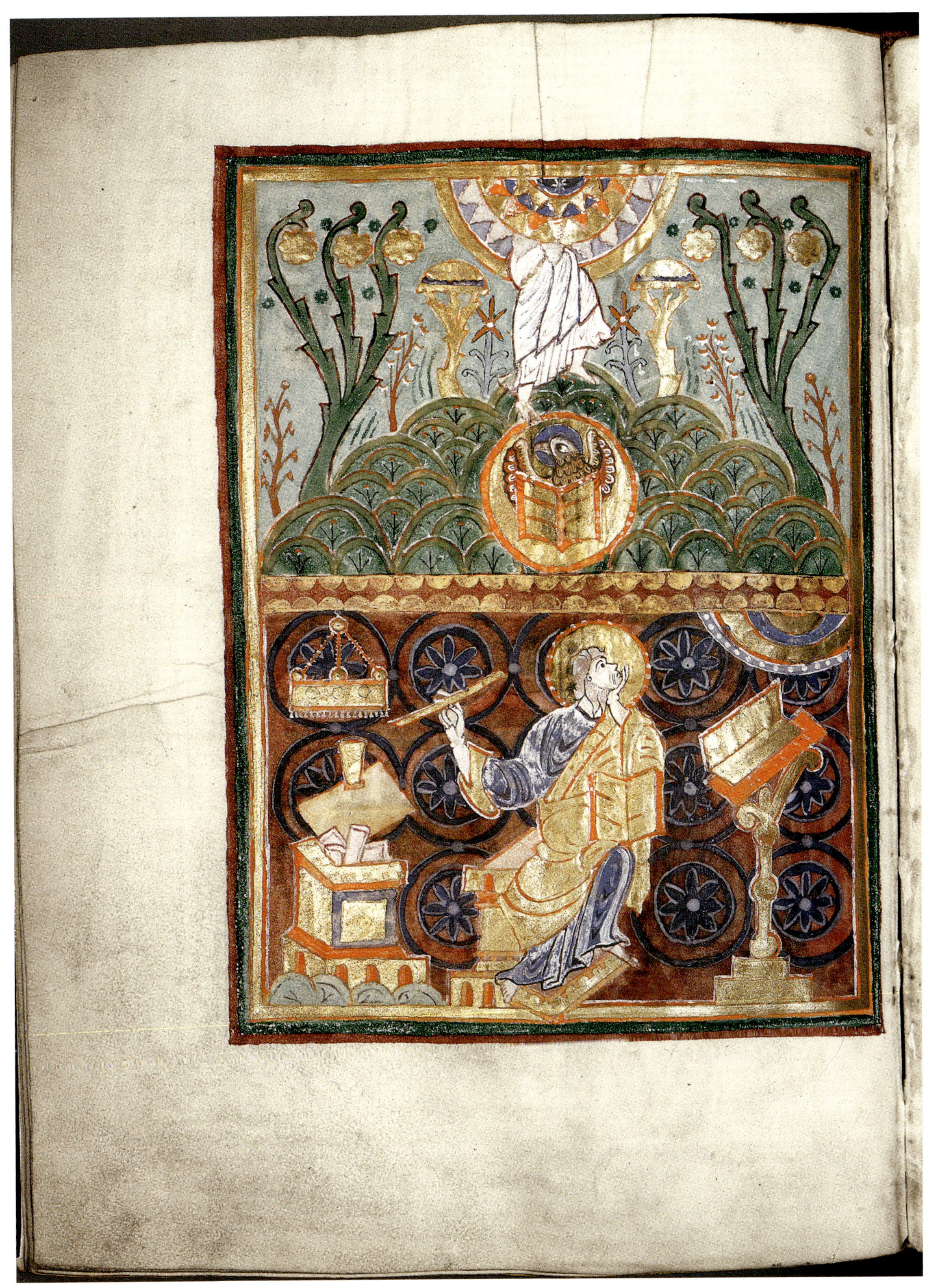

COLOR PLATE 17   Hildesheim, Dom- und Diözesanmuseum, Domschatz 18 (Bernward Gospels), fol. 175v, *Ascension* (above) and *Portrait of John* (below)

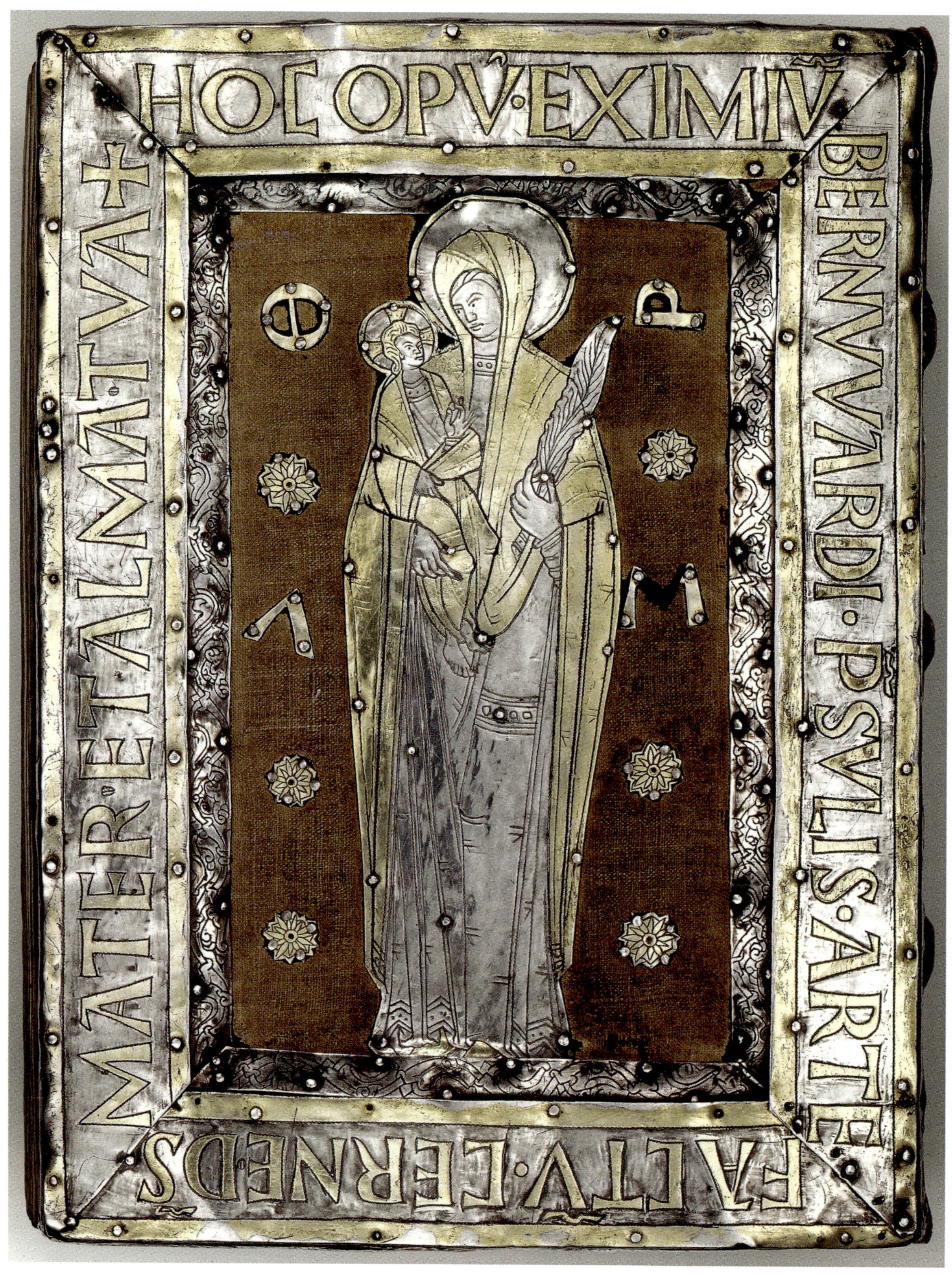

COLOR PLATE 18   Hildesheim, Dom- und Diözesanmuseum, Domschatz 18
(Bernward Gospels), back cover

NOTES

ABBREVIATIONS

Bernward und das Zeitalter Brandt, Michael, and Arne Egge-brecht, eds. *Bernward von Hildes-heim und das Zeitalter der Ottonen: Katalog der Ausstellung.* 2 vols. Hildesheim: Bernward Verlag, 1993.

CCCM Corpus Christianorum: Continuatio Mediaevalis

CCSL Corpus Christianorum: Series Latina

Clm Codex Latinus Monacensis, Bayerisches Staatsbibliothek, Munich

DS Hildesheim Dom- und Diözesanmuseum, Domschatz (inventory number)

HAB Herzog August Bibliothek, Wolfenbüttel

Kostbare Evangeliar Brandt, Michael, ed. *Das kostbare Evangeliar des heiligen Bernward.* With contributions by Rainer Kahsnitz and Hans Jakob Schuffels. Munich: Prestel, 1993.

MGH Monumenta Germaniae Historicae

MGH SS MGH Scriptores in Folio. 38 vols. 1826–2000.

MGH SS rer. Germ. MGH SS rerum Germanicarum in usum scholarum separatim editi. 71 vols. 1871–1999.

MGH SS rer. Germ. n.s. MGH SS rerum Germanicarum: Nova Series. 17 vols. 1922–1994.

PL Patrologiae Cursus Completus: Series Latina. Edited by Jacques-Paul Migne. 221 vols. Paris: Migne, 1844–91.

Biblical citations are taken from *The New Oxford Annotated Bible: New Revised Standard Edition with the Apocrypha,* edited by Michael D. Coogan with Marc Z. Brettler, Carol A. Newsom, and Pheme Perkins, 3rd ed. (Oxford: Oxford University Press, 2001).

INTRODUCTION

1. Carola Jäggi, "Stifter, Schreiber oder Heiliger? Überlegungen zum Dedikationsbild der Bernward-Bibel," in *Für irdischen Ruhm und himmlischen Lohn: Stifter und Auftraggeber in der mittelalterlichen Kunst, Festschrift für Beat Brenk*, ed. Hans-Rudolf Meier, Carola Jäggi, and Philippe Büttner (Berlin: Reimer, 1995), 65–75. Marlis Stähli identifies the male figure in the painting as Moses in *Die Handschriften im Domschatz zu Hildesheim,* ed. Helmar Härtel (Wiesbaden: In Kommission bei O. Harrassowitz, 1984), 148. Carl Nordenfalk believes him to represent Jerome; see "Noch eine turonische Bilderbibel," in *Festschrift Bernhard Bischoff zu seinem 65. Geburtstag*, ed. Johanne Autenrieth and Franz Brunhölzl (Stuttgart: Hiersemann, 1971), 153–63, esp. 155. As Jäggi shows and I discuss below, however, it is probable that the miniature represents all three characters simultaneously.

2. The codex's textual model was a now-lost Carolingian Bible from Tours. Nordenfalk, "Noch eine turonische Bilderbibel." Turonian Bibles often include frontispieces to the New Testament that depict Jerome as the translator of the Bible and frontispieces to Exodus that show Moses on Mount Sinai receiving the tablets of the Law. Herbert L. Kessler, *The Illustrated Bibles from Tours* (Princeton: Princeton University Press, 1977). There is no way of knowing for sure how

the Turonian Bible in Hildesheim was illustrated, although as Nordenfalk points out, it may be the source for the Genesis scenes decorating bronze doors that were made under Bernward's direction between 1007 and 1015. For an alternative view, see Søren Kaspersen, "Cotton-Genesis, die Toursbibeln und die Bronzetüren: Vorlage und Aktualität," in *Bernwardinische Kunst: Bericht über ein wissenschaftliches Symposium in Hildesheim vom 10.10. bis 13.10.1984* (Göttingen: Goltze, 1988), 79–103.

3. One example is the presentation of the ideal king in manuscripts associated with Charles the Bald. William J. Diebold, "The Ruler Portrait of Charles the Bald in the S. Paolo Bible," *Art Bulletin* 76 (1994): 6–18; Paul E. Dutton and Herbert L. Kessler, *The Poetry and Paintings of the First Bible of Charles the Bald* (Ann Arbor: University of Michigan Press, 1997).

4. On the bishop's antiquarianism, see Lawrence Nees, "Aspects of Antiquarianism in the Art of Bernward and Its Contemporary Analogues," in *1000 Jahre St. Michael in Hildesheim: Kirche-Kloster-Stifter*, ed. Gerhard Lutz and Angela Weyer (Göttingen: Michael Imhof Verlag, 2012), 153–70; in the same volume, on medium, see Jennifer P. Kingsley, "VT CERNIS and the Materiality of Bernwardian Art," 171–84, and on the Christological and theological cast of Bernward's patronage, see Klaus Gereon Beuckers, "Bernward und Willigis: Zu einem Aspekt der bernwardinischen Stiftungen," 142–52.

5. On the so-called imperial church system, see Leo Santifaller, *Zur Geschichte des ottonisch-salischen Reichskirchensystems*, 2nd ed. (Vienna: Böhlau, 1964), and Josef Fleckenstein, *Die Hofkapelle der deutschen Konige*, pt. 2, *Die Hofkapelle im Rahmen der ottonisch-salischen Reichskirche* (Stuttgart: Hiersemann, 1966), but cf. Timothy Reuter, "The Imperial Church System of the Ottonian and Salian Rulers: A Reconsideration," *Journal of Ecclesiastical History* 33 (1982): 347–74. Fleckenstein responds to Reuter in "Problematik und Gestalt der ottonisch-salischen Reichskirche," in *Reich und Kirche vor dem Investiturstreit: Vorträge beim wissenschaftlichen Kolloquium aus Anlaß des achtzigsten Geburtstages von Gerd Tellenbach*, ed. Karl Schmid (Sigmaringen: Thorbecke, 1985), 83–98. For a sensitive overview of the historiography on the German imperial church, see John S. Ott and Anna Trumbore Jones, "Introduction: The Bishop Reformed," in *The Bishop Reformed: Studies of Episcopal Power and Culture in the Central Middle Ages*, ed. John S. Ott and Anna Trumbore Jones (Aldershot: Ashgate, 2007), 1–20. For a discussion of Bernward's political intentions in founding Saint Michael's, see Bernhard Gallistl, "Bernward of Hildesheim: A Case of Self-Planned Sainthood?" in *The Invention of Saintliness*, ed. Anneke B. Mulder-Bakker (London: Routledge, 2002), 145–62, esp. 152–55.

6. A biographical sketch of the bishop is in Hans Jakob Schuffels, "Bernward Bischof von Hildesheim: Eine biographische Skizze," in *Bernward und das Zeitalter*, 1:29–43, and more recently Christine Wulf, "Bernward von Hildesheim, ein Bischof auf dem Weg zur Heiligkeit," *Concilium medii aevi* 11 (2008): 1–19. For evidence of Bernward's career in the imperial chapel, see Heinrich Fichtenau, "Diplomatiker und Urkundenforscher," *Mitteilungen des Instituts für Österreichische Geschichtsforschung* 100 (1992): 9–49; Hans Jakob Schuffels, "*Aulicus scriba doctus*: Bernward in der Königskanzlei," in *Bernward und das Zeitalter*, 2:247–54. For a recent discussion of the bishop, see also Wolfgang Christian Schneider, *Bernward von Hildesheim: Bischof—Politiker—Künstler—Theologe* (Hildesheim: Olms, 2010).

7. On the tendency of local comital dynasties to dominate bishoprics, see Michel Parisse, "Princes laïques et/ou moines, les évêques du Xᵉ siècle," in *Il secolo di ferro: Mito e realtà del secolo X. 19–25 aprile 1990* (Spoleto: Centro italiano di studi sull'alto medioevo, 1991), 1:449–513. Bernward's two predecessors, Bishops Osdag (985–89) and Gerdag (990–92), were relatives, while Bernward's sister Judith was an abbess in the diocese (of Ringelheim) and his brother Tammo succeeded their father, Dietrich, as count palatine of Saxony.

8. The most notable conflict over property in Bernward's episcopacy was a jurisdictional dispute between the bishop of Hildesheim and the archbishop of Mainz regarding who had authority over the rich

nunnery of Gandersheim. Knut Görich, "Der Gandersheimer Streit zur Zeit Ottos III: Ein Konflikt um die Metropolitanrechte des Erzbischofs Willigis von Mainz," *Zeitschrift der Savigny-Stiftung für Rechtsgeschichte: Kanonistische Abteilung* 79 (1993): 56–94. Additional legal documents concerning the Hildesheim diocese's tithes and properties include Karl Janicke, ed., *Die Urkundenbuch des Hochstifts Hildesheim und seiner Bischöfe*, vol. 1 (1896; repr., Osnabrück: Zeller, 1965), 38, no. 49; 296, no. 256a+b; and 302, no. 258. On the Hildesheim mint, see Hans Drescher, "HILDENESHEM und MVNDBVRUC: Bischof Bernward als Münzherr," in *Bernward und das Zeitalter*, 1:323–35.

9. Ulrich Faust, "Das Hildesheimer Benediktinerkloster Sankt Michael in den monastischen Reformbewegungen," in *Bernward und das Zeitalter*, 1:397–406, and in the same volume, Otto Gerhard Oexle, "Bernward von Hildesheim und die religiösen Bewegungen seiner Zeit," 1:355–68; Warren Sanderson, "Gorze Reform Architecture," in *The White Mantle of Churches: Architecture, Liturgy, and Art Around the Millennium*, ed. Nigel Hiscock (Turnhout: Brepols, 2003), 81–90.

10. Thangmar, *Vita Bernwardi episcopi Hildesheimensis*, ed. Georg Heinrich Pertz, MGH SS 4.754–82 (Hannover: Impensis bibliopolii aulici Hahniani, 1841), excerpts from chaps. 1, 6, and 8, on pp. 758–62; English trans. Caecilia Davis-Weyer, *Early Medieval Art, 300–1150: Sources and Documents* (Toronto: University of Toronto Press, 1986), 122–23. The dating of the biography is somewhat disputed. A twelfth-century date is advocated by Knut Görich and Hans H. Kortüm, "Otto III, Thangmar und die Vita Bernwardi," *Mitteilungen des Instituts für Österreichische Geschichtsforschung* 98 (1990): 1–57, and Josef Nolte, "Tercii Ottonis imperatoris didascalus: Die *Vita Bernwardi* von Thangmar," in *Vormoderne Lebensläufe*, ed. Rudolf W. Keck and Erhard Wiersing (Cologne: Böhlau, 1994), 131–49. Marcus Stumpf has argued that most of the text draws on an authentic eleventh-century source composed by Thangmar in "Zum Quellenwert von Thangmars Vita Bernwardi," *Deutsches Archiv für Erforschung des Mittelalters* 53 (1997): 461–96. The most recent study of Bernward's biography and its varied iterations is Martina Giese, *Die Textfassungen der Lebensbeschreibung Bischof Bernwards von Hildesheim* (Hannover: Hahnsche Buchhandlung, 2006). Giese concludes that a core of the *Vita* was redacted based on a dossier compiled to support Hildesheim's jurisdictional claims to Gandersheim, and that this formed the basis of a first, eleventh-century biography of Bernward, but that substantial additions were made to that core in the twelfth century.

11. On the courtier bishop, see C. Stephen Jaeger, *The Origins of Courtliness: Civilizing Trends and the Formation of Courtly Ideals, 923–1210* (Philadelphia: University of Pennsylvania Press, 1985), and his *Envy of Angels: Cathedral Schools and Social Ideas in Medieval Europe, 950–1200* (Philadelphia: University of Pennsylvania Press, 1994).

12. See especially "'Both Mary and Martha': Bishop Lietbert of Cambrai and the Construction of Episcopal Sanctity in a Border Diocese Around 1100," in Ott and Jones, *Bishop Reformed*, 137–60, and in the same volume, Thomas Head, "Postscript: The Ambiguous Bishop," 250–64.

13. A parallel example is Matilda of Canossa, countess of Tuscany from 1076 to 1115. Christine B. Verzar, "Picturing Matilda of Canossa: Medieval Strategies of Representation," in *Representing History, 900–1300: Art, Music, History,* ed. Robert A. Maxwell (University Park: The Pennsylvania State University Press, 2010), 73–90.

14. On medieval portraiture, see Kurt Bauch, *Das mittelalterliche Grabbild: Figürliche Grabmäler des 11. bis 15. Jahrhunderts in Europa* (Berlin: W. de Gruyter, 1976); Peter Bloch, "Herrscherbild—Grabbild—Stifterbild," in *Bilder vom Menschen in der Kunst des Abendlandes,* ed. Peter Bloch (Berlin: Mann, 1980), 107–20, with a catalog of examples on 121–42; Otto Gerhard Oexle, "Memoria und Memorialbild," in *Memoria: Der geschichtliche Zeugniswert des liturgischen Gedenkens im Mittelalter*, ed. Karl Schmid and Joachim Wollasch (Munich: Fink, 1984), 384–440; Bruno Reudenbach, "Individuum ohne Bildnis? Zum Problem künstlerischer Ausdrucksformen

von Individualität im Mittelalter," in *Individuum und Individualität im Mittelalter*, ed. Jan A. Aertsen and Andreas Speer (Berlin: W. de Gruyter, 1996), 807–18. On the emergence of a new type of episcopal portraiture in the Ottonian era, see Evan A. Gatti, "Developing an Iconography of the Episcopacy: Liturgical Portraiture and Episcopal Politics in Late Tenth- and Early Eleventh-Century Manuscripts" (Ph.D. diss., University of North Carolina at Chapel Hill, 2005); see also Gatti, "Building the Body of the Church: A Bishop's Blessing in the Benedictional of Engilmar of Parenzo," in Ott and Jones, *Bishop Reformed*, 92–121. For a discussion of how representational conventions could be manipulated to convey something of the medieval individual, see Thomas E. A. Dale, "The Individual, the Resurrected Body, and Romanesque Portraiture: The Tomb of Rudolf von Schwaben in Merseburg," *Speculum* 77 (2002): 707–43.

15. The term "self-fashioning" was introduced by Stephen Greenblatt to suggest the process of constructing identity and public personae according to particular social standards; see *Renaissance Self-Fashioning from More to Shakespeare* (Chicago: University of Chicago Press, 1980). For an example of Bernward's self-fashioning, see Wolfram von Steinen, "Bernward von Hildesheim über sich selbst," *Deutsches Archiv für Erforschung des Mittelalters* 12 (1956): 331–62. On the relationship between hagiographic types and the individual in medieval texts, see Adelheid Krah, "Wo bleibt der Mensch? Das Dilemma der Typologisierungen des Sujets in hagiographischen Texten des Mittelalters," *Mitteilungen des Instituts für Österreichische Geschichtsforschung* 111 (2003): 267–85.

16. William North and Anthony Cutler, "Ivories, Inscriptions, and Episcopal Self-Consciousness in the Ottonian Empire: Berthold of Toul and the Berlin Hodegetria," *Gesta* 42 (2003): 1–17. Various exhibitions in Germany have shown the richness of Ottonian prelates' patronage. See Anton Legner, ed., *Monumenta Annonis: Köln und Siegburg, Weltbild und Kunst im hohen Mittelalter: Eine Ausstellung des Schnütgen-Museums der Stadt Köln in der Cäcilienkirche vom 30. April bis zum 27. Juli 1975* (Cologne: Das Museum, 1975); Franz Ronig, ed., *Egbert: Erzbischof von Trier,*

977–993: Gedenkschrift der Diözese Trier zum 1000. Todestag, 2 vols. (Trier: Rheinisches Landesmuseum, 1993); *Bernward und das Zeitalter*; Christoph Stiegemann and Martin Kroker, eds., *Für Königtum und Himmelreich: 1000 Jahre Bischof Meinwerk von Paderborn* (Regensburg: Schnell & Steiner, 2009).

17. Karl A. O. Henkel, *Die Bernwardinische Kunst: Bischof Bernward und seine Werke* (Hildesheim: F. Borgmeyer, 1937); Rudolf Wesenberg, *Bernwardinische Plastik: Zur ottonischen Kunst unter Bischof Bernward von Hildesheim* (Berlin: Deutscher Verein für Kunstwissenschaft, 1955); *Bernwardinische Kunst: Bericht.*

18. The earliest studies of the codex are Johannes M. Kratz, *Der Dom zu Hildesheim: Seine Kostbarkeiten, Kunstschätze und sonstige Merkwürdigkeiten* (Hildesheim: Gerstenberg, 1840), 117–23; Stephan Beissel, *Das heiligen Bernward Evangelienbuch im Dome zu Hildesheim: Mit Handschriften des 10. und 11. Jahrhunderts in kunsthistorischer und liturgischer Hinsicht verglichen* (Hildesheim, 1891); Hans Heinz Josten, *Neue Studien zur Evangelienhandschrift Nr. 18 des Hl. Bernward Evangelienbuch im Domschatze zur Hildesheim: Beiträge zur Geschichte der Buchmalerei im frühen Mittelalter* (Strassburg: J. H. E. Heitz, 1909).

19. This includes the front- and endleaves now bound to the book covers. Rainer Kahsnitz, "Inhalt und Aufbau der Handschrift," in *Kostbare Evangeliar,* 18. In contrast, Marlis Stähli counts 232 folios in thirty-one quires; these are the pages that were numbered in the top right corner of every recto face at some postmedieval date. Stähli, *Handschriften im Domschatz,* 17.

20. Characteristic features of this scribe's hand include the curving of the ends of the *m* and *n*; the way the bottom loop of the *g* starts from the right corner of the letter, creating a very short vertical before continuing with an elongated curve; the *e-t* ligature; and other favored abbreviations and punctuation marks. For examples, see Anton Chroust, *Monumenta palaeographica: Denkmäler der Schreibkunst des Mittelalters: Schrifttafeln in lateinischer und deutscher Sprache,* 2nd ser., vol. 3 (Munich, 1917), plate 7. The hand closely resembles that of a scribe who produced documents in Hildesheim over a span of twenty-five years:

the Hildesheim Annals for the years 995–99 (Paris, Bibliothèque nationale, lat. 6114, fols. 24v–30v); parts of a tenth-century collection of church rights (Wolfenbüttel, HAB, Cod. Guelf. 454 Helmstedt, 1r–60r, 80v–85v, 110r–165v), and portions of a document that records, among other events, the synod convoked by Bernward on 10 October 1020 (Wolfenbüttel, HAB, Cod. Guelf. 32 Helmstedt, fol. 19r). Otto von Heinemann, *Die Handschriften der Herzoglichen Bibliothek zu Wolfenbüttel*, vol. 1, pt. 1 (Wolfenbüttel: Zwissler, 1884), 356; *Bernward und das Zeitalter*, 2:474–89, VII-20, VII-25, VII-27. The cathedral school in Hildesheim is one place where local scribes may have been trained. For a history of the school, see Julius Seiters, "Die Domschule zu Hildesheim im Mittelalter," *Die Diözese Hildesheim in Vergangenheit und Gegenwart* 69 (2001): 21–62.

21.   The Bernward Gospels uses the so-called monarchian prologues that appear in most Ottonian gospel books. Friedrich Stegmüller, *Repertorium Biblicum Medii Aevi*, vol. 1, *Initia Biblica. Apocrypha. Prologuei* (Madrid: Consejo Superior de Investigaciones Científicas, 1950), 280–88; for Matthew, *RB* 590; for Mark, *RB* 607; for Luke, *RB* 620; and for John, *RB* 624.

22.   The manuscripts produced in Corvey and Hildesheim share many traits, on which see Gerd Bauer, "Corvey oder Hildesheim? Zur Ottonischen Buchmalerei in Norddeutschland," 2 vols. (Ph.D. diss., Universität Hamburg, 1977). The two places were linked by the Hellweg, a major trade road of the period.

23.   With some minor exceptions, the order and selection of the *comes* accord with a type labeled Σ in Theodor Klauser's categorization of medieval capitularies, a format first developed in eighth-century Rome. The feasts for the last two months of the liturgical year stem from a different source: the so-called group Δ, which, although based on an earlier Roman capitulary, included material of the Gallican liturgy by the Carolingian period. Theodor Klauser, *Das römische Capitulare evangeliorum: Texte und Untersuchungen zu seiner ältesten Geschichte*, vol. 1, *Typen* (Münster: Aschendorff, 1935), 93–172; Bauer, "Corvey oder Hildesheim?," 1:56–92. A different labeling scheme

is adopted by Antoine Chavasse. See the summary of his findings in Chavasse, "Evangéliaire, épistolier, antiphonaire et sacramentaire: Les livres romains de la messe aux VIIe et VIIIe siècles," *Ecclesia orans* 6 (1989): 177–255. For an examination of Klauser's categories and their correspondences with Chavasse's breakdown, see Cyrille Vogel, *Medieval Liturgy: An Introduction to the Sources*, rev. ed., trans. William G. Storey and Niels Krogh Rasmussen, with John K. Brooks-Leonard (Washington, D.C.: Pastoral Press, 1986), 342–48.

24.   Also notable is the absence of canon tables— an important element, both decorative and practical, that records the concordances between each gospel. Instead, those connections are noted in the margins throughout the text. Kahsnitz suggests the Eusebian canon tables may have been lost in "Inhalt und Aufbau," 20.

25.   Josten, *Neue Studien*, 28; Kahsnitz, "Inhalt und Aufbau," 18–19.

26.   For a detailed technical account of the book covers, including the dating of each part, see Michael Brandt, "Der Einband," in *Kostbare Evangeliar*, 56–61.

27.   Stähli, *Handschriften im Domschatz*, 75–98. The dating of the Hezilo Codex remains disputed. Josten, *Neue Studien*, 88; Albert Boeckler, *Abendländische Miniaturen bis zum Ausgang der romanischen Zeit* (Berlin: W. de Gruyter, 1930); Stähli, *Handschriften im Domschatz*, 99–101; Gerd Bauer, "'Neue' Bernward-Handschriften," in *Bernwardinische Kunst: Bericht*, 211–13; Ulrich Kuder, in *Bernward und das Zeitalter*, 2:512–14. In the recent studies, Stähli and Bauer argue for a date in the last third of the tenth century, while Kuder argues for an eleventh-century date.

28.   Two other manuscripts made for Bernward include added drawings. The so-called Guntbald Gospels (DS 33), for example, contains sketches that seem to test compositions not ultimately used in (or perhaps never meant for) the manuscript's decoration (sketches on fol. 1v and 270r). However, in these cases the reused parchment pieces serve as endleaves. They are not within the gospel proper, so they do not seem to be vestiges of another system of decoration for that gospel. See Ulrich Knapp and Elisabeth Scholz, eds., *Buch und Bild im Mittelalter* (Hildesheim: Gerstenberg,

1999), 59, figs. 82 and 83. Bernward's small Carolingian gospel book (DS 13) also includes added sketches of the evangelists in the lower margin of the illuminated initials opening each gospel; these probably date to the tenth century and may be an attempt to update the otherwise aniconic decoration. Stähli, *Handschriften im Domschatz*, 1; Knapp and Scholz, eds., *Buch und Bild*, 43 and figs. 52–55.

29.   For a thorough discussion of the proposed sources for the paintings, see Kahsnitz, "Inhalt und Aufbau," 18–30 and 56–58. Kahsnitz particularly emphasizes the importance of models from medieval Corvey, Rome, Byzantium, and varied Carolingian centers. Robert Deshman has suggested that the iconography of the Ascension in the Bernward Gospels derived from Anglo-Saxon manuscript painting; see his "Another Look at the Disappearing Christ: Corporeal and Spiritual Vision in Early Medieval Images," *Art Bulletin* 79 (1997): 518–46. The crowned Virgin in the dedicatory miniature has a probable source in Rome. See Mariëlle Hageman, "Between the Imperial and the Sacred: The Gesture of Coronation in Carolingian and Ottonian Images," in *New Approaches to Medieval Communication*, ed. Marco Mostert (Turnhout: Brepols, 1999), 127–63, although cf. the remarks regarding the portrayal of Mary as queen in Ottonian art in Kristin Collins, "Redeemer, Mother, and Ruler: Images of the Virgin in Ottonian Germany" (Ph.D. diss., University of Texas at Austin, 2006), and as Ecclesia in the tenth-century sacramentary of Warmund of Ivrea, in Pierre-Alain Mariaux, *Warmond d'Ivrée et ses images: Politique et création iconographique autour de l'an mil* (Bern: Lang, 2002), 218–25. Byzantine silks provided inspiration for much of the manuscript's ornament. Stephen Wagner, "Silken Parchments: Design, Context, Patronage, and Function of Textile-Inspired Pages in Ottonian and Salian Manuscripts" (Ph.D. diss., University of Delaware, 2004), 143–62.

30.   An exception is Lieselotte E. Stamm-Saurma, "Die 'auctoritas' des Zitates in der bernwardinischen Kunst," in *Bernwardinische Kunst: Bericht*, 105–26.

31.   Deshman, "Another Look."

32.   It was long posited that a scribe and deacon named Guntbald played a major role in Hildesheim's scriptorium. Guntbald names himself in two codices made in Hildesheim whose script is in a Regensburg hand: the Guntbald Gospels (DS 33) and a sacramentary (DS 19). Bernhard Bischoff described the characteristics of Regensburg writing as a "schrägovale Stil" in *Kalligraphie in Bayern 8–12 Jahrhundert* (Wiesbaden: Reichert, 1981), 34–38. Guntbald's book-hand has been further identified in a psalter that remained at Saint Michael's monastery until the seventeenth century; see *Bernward und das Zeitalter,* 2:559–64 and 566–68. Hans Jakob Schuffels also attributed to Guntbald a pericope book now in Nuremberg (Germanisches Nationalmuseum, MS 29 770) that, according to Ulrich Kuder, includes some lines by a Halberstadt hand (*Bernward und das Zeitalter,* 2:564–66, VIII-27). Gerd Bauer attributes this work to Bernward's patronage based on Schuffels's claim that certain lines resemble the hand of a Hildesheim scribe. Bauer writes that Schuffels expressed this opinion at an unpublished lecture in Munich, "Bischof Bernward und die Buchproduktion in Hildesheim" (lecture at Herrscherbild und Buchproduktion im hohen Mittelalter, a symposium held in Munich, 30 April 1983), cited by Bauer in "'Neue' Bernward-Handschriften," 213n40. The manuscript came to Nuremberg's collection in the nineteenth century from the monastery of Neumarkt in southern Germany; its earlier provenance is unknown. Although readings for Sunday Mass correspond to other manuscripts written in Hildesheim, the weekly Mass readings and the selection of saints' feast days differ from these substantially, and in my opinion it is consequently difficult to connect the work to Bernward. Ernst W. Bredt, *Katalog der mittelalterlichen Miniaturen des Germanischen Nationalmuseums* (Nuremberg: Verlag des Germanischen Museums, 1903), no. 2; Rainer Kahsnitz, "Die Kunsthandwerk des späten Mittelalters," in *Das Germanische Nationalmuseum Nürnberg 1852–1977*, ed. Bernward Deneke and Rainer Kahsnitz (Berlin: Deutscher Kunstverlag, 1978), 736. Francis Tschan believed that Guntbald directed the Hildesheim scriptorium; see his *Saint Bernward of Hildesheim* (Notre Dame: University of Notre Dame, 1942–52), 2:54. Georg Swarzenski proposed that Guntbald was also a painter and that his move from Regensburg to

Hildesheim resulted in the transmission of pictorial motifs: *Die Regensburger Buchmalerei des X. und XI. Jahrhunderts: Studien zur Geschichte der deutschen Malerei des frühen Mittelalters* (Leipzig: E. Hermann, Senior, 1900; repr., Stuttgart: Hiersemann, 1969), 85, an assertion repeated by Ulrich Kuder in *Bernward und das Zeitalter*, 1:191–201, but cf. Adam Cohen's persuasive demonstration that Guntbald was not a trained artist in *The Uta Codex: Art, Philosophy, and Reform in Eleventh-Century Germany* (University Park: The Pennsylvania State University Press, 2000), 147–48 and 150–51, figs. 53–54. Moreover, Eliza Garrison has shown the extent to which the artistic style associated with Regensburg workshops generally increased in visibility during Henry II's reign. See Garrison, "The Art Policy of Emperor Henry II (1002–1024)" (Ph.D. diss., Northwestern University, 2005) and her book *Ottonian Imperial Art and Portraiture: The Art Patronage of Otto III and Henry II* (Burlington: Ashgate, 2012).

33.   While this might be taken as a given—the role of medieval patrons in conceiving pictures has been amply demonstrated—it bears establishing through the evidence of the codex itself. Relationships between artists and patrons in the designing of medieval artworks were complicated. Beat Brenk, "Le texte et l'image dans la 'vie des saints' au Moyen Âge: Rôle du concepteur et rôle du peintre," in *Texte et image: Actes du colloque international de Chantilly, 13 au 15 octobre 1982* (Paris: Les Belles Lettres, 1984), 31–39; Herbert L. Kessler, "On the State of Medieval Art History," *Art Bulletin* 70 (1988): 166–87; Piotr Skubiszewski, "L'intellectuel et l'artiste face à l'oeuvre à l'époque qui peint," in *Le travail au Moyen Âge: Une approche interdisciplinaire: Actes du Colloque international de Louvain-la-Neuve, 21–23 mai 1987* (Louvain-la-Neuve: Institut d'études médiévales de l'Université catholique de Louvain, 1990), 263–321. An eleventh-century patron whose correspondence is a precious record of his intimate involvement in the design of artworks is Abbot Wibald of Stavelot. His letter to the artist G (Liège, Archives de l'Etat, Fonds de Stavelot, MS 341, fol. 30v) is reproduced in *Wibald, abbé de Stavelot-Malmédy et de Corvey (1130–1158: Catalogue)* (Stavelot: Musée de l'ancienne Abbaye, 1982), 48.

34.   At least two manuscripts made their way from Corvey to Hildesheim: Wolfenbüttel, HAB, Codex Guelf. 426 Helmstedt and Wolfenbüttel, HAB, Codex Guelf. 427 Helmstedt. A treasury list in a tenth-century hand on 426 Helmst, fol. 171v, seems to be that of Lamspringe, a house for canonesses in the diocese that was about twelve miles south of Hildesheim. Bernhard Bischoff and Florentine Mütherich, eds., *Mittelalterliche Schatzverzeichnisse*, pt. 1, *Von der Zeit Karls des Grossen bis zur Mitte des 13. Jahrhunderts* (Munich: Prestel, 1967), 48, no. 40. The basis for the list's attribution to Lamspringe is its reproduction in a late medieval inventory there. The ornament of the codex's metal back cover is so reflective of the vegetation carved on Bernward's bronze doors that Adolf Goldschmidt raised the possibility that the covers might have been produced in Hildesheim. Goldschmidt, "Ein sächsischer Buchdekel aus ottonischer Zeit," in *Festschrift zum 60. Geburtstag von Paul Clemen 31. Oktober 1926*, ed. Wilhelm Worringer, Heribert Reinards, and Leopold Seligmann (Düsseldorf: Instituts für Siedlungs- und Wohnungswesen und des Zentralinstituts für Raumplanung der Universität Münster, 1926), 277–80. Michael Peter, however, compares it to Essen's candelabra and work on Henry II's ambo, suggesting that it was manufactured in the Rhineland. Matthias Puhle, ed., *Otto der Grosse: Magdeburg und Europa* (Mainz: Philipp von Zabern, 2001), 2:189, IV-14. In 427 Helmst, two separate relic lists written in different early eleventh-century hands appear on the front- and endleaves. While the latter places particular emphasis on the patron saint of Lamspringe, the former describes a reliquary "on the lid of which is incised the lamb of God" that seems loosely to describe one of Bernward's reliquaries. Von Heinemann, *Handschriften*, 1:333–34, no. 462; Bischoff and Mütherich, *Mittelalterliche Schatzverzeichnisse*, 48, no. 41. A silk pasted into the back cover of the Bernward Gospels and another found covering relics sealed by Bernward's predecessor attest to the presence of Byzantine textiles in Hildesheim. Regula Schorta, "Seidengewebe und Schliesse," in *Kostbare Evangeliar*, 61–62, and "The Textiles Found in the Shrine of the Patron Saints of Hildesheim Cathedral," *Bulletin du CIETA* 77 (2000): 45–56.

35. On the abbey, see *Stadt Hildesheim: Kirchliche Bauten* (Hannover: Provinzialverwaltung, 1911), 197–228; August C. Gothe, "St. Michael zu Hildesheim: Ergebnis der Untersuchungen 1939/40," *Alt-Hildesheim* 22 (1951): 22–28; Hartwig Beseler and Hans Roggenkamp, *Die Michaeliskirche in Hildesheim* (Berlin: Mann, 1954); Günther Binding, *Bischof Bernward als Architekt der Michaeliskirche in Hildesheim* (Cologne: Abt. Architektur des Kunsthistorischen Instituts, 1987); Johannes Cramer, Werner Jacobsen, and Dethard von Winterfeld, "Die Michaeliskirche," in *Bernward und das Zeitalter,* 1:369–82, and most recently Christoph Schulz-Mons, *Das Michaeliskloster in Hildesheim: Untersuchungen zur Gründung durch Bischof Bernward 993–1022,* 2 vols. (Hildesheim: Gerstenberg, 2010).

36. Hunc ego Bernwardus codicem conscribere feci
Atq[ue] meas ut cernis opes super addere
    iubens
Dilecto d[omi]ni dederam s[an]c[t]o Michaheli
Sit anathema d[e]i quisq[ui]s sibi dempserit
    illum.

37. The saints who appear in the manuscript's dedicatory painting—Mary, Christ, Michael, and Gabriel—are the patrons of the monastery's crypt altar. Fragments of an inscription in the crypt indicate that the altar there was dedicated to Christ, the Virgin, the archangel Michael, and the whole celestial army: "anno dominice incarnationIS Mxv ordinationis beRNWARDI VENErabilis presulis hild[eshemensis] anno xxIII INDICT[IONE] XIII iiii k[alendas] oct[obris] in honore d[omi]ni beate genitRICIS ET archangeli michaelis et totius militie cELEstis hec cripta a bernwardo ep[iscop]o dedicata est." (Capitalized letters are those that remain extant.) The inscription is reconstructed by Wilhelm Berges and Hans Jürgen Rieckenberg, *Die älteren Hildesheimer Inschriften bis zum Tode Bischof Hezilos (†1079)* (Göttingen: Vandenhoeck & Ruprecht, 1983), 54–62 and 172–80. See also Christine Wulf and Hans Jürgen Rieckenberg, *Die Inschriften der Stadt Hildesheim,* 2 vols. (Wiesbaden: Reichert, 2003). Christ and the Virgin are also named as recipients of the codex twice, once in the dedicatory painting's inscriptions, and a second time on the manuscript's covers. The correspondence between the pictorial and textual dedications of the Bernward Gospels and that of the crypt altar suggests a date around its consecration in 1015.

38. Opinions differ as to the authenticity of the document, although it is generally agreed that its introduction, from which I quote here, is Bernward's. Janicke, ed., *Urkundenbuch,* vol. 1, no. 62; Hatto Kallfelz, ed., *Lebensbeschreibungen einiger Bischöfe des 10.–12. Jahrhunderts,* 2nd ed. (Darmstadt: Wissenschaftliche Buchgesellschaft, 1986), 350–55; Steinen, "Bernward von Hildesheim über sich selbst." My English translation is adapted from Gallistl, "Bernward of Hildesheim," 147–48.

39. Four foundation stones from the complex bear the date 1010. *Bernward und das Zeitalter,* 2:533, VIII-10. Based on the documentary evidence of the bishop's travels and activities in Hildesheim, it is probable that his illness spanned a period from about 1013 to about 1018. The most recent time line of Bernward's episcopacy is in Schulz-Mons, *Das Michaeliskloster in Hildesheim,* 1:523–27.

40. Gerd Althoff, *Amicitiae und Pacta: Bündnis, Einung, Politik und Gebetsgedenken im beginnenden 10. Jahrhundert,* MGH Schriften 37 (Hannover: Hahnsche Buchhandlung, 1992); Christine Sauer, *Fundatio und Memoria: Stifter und Klostergründer im Bild 1100 bis 1350* (Göttingen: Vandenhoeck & Ruprecht, 1993), esp. chap. 5; Marie-Louis Laudage, *Caritas und Memoria mittelalterlicher Bischöfe* (Cologne: Böhlau, 1993), esp. 318–25; Rudolf Schieffer, *Das Grab des Bischofs in der Kathedrale* (Munich: Verlag der Bayerischen Akademie der Wissenschaften, 2001).

41. Caroline Walker Bynum, *The Resurrection of the Body in Western Christianity, 200–1336* (New York: Columbia University Press, 1995). On the role of the miracle story in tomb decoration, see Jan Stanislaw Partyka, *La résurrection de Lazare dans les monuments funéraires des nécropoles chrétiennes à Rome: Peintures, mosaïques et décor des épitaphes; Étude archéologique, iconographique et iconologique* (Warsaw: Zakład Archeologii Śródziemnomorskiej Polskiej Akademii Nauk, 1993). On medieval rituals and pictures relating

to death, see Paul Binski, *Medieval Death: Ritual and Representation* (Ithaca: Cornell University Press, 1996).

42. Patristic and medieval theology presented vague ideas about what happened to the dead between their burial and the Day of Judgment, at least until the establishment of the doctrine of Purgatory in the twelfth century. Jacques Le Goff, *The Birth of Purgatory*, English trans. Arthur Goldhammer (Chicago: University of Chicago Press, 1984). Yet the notion that alms and commemorative prayers could benefit the dead was already highly developed in the Ottonian period. Giles Constable, "The Commemoration of the Dead in the Early Middle Ages," in *Early Medieval Rome and the Christian West: Essays in Honour of Donald A. Bullough*, ed. Julia M. H. Smith (Leiden: Brill, 2000), 169–96. During the course of the eleventh century, the role of prayers in interceding for the dead became increasingly important. Umberto Longo, "Riti e agiografia: L'istituzione della commemoratio omnium fidelium defunctorum nelle Vitae di Odilone di Cluny," *Bullettino dell'Istituto italiano per il Medio Evo* 103 (2002): 163–200; Michael E. Hoenicke Moore, "Demons and the Battle for Souls at Cluny," *Studies in Religion* 32 (2003): 485–97; Herbert Schneider, "L'intercession des vivants pour les morts: L'exemple des synodes du haut Moyen Âge," in *L'intercession du Moyen Âge à l'époque moderne: Autour d'une pratique sociale*, ed. Jean-Marie Moeglin (Geneva: Droz, 2004), 41–65.

43. On mnemotechnics, the classic study is Frances Yates, *The Art of Memory* (Chicago: University of Chicago Press, 1966). More recently, see Mary Carruthers, *The Book of Memory: A Study of Memory in Medieval Culture* (New York: Cambridge University Press, 1990). Liturgical memory and its relationship to history has been a central concern of scholarship in the humanities. Most relevant for understanding medieval remembering of this type (rather than mnemotechnics) are liturgical practices that have been of particular interest to German historians. I cite only a few illustrative examples of this scholarship here: Otto Gerhard Oexle, "Memoria und Memorialüberlieferung im früheren Mittelalter," *Frühmittelalterliche Studien* 10 (1976): 70–95; Schmid and Wollasch, eds., *Memoria*;

Dieter Geuenich and Otto Gerhard Oexle, eds., *Memoria in der Gesellschaft des Mittelalters* (Göttingen: Vandenhoeck & Ruprecht, 1994); Otto Gerhard Oexle, *Memoria als Kultur* (Göttingen: Vandenhoeck & Ruprecht, 1995). See also, more recently, Gerd Althoff, Johannes Fried, and Patrick Geary, eds., *Medieval Concepts of the Past: Ritual, Memory, Historiography* (Washington, D.C.: German Historical Institute, 2002). An important question these works do not address is the role of gender in memory, on which see Elisabeth van Houts, *Memory and Gender in Medieval Europe, 900–1200* (Toronto: University of Toronto Press, 1999), and Houts, ed., "Introduction: Medieval Memories," in *Medieval Memories: Men, Women, and the Past, 700–1300* (New York: Longman, 2001).

44. Andrew Hughes, *Medieval Manuscripts for Mass and Office: A Guide to Their Organization and Terminology* (Toronto: University of Toronto Press, 1982); Éric Palazzo, "Le livre dans les trésors du Moyen-Âge: Contribution à l'histoire de la *Memoria* médiévale," *Annales: Histoire, sciences sociales* 52 (1997): 93–118, and Palazzo, *A History of Liturgical Books from the Beginning to the Thirteenth Century*, trans. Madeleine Beaumont (Collegeville, Minn.: Liturgical Press, 1998); John Lowden, "Illuminated Books and the Liturgy: Some Observations," in *Objects, Images, and the Word: Art in the Service of the Liturgy*, ed. Colum Hourihane (Princeton: Index of Christian Art, Dept. of Art and Archaeology, Princeton University in association with Princeton University Press, 2003), 17–53.

45. Rainer Kahsnitz suggests that this was not the original location of the miniature and that it probably appeared among the first folios of the manuscript, which would be more usual for Ottonian manuscripts, in "Inhalt und Aufbau," 19. Whether the painting appeared closer to the beginning of the codex than it does at present does not affect the arguments made here.

CHAPTER 1

1. The classic study on gift exchange is Marcel Mauss, "Essai sur le don: Forme et raison de l'échange

dans les sociétés archaïques," *Année sociologique,* 2nd ser. (1923–24). A response is Maurice Godelier, *The Enigma of the Gift,* trans. Nora Scott (Chicago: University of Chicago Press, 1999). For the early medieval vocabulary of giving, see Bernhard Jussen, "Religious Discourses of the Gift in the Middle Ages: Semantic Evidence (Second to Twelfth Centuries)," in *Negotiating the Gift: Pre-Modern Figurations of Exchange*, ed. Gadi Algazi, Valentin Groebner, and Bernhard Jussen (Göttingen: Vandenhoeck & Ruprecht, 2003), 173–92. A useful overview of the current scholarship on medieval giving is Arnoud-Jan Bijsterveld, "Afterword: The Study of Gift-Giving Since the 1990s," in *Do ut des: Gift Giving, "Memoria," and Conflict Management in the Medieval Low Countries* (Hilversum: Verloren, 2007), 40–50.

2. The inscriptions' arrangement around the frame on the left separates the text into two main segments, one reading from the top and down the right side:

> Hoc evangelicu[m] devota m[en]te libellum:
> Virginitatis amor pr[ae]stat tibi, s[an]c[t]a
> Maria :✠:

The other title reads down the left side and wraps around the bottom:

> Praesul Bernward[us], vix solo nomine
> dignus:
> ornatus tanti, vestitu pontificali

The final line is on the facing page:

> ✠: Offert, Chr[ist]e, tibi s[an]c[t]aeque tuae
> genetrici.

3. The Magi were the focus of mimetic devotion in the Middle Ages. Early Byzantine pilgrimage art, for example, garbed pilgrims in the clothing of the Magi. Gary Vikan, "Pilgrims in Magi's Clothing: The Impact of Mimesis on Early Byzantine Pilgrimage Art," in *The Blessings of Pilgrimage*, ed. Robert Ousterhout (Urbana: University of Illinois Press, 1990), 97–107. The tradition continued in later Byzantine art as well, such as in the Ravenna mosaic that famously assimilates the Empress Theodora to the Magi. Natalia Teteriatnikov, "The 'Gift-Giving' Image: The Case of the Adoration of the Magi," *Visual Resources* 13 (1998): 381–91. Such images helped shape an artistic tradition in which dedicatory scenes involving the Virgin Mary were viewed in the context of the Adoration of the Magi, on which see the discussion of the dedicatory painting from the Uta Codex (ca. 1025) in Adam Cohen, *The Uta Codex: Art, Philosophy, and Reform in Eleventh-Century Germany* (University Park: The Pennsylvania State University Press, 2000), 41–46.

4. This is not the only example of an unconventional donor portrait figuring Bernward. As described in the introduction, the bishop's Bible (DS 61, fol. 1r, plate 1) shows Bernward in the guise of Moses, Jerome, and John the Evangelist, displaying a book that he presents to the Virgin Mary. Carola Jäggi, "Stifter, Schreiber oder Heiliger? Überlegungen zum Dedikationsbild der Bernward-Bibel," in *Für irdischen Ruhm und himmlischen Lohn: Stifter und Auftraggeber in der mittelalterlichen Kunst, Festschrift für Beat Brenk,* ed. Hans-Rudolf Meier, Carola Jäggi, and Philippe Büttner (Berlin: Reimer, 1995), 65–75.

5. For example, the late tenth-century lectionary of Bishop Evergerus of Cologne (Cologne, Cathedral Library 143, fols. 3v–4r); Peter Bloch and Hermann Schnitzler, *Die ottonische Kölner Malerschule*, 2 vols. (Düsseldorf: Schwann, 1967–70), 1:13, plates 2 and 3, and color plates I and II; also the early eleventh-century lectionary of Henry II (Bamberg, Staatsbibl. MS Bibl. 95, fols. 7v–8r); Josef Kirmeier, Aloïs Schütz, and Evamaria Brockhoff, eds., *Schreibkunst: Mittelalter-liche Buchmalerei aus dem Kloster Seeon* (Regensburg: F. Pustet, 1994), color figs. on p. 75. For more examples, see Joachim Prochno, *Das Schreiber- und Dedikati-onsbild in der deutschen Buchmalerei,* pt. 1, *Bis zum Ende des 11. Jahrhunderts (800–1100)* (Leipzig: Teubner, 1929).

6. On the significance of the medieval gift's transformation, see Eliana Magnani S. Christen,

"Transforming Things and Persons: The Gift *pro anima* in the Eleventh and Twelfth Centuries," in Algazi, Groebner, and Jussen, *Negotiating the Gift*, 269–84.

7. On the different meanings highlighted by various types of dedication iconography within the donor portrait genre, see Prochno, *Schreiber- und Dedikationsbild*, and Peter Bloch, "Zum Dedikationsbild im Lob des Kreuzes des Hrabanus Maurus," in *Das erste Jahrtausend*, ed. Victor H. Elbern (Düsseldorf: Schwann, 1962), 471–94.

8. Michael Brandt has recently suggested that the liturgical objects, especially the inclusion of five candlesticks, help present the bishop as a new Solomon, builder of the Jewish Temple and a prototypical model for medieval patrons. See Brandt, "Bernward d'Hildesheim et ses trésors," *Cahiers de Saint-Michel de Cuxa* 41 (2010): 133–43.

9. Evan Gatti persuasively argues that a new type of portraiture developed for bishops in the Ottonian era that showed living bishops in liturgical postures. In that context, Gatti reads the Bernward Gospels painting as the representation of an altar dedication, although both the inscriptions and the painted elements discussed above, such as showing Bernward in the pose of a Magus, also draw heavily on the tradition of medieval donor images. These details set the Bernward Gospels painting apart. See Evan A. Gatti, "Developing an Iconography of the Episcopacy: Liturgical Portraiture and Episcopal Politics in Late Tenth- and Early Eleventh-Century Manuscripts" (Ph.D. diss., University of North Carolina at Chapel Hill, 2005), and "Building the Body of the Church: A Bishop's Blessing in the Benedictional of Engilmar of Parenzo," in *The Bishop Reformed: Studies of Episcopal Power and Culture in the Central Middle Ages*, ed. John S. Ott and Anna Trumbore Jones (Aldershot: Ashgate, 2007), 92–121.

10. Bernhard Bruns first suggested that the dedication opening presents a relationship between the earthly and heavenly church in "Das Widmungsbild im Kostbaren Evangeliar des heiligen Bernward," *Die Diözese Hildesheim in Vergangenheit und Gegenwart* 65 (1997): 29–55.

11. On the right door: "Porta paradisi primeva[m] clausa per aevam." On the left: "Nunc est per s[an]c[t]am cunctis patefacta Maria[m]."

12. Gregory the Great, *Dialogorum*, chap. 48, PL 77.425–28.

13. On how this concept underlay early medieval Eucharistic debates, see Enrico Mazza, *The Celebration of the Eucharist: The Origin of the Rite and the Development of Its Interpretation* (Collegeville, Minn.: Liturgical Press, 1999), 182–92.

14. "Hoc sermone D[eu]m concepit et edidit illu[m]."

15. "Virgo D[e]i Genetrix Gabriehelis credula dictis."

16. "Ave stella maris karismate lucida p[ro]lis
Ave spiritui s[an]c[t]o templu[m] reseratu[m]
Ave porta d[e]i post partu[m] clausa p[er] evum."

17. These metaphors may have stemmed from Byzantine sources. Already in the fifth century Constantinopolitan exegetes had developed elaborate metaphors for the Incarnation and the Virgin's place in it. Nicholas Constas, "Weaving the Body of God: Proclus of Constantinople, the Theotokos, and the Loom of the Flesh," *Journal of Early Christian Studies* 3 (1995): 169–94. The Akathistos hymn of the sixth century, formulated as hails to Mary, offered a series of chants in which, among many titles, Mary is named the redeemer of Adam and Eve, star manifesting the sun, and key to the door of Paradise. Egon Wellesz, ed., *The Akathistos Hymn* (Copenhagen: Munksgaard, 1957); Leena Mari Peltomaa, *The Image of the Virgin Mary in the Akathistos Hymn* (Leiden: Brill, 2001). This hymn was translated at Charlemagne's court at the end of the eighth century, and its impact already appears in the art of that period. Suzanne Lewis, "A Byzantine *Virgo militans* at Charlemagne's Court," *Viator* 11 (1980): 71–94.

18. Hrotsvit, *Opera Omnia*, ed. Walter Berschin (Munich: Saur, 2001), 4-35. A critical examination of the poem appears in Monique Goullet, "Hrotsvita de Gandersheim, *Maria*," in *Marie: Le culte de la Vierge dans la société médiévale*, ed. Dominique Iogna-Prat,

Éric Palazzo, and Daniel Russo (Paris: Beauchesne, 1996), 441–70. The text may have been produced for the court and seems to have been well known in Saxony. For example, a copy was made at Magdeburg in the tenth century. Matthias Puhle, ed., *Otto der Grosse: Magdeburg und Europa* (Mainz: Philipp von Zabern, 2001), 2:357–8, V-32.

19.   "Mandans, egregiam Mariam vocitare puellam, / 'Stella maris' lingua quod consonant ergo latina; / Hoc nomen merito sortitur sancta puella, / Est quia praeclarum sidus, quod fulget in evum / Regis [in] aeterni claro diademate Christi," in Hrotsvit, "Historia Nativitatis," lines 275–79. The description of Mary as "shining" also appears in a work produced in Corvey at the end of the tenth century. The Crucifixion in a sacramentary (Leipzig, Universitätsbibliothek, Rep. I 57, fol. 1v) shows Mary looking up at her son on the cross. A titulus running down the side of the frame states, "fulgida stella maris pro cunctis posce misellis" (shining star of the sea pray for all the wretched). *Bernward und das Zeitalter*, 2:407–10, VI-68.

20.   On the iconography of the crowned Virgin, see Mariëlle Hageman, "Between the Imperial and the Sacred: The Gesture of Coronation in Carolingian and Ottonian Images," in *New Approaches to Medieval Communication*, ed. Marco Mostert (Turnhout: Brepols, 1999), 127–63; Kristin Collins, "Redeemer, Mother, and Ruler: Images of the Virgin in Ottonian Germany" (Ph.D. diss., University of Texas at Austin, 2006). Although Hrotsvit states that Mary is the gem that shines from her son's diadem, later writers applied this metaphor to the jewels of Mary's crown, and it is unclear when this association originated. An anonymous work from the thirteenth century states that Mary wore a crown ornamented by seven stars, which shone with the *dona charismatum* of the Holy Spirit: *Libellus de corona Virginis*, chap. 7, PL 96.295. This work was mistakenly attributed to Ildefonsus of Toledo by Peter of Alva in the seventeenth century. See Robert M. Maloy, "The Sermonary of St. Ildephonsus of Toledo: A Study of the Scholarship and Manuscripts," *Classical Folia* 25 (1971): 137–99; Francisco Javier Tovar Paz, *Tractatus, sermones atque homiliae:*

El cultivo del género literario del discurso homilético en la Hispania tardoantigua y visigoda (Cáceres: Universidad de Extramadura, 1994), 208–20. The portrayal of Mary as the Queen of Heaven can also be connected to Hrotsvit's poem, where she names Mary *regina* at several points. The poem begins: "Unica spes mundi, dominatrix inclita celi / Sancta parens regis, lucida stella maris." Hrotsvit, "Historia Nativitatis," lines 13–14. Further in the poem, the angel Gabriel hails her as *regina perennis* and *dominatrix inclita celi*, in lines 516–17.

21.   "Quis opus ad templi pertingens namque sacrati / Traditur ornatum studiose perficiendum / Purpura cum bysso, linum cum vellere Serum; / Purpura sed sanctae fulgens operanda Mariae / Creditur ad velum domini templi pretiosum." Hrotsvit, "Historia Nativitatis," lines 499–503. Hrotsvit drew this idea from apocryphal stories of Mary's youth that circulated widely in the tenth century. *Libri de nativitate Mariae*, ed. Jan Gijsel and Rita Beyers (Turnhout: Brepols, 1997). On dating the Latin translation, see Jean-Daniel Kaestli, "Le Protévangile de Jacques en latin: État de la question et perspectives nouvelles," *Revue d'histoire des textes* 26 (1996): 41–102. For the connection between Hrotsvit's poem and the text of Pseudo-Matthew, see Jan Gijsel, "Zu welcher Textfamilie des Pseudo-Matthäus gehört die Quelle von Hrotsvits Maria?" *Classica et mediaevalia* 32 (1979–80): 279–88.

22.   Carol Herselle Krinsky, "Representations of the Temple of Jerusalem Before 1500," *Journal of the Warburg and Courtauld Institutes* 33 (1970): 1–19; Stanley Ferber, "The Temple of Solomon in Early Christian and Byzantine Art," in *The Temple of Solomon: Archaeological Fact and Medieval Tradition in Christian, Islamic, and Jewish Art*, ed. Joseph Gutmann (Missoula, Mont.: Scholars Press for American Academy of Religion, 1976), 21–43; Walter Cahn, "Solomonic Elements in Romanesque Art," in Gutmann, *Temple of Solomon*, 45–72; Helen Rosenau, *Vision of the Temple: The Image of the Temple of Jerusalem in Judaism and Christianity* (London: Oresko Books, 1979); Stefania Tuzi, *Le colonne e il Tempio di Salomone: La storia, la leggenda, la fortuna* (Rome: Gangemi, 2002), esp. 41–98.

23.   Ernst Guldan, *Eva und Maria: Eine Antithese als Bildmotiv* (Graz: Böhlau, 1966), 18, 44n5, and 45nn11–13. The medieval tropes for the Virgin have been edited by Ann-Katrin Andrews Johansson, *The Feasts of the Blessed Virgin Mary* (Stockholm: Almqvist and Wiksell, 1998). On the study of the relationships among the tropes, Mary's cult, and liturgical practice, see Éric Palazzo and Ann-Katrin Andrews Johansson, "Jalons liturgiques pour une histoire de culte de la Vierge dans l'Occident latin (V^e–XIe siècles)," in Iogna-Prat, Palazzo, and Russo, *Marie: Le culte*, 14–43. The angels' gestures of coronation reinforce the reference to Mary's Assumption, as the Virgin's crowning as Queen of Heaven was a central component of exegetical commentary on that feast. Henk van Os, "Krönung Mariens," in *Lexikon der christlichen Ikonographie*, ed. Engelbrecht Kirschbaum and Günter Bandmann (Rome: Herder, 1968–76), 2:671–72; Philippe Verdier, *Le couronnement de la Vierge: Les origines et les premiers développements d'un thème iconographique* (Paris: Vrin, 1980).

24.   The attribution is based on the ornament and technique of the oldest gem fastenings associated with the sculpture, which are on the left segment at the base of the Virgin's head-cloth. Although much of the original revetment of the statue was stolen in the thirteenth century, the wooden core was deeply carved in some detail, and remnants of both gold and silver in the core give indications of the original materials. The current revetment closely traces that core so that what we see today reflects, to the best of conservators' knowledge, the original appearance of the statue. For an overview of the history of the statue and related technical questions, see Michael Brandt, "'. . . und geziehrt mit Edelgesteinen': Zur grossen Madonna im Hildesheimer Domschatz," in *Bernwardinische Kunst: Bericht über ein wissenschaftliches Symposium in Hildesheim vom 10.10. bis 13.10.1984* (Göttingen: Goltze, 1988), 195–210; Brandt, ed., *Der Schatz von St. Godehard* (Hildesheim: Diözesan-Museum, 1988), 37–84, no. 4; and *Bernward und das Zeitalter,* 2:500–503, VII-32, with references to the earlier literature.

25.   Franz Arens, *Der Liber Ordinarius der Essener Stiftskirche* (Paderborn: A. Pape, 1908), 34. That crown, presented by Otto III to the nunnery, may have been reduced in size to fit the statue. Hermann Schnitzler, *Rheinische Schatzkammer: Die Romanik* (Düsseldorf: Schwann, 1957), 1:31–32, no. 40. On the crown, see also Heinz Biehn, *Die Kronen Europas und ihre Schicksale* (Wiesbaden: Limes Verlag, 1957), 94–95; Leonhard Küppers and Paul Mikat, *Der Essener Münsterschatz* (Essen: Fredebeul & Koene, 1966), 40. On the statue, see Ilene H. Forsyth, *The Throne of Wisdom: Wood Sculptures of the Madonna in Romanesque France* (Princeton: Princeton University Press, 1972), 112–21; Frank Fehrenbach, *Die Goldene Madonna in Essener Münster: Der Körper der Königin* (Ostfildern: Edition Tertium, 1996); Karen Blough, "The Princess-Abbesses of Essen and the Golden Virgin," in *De re metallica: The Uses of Metal in the Middle Ages*, ed. Robert Odell Bork with Scott Montgomery et al. (Aldershot: Ashgate, 2005), 147–62. The earliest documentation for Western reliquary statues dates to the 880s: Jean Hubert and M.-C. Hubert, "Piété chrétienne ou paganisme? Les statues-reliquaires de l'Europe carolingienne," in *Christianizzazione ed organizzazione ecclesiastica delle campagne nell' alto medioevo: Espansione e resistenze* (Spoleto: Centro italiano di studi sull'alto medioevo, 1982), 235–75. Jean Wirth argues, however, that the type of the enthroned reliquary statue dates to the mid-tenth century. See Wirth, *La datation de la sculpture médiévale* (Geneva: Droz, 2004), 221–35; see also Beate Fricke, *Ecce Fides: Die Statue von Conques, Götzendienst und Bildkultur im Westen* (Munich: Fink, 2007), 39–56.

26.   Evidence increasingly suggests that there was a tendency to conflate material object, oneiric image, and spiritual prototype around the turn of the millennium: Marcia Kupfer, "The Cult of Images in Light of Pictorial Graffiti at Doué la Fontaine," *Early Medieval Europe* 19 (2011): 125–52.

27.   On the elastic nature of medieval copying, see Richard Krautheimer, "Introduction to an 'Iconography of Mediaeval Architecture,'" *Journal of the Warburg and Courtauld Institutes* 5 (1942): 1–33. Publications since Krautheimer that have developed the vocabulary to describe medieval copying include

Hans Swarzenski, "The Role of Copies in the Formation of the Styles of the Eleventh Century," in *Romanesque and Gothic Art* (Princeton: Princeton University Press, 1963), 7–18; Madeline Caviness, "'De convenientia et cohaerentia antiqui et novi Operis': Medieval Conservation, Restoration, Pastiche, and Forgery," in *Intuition und Kunstwissenschaft: Festschrift für Hans Swarzenski*, ed. Peter Bloch (Berlin: Mann, 1973), 205–21; Jonathan J. G. Alexander, "Facsimiles, Copies, and Variations: The Relationship to the Model in Medieval and Renaissance Illuminated Manuscripts," in *Retaining the Original: Multiple Originals, Copies, and Reproductions*, ed. Kathleen Preciado (Washington, D.C.: National Gallery of Art, 1989), 61–72; Bruno Reudenbach, "Authentizitätsverheissungen im mittelalterlichen Reliquienkult und in der Gegenwartskunst," in *Zeitenspiegelung: Zur Bedeutung von Traditionen in Kunst und Kunstwissenschaft: Festschrift für Konrad Hoffmann zum 60. Geburtstag am 8. Oktober 1998*, ed. Peter K. Klein and Regine Prange (Berlin: Reimer, 1998), 375–85.

28.   Louis Bréhier, "Deux inventaires du trésor de la cathédrale de Clermont au Xᵉ siècle," *Études archéologiques: Mémoires de la Société des "Amis de l'Université de Clermont-Ferrand"* 2 (1910): 205–10; René Rigodon, "Vision de Robert, abbé de Mozat, au sujet de la basilique de la Mère de Dieu edifiée dans la Ville des Arvernes, relation par le diacre Arnaud (ms de Clermont 145, f. 130–134)," *Bulletin historique et scientifique de l'Auvergne* 70 (1950): 22–55. See also Forsyth, *Throne of Wisdom*, 31 and 50; Monique Goullet and Dominique Iogna-Prat, "La Vierge en majesté de Clermont-Ferrand," in Iogna-Prat, Palazzo, and Russo, *Marie: Le culte*, 383–405.

29.   For examples, see Otto Lehmann-Brockhaus, ed., *Schriftquellen zur Kunstgeschichte des 11 und 12 Jahrhunderts für Deutschland, Lotharingen und Italien*, 2 vols. (Berlin: Deutscher Verein für Kunstwissenschaft, 1938), and Bernhard Bischoff and Florentine Mütherich, eds., *Mittelalterliche Schatzverzeichnisse*, pt. 1, *Von der Zeit Karls des Grossen bis zur Mitte des 13. Jahrhunderts* (Munich: Prestel, 1967); Gerhard Weilandt, *Geistliche und Kunst: Ein Beitrag zur Kultur der ottonisch-salischen Reichskirche und zur Veränderung künstlerischer Traditionen im späten 11. Jahrhundert* (Cologne: Böhlau, 1992), 167–98.

30.   *Bernward und das Zeitalter*, 2:476, VII-20.

31.   ". . . in vitreo scrinio continetur hoc . . . hoc continetur in scrinio in cuius operculo agnus Dei incisus est. . . . Hoc continetur in scrinio quod viridi colore depictum est . . . continentur in scrinio oblongo sine viredine rubro tantum picto . . . haec continentur in scrinio quod in operculo imaginem throni Domini pretendit. . . . " Bischoff and Mütherich, *Mittelalterliche Schatzverzeichnisse*, 48, no. 41.

32.   In the early Carolingian period, the inventories of the treasury were made regularly for the ruler by officials entrusted with creating an up-to-date record of each church's possessions. However, the custom of inventorying ecclesiastical goods for the ruler ended with the death of Charles the Bald, after which the treasury list served primarily as a record for the community that owned the objects. Emile Lesne, *Histoire de la propriété ecclésiastique en France* (Lille: Fac. Cath, 1910), 3:1–25.

33.   As noted above, the classic study is Frances Yates, *The Art of Memory* (Chicago: University of Chicago Press, 1966), and see also Mary Carruthers, *The Book of Memory: A Study of Memory in Medieval Culture* (New York: Cambridge University Press, 1990).

34.   Carruthers, *Book of Memory*, esp. 80–156; Mary Carruthers, *The Craft of Thought: Meditation, Rhetoric, and the Making of Images, 400–1200* (New York: Cambridge University Press, 1998); Mary Carruthers and Jan M. Ziolkowski, eds., *The Medieval Craft of Memory: An Anthology of Texts and Pictures* (Philadelphia: University of Pennsylvania Press, 2002). These mnemotechnic practices translated to actual pictures. Carol Gibson-Wood, "The Utrecht Psalter and the Art of Memory," *RACAR: Revue d'art canadienne* 14 (1987): 9–15.

35.   Carruthers, *Book of Memory*, 221–57; Carruthers, *Craft of Thought*, 237–38. Amy Remensnyder has coined the term "imaginative memory" to capture the creative aspects of this type of memory-making. Amy G. Remensnyder, "Legendary Treasure at

Conques: Reliquaries and Imaginative Memory," *Speculum* 71 (1996): 884–906.

36.   Sarah Blick, "Exceptions to Krautheimer's Theory of Copying," *Visual Resources: An International Journal of Documentation* 20 (2004): 123–42.

37.   Johannes M. Kratz, *Der Dom zu Hildesheim: Seine Kostbarkeiten, Kunstschätze und sonstige Merkwürdigkeiten* (Hildesheim: Gerstenberg, 1840), 175; Rudolf Wesenberg, *Bernwardinische Plastik: Zur ottonischen Kunst unter Bischof Bernward von Hildesheim* (Berlin: Deutscher Verein für Kunstwissenschaft, 1955), 59–62 and 171.

38.   Although there are also technical reasons for hollowing out a wooden statue, and as Ilene Forsyth's study indicates, few Marian statues seem to have actually contained relics. See Forsyth, *Throne of Wisdom*, 43n38 and 122.

39.   A service book at Essen gathering material from the fourteenth century and earlier may describe an early medieval processional use of a golden Madonna statue. On the feast of the Purification, the Essen statue was vested and crowned. It was also carried in procession on the feast of the Assumption. Arens, *Liber Ordinarius*, 4, 33–35, 80–89, 104–7, 168–73, 181–85; Forsyth, *Throne of Wisdom*, 43nn36–37. The *Officium stellae* play performed at Epiphany also refers to the use of an image of the Virgin and Child. A recent discussion of this and other plays' performances in the tenth and eleventh centuries is Johann Drumbl, "Stage and Players in the Early Middle Ages," *European Medieval Drama* 1 (1997): 51–75. The classic study is Karl Young, *The Drama of the Medieval Church*, 2 vols. (Oxford: Clarendon Press, 1933), but cf. O. B. Hardison, *Christian Rite and Christian Drama in the Middle Ages* (Baltimore: Johns Hopkins University Press, 1965). Examples of the Epiphany play not known by Young appear in Norbert King, *Mittelalterliche Dreikönigsspiele: Eine Grundlagenarbeit zu den lateinischen, deutschen und französischen Dreikönigsspielen und -spielszenen bis zum Ende des 16. Jahrhunderts* (Freiburg: Universitätsverlag Freiburg, 1979).

40.   "In dussem jare am ersten dage Augusti, do de heiliche processio mit dem hilligedom umme de stat Hildensem geschein und ein ider to dische gan wolde, wart ein grot glockenslach dorch de ganzen stat Hildensem." Johannes Oldekop, *Chronik*, ed. Karl Euling (Stuttgart: Hiersemann, 1891), 135, lines 7–11. The term *hilligedom* in this passage, like its modern German equivalent *heiligtum*, refers generically to a holy thing. It may refer to all of the cathedral's major reliquaries and sacred images, which at the time were much more numerous than during Bernward's episcopacy, or only some of them. Michael Brandt, "Bau und Kult— Der Dom und seine Heiligen," in *Ego sum Hildensemensis: Bischof, Domkapitel und Dom in Hildesheim 815 bis 1810*, ed. Ulrich Knapp (Petersberg: Michael Imhof Verlag, 2000), 149–64.

41.   The Marian feasts are already recorded in Bernward's sacramentary (MS 19, fols. 175r, 204r, 206v). Later sources for Saint Michael's liturgical practice include the so-called Ratmann Sacramentary/Missal, rewritten around the year 1400 (MS 37), and the epistolary of 1520 (MS 67). On the history of Saint Michael's monastery, see Ulrich Faust, *Die Benediktinerklöster in Niedersachsen, Schleswig-Holstein und Bremen* (St. Ottilien: EOS Verlag, 1979), 218–52.

42.   Brandt, "Bau und Kult."

43.   Bernard of Angers, *Liber miraculorum Sancte Fidis,* ed. Luca Robertini (Spoleto: Centro italiano di studi sull'alto medioevo, 1994), 2.4; English trans. Pamela Sheingorn in *Book of Sainte Foy* (Philadelphia: University of Pennsylvania Press, 1995), 120–21.

44.   Kathleen Ashley and Pamela Sheingorn, *Writing Faith: Text, Sign, and History in the Miracles of Sainte Foy* (Chicago: University of Chicago Press, 1999).

45.   Ellert Dahl, "Heavenly Images: The Statue of St. Foy of Conques and the Significance of the Medieval 'Cult-Image' in the West," *Acta ad archaeologium et artium historiam pertinentia* 8 (1978): 175–91; Annegret Friedrich, "'Ich seh' dir nicht in die Augen, Kleines': Zur Rezeption der Essener Goldenen Madonna," in Klein and Prange, *Zeitenspiegelung*, 21–32. The French sociologist Maurice Halbwachs developed the theoretical basis for understanding memory as the collective re-presentation of communities' pasts, what

has sometimes also been termed social or historical memory. Maurice Halbwachs, *Les cadres sociaux de la mémoire* (Paris: F. Alcan, 1925), *La topographie légendaire des Évangiles en Terre Sainte: Étude de mémoire collective* (Paris: Presses universitaires de France, 1941), and *La mémoire collective* (Paris: Presses universitaires de France, 1950). Cf. Patrick H. Hutton, *History as an Art of Memory* (Hanover: University Press of New England, 1993), 73–90. See also Pierre Nora, *Les lieux de mémoire*, 3 vols. (Paris: Gallimard, 1984–92), and more recently, "General Introduction: Between Memory and History," in *Realms of Memory: Rethinking the French Past*, vol. 1, trans. Arthur Goldhammer (New York: Columbia University Press, 1996), on which cf. Nancy Wood, "Memory's Remains: *Les lieux de mémoire*," *History and Memory* 6 (1994): 123–49, and Peter Carrier, "Places, Politics, and the Archiving of Contemporary Memory in Pierre Nora's *Les lieux de mémoire*," in *Memory and Methodology*, ed. Susannah Radstone (Oxford: Berg, 2000), 37–57. See also James Fentress and Chris Wickham, *Social Memory* (Cambridge: Blackwell, 1992).

46.   Although no textual source documents the origins of the Marian statue, the attribution to Bernward's patronage has never been questioned—the oldest embellishments on the sculpture are consistent with Bernwardian metalwork and correspond closely to pieces from the so-called treasure of the empress Gisela (d. 1034). Joseph Braun, *Meisterwerke der deutschen Goldschmiedekunst der vorgotischen Zeit* (Munich: Riehn & Reusch, 1922), 21; Wilhelm Pinder, *Die Kunst der deutschen Kaiserzeit* (Leipzig: H. F. Menck, 1940), 193. Wesenberg pointed out as well the close stylistic relationship between the sculpture's wooden core and the rendering of Mary on Bernward's bronze doors, which bear the bishop's name and the date 1015; see Wesenberg, *Bernwardinische Plastik*, 59–62.

47.   Evidence for this attribution is the inscription on the doors. It begins on the left panel, with "An[no] Dom[inicae] inc[arnationis] MXV B[ernwardus] ep[iscopus] dive mem[oriae] has valvas fusilis," and continues on the right, "In facie[m] angel[i]ci te[m]pli

ob monim[en]t[um] sui fecit suspendi." On the inscription, see Dieter von Nahmer, "Die Inschrift auf der Bernwardstür in Hildesheim im Rahmen Bernwardinischer Texte," and Hans Drescher, "Einige technische Beobachtungen zur Inschrift auf der Hildesheimer Bernwardstür," both in *Bernwardinische Kunst: Bericht*, 51–70 and 71–75, respectively. These authors argue that the inscriptions were designed by Bishop Bernward himself.

48.   Adam Cohen and Anne Derbes contend that the Bernward Gospels dedication opening presented a summary of the themes of Saint Michael's bronze doors. See their "Bernward and Eve at Hildesheim," *Gesta* 40 (2001): 19–38.

49.   The intended location of the doors remains contentious, because Saint Michael's was not finished at Bernward's death and the doors are documented at the cathedral in 1035. On the case for the cathedral, see Rainer Kahsnitz in *Bernward und das Zeitalter*, 2:503–12, no. VII-33, and Matthias Untermann, "St. Michael und die Sakralarchitektur um 1000. Forschungsstand und Perspectiven," in *1000 Jahre St. Michael in Hildesheim: Kirche-Kloster-Stifter*, ed. Gerhard Lutz and Angela Weyer (Göttingen: Michael Imhof Verlag, 2012), 62. For the traditional response that the doors were for Saint Michael's, see Bernhard Schütz, "Zum ursprünglichen Anbringungsort der Bronzetür Bischof Bernwards von Hildesheim," *Zeitschrift für Kunstgeschichte* 57 (1994): 569–99; and Bernhard Gallistl, "In Faciem Angelici Templi: Kultgeschichtliche Bemerkungen zu Inschrift und ursprünglicher Platzierung der Bernwardstür," *Jahrbuch für Geschichte und Kunst im Bistum Hildesheim* 75/76 (2007/2008): 59–92. For an overview of all the evidence on both sides and the suggestion that wherever they were intended to go, the doors were not used before 1035, see Christoph Schulz-Mons, *Das Michaeliskloster in Hildesheim: Untersuchungen zur Gründung durch Bischof Bernward 993–1022* (Hildesheim: Gerstenberg, 2010), 1:280–330.

50.   Thangmar, *Vita Bernwardi episcopi Hildesheimensis*, ed. Georg Heinrich Pertz, MGH SS 4 (Hannover: Impensis Bibliopolii Aulici Hahniani, 1841), chaps. 16–17 on pp. 765–66. For more on the conflict,

see Knut Görich, "Der Gandersheimer Streit zur Zeit Ottos III: Ein Konflikt um die Metropolitanrechte des Erzbischofs Willigis von Mainz," *Zeitschrift der Savigny-Stiftung für Rechtsgeschichte: Kanonistische Abteilung* 79 (1993): 56–94.

51. The connection between the doors and the dedicatory painting of the Bernward Gospels has been stressed by Guldan, *Eva und Maria,* 13–20; William Tronzo, "The Hildesheim Doors: An Iconographic Source and Its Implications," *Zeitschrift für Kunstgeschichte* 46 (1983): 357–66, and Cohen and Derbes, "Bernward and Eve."

52. *Bernward und das Zeitalter,* 2:578–81, no. VIII-31.

53. Thangmar, *Vita Bernwardi,* chap. 41, on p. 776.

54. The processional crosses at Essen perform a similar function. Christina Nielson, "Hoc opus eximium: Artistic Patronage in the Ottonian Empire" (Ph.D. diss., University of Chicago, 2002), chap. 2.

55. Hermann Schnitzler, "Das sogenannte grosse Bernwardkreuz," in *Karolingische und ottonische Kunst: Werden, Wesen, Wirkung,* ed. Friedrich Gerke, Georg von Opel, and Hermann Schnitzler (Wiesbaden: Steiner, 1957), 382–94.

56. Jäggi, "Stifter, Schreiber oder Heiliger?"

57. Regula Schorta, "The Textiles Found in the Shrine of the Patron Saints of Hildesheim Cathedral," *Bulletin du CIETA* 77 (2000): 45–56.

58. Herbert L. Kessler also points this out in *Seeing Medieval Art* (Orchard Park, N.Y.: Broadview Press, 2004), 174.

59. Rüdiger Becksmann, "Vor- und frühromanische Glasmalerei in Deutschland: Quellen—Funde—Hypothesen," *Zeitschrift des Deutschen Vereins für Kunstwissenschaft* 52–53 (1998–99): 197–212.

60. Francesca Dell'Acqua, *"Illuminando colorat": La vetrata tra l'età tardo imperiale e l'alto medioevo; Le fonti, l'archeologia* (Spoleto: Centro italiano di studi sull'alto medioevo, 2003).

61. Rosemary Cramp, "Window Glass from the Monastic Site of Jarrow: Problems of Interpretation," *Journal of Glass Studies* 17 (1975): 88–96, and Cramp, "Window Glass from the British Isles 7th–10th Century," in *Il colore nel medioevo: Arte, simbolo, tecnica; La vetrata in Occidente dal IV all'XI secolo,* ed. Francesca Dell'Acqua and Romano Silva (Lucca: Istituto storico lucchese, 2001), 67–85; Dell'Acqua, *"Illuminando Colorat,"* 27.

62. Becksmann, "Vor- und frühromanische Glasmalerei in Deutschland."

63. The origins of this metaphor may date to the sixth or fifth century. Henri Barré, "Le sermon 'Exhortatur' est-il de Saint Ildefonse?" *Revue bénédictine* 67 (1957): 10–33; Andrew Breeze, "The Blessed Virgin and the Sunbeam Through Glass," *Celtica* 23 (1999): 19–29.

64. My translation is indebted to Friedrich von der Leyen's modern German translation in *Deutsche Dichtung des Mittelalters* (Frankfurt am Main: Insel-Verlag, 1962), 136–77, no. 742.

65. Hans Drescher, "Zur Technik bernwardinischer Silber- und Bronzegüsse," in *Bernward und das Zeitalter,* 1:337–51; *Bernward und das Zeitalter,* 2:581, VIII-32. Liturgical objects were often buried with their clerical patrons, which made the works serve as identifying insignia, similar to a seal or ring. Victor H. Elbern, *Der eucharistische Kelch im frühen Mittelalter* (Berlin: Deutscher Verein für Kunstwissenschaft, 1964), 44–57; Frans van Molle, "Notes sur quelques calices funéraires du XIe siècle en France et en Belgique," in *Les monuments historiques de la France* 12 (1966): 113–19; Neil Stratford, Pamela Tudor-Craig, and Anna M. Muthesius, "Archbishop Hubert Walter's Tomb and Its Furnishings," in *Medieval Art and Architecture at Canterbury Before 1220* (London: British Archaeological Association, 1982), 20–26.

66. According to his later biography, Bernward had three chalices made: one of onyx, one of crystal, and one of gold. They are discussed within a longer passage describing Bernward's patronage. Thangmar, *Vita Bernwardi,* chap. 8, on pp. 761–62.

67. The portable altar may have been placed inside the cathedral's main altar by Bernward's successor, Hezilo, in 1061. *Bernward und das Zeitalter,* 2:478–9, VII-22. Ursula Nilgen first identified the crib in the Bernward Gospels Epiphany painting as a portable altar; see "The Epiphany and the Eucharist: On the

Interpretation of Eucharistic Motifs in Mediaeval Epiphany Scenes," trans. Renate Franciscono, *Art Bulletin* 49 (1967): 314.

68.   Paul Tirot, "Histoire des prières d'offertoire dans la liturgie romaine du VIIe au XVIe siècle," *Ephemerides liturgicae* 98 (1984): 148–97.

69.   Jussen, "Religious Discourses"; Christen, "Transforming Things and Persons"; Arnold Angenendt, "*Donationes pro anima*: Gift and Countergift in the Early Medieval Liturgy," in *The Long Morning of Medieval Europe: New Directions in Early Medieval Studies*, ed. Jennifer R. Davis and Michael McCormick (Aldershot: Ashgate, 2008), 131–54.

70.   This may help explain records of gifts that stipulate that the grain or grapes collected from a particular donated parcel of land should be used for making the bread or wine of the Eucharist. Philippe Buc, "Conversion of Objects," *Viator* 28 (1997): 99–142. On the Eucharist in this period, see Henri de Lubac, *Corpus Mysticum: L'eucharistie et l'Église au Moyen Âge; Étude historique* (Paris: Aubier, 1944); Robert Cabié, *The Church at Prayer: An Introduction to the Liturgy*, vol. 2, *The Eucharist*, ed. Aimé Georges Martimort, trans. Matthew J. O'Connell (Collegeville, Minn.: Liturgical Press, 1992); and, more recently, Burcht Pranger, "Le sacrement de l'eucharistie et la prolifération de l'imaginaire aux XIe et XIIe siècles," in *Fête-Dieu (1246–1996)*, vol. 1, *Actes du colloque de Liège, 12–14 septembre 1996*, ed. André Haquin (Turnhout: Brepols, 1999), 97–116.

71.   This was first noted by Albert Boeckler, "Das Erhardbild im Utacodex," in *Studies in Art and Literature for Belle da Costa Greene*, ed. Dorothy Miner (Princeton: Princeton University Press, 1954), 225–30.

72.   Cohen, *Uta Codex*, 87–96 (St. Erhard page) and 53–86 on the facing miniature (symbolic crucifixion).

73.   Ibid., esp. 87–96.

74.   *Ex Arnoldi libris de S. Emmerammo*, ed. Georg Heinrich Pertz, MGH SS 4 (Hannover: Impensis Bibliopolii Aulici Hahniani, 1841), bk. 1, pp. 543–74, esp. 551. The passage containing the description of the objects is excerpted in Max Piendl, "Fontes monasterii

s. Emmerami Ratisbonensis: Bau- und kunstgeschichtliche Quellen," in *Quellen und Forschungen zur Geschichte des ehemaligen Reichsstiftes St. Emmeram in Regensburg* (Kallmünz: M. Lassleben, 1961), 17–18, no. 15. On the author of the *vita*, see Bernhard Bischoff, "Literarisches und künstlerisches Leben in St. Emmeram (Regensburg) während des frühen und hohen Mittelalter," in *Mittelalterliche Studien: Ausgewählte Aufsätze zur Schriftkunde und Literaturgeschichte* (Stuttgart: Hiersemann, 1966–81), 2:77–115, esp. 84ff. Adam Cohen discusses the reproduction of these objects in detail in *Uta Codex*, 93–94.

75.   On the altar, see most recently Uta Appel Tallone, *Das Arnulfziborium in der Schatzkammer der Münchener Residenz: Eine monographische Untersuchung* (Herne: Verlag für Wissenschaft und Kunst, 2003).

76.   Cohen, *Uta Codex*, 94; James Trilling, *The Medallion Style: A Study in the Origins of Byzantine Taste* (New York: Garland, 1985).

77.   Gudrun Sporbeck, "Die liturgischen Gewänder im Mittelalter: Paramente und Reliquienkult nach Ausweis kölnischer Grabornate und Textilien des 11. Jahrhunderts," in *Kunst und Liturgie im Mittelalter: Akten des internationalen Kongresses der Bibliotheca Hertziana und des Nederlands Instituut te Rome, Rom, 28.–30. September 1997*, ed. Nicolas Bock (Munich: Hirmer, 2000), 191–204.

78.   On the pseudo-Dionysian thought underlying the painting, see Cohen, *Uta Codex*, 79–84; the suggestion that the golden objects may serve anagogically is on 93 and elaborated on 95–96.

79.   Ibid., 95n75.

80.   Ibid., 95.

81.   On the historical moment of making and using the codex, see ibid., 183–196.

82.   On forgetting and memory, see Patrick Geary, *Phantoms of Remembrance: Memory and Oblivion at the End of the First Millennium* (Princeton: Princeton University Press, 1994), and with reference to bishops more specifically, Atsuko Iwanami, "Memoria et oblivio: Zur Entwicklungen des Begriffs memoria in den bischöflichen Urkunden des Früh- und

Hochmittelalters, insbesondere im Maas-Rheingebiet," in *Urkundensprachen im germanisch-romanischen Grenzgebiet: Beiträge zum Kolloquium am 5/6 Oktober in Trier*, ed. Kurt Gärtner and Günter Holtus (Mainz: Philipp von Zabern, 1997), 151–59.

83. Peter Bloch and Erich Zimmerman, *Der Darmstädter Hitda-Codex: Bilder und Zierseiten aus der Handschrift 1640 der Hessischen Landes- und Hochschulbibliothek* (Berlin: Propyläen, 1968); Michael Schaefer, *Hitda-Codex: Evangeliar des Stifts St. Walburga in Meschede; Handschrift 1640 der Hessischen Landes- und Hochschulbibliothek in Darmstadt* (Meschede: Heimatbund der Stadt Meschede, 2003).

84. "Haec munera Hidda peregrina istius loci procuratrix Deo et sanctae Waltburgi dono dedit pro se suisque ex voto. Cruces III auro et lapidibus ornatas et unum ex auro et ebore. Imaginem sanctae Mariae auro et lapidibus factam et palliolum, quo portatur. Librum I auro et gemmis, et duos aureos. Thurribulum aureum I. Vexilla IIII. Ampullas III, unam onichinam, II cristallinas. Mappulas III. Casulam I cum serica cum stola aurea. III Icones. Scrinia tria. Dorsalia II. Cortinas IIII. Corium unum. Vascula II ad usum sacrificii, unum lapideum et aliud eburneum. Cervicalia III coccinea ad portandum libros. Si quis ex alisquid abstraxerit de usu sanctorum vel minuerit, sit anathema." In Bischoff and Mütherich, *Mittelalterliche Schatzverzeichnisse*, 62, no. 54. For more on this inventory, see Klemens Honselmann, "Eine Schenkung der Äbtissin Hitda von Meschede," *Westfälische Zeitschrift* 112 (1962): 305–7.

85. Bloch and Zimmerman, *Der Darmstadter Hitda-Codex*, 15.

86. Ibid., 17.

87. "Hoc visibile imaginatum figurat illud invisibile veru[m], cuius splendor penetrat mundu[m], cum bis binis candelabris, ipsius novi sermonis" (fol. 6v); trans. Herbert L. Kessler, "'Hoc Visibile Imaginatum Figurat Illud Invisibile Verum': Imagining God in Pictures of Christ," in *Seeing the Invisible in Late Antiquity and the Early Middle Ages*, ed. Giselle de Nie, Karl F. Morrison, and Marco Mostert (Turnhout: Brepols, 2005), 293–328. On the influence of neo-Platonic

ideas in this miniature, see Anton von Euw, "Die Majestas-Domini-Bilder der ottonischen Kölner Malerschule im Licht des platonischen Weltbildes: Codex 192 der Kölner Dombibliothek," in *Kaiserin Theophanu: Begegnung des Ostens und Westens um die Wende des ersten Jahrtausends: Gedenkschrift des Kölner Schnütgen-Museums zum 1000. Todesjahr der Kaiserin*, ed. Anton von Euw, Peter Schreiner, and Gudrun Sporbeck (Cologne: Schnütgen-Museum, 1991), 1:251–80 and 1:379–98.

88. Silk patterns ornament most of the paintings of the Bernward Gospels. Stephen Wagner, "Silken Parchments: Design, Context, Patronage, and Function of Textile-Inspired Pages in Ottonian and Salian Manuscripts" (Ph.D. diss., University of Delaware, 2004), 143–62.

89. Treasury lists frequently appear in service books, which also tend to be stored in treasuries. Both trends contribute to the conflation of liturgical books with the treasury. Éric Palazzo, "Le livre dans les trésors du Moyen-Âge: Contribution à l'histoire de la *Memoria* médiévale," *Annales: Histoire, sciences sociales* 52 (1997): 93–118.

90. Titos Papamastorakis has shown how the display of accumulated wealth on Byzantine icons operated on three levels: to thank the saint, to create the anticipation of a future return from the saint, and to underscore the donors' rightful and legitimate inclusion among an elite community. Titos Papamastorakis, "The Display of Accumulated Wealth in Luxury Icons: Gift Giving from the Byzantine Aristocracy to God in the Twelfth Century," in *Byzantines eikones: Techne, technike kai technologia*, ed. Maria Vassilaki (Heraklion: Panepistēmiakes Ekdoseis Krētēs, 2002), 35–37. The thesaurization of the Bernward Gospels functions similarly—not only to illustrate the bishop's merit by means of the gift's materials, but also to locate him among an elite network of patrons. William North and Anthony Cutler have suggested that Ottonian bishops expressed their roles as cultural impresarios by the ways in which they manipulated one such luxury material, Byzantine ivory spolia, in "Ivories, Inscriptions, and Episcopal Self-Consciousness in

the Ottonian Empire: Berthold of Toul and the Berlin Hodegetria," *Gesta* 42 (2003): 1–17.

91.   Pierre-Alain Mariaux, "Collecting (and Display)," in *A Companion to Medieval Art: Romanesque and Gothic in Northern Europe,* ed. Conrad Rudolph (Oxford: Blackwell, 2006), 213–32.

92.   Bischoff and Mütherich, *Mittelalterliche Schatzverzeichnisse.*

93.   Lesne, *Histoire de la propriété ecclésiastique.* In that sense they are similar to other medieval documents that relate to a community's history, such as foundation legends. Amy G. Remensnyder, *Remembering Kings Past: Monastic Foundation Legends in Medieval Southern France* (Ithaca: Cornell University Press, 1995).

94.   On the way in which collecting manipulates context and memory, see Susan Stewart, *On Longing: Narratives of the Miniature, the Gigantic, the Souvenir, the Collection* (Baltimore: Johns Hopkins University Press, 1984), 132–66. See also Krzysztof Pomian, *Collectionneurs, amateurs et curieux* (Paris: Gallimard, 1987), 1–44; a section is reprinted in "The Collection: Between the Visible and the Invisible," in *Interpreting Objects and Collections,* ed. Susan Pearce (London: Routledge, 1994), 160–74; 170ff homes in on the formation of collections as attempts to make connections between the visible and the invisible. Pomian points out how in these instances the link between model and image was much stronger than one consisting merely of resemblance, attributing to images the power to represent the active force of a person. While here Pomian specifically means cult images of gods and saints, the attributes he specifies are relevant to considering the significance of the Bernward Gospels depiction, which presents several types of objects not only as reproductions of works in the treasury but also as material membranes that act in the mode of Christ's Incarnation.

95.   For examples, see Danielle Gaborit-Chopin, "Trésors de Neustrie," in *La Neustrie: Les pays au nord de la Loire de 650 à 850,* ed. Hartmut Atsma and Karl Ferdinand Werner (Sigmaringen: Thorbecke, 1989), 2:259–60; Xavier Barral i Altet, "Définition et fonction d'un trésor monastique autour de l'an mil: Sainte Foy de Conques," in *Haut Moyen Âge: Culture, éducation et société; Études offertes à Pierre Riché,* ed. Michel Sot (La Garennes-Colome: Éditions européennes Erasme, 1990), 401–8; Cynthia Hahn, "The Meaning of Early Medieval Treasuries," in *Reliquiare im Mittelalter,* ed. Bruno Reudenbach and Gia Toussaint (Berlin: Akademie Verlag, 2005), 1–20, and Hahn, "Relics and Reliquaries: The Construction of Imperial Memory and Meaning, with Particular Attention to Treasuries at Conques, Aachen, and Quedlinburg," in *Representing History, 900–1300: Art, Music, History,* ed. Robert A. Maxwell (University Park: The Pennsylvania State University Press, 2010), 133–49.

96.   By the eleventh century, the treasury metaphor for memory was completely conventional, transmitted in large part through the writings of Augustine. Gillian R. Evans, "Two Aspects of Memoria in Eleventh and Twelfth Century Writings," *Classica et Mediaevalia* 32 (1980): 263–78. On the same metaphor in mnemotechnics, see Carruthers, *Book of Memory,* 33–45.

97.   Jan Assmann and John Czaplicka, "Collective Memory and Cultural Identity," *New German Critique* 65 (1995): 125–33. See also Jan Assmann, *Das kulturelle Gedächtnis: Schrift, Erinnerung und politische Identität in den frühen Hochkulturen* (Munich: Beck, 1992).

98.   Christen, "Transforming Things and Persons"; Angenendt, "*Donationes pro anima,*" 131–54.

CHAPTER 2

1.   The Baptist's biography would not be illustrated by a full cycle in the West until the end of the twelfth century. Engelbrecht Kirschbaum and Günter Bandmann, *Lexikon der christlichen Ikonographie* (Rome: Herder, 1968–76), 7:170–90; Véronique Rouchon Mouilleron, "Entre Orient et Occident: L'image de saint Jean du XIe au XIVe siècle," *Revue de l'art* 158 (2007): 35–45.

2.   Donatien de Bruyne, *Préfaces de la Bible latine* (Namur: A. Godenne, 1920), 170–73.

3.   Herbert L. Kessler, "*Facies bibliothecae revelata*: Carolingian Art as Spiritual Seeing," in *Testo e*

immagine nell'alto medioevo: 15–21 aprile 1993 (Spoleto: Centro italiano di studi sull'alto medioevo, 1994), 533–94; Jennifer O'Reilly, "St. John as a Figure of the Contemplative Life: Text and Image in the Art of the Anglo-Saxon Benedictine Reform," in *St. Dunstan: His Life, Times, and Cult*, ed. Nigel Ramsay, Margaret Sparks, and Tim Tatton-Brown (Woodbridge: Boydell Press, 1992), 165–85; Jeffrey Hamburger, *St. John the Divine: The Deified Evangelist in Medieval Art and Theology* (Berkeley: University of California Press, 2002), 1–20 and 185–202.

4. Peter Bloch and Ursula Nilgen, "Evangelisten," in *Reallexikon zur deutschen Kunstgeschichte*, vol. 6, ed. Ludwig H. Heydenreich and Karl-August Wirth (Stuttgart: Metzler, 1973), cols. 448–88.

5. Rainer Kahsnitz, "Inhalt und Aufbau der Handschrift," in *Kostbare Evangeliar*, esp. 21–24 and 33–37.

6. Anton Baumstark, "Eine Antike Bildkomposition in christlich-orientalischen Umdeutungen," *Monatshefte für Kunstwissenschaft* 8 (1915): 111–23; Josepha Weitzmann-Fiedler, "Ein Evangelientyp mit Aposteln als Begleitfiguren," in *Adolph Goldschmidt zu seinem siebensigsten Geburtstag am 15. Januar 1933* (Berlin: Würfel Verlag, 1935), 30–34; George Galavaris, *The Illustrations of the Prefaces in Byzantine Gospels* (Vienna: Verlag der Österreichischen Akademie der Wissenschaften, 1979), 50–72; Robert S. Nelson, *The Iconography of Preface and Miniature in the Byzantine Gospel Book* (New York: New York University Press for the College Art Association of America, 1980), 75–91.

7. Robert Deshman, "Another Look at the Disappearing Christ: Corporeal and Spiritual Vision in Early Medieval Images," *Art Bulletin* 79 (1997): 518–46.

8. This is the central point of patristic commentary on the New Testament, including Jerome's *Plures fuisse* gospel preface, an exegetical text usually included in gospel books that analyzes the relationship between the four gospels. Carolingian gospels frequently express this concept in their illustrations. Robert M. Walker, "Illustrations to the Priscillian Prologues in the Gospel Manuscripts of the Carolingian Ada School," *Art Bulletin* 30 (1948): 1–10; Paul A. Underwood, "The Fountain of Life in Manuscripts of the Gospels," *Dumbarton Oaks Papers* 5 (1950): 43–138; Herbert L. Kessler, *The Illustrated Bibles from Tours* (Princeton: Princeton University Press, 1977), 36–58. Jennifer O'Reilly traces related ideas in insular gospel books in "Patristic and Insular Traditions of the Evangelists: Exegesis and Iconography," in *Le isole britanniche e Roma in età romanobarbarica*, ed. Anna Maria Luiselli Fadda and Éamonn Ó Carragáin (Rome: Herder, 1998), 49–94. The idea of the harmony of the knowledge contained in the gospels also occurs in Ottonian books. Adam Cohen, *The Uta Codex: Art, Philosophy, and Reform in Eleventh-Century Germany* (University Park: The Pennsylvania State University Press, 2000), 97–134.

9. Galavaris, *Illustrations of the Prefaces*, 50–72; Nelson, *Iconography of Preface and Miniature*, 75–91; Carl Nordenfalk, "Der inspirierte Evangelist," *Wiener Jahrbuch für Kunstgeschichte* 36 (1983): 175–90 and 249–60.

10. Rainer Kahsnitz, "'Matheus ex ore Christi scripsit': Zum Bild der Berufung und Inspiration der Evangelisten," in *Byzantine East, Latin West: Art-Historical Studies in Honor of Kurt Weitzmann*, ed. Doula Mouriki, Christopher Moss, and Katherine Kiefer (Princeton: Princeton University Press, 1995), 169–80.

11. Gunther Franz and Franz J. Ronig, eds., *Codex Egberti Teilfaksimile-Ausgabe des Ms. 24 der Stadtbibliothek Trier* (Wiesbaden: Reichert, 1983), 2:28v–29r and 3v–6r. See also, more recently, Gunther Franz, ed., *Der Egbert Codex: Das Leben Jesu. Ein Höhepunkt der Buchmalerei vor 1000 Jahren; Handschrift der Stadtbibliothek Trier* (Stuttgart: Theiss, 2005).

12. A recent study on this manuscript is Anja Grebe, *Codex Aureus: Das goldene Evangelienbuch von Echternach* ([Darmstadt]: Primus, 2007). The Calling of Matthew is fig. 37 on p. 59.

13. Hans Heinz Josten, *Neue Studien zur Evangelienhandschrift Nr. 18 des Hl. Bernward Evangelienbuch im Domschatze zur Hildesheim: Beiträge zur Geschichte der Buchmalerei im frühen Mittelalter* (Strassburg:

J. H. E. Heitz, 1909), 55. Kahsnitz repeats the reference in "Inhalt und Aufbau," 33 and 53n88. Josten seems to be using as his source the verses for a fresco cycle at Mainz that were composed by Ekkehard IV for Archbishop Aribo between 1022 and 1031, specifically verses 700–705 on Zacchaeus the tax collector.

14.   It is important to acknowledge, however, that at the time of Archbishop Aribo of Mainz's death in 1031, the frescoes remained unrealized. Arwed Arnulf's close study of the verses and their glosses (also by Ekkehard IV) does, however, suggest that some of the tituli reflect a knowledge of actual paintings (possibly even including fragments of older frescoes damaged by a 1009 fire at the cathedral). Arwed Arnulf, *Versus ad Picturas: Studien zur Titulusdichtung als Quellengattung der Kunstgeschichte von der Antike bis zum Hochmittelalter* (Munich: Deutscher Kunstverlag, 1997), 201–28.

15.   Weitzmann-Fiedler, "Evangelientyp," plates.

16.   Deshman, "Another Look," 537–39.

17.   The Jewish priests in the scene of Judas receiving thirty coins to betray Christ wear the same headgear (fol. 118r; plate 12), although the Magi are similarly coiffed in the manuscript's Adoration scene (fol. 18r; plate 4), so this type of headdress is not used consistently in the manuscript as an identifier for Jews. Other aspects of the foremost figure's garb do reflect, albeit with some variations, the description of the vestments of the high priest in Exodus 28. The colors of his outfit are primarily purple, gold, and scarlet over white. Gold medallions fasten the cloak at the shoulders. The edges of a maniple peek out below the coat, and from its hem hangs a fringe of twelve threads, symbolizing the twelve tribes of Israel. For other variations in medieval representations of Jewish priests, see Paul E. Dutton and Herbert L. Kessler, *The Poetry and Paintings of the First Bible of Charles the Bald* (Ann Arbor: University of Michigan Press, 1997), plate 7, and Cohen, *Uta Codex*, plate 5.

18.   Joseph Braun, "Die Stola," in *Die liturgische Gewandung im Occident und Orient nach Ursprung und Entwicklung, Verwendung und Symbolik* (Darmstadt: Wissenschaftliche Buchgesellschaft, 1964), 562–608.

19.   The closest textual parallel for this scene is not, however, the opening of Mark's gospel, but the concordant passage in John (1:6–50), which emphasizes that Christ's first two disciples came from among John's followers. In the text, Andrew and Simon join Christ at the moment when John the Baptist recognizes Christ as the son of God, proclaiming, "Behold the lamb of God." Christ called the second pair of disciples, Philip and Nathaniel, on the second day, at the moment of his departure for Galilee. Consistent with John's version, but not Mark's, the Bernward Gospels miniature divides Christ's audience into two groups of two. Philip places his arm around Nathaniel, bringing him toward Christ.

20.   *Commentariorum in Genesim*, bk. 1, chap. 12, PL 107.479. For more on what water, and especially the paradisiacal fountain, could represent in the Middle Ages, see Underwood, "Fountain of Life."

21.   As Kahsnitz points out, an unusual aspect of this infancy cycle is the absence of the Baptist's nativity, usually a central episode of such series. See the pericope book of Henry II (Munich, Bayerische Staatsbibliothek, Clm 4452, fols. 149v–150r) reproduced in Kahsnitz, "Inhalt und Aufbau," 39–40, and the Gospels of Henry III (Escorial, Real biblioteca del monasterio, Cod. Vitr. 17, fols. 94–95), repr. in Albert Boeckler, *Das Goldene Evangelienbuch Heinrichs III* (Berlin: Deutscher Verein für Kunstwissenschaft, 1933), plates 110–11.

22.   For a general introduction to the figure of the Baptist in the gospels and its early Christian commentary, see Josef Ernst, *Johannes der Täufer: Interpretation, Geschichte, Wirkungsgeschichte* (Berlin: W. de Gruyter, 1989). On these ideas in the development of a medieval feast cycle for the Baptist, see Luce Pietri, *La ville de Tours du IVe au VIe siècle: Naissance d'une cité chrétienne* (Rome: École française de Rome, 1983), 462–65.

23.   Joseph T. Lienhard, "John the Baptist in Augustine's Exegesis," in *Augustine: Biblical Exegete*, ed. Frederick van Fleteren and Joseph C. Schnaubelt (New York: Peter Lang, 2001), 197–213.

24.   Bede the Venerable, *Opera*, pars 3, *Opera homiletica,* ed. David Hurst, O.S.B., CCSL 122 (Turnhout: Brepols, 1955), homily 2, chap. 20, on pp. 328–34.

25.   Among others: Haimo of Auxerre, *Homilia II: In nativitate sancti Joannis Baptistae*, PL 118.755. Migne mistakenly attributes this text to Haimo, bishop of Halberstadt. See also Hrabanus Maurus, *Homiliae in evangelia et epistolas*, homily 104, PL 110.341–43.

26.   Both mimetic dress and gesture are typical strategies of assimilating the devout to figures of the gospels during medieval liturgical rites that enact biblical stories. C. Clifford Flanigan, "Medieval Liturgy and the Arts: Visitatio Sepulchri as Paradigm," in *Liturgy and the Arts in the Middle Ages: Studies in Honour of C. Clifford Flanigan*, ed. Eva Louise Lillie and Nils Holger Petersen (Copenhagen: Museum Tusculanum Press, University of Copenhagen, 1996), 9–35.

27.   Annabel J. Wharton, "Ritual and Reconstructed Meaning: The Neonian Baptistery in Ravenna," *Art Bulletin* 69 (1987): 365. Although in practice an infant might be baptized in his local village, to be confirmed as an initiate in the faith required the action of the bishop. That confirmation was understood as an extension of baptism. Ulrich Schwalbach, *Firmung und religiöse Sozialisation* (Innsbruck: Tyrolia-Verlag, 1979), 21–23.

28.   Wharton, "Ritual and Reconstructed Meaning," 365–69.

29.   On the liturgical content of the book covers, see Roger E. Reynolds, "A Visual Epitome of the Eucharistic Ordo from the Era of Charles the Bald: The Ivory Mass Cover of the *Drogo Sacramentary*," in *Charles the Bald: Court and Kingdom*, ed. Margaret T. Gibson and Janet L. Nelson (Aldershot: Ashgate, 1990), 241–60. For an image of the front cover, see Peter Lasko, *Ars Sacra, 800–1200*, 2nd ed. (New Haven: Yale University Press, 1994), fig. 46.

30.   Bertram Colgrave, ed. and trans., *Two Lives of Saint Cuthbert: Texts, Translation, and Notes* (1940; repr., Cambridge: Cambridge University Press, 1985), 67. See additional Merovingian and early Anglo-Saxon saints' lives in Charles W. Jones, *Saints' Lives and Chronicles in Early England: Together with the First English Translations of the Oldest Life of Pope St. Gregory the Great by a Monk of Whitby and the Life of St. Guthlac of Crowland by Felix* (Ithaca: Cornell University Press, 1947); Clinton Albertson, ed. and trans., *Anglo-Saxon Saints and Heroes* (New York: Fordham University Press, 1967); Thomas F. X. Noble and Thomas Head, eds., *Soldiers of Christ: Saints and Saints' Lives from Late Antiquity and the Early Middle Ages* (University Park: The Pennsylvania State University Press, 1995); Paul Fouracre and Richard A. Gerberding, eds., *Late Merovingian France: History and Hagiography, 640–720* (Manchester: Manchester University Press, 1996).

31.   *Vita Willibrordi archiepiscopi Traiectensis,* ed. Bruno Krusch and Wilhelm Levison, MGH SS rerum Merovingicarum 7 (Hannover: Hahnsche Buchhandlung, 1920), bk. 1, chap. 2, on p. 117, line 5; English trans. in *The Anglo-Saxon Missionaries in Germany: Being the Lives of SS. Willibrord, Boniface, Sturm, Leoba and Lebuin, together with the Hodoeporicon of St. Willibald and a Selection from the Correspondence of St. Boniface,* ed. and trans. Charles H. Talbot (New York: Sheed and Ward, 1954), 4; *Vita Remigii episcopi,* ed. Bruno Krusch, MGH SS rerum Merovingicarum 3 (Hannover: Impensis Bibliopolii Hahniani, 1896), chap. 1, 262.

32.   "Consecratio Cornelii ante baptismum et sancti Remigii non solum ante baptismum, sed etiam ante nativitatem. Ortus est autem ex anu et vetulodiu sterilibus per repromissionem, ut Isaac et Iohannes, vir iste sanctus, antequam natus, nomine designatus, antequam mundo cognitus, in pago laudunensi alto parentum sanguine, ut mostratur in ortu, qualis futurus erat in actu." *Vita Remigii episcopi*, chap. 1, on p. 261, lines 12–14.

33.   "Iohannes populum suo inluminaturus alloquio, in utero materno propheticam suscepit gratiam. Et beatus Remigius gentem Francorum a tenebris ignorantiae ad lucem perducturus evangelii, itidem divina donatus est gratia, ut, quod perfecturus erat ministerio, cum participibus suis pari claresceret munere; et qui, ut dictum est, aecclesiam Dei, spetiali autem cura

Remorum civitatem atque provinciam remigio alarum sanctarum, scilicet verbo et exemplo, meritis et orationibus, erat Dei predestinatione recturus, et perfecto certamine, spiritu caelestia regna petiturus, angelorum utique subvectus auxiolio, Remigius est iure Dei preceptione vocatus." Ibid., chap. 1, on p. 262, lines 2–6.

34. On Ottonian bishops' lives more generally, see Stephanie Coué, *Hagiographie im Kontext: Schreibanlass und Funktion von Bischofsviten aus dem 11. und vom Anfang des 12. Jahrhunderts* (Berlin: W. de Gruyter, 1997); as Stephanie Haarländer, *Vitae episcoporum: Eine Quellengattung zwischen Hagiographie und Historiographie, untersucht an Lebensbeschreibungen von Bischöfen des Regnum Teutonicum im Zeitalter der Ottonen und Salier* (Stuttgart: Hiersemann, 2000).

35. "Iamque ut caeteros taceamus, Iohannis ipse, quo nemo in natis mulierum maior, teste evangelio, signum fecit nullum, et dum in carcere gladio feriretur, utrum vel extrema qualibet nota a quolibet homicidarum seu latronum distiterit, perpetuo omnium scripturarum silentio consopitur." *Vita Iohannis abbatis Gorzienzis auctore Iohanne abate S. Arnulfi*, ed. Georg Heinrich Pertz, MGH SS 4 (Hannover: Impensis Bibliopolii Aulici Hahniani, 1841), praefatio, on p. 338, lines 14–17.

36. Giulia Barone, "Une hagiographie sans miracles: Observations en marge de quelques vies du Xᵉ siècle," in *Les fonctions des saints dans le monde occidental (IIIᵉ–XIIIᵉ siècle): Actes du colloque* (Rome: École française de Rome, 1991), 435–46. The classic study of tenth-century reforms is Kassius Hallinger, *Gorze-Kluny: Studien zu den monastischen Lebensformen und Gegensätzen im Hochmittelalter*, 2 vols. (Rome: Herder, 1950–51). See also Raymond Kottje, "Monastische Reform oder Reformen?" in *Monastische Reformen im 9. und 10. Jahrhundert*, ed. Raymond Kottje and Helmut Maurer (Sigmaringen: Thorbecke, 1989), 9–13.

37. "Qui vero judaizantes signa quaerunt, quid faciunt de Joanne Baptista, qui post nativitatem suam nullum signum legitur edidisse?" Odo of Cluny, *De vita Sancti Geraldi Auriliacensis*, bk. 2, praefatio, PL 133.670.

38. Paul Rousset, "L'idéal chevaleresque dans deux Vitae clunisiennes," in *Études de civilisation médiévale (IXᵉ–XIIᵉ siècles): Mélanges offerts à Edmond-René Labande* (Poitiers: C.E.S.C.M., 1974), 623–33; Stuart Airlie, "The Anxiety of Sanctity: St Gerald of Aurillac and His Maker," *Journal of Ecclesiastical History* 43 (1992): 372–95; Paolo Facciotto, "La 'Vita Geraldi' di Oddone di Cluny, un problema aperto," *Studi Medievali*, 3rd ser., 33 (1992): 243–63.

39. Peter Damian, *Vita beati Romualdi,* ed. Giovanni Tabacco (Rome: Istituto storico italiano per il medio evo, 1957), 11. Colin Phipps, "Romuald—Model Hermit: Eremitical Theory in Peter Damian's *Vita Beati Romualdi*, Chapters 16–27," *Studies in Church History* 22 (1985): 65–77.

40. "Factum est et alia tempestate, ut messis omnino deperiret prae siccitate, et alter Helias, salvo Iohanne baptista, ad nota praesidia confugiens, a Deo monuit esse quaerendum, et clerum et populum hortatur tridui afflicatione secum adterendum, et ut pariter cotidie votici sanctorum frequentarent patrocinia, et conculcatos et humilis eorum adiuvarent merita." Lantbert of Deutz, *Vita Heriberti archiepiscopi Coloniensis auctore Lantberto*, ed. Georg Heinrich Pertz, MGH SS 4 (Hannover: Impensis Bibliopolii Aulici Hahniani, 1841), chap. 8, on p. 745, lines 40–44.

41. "Per quem et multorum saluti consulendum providit," in *Vita Theodorici abbatis Andaginensis*, ed. W. Wattenbach, MGH SS 12 (Hannover: Impensis Bibliopolii Hahniani, 1856), incipit, on p. 38, line 44.

42. Terrence Kardong, *Benedict's Rule: A Translation and Commentary* (Collegeville, Minn.: Liturgical Press, 1996), 493–97 and 505–14.

43. Franz Mennemeyer, "Kult und Brauchtum Johannis des Täufers in Westfalen" (Ph.D. diss., University of Münster, 1940); Thomas Rensing, "Johannes der Täufer: Patron des Westwerks von Corvey und des Königtums," *Westfalen* 42 (1964): 243–328.

44. An inscription dated to 1061 on the back of the high altar records the cathedral's renovation by Bishop Hezilo (1054–71) after a fire. It lists John the Baptist first among a list of saints to whom the church's altars were consecrated and of whom the cathedral owned

relics. Christine Wulf, elaborating on the work of
Hans Jürgen Rieckenberg, in *Die Inschriften der Stadt
Hildesheim*, 2 vols. (Wiesbaden: Reichert, 2003), 217.
The source for Saint Michael's altar is the *Chronica
episcoporum Hildensheimensium*, ed. Gottfried Wil-
helm Leibniz (Hannover, 1710), 784–806.

45. Marlis Stähli, *Die Handschriften im Domschatz zu Hildesheim,* ed. Helmar Härtel (Wiesbaden:
In Kommission bei O. Harrassowitz, 1984), 52.

46. On this see most recently Bernhard Gallistl, *Die Bernwardsäule und die Michaeliskirche zu
Hildesheim* (Hildesheim: Olms, 1993).

47. Ottonian biographical writing in general
seems to look for ways to reconcile more traditional,
often monastically inspired models of sanctity with
the exercise of authority in the world. Patrick Corbet
argues that in the construction of queens as saints,
Ottonian texts seek to make sanctity compatible
with the exercise of governing authority in *Les saints
ottoniens: Sainteté dynastique, sainteté royale et sainteté
féminine autour de l'an Mil* (Sigmaringen: Thorbecke,
1986). Jean-Charles Picard makes a similar argument
for bishops' lives in "Le modèle épiscopale dans deux
vies du Xᵉ siècle: Saint Innocentius de Tortona et Saint
Prosper de Reggio Emilia," in *Les fonctions des saints
dans le monde occidental (IIIᵉ–XIIIᵉ siècle)* (Rome:
École française de Rome, 1991), 371–84. See also Guy
Lobrichon, "L'engendrement des saints: Le débat des
savants et la revendication d'une sainteté exemplaire
en France du Nord au XIᵉ et au début du XIIᵉ siècle,"
in *Les fonctions des saints*, 143–60.

48. John S. Ott, "'Both Mary and Martha': Bishop
Lietbert of Cambrai and the Construction of Episco-
pal Sanctity in a Border Diocese Around 1100," in *The
Bishop Reformed: Studies of Episcopal Power and Culture
in the Central Middle Ages*, ed. John S. Ott and Anna
Trumbore Jones (Aldershot: Ashgate, 2007), 137–60. See
also, in the same volume, Valerie Ramseyer, "Pastoral
Care as Military Action: The Ecclesiology of Archbishop
Alfanus of Salerno (1058–1085)," 189–208, and Thomas
Head, "Postscript: The Ambiguous Bishop," 250–64.

49. It was relatively common in the Middle Ages
to present John the Baptist in relation to the four

evangelists, often as a symbolic shorthand for the
Christian Church. For example, the front of the seat
of Archbishop Maximianus's ivory throne in Ravenna
shows the Baptist flanked on each side by the evange-
lists. Otto G. von Simson, *Sacred Fortress: Byzantine
Art and Statecraft in Ravenna* (Chicago: University
of Chicago Press, 1948), 64–66. A late eighth-century
gospel book from Flavigny assimilates the figures of
Christ, the Evangelists, their symbols, and John the
Baptist to columns to form an image of the Living
Ecclesia. Robert Deshman, "The Imagery of the Living
Ecclesia and the English Monastic Reform," in *Sources
for Anglo-Saxon Culture*, ed. Paul E. Szarmach with
Virginia D. Oggins (Kalamazoo: Medieval Institute
Publications, Western Michigan University, 1986),
261–82. On a now-lost tenth-century retable of Xanten
Cathedral, commissioned by Bruno and Volkmar of
Cologne, the Baptist is immediately next to the group
of four evangelists; he appears among a series of Old
Testament prophets—positioned as the linchpin
between the prophecy of the Old Testament and the
Word of the New Testament. The object is known
today only through a seventeenth-century drawing.
Udo Grote, *Der Schatz von St. Viktor: Mittelalterliche
Kostbarkeiten aus dem Xantener Dom* (Regensburg:
Schnell & Steiner, 1998), 25.

50. The two Johns were also considered joint heirs
in Christ. Hamburger, *St. John the Divine*, 65–83.

51. Kathleen Corrigan, "The Witness of John the
Baptist on an Early Byzantine Icon in Kiev," *Dumbar-
ton Oaks Papers* 42 (1988): 1–11; George Henderson,
"The John the Baptist Panel on the Ruthwell Cross,"
Gesta 24 (1985): 3–12; Éamonn Ó Carragáin, "John the
Baptist and the Agnus Dei: Ruthwell (and Bewcastle)
Revisited," *The Antiquaries' Journal* 81 (1999): 131–53;
Ó Carragáin, *Ritual and the Rood: Liturgical Images
and the Old English Poems of the "Dream of the Rood"
Tradition* (London: British Library, 2005), 83–84 and
95–110.

52. The depiction of the evangelists as visionaries
is not, however, without parallel in Ottonian art. Konrad Hoffmann, "Die Evangelistenbilder des Münchener
Otto-Evangeliars (Clm 4453)," *Zeitschrift des Deutschen

Vereins für Kunstwissenschaft 20 (1966): 17–46. Florentine Mütherich and Karl Dachs, *Das Evangeliar Ottos III: Clm 4453 der Bayerischen Staatsbibliothek München* (Munich: Prestel, 2001), plates 16, 30, 42, and 56.

53.   For more on the eleventh-century hagiographic interest in the Baptist as a Christo-mimetic type, see Phyllis G. Jestice, "A New Fashion in Imitating Christ: Changing Spiritual Perspectives Around the Year 1000," in *The Year 1000: Religious and Social Response to the Turning of the First Millennium*, ed. Michael Frassetto (New York: Palgrave Macmillan, 2002), 165–85.

CHAPTER 3

1.   For a pointed exploration of the use of representational or stylistic modes to express content, see Jan Bialostocki, "Das Modusproblem in den bildenden Künsten: Zur Vorgeschichte und zum Nachleben des 'Modusbriefes' von Nicholas Poussin," in *Stil und Ikonographie: Studien zur Kunstwissenschaft* (Dresden: VEB Verlag der Kunst, 1966), 9–35. Meyer Schapiro has argued that different "modes" were practiced by the same artists in the Middle Ages to create meaning; see "Style," in *Anthropology Today: An Encyclopedic Inventory*, ed. Alfred L. Kroeber (Chicago: University of Chicago Press, 1953), 287–312; repr. in *Theory and Philosophy of Art: Style, Artist, and Society* (New York: George Braziller, 1994), 51–102 (see esp. 94–96). On the sensitivity of medieval viewers to pictorial modes or styles, see Henry Maguire, "Style and Ideology in Byzantine Imperial Art," *Gesta* 28 (1989): 217–31; Maguire, "Disembodiment and Corporality in Byzantine Images of the Saints," in *Iconography at the Crossroads: Papers from the Colloquium Sponsored by the Index of Christian Art, Princeton University, 23–24 March 1990*, ed. Brian Cassidy (Princeton: Index of Christian Art, Dept. of Art and Archaeology, Princeton University, 1993), 75–90; Thomas E. A. Dale, *Relics, Prayer, and Politics in Medieval Venetia: Romanesque Painting in the Crypt of Aquilea Cathedral* (Princeton: Princeton University Press, 1997); Madeline Caviness, "Images of

Divine Order and the Third Mode of Seeing," *Gesta* 22 (1983): 99–120; repr. in *Art in the Medieval West and Its Audience* (Aldershot: Ashgate, 2001), 1–22.

2.   Robert Deshman first suggested that the unusual form of the Bernward Gospels Ascension served as a prompt for spiritual seeing in "Another Look at the Disappearing Christ: Corporeal and Spiritual Vision in Early Medieval Images," *Art Bulletin* 79 (1997): 518–46. This imagery, first christened the "disappearing Christ" by Meyer Schapiro, seems to have been invented in Anglo-Saxon England around the millennium. Meyer Schapiro, "The Image of the Disappearing Christ: The Ascension in English Art Around the Year 1000," *Gazette des beaux-arts*, 6th ser., 23 (1943): 133–52, repr. in Schapiro, *Late Antique, Early Christian, and Medieval Art* (New York: George Braziller, 1979), 267–87.

3.   I use the word *imago* here deliberately because its Latin meaning is broader than the usual English translation of the term ("image"). *Imago* is multivalent and refers equally to material pictures, visions, and images produced by narrative text. It is also the medieval term employed when suggesting a relationship of likeness between "image" and prototype that is central to the notion that Christ is the *imago Dei*—the "image" of God. Jean-Claude Schmitt, "*Imago*: De l'image à l'imaginaire," in *L'image: Fonctions et usages des images dans l'Occident médiéval*, ed. Jérôme Baschet and Jean-Claude Schmitt (Paris: Le Léopard d'or, 1996), 29–57.

4.   Medieval art characteristically separates and marks the representation of visionary space by formal means, on which see David Ganz, *Medien der Offenbarung: Visionsdarstellungen im Mittelalter* (Berlin: Reimer, 2008), esp. 52–100 and 143–76. On the migration of scientific schemata into visionary images of the Maiestas Domini in Carolingian and Ottonian art, see Bianca Kühnel, *The End of Time in the Order of Things: Science and Eschatology in Early Medieval Art* (Regensburg: Schnell & Steiner, 2003).

5.   For more on the iconographic conventions for the Nativity and Adoration, see Gertrud Schiller, *Ikonographie der christlichen Kunst* ([Gütersloh]: Gütersloher Verlagshaus G. Mohn, 1966), 1:69–98 and 110–24.

6. Other examples range widely and include early eleventh-century representations from Reichenau (Bamberg Staatsbibliothek, Bibl. 140, fol. 63v), in Alois Fauser, *Die Bamberger Apokalypse* (Wiesbaden: E. Wasmuth, 1958), 38–39; color plate 55; pictures from Echternach (Brussels, Bibliothèque royale, MS 9428, fol. 7v, ca. 1050), at the Index of Christian Art, Index photo: 32 B91 LRl 9,7B 050792 Phot.; images produced in Cologne (Darmstadt Landesbibliothek MS 1640, Hitda Codex, fol. 21r), in Peter Bloch and Hermann Schnitzler, *Die ottonische Kölner Malerschule* (Düsseldorf: Schwann, 1967–70), 1: plate 127.

7. Bernhard Bruns, "Das Epiphaniebild im Kostbaren Evangeliar des hl. Bernward," *Die Diözese Hildesheim in Vergangenheit und Gegenwart* 61 (1993): 11–19. Gregory the Great glossed the ox as representing the Jews, and the ass, the Gentiles, in *Moralia in Job*, bk. 1, chap. 16, ed. Marc Adriaen, *S. Gregorii Magni Moralia in Job*, CCSL 143–143A, B (Turnhout: Brepols, 1979–85), 143:36–37. By the twelfth century, the motif evolved, and the identification of the ox with the Jews and the ass with the Gentiles was apparently reversed. Erwin Panofsky, *Early Netherlandish Painting: Its Origins and Character* (Cambridge, Mass.: Harvard University Press, 1953), 1:470n1; Ruth Mellinkoff, "One Is Good, Two Are Better: The Twice-Appearing Ass in a Thirteenth-Century English Nativity," in *New Offerings, Ancient Treasures: Studies in Medieval Art for George Henderson*, ed. Paul Binski and William Noel (Stroud: Sutton, 2001), 325–42.

8. Anke Vasiliu, "Le mot et le verre: Une définition médiévale du Diaphane," *Journal des savants* 1 (1994): 135–62; Deshman, "Another Look"; Hans Belting, *Bild-Anthropologie: Entwurfe für eine Bildwissenschaft* (Munich: Fink, 2001), 189–211; Herbert L. Kessler, *Seeing Medieval Art* (Orchard Park, N.Y.: Broadview Press, 2004), 173–76; Chris Webb, "Greek, Roman, Hebrew, and Byzantine Interpretations of Light and Its Origins," *Greek Orthodox Theological Review* 54 (2009): 155–67.

9. On using ornament to support content in medieval art, see Jean-Claude Bonne, "De l'ornemental dans l'art médiéval (VII–XII siècle): Le modèle insulaire," in Baschet and Schmitt, *L'image*, 207–51, and Bonne, "Les ornements de l'histoire: A propos de l'ivoire carolingien de Saint Rémi," *Annales: Histoire, sciences sociales* 1 (1996): 37–70.

10. Ursula Nilgen first suggested the parallel in "The Epiphany and the Eucharist: On the Interpretation of Eucharistic Motifs in Mediaeval Epiphany Scenes," trans. Renate Franciscono, *Art Bulletin* 49 (1967): 314. On the liturgical uses of the portable altar, see Éric Palazzo, *L'espace rituel et le sacré dans le Christianisme: La liturgie de l'autel portatif dans l'Antiquité et au Moyen Âge* (Turnhout: Brepols, 2008).

11. The analogy between altar and crib, Christ and Eucharistic bread, becomes particularly important starting in the fourth century. By the eleventh century, the trope appears frequently in the liturgy and especially in the staging of Epiphany plays. Adolf Katzenellenbogen, *The Sculptural Programs of Chartres Cathedral* (Baltimore: Johns Hopkins University Press, 1959), 12–15; Alphonse A. Barb, "Krippe, Tisch und Grab," in *Mullus: Festschrift Theodor Klauser* (Münster: Aschendorff, 1964), 17–27; Kurt Weitzmann, "*Loca Sancta* and the Representational Arts of Palestine," *Dumbarton Oaks Papers* 28 (1974): 36–39; Nilgen, "Epiphany and the Eucharist"; Barbara G. Lane, "'Ecce Panis Angelorum': The Manger as Altar in Hugo's Berlin Nativity," *Art Bulletin* 57 (1975): 476–86.

12. Indeed, in sermons composed and revised between 1018 and 1050 against heresies which they labeled Manichean, Ademar of Chabannes and Gerard of Arras-Cambrai would each use reports of visions of the Eucharist as an infant and of the choir of angels as evidence for the real presence of Christ in the Eucharist. On these miracles, see Benedicta Ward, *Miracles and the Medieval Mind*, rev. ed. (Philadelphia: University of Pennsylvania Press, 1987), 13–18; Miri Rubin, *Corpus Christi: The Eucharist in Late Medieval Culture* (Cambridge: Cambridge University Press, 1991), 112–13; Michael Frassetto, "Reaction and Reform: Reception of Heresy in Arras and Aquitaine in the Early Eleventh Century," *Catholic Historical Review* 83 (1997): 385–400. There is no evidence to suggest that such controversy informs the inclusion of the motif

in the Bernward Gospels; rather, it illustrates what the bishop would probably have considered a conventional understanding of the Eucharist. Although most studies of the Eucharist skip from the Carolingian to the mid-eleventh-century controversy launched by the writings of Berengar of Tours, some information on tenth-century ideas about the Eucharist can be found in Charles R. Shrader, "The False Attribution of an Eucharistic Tract to Gerbert of Aurillac," *Mediaeval Studies* 35 (1973): 178–204; Pierre-Alain Mariaux, "'Faire Dieu': Quelques remarques sur les relations entre confection eucharistique et création d'image (IXe–XIIe siècles)," in *Ästhetik des Unsichtbaren: Bildtheorie und Bildgebrauch in der Vormoderne,* ed. David Ganz and Thomas Lentes (Berlin: Reimer, 2004), 94–106, and Mariaux, "The Bishop as Artist? The Eucharist and Image Theory Around the Millennium," in *The Bishop: Power and Piety at the First Millennium*, ed. Sean Gilsdorf (Münster: LIT-Verlag, 2004), 155–68.

13. Joseph A. Jungmann, *The Mass of the Roman Rite: Its Origins and Development,* trans. Francis A. Brunner (New York: Benziger, 1951), 2:125–28. This work was originally published as *Missarum Sollemnia: Eine genetische Erklärung der römischen Messe,* 2 vols. (Vienna: Herder, 1949); citations are to the translation. This is a point emphasized by Gregory the Great, among other commentators, in his *Dialogorum,* chap. 58, PL 77.425.

14. Note the circles articulating the golden mound in the central Magus's hands. In the early eleventh century, an offertory procession took place at the beginning of Mass, and coins were presented as part of that offertory. By the twelfth century, when the coins offered were made of gold, liturgists compared their donors explicitly to the "wise men from the east." Honorius Augustodinensis, *Gemma anima*, I, chap. 27, PL 172.553; also in Sicard of Cremona, *Mitralis de Officiis*, ed. Gábor Sarbak and Lorenz Weinrich, CCCM 228 (Turnhout: Brepols, 2008), bk. 3, chap. 5, lines 55–60 on p. 168. This mimetic assimilation may have already been in place in the eleventh century. Contemporary rubrics of the offertory *secreta* and *benedictio*

for the feast of the Epiphany compare contemporary gift givers to the Magi. For the history of the offertory, see Jungmann, *Mass of the Roman Rite*, 2:9–130.

15. The literature on the various phases of the Carolingian debates about religious images is extensive. For a recent and thorough exploration of the relevant texts, see Thomas F. X. Noble, *Images, Iconoclasm, and the Carolingians* (Philadelphia: University of Pennsylvania Press, 2009).

16. For an introduction to how early medieval pictures make arguments about the role of images in perceiving God, see especially Herbert L. Kessler, *Spiritual Seeing: Picturing God's Invisibility in Medieval Art* (Philadelphia: University of Pennsylvania Press, 2000), and his *Seeing Medieval Art*. See also Kessler, "'Hoc Visibile Imaginatum Figurat Illud Invisibile Verum': Imagining God in Pictures of Christ," in *Seeing the Invisible in Late Antiquity and the Early Middle Ages*, ed. Giselle de Nie, Karl F. Morrison, and Marco Mostert (Turnhout: Brepols, 2005), 293–328, and "Image and Object: Christ's Dual Nature and the Crisis of Early Medieval Art," in *The Long Morning of Medieval Europe: New Directions in Early Medieval Studies*, ed. Jennifer R. Davis and Michael McCormick (Aldershot: Ashgate, 2008), 291–320.

17. In brief, the first level of seeing is corporeal sight, which employs the eyes of the body and is limited to perceiving the things of the earth. The second level, spiritual vision, requires a spiritual understanding in the heart that allows sight to look beyond the physically perceptible world. The last and highest mode of seeing is intellectual sight; it permits the direct vision of God. These ideas are developed most fully in Augustine's *De trinitate* and *Confessions*. For a study of these concepts in Augustinian thought, see Margaret Miles, "Vision: The Eye of the Body and the Eye of the Mind in Saint Augustine's 'De trinitate' and 'Confessions,'" *Journal of Religion* 63 (1983): 125–42, and Deshman, "Disappearing Christ," esp. 537–38.

18. Yves Christe, *L'Apocalypse de Jean: Sens et développements de ses visions synthétiques* (Paris: Picard, 1996), 192–93, and Adam Cohen, *The Uta Codex: Art, Philosophy, and Reform in*

Eleventh-Century Germany (University Park: The Pennsylvania State University Press, 2000), 123–28.

19. The use of spherical shapes to denote the heavens and angular shapes to mark the earth is common in Christian art. In the eighth century, Alcuin specifically identifies the four-cornered shape of the lozenge with the created world. For more on this trope, see Herbert L. Kessler, *The Illustrated Bibles from Tours* (Princeton: Princeton University Press, 1977), 51–52; for an example, see fig. 76.

20. Christe, *Apocalypse de Jean*, 123–31; Anne-Orange Poilpré, *Majestas Domini: Une image de l'Église en Occident, V^e–IXe siècle* (Paris: Cerf, 2005). On the association of this motif with rulership, see Søren Kaspersen, "Majestas Domini, regnum et sacerdotium: Zu Entstehung und Leben des Motivs bis zum Investiturstreit," *Hafnia: Copenhagen Papers in the History of Art* 8 (1981): 83–146. On the Maestas Domini as an image of eschatological judgment, see Daniel Russo, "Le Christ entre Dieu et homme dans l'art du Moyen Âge en Occident, IXe–XVe siècles: Essai d'interprétation iconographique," in *Le Moyen Âge aujourd'hui: Trois regards contemporains sur le Moyen Âge; Histoire, théologie, cinema; Actes de la Rencontre de Cerisy-la-Salle, juillet 1991*, ed. Jacques Le Goff and Guy Lobrichon (Paris: Le Léopard d'or, 1997), 247–79.

21. Among other examples, in the Carolingian Metz Sacramentary (Paris, lat. 1141, fol. 6r), the sea monster appears below Christ in the illustration for the text of the Sanctus preceding the Canon of the Mass, and in the Uta Codex's John frontispiece, the sea serpent faces toward the frame of the roundel (Munich, Clm. 13601, fol. 89v). Florentine Mütherich, *Sakramentar von Metz: Fragment: Ms. Lat. 1141, Bibliothèque nationale, Paris, vollständige Faksimile-Ausgabe* (Graz: Akademiche Druck- und Verlagsanstalt, 1972), vol. 2, fol. 6r; Cohen, *Uta Codex*, color plate 12.

22. Beat Brenk, *Tradition und Neuerung in der christlichen Kunst des ersten Jahrtausends* (Graz: Böhlaus in Kommission, 1963), 55–70 and 107–42; Yves Christe, *La vision de Matthieu (Matth. XXIV–XXV): Origine et développement d'une image de la Seconde Parousie* (Paris: Klincksieck, 1973).

23. Adam Cohen has carefully compared all three miniatures and suggests that they may have shared a common model. Cohen, *Uta Codex*, 128nn85–86. Yet as Cohen himself points out, finding that specific model has proved impossible. Moreover, there is no clear link among all three manuscripts that can account for such commonalities. As Cohen recognizes, there are also significant pictorial differences among the three miniatures that suggest a unique emphasis in each one's content. Finally, recent research into the illustrations of the prologue to John's gospel underscores the extent to which certain of the pictorial themes and motifs to which Cohen refers are recurrent in this type of picture. François Boespflug and Yolanta Zaluska, "Le prologue de l'évangile selon Saint Jean dans l'art médiéval, IXe–XIIIe siècles: L'image comme commentaire," *Folia historiae atrium* 8–9 (2002): 11–45. In my opinion, the question of a common model is less important than what the comparison of the three miniatures indicates about Ottonian conceptions of the significance of this gospel passage, and how that, in turn, elucidates the nature of the vision painted in the Bernward Gospels. Consequently, I restrict my discussion to highlighting those shared traits that clarify the unique content of the Bernward Gospels.

24. This Platonic content derives in part from Calcidius's translation of Plato's *Timaeus*, a text that the phrasing of Bishop Bernward's testament suggests he knew intimately. Fidel Rädl, "Calcidius und Paulus begründen ein Vermächtnis: Zu Bernwards Dotationsurkunde für St. Michael in Hildesheim," in *Latin Culture in the Eleventh Century: Proceedings of the Third International Conference on Medieval Latin Studies, Cambridge, September 9–12, 1998*, ed. Michael W. Herren, Christopher J. McDonough, and Ross G. Arthur (Turnhout: Brepols, 2002), 2:328–49. The importance of the *Timaeus* for the design of the Bernward Gospels is discussed at greater length in the next chapter.

25. Cohen, *Uta Codex*, 125.

26. For example, see the diagram in *Timaeus a Calcidio Translatus Commentarioque Instructus*, ed. Jan Hendrik Waszink (London: The Warburg Institute; Leiden: Brill, 1962), paragraph 67, on p. 114, which is

the basis of an image of Christ Enthroned produced in Cologne around the year 1000. Anton von Euw, "Die Majestas-Domini-Bilder der ottonischen Kölner Malerschule im Licht des platonischen Weltbildes: Codex 192 der Kölner Dombibliothek," in *Kaiserin Theophanu: Begegnung des Ostens und Westens um die Wende des Ersten Jahrtausends: Gedenkschrift des Kölner Schnütgen-Museums zum 1000. Todesjahr der Kaiserin*, ed. Anton von Euw, Peter Schreiner, and Gudrun Sporbeck (Cologne: Schnütgen-Museum, 1991), 1:251–801 and 1:379–98.

27. Haimo of Auxerre, *Expositionis in Apocalypsin Beati Joannis*, bk. 1, chap. 1, PL 117.276; Ambrosus Autpertus, "In Apocalypsin," *Ambrosii Autperti Opera*, ed. Robert Weber, CCCM 27 (Turnhout: Brepols, 1975), bk. 4, chap. 6, pt. A on p. 276; Alcuin, *Commentariorum in Apocalypsin libri quinque*, bk. 4, chap. 6, PL 100.1123. On medieval commentary on the Apocalypse, including its foregrounding of incarnational themes, see E. Ann Matter, "Exegesis of the Apocalypse in the Early Middle Ages," in *The Year 1000: Religious and Social Response to the Turning of the First Millennium*, ed. Michael Frassetto (New York: Palgrave Macmillan, 2002), 29–40.

28. A widely circulating commentary on the opening of John's gospel makes a similar point. Donatien de Bruyne, *Préfaces de la Bible latine* (Namur: A. Godenne, 1920), 173. Pictures also frequently established links between the two *in principio* phrases. Illustrators of Genesis, for example, borrowed the layout of the *IN* initials used primarily in frontispieces for the gospel of John. Harry Bober, "In Principio: Creation Before Time," in *De artibus opuscula XL: Essays in Honor of Erwin Panofsky*, ed. Millard Meiss (New York: New York University Press, 1961), 1:13–28; Richard H. Putney, "Creatio et Redemptio: The Genesis Monogram of the St. Hubert Bible" (Ph.D. diss., University of Delaware, 1985). Frontispieces to John, in turn, invoked details from Genesis. Kühnel, *End of Time*, esp. 185–98 and 239–47. The connection between the two *in principio* helped position John the Evangelist in medieval thought as a type of deified creator. Jeffrey Hamburger, *St. John the Divine: The Deified Evangelist in Medieval Art and Theology* (Berkeley: University of California Press, 2002), 21–42.

29. Some aspects of the Bernward Gospels painting draw on Carolingian models from Tours. It is probable that there was a Turonian Bible available in Hildesheim in this period. Nordenfalk, "Noch eine turonische Bilderbibel," 153–63; Peter Klein, "Die frühen Apocalypse-Zyklen und verwandte Denkmaler" (Ph.D. diss., University of Bamberg, 1980), 423–27; Yves Christe, "Trois images carolingiennes en forme de commentaires sur l'Apocalypse," *Cahiers archéologiques: Fin de l'antiquité et Moyen Âge* 25 (1976): 77–92.

30. Augustine, "Sermo CCLXIV," in *Opera Omnia*, ed. Cornelius Mayer (Charlottesville: InteLex, 2000), trans. as *The Works of Saint Augustine: A Translation for the Twenty-First Century*, ed. Boniface Ramsey, 2nd release (New York: New City Press, 1991–). Past Masters Database, http://library.nlx.com, © 2002.

31. Kessler, "'Hoc Visibile Imaginatum."

32. "Scio enim, quod Redempt[or] meu[s] [vi]vit, et in novissimo die de terra surrecturus sum, et rursum circumdabor pelle mea, et in carne mea videbo D[eu]m salvatorem meum, qu[e]m visurus sum ego ipse, et oculi mei conspecturi sunt et non ali[us]. Reposita est haec spes in sinu meo." The lid has broken into several large pieces, cutting away parts of some letters. Rudolf Wesenberg, *Bernwardinische Plastik: Zur ottonischen Kunst unter Bischof Bernward von Hildesheim* (Berlin: Deutscher Verein für Kunstwissenschaft, 1955), 159–60, 182–83, and 314–18; Karl-August Wirth, "Die Nachrichten über Begräbnis und Grab Bischof Bernwards von Hildesheim in Thangmars Vita Bernwardi," *Zeitschrift für Kunstgeschichte* 22 (1959): 305–23; Ulrich Teuscher, "Das ikonologische Programm der Grabanlage Bernwards," in *Bernward und Godehard von Hildesheim: Ihr Leben und Wirken*, ed. Konrad Algermissen (Hildesheim: Lax, 1960), 202–15; Peter Lasko, "The Tomb of St. Bernward of Hildesheim," in *Romanesque and Gothic: Essays for George Zarnecki*, ed. Neil Stratford (Woodbridge: Boydell Press, 1987), 1:147–52; Rainer Kahsnitz, "Bischof Bernwards Grab," in *Bernward und das Zeitalter*, 1:383–96.

33. Medieval commentary on the evangelists associated each with a particular symbol that had been described in visions by Ezekiel (1:1–28) and John (Rev. 4:1–11): angel/man, lion, ox, and eagle. Although the second-century Irenaeus was the first to link each evangelist to one of these creatures, Jerome codified what became the conventional medieval correlation of Matthew with the angel/man, Mark with the lion, Luke with the ox, and John with the eagle. On the evangelist symbols in general, see Frederik van der Meer, *Maiestas Domini: Théophanies de l'Apocalypse dans l'art chrétien* (Rome: Pontificio istituto di archeologia cristiana, 1938), 78–84. On variations in the exegetical tradition, especially in Byzantium, see George Galavaris, *The Illustrations of the Prefaces in Byzantine Gospels* (Vienna: Verlag der Österreichischen Akademie der Wissenschaften, 1979), 36–49; Robert S. Nelson, *The Iconography of Preface and Miniature in the Byzantine Gospel Book* (New York: New York University Press for the College Art Association of America, 1980), 15–53.

34. Karl Lehmann, "The Dome of Heaven," *Art Bulletin* 27 (1945): 1–27, but cf. Thomas Mathews, "Cracks in Lehmann's 'Dome of Heaven,'" *Notes on the History of Art* 1 (1982): 12–16; E. Baldwin Smith, *Architectural Symbolism of Imperial Rome and the Middle Ages* (Princeton: Princeton University Press, 1956); Theodor Klauser, *Das Ciborium in der älteren christlichen Buchmalerei* (Göttingen: Aschendorff, 1961), 191–208; Jacques Bousquet, "Des antependiums aux retables: Le problème du décor des autels et de son emplacement," *Cahiers de Saint-Michel de Cuxa* 13 (1982): 201–32.

35. For parallels, see Jane Rosenthal, "The Unique Architectural Settings of the Arenberg Evangelists," in *Sources of Anglo-Saxon Culture*, ed. Paul Szarmach with Virginia D. Oggins (Kalamazoo: Medieval Institute Publications, Western Michigan University, 1986), 261–82; and in the same volume, Robert Deshman, "The Imagery of the Living Ecclesia and the English Monastic Reform," 261–82.

36. André Grabar, "Observations sur l'arc de triomphe de la croix dit arc d'Éginhard et sur d'autres bases de la croix," *Cahiers archéologiques: Fin de l'antiquité et Moyen Âge* 27 (1978): 61–83; Robert Deshman, "The Exalted Servant: The Ruler Theology of the Prayerbook of Charles the Bald," *Viator* 11 (1980): 385–417; Elizabeth Leesti, "Carolingian Crucifixion Iconography: An Elaboration of a Byzantine Theme," *RACAR: Revue d'art canadienne* 20 (1993): 3–15; Martin Büchsel, "Die Kreuzigung zwischen Antike und Christentum," *Jahrbuch der Kunsthistorischen Sammlungen in Wien* 89–90 (1993–94): 7–33; Piotr Skubiszewski, "Le titre de 'Roi de gloire' et les images du Christ: Un concept théologique, l'iconographie et les inscriptions," in *Épigraphie et iconographie: Actes du Colloque tenu à Poitiers les 5–8 octobre 1995*, ed. Robert Favreau (Poitiers: Université de Poitiers, Centre national de la recherche scientifique, Centre d'études supérieures de civilisation médiévale, 1996), 229–58; Elizabeth Coatsworth, "The 'Robed Christ' in Pre-Conquest Sculptures of the Crucifixion," *Anglo-Saxon England* 29 (2000): 153–76; Egon Warners, "Ok Dani gaerdi kristna: Der grosse Jellingstein im Spiegel ottonischer Kunst," *Frühmittelalterliche Studien* 34 (2000): 132–58.

37. The visual conflation of the cross and the tree of life first appears at the end of the tenth century. One example close to Hildesheim is a sacramentary fragment from Corvey (Leipzig, Universitätsbibliothek, Rep. I 4° 57, fol. 1v). It portrays a serpent climbing up the hewn timber of the green cross. In *Bernward und das Zeitalter*, 2:407–10, VI-68. On the history of the motif, see Romuald Bauerreiss, *Arbor vitae: Der "Lebensbaum" und seine Verwendung in Liturgie, Kunst und Brauchtum des Abendlandes* (Munich: Neuer Filser-Verlag, 1938). It is also a literary trope. See Thomas N. Hall, "The Cross as Green Tree in the *Vindicta Salvatoris* and the Green Rod of Moses in *Exodus*," *English Studies: A Journal of English Language and Literature* 72 (1991): 297–307.

38. *Mise[g?]ratio xpi / Redemptio mundi.* Kahsnitz sees the first word as *misegratio*, while acknowledging the strangeness of the word and that the space between the *s* and the *r* seems only to allow for one letter. The *g* hangs off of the *e* awkwardly and may be an error. Rainer Kahsnitz, "Inhalt und Aufbau der Handschrift,"

in *Kostbare Evangeliar*, 42–43. The meaning of the
inscription, however, is clear despite this possible error.
Both lines appear in prayers addressed to the cross
in this period. André Wilmart, "Prières médiévales
pour l'adoration de la croix," *Ephemerides liturgicae* 46
(1932): 22–65.

39. Brenk, *Tradition und Neuerung*, 55–60. Christe,
Vision de Matthieu.

40. Kühnel, *End of Time*, chap. 4. For more on
this, see also Rachel Fulton, *From Judgment to Passion:
Devotion to Christ and the Virgin Mary, 800–1200*
(New York: Columbia University Press, 2002); Richard
Landes, *Relics, Apocalypse, and the Deceits of History:
Ademar of Chabannes, 989–1034* (Cambridge, Mass.:
Harvard University Press, 1995), and Landes, "The Fear
of an Apocalyptic Year 1000: Augustinian Historio-
graphy, Medieval and Modern," *Speculum* 75 (2000):
97–145.

41. For a discussion of diagrams that combine
the quincunx in a square with the cross as an eschatological motif, see Kühnel, *End of Time*, esp. 52–62 and
148–59. On how medieval diagrams help visualize the
nature of Christ, see Herbert L. Kessler, "Images of
Christ and Communication with God," in *Comunicare
et significare nell'alto Medioevo: 15–20 aprile 2004* (Spoleto: Centro italiano di studi sull'alto medioevo, 2005),
1:1099–136.

42. Olivier Boulnois, *Au delà de l'image: Une
archéologie du visuel au Moyen-Âge V^e–XVIe siècle*
(Paris: Seuil, 2008).

43. Deshman, "Another Look"; Schapiro,
"The Image of the Disappearing Christ."

44. See the discussion in Deshman, "Another
Look," 538.

45. Hamburger, *St. John the Divine*, esp. 185–203.

46. Robert Deshman, *The Benedictional of Aethelwold* (Princeton: Princeton University Press, 1995),
109–14 and 177–79, and Jennifer O'Reilly, "St. John as
a Figure of the Contemplative Life: Text and Image
in the Art of the Anglo-Saxon Benedictine Reform,"
in *St. Dunstan: His Life, Times, and Cult*, ed. Nigel
Ramsay, Margaret Sparks, and Tim Tatton-Brown
(Woodbridge: Boydell Press, 1992), 165–85. Examples

from the period that identify John the Evangelist as
a priest range in type from a picture showing John
celebrating Mass in a sacramentary produced in Fulda
around 975 (Göttingen, Universitätstbibliothek, MS 231,
fol. 15v; repr. in Henry Mayr-Harting, *Ottonian Book
Illumination: An Historical Study* [London: H. Miller,
1991], 2:130, fig. 81), to a pair of ivory clasps made in
Italy around 1100. For this and other medieval depictions of the Evangelist as either a deacon or priest, see
Hamburger, *St. John the Divine*, figs. 10, 18, and 61. See
also Ernst Zeh, "Johannes Evangelist im Priestergewand: Eine ikonographische Vorstudie," *Jahrbuch für
das Bistum Mainz* 6 (1951–54): 254–65.

47. Hamburger, *St. John the Divine*, 65–82.

48. This derives from Early Christian painting,
and numerous Carolingian pictures of the Ascension
show Christ striding up a hill in this way, remaining
partially in contact with the earth. For example, in the
San Paolo Bible (Rome, Monastery of San Paolo fuori
le mura, Bible, fol. 292v), the sole of Christ's left foot
is visible and the toes of his right foot depart from the
earth. Joachim E. Gaehde, "La decorazione: Le miniature," in *Commentario della Bibbia di San Paolo fuori
le mura* (Rome: Istituto poligrafico e Zecca dello Stato,
Libreria dello Stato, 1993); Kessler, "Images of Christ,"
1128, fig. 33.

49. Deshman, "Another Look," 538–40.

50. As he does on Bernward's bronze doors, for
example: see *Bernward und das Zeitalter*, 2:503–12,
no. VII-33.

51. Kahsnitz, "Inhalt und Aufbau," 46–47. The
Transfiguration in the Uta Codex, for example, uses
the same open-armed pose; see Cohen, *Uta Codex*,
fig. 79. Another contemporary manuscript, produced
in Echternach, portrays Christ in the same way, but
in the context of an Ascension, also a moment that
revealed Christ's divine nature (Nuremberg, Germanisches Nationalmuseum Bibliothek, MS 156 142,
fol. 112r; reproduced in Rainer Kahsnitz and Elisabeth
Rücker, eds., *Das Goldene Evangelienbuch von Echternach: Codex Aureus Epternacensis Hs 156142 aus
dem Germanischen Nationalmuseum Nürnberg*, vol. 1
[Faksimileband] [Frankfurt am Main: S. Fischer Verlag

in Zusammenarbeit mit Verlag Müller und Schindler, 1982], fol. 112).

52.   For the history of the celebration of the Raising of Lazarus during the Feast of Lent, see Daniel Saulnier, "La résurrection de Lazare," *Études grégoriennes* 25 (1997): 7–11.

53.   On Lazarus as a type for Christ, see Moshe Barasch, "Das Bild des Unsichtbaren: Zu den frühen Christusbildern," *Visible Religion* 2 (1983): 1–13.

54.   Jan Stanislaw Partyka, *La résurrection de Lazare dans les monuments funéraires des nécropoles chrétiennes à Rome: Peintures, mosaïques et décor des épitaphes; Étude archéologique, iconographique et iconologique* (Warsaw: Zakład Archeologii Śródziemnomorskiej Polskiej Akademii Nauk, 1993). On Christianity's attitudes toward death as apparent in pictures, see Paul Binski, *Medieval Death: Ritual and Representation* (Ithaca: Cornell University Press, 1996).

55.   See especially the discussion of the writings of Berno of Reichenau, Rather of Verona, Atto of Vercelli, and the text *Sermo de informatione episcoporum* in Mariaux, "Bishop as Artist," 157–59.

CHAPTER 4

1.   On the varied modes of haptic perception, see Mark Paterson, *Senses of Touch: Haptics, Affects, and Technologies* (Oxford: Berg, 2007).

2.   Ademar of Chabannes's (d. 1034) description of (or instructions for making) a small crucifix illustrates the sensitivity of medieval patrons, viewers, and artists to minute details of iconography. Among other elements, Ademar carefully describes the number of hairs to be carved on each side of Christ's head as well as the shape of the eye, eyelid, and eyebrow and mentions that the left shoulder and arm should be slightly higher than the right. The full text is edited and translated into German by Bernhard Bischoff, *Anecdota Novissima: Texte des vierten bis sechzehnten Jahrhunderts* (Stuttgart: Hiersemann, 1984), 226–32.

3.   Gertrud Schiller, *Ikonographie der christlichen Kunst* ([Gütersloh]: Gütersloher Verlagshaus G. Mohn, 1986), 3:276–288.

4.   Robert Deshman, "Another Look at the Disappearing Christ: Corporeal and Spiritual Vision in Early Medieval Images," *Art Bulletin* 79 (1997), esp. 537–8.

5.   This Augustinian interpretation remained popular in the tenth and eleventh centuries, appearing, for example, in the "Sermo in veneratione sanctae Mariae Magdalenae" generally attributed to Odo of Cluny, although Dominique Iogna-Prat suggests that the work belongs to the intellectual environment of Vezelay and may date anytime between the mid-ninth and mid-eleventh century. See Iogna-Prat, "La Madeleine du *Sermo in veneratione sanctae Mariae Magdalenae* attribué à Odon de Cluny," *Mélanges de l'École française de Rome: Moyen Âge* 104 (1992): 37–67. Suffice it to say that this Augustinian idea was, in the Middle Ages, a conventional and oft-repeated interpretation of the Noli me tangere.

6.   These ideas were picked up by later commentators such as Leo the Great, Maximus of Turin, Cesarius of Arles, and (especially important for the Anglo-Saxons) Bede. Deshman, "Another Look," 534nn114–19. See also Kessler, "Images of Christ," 293–328.

7.   Constance Classen, *Worlds of Sense: Exploring the Senses in History and Across Cultures* (London: Routledge, 1993); Robert Jütte, *Geschichte der Sinne: Von der Antike bis zum Cyberspace* (Munich: Beck, 2000). On the representation of the senses in art, see Carl Nordenfalk, "Les cinq sens dans l'art du moyen âge," *Revue de l'art* 34 (1976): 17–28, and Nordenfalk, "The Five Senses in Late Medieval and Renaissance Art," *Journal of the Warburg and Courtauld Institutes* 48 (1985): 1–22.

8.   Deshman, "Another Look," esp. 537–38.

9.   It is common for art historians to privilege the investigation of visual perception over the other senses, although this trend has shifted somewhat in the last decade. A particularly fruitful area of research has been on synaesthesia in the Byzantine liturgical experience of icons. Liz James, "Senses and Sensibility in Byzantium," *Art History* 27 (2004): 522–37; Bissera V. Pentcheva, "The Performative Icon," *Art Bulletin* 88 (2006): 631–55, and Pentcheva, *The Sensual Icon: Space, Ritual, and the Senses in Byzantium* (University

Park: The Pennsylvania State University Press, 2010). Elizabeth Sears has noted the pictorialization of hearing in a Western manuscript, the Utrecht Psalter, in "The Iconography of Auditory Perception in the Early Middle Ages: On Psalm Illustration and Psalm Exegesis," in *The Second Sense: Studies in Hearing and Musical Judgment from Antiquity to the Seventeenth Century*, ed. Charles Burnett (London: The Warburg Institute, 1991): 19–38. Other scholars have searched for tactile and gustatory experiences of and in works of art: see Volker Schier and Corine Schleif, "Seeing and Singing, Touching and Tasting the Holy Lance: The Power and Politics of Embodied Religious Experiences in Nuremberg, 1424–1524," in *Signs of Change: Transformations of Christian Traditions and Their Representation in the Arts, 1000–2000*, ed. Nils Petersen, Claus Cluver, and Nicholas Bell (New York: Rodopi, 2004), 401–87; Glenn W. Most, *Doubting Thomas* (Cambridge, Mass.: Harvard University Press, 2005). Jacqueline Jung considers the description of a tactile visionary experience in "The Tactile and the Visionary: Notes on the Place of Sculpture in the Medieval Imagination," in *Looking Beyond: Visions, Dreams, and Insights in Medieval Art and History*, ed. Colum Hourihane (University Park: The Pennsylvania State University Press, 2010), 203–40.

10.   The programmatic emphasis on sight and touch together in the Bernward Gospels may seem surprising in that it excludes the other senses: taste, smell, and especially hearing. The latter is more commonly paired with sight in hierarchies of the senses. Yet in the different optical theories formulated in antiquity that influenced the medieval understanding of sight, vision operates in a process of emission or extramission. Consequently, vision involves contact. The eye "touches" what it sees. As Augustine explained it in *De trinitate,* "We see bodies through the eyes of the body, because . . . the rays shine forth through those eyes and touch whatever we discern" (per oculos enim corporis corpora videmus, quia radios qui per eos emicant et quidquid cernimus tangunt). Augustine, *De trinitate*, IX, 3, 3, in *Opera Omnia*, ed. Cornelius Mayer (Charlottesville: InteLex, 2000), trans. as *The Works*

of Saint Augustine: A Translation for the Twenty-First Century, ed. Boniface Ramsey, 2nd release (New York: New City Press, 1991–), Past Masters Database, http://library.nlx.com, © 2002. Margaret Miles argues that the extramission theory also informed Augustine's model for spiritual sight; see Miles, "Vision: The Eye of the Body and the Eye of the Mind in Saint Augustine's 'De trinitate' and 'Confessions,'" *Journal of Religion* 63 (1983): 125–42. What may also play a role in this pairing is the etymological understanding of the terms for the optic and haptic senses transmitted through medieval encyclopedias. Isidore of Seville, whose *Etymologies* was among the most copied texts of the Middle Ages, positions vision as the most vivid and important sense, but emphasizes that touch allows the sensing of what cannot be judged with the other senses: "*tactus* is so called, because it strokes [*pertractare*] and 'makes contact' [*tangere*, ppl. *tactus*], and distributes the power of this sense through all the limbs. *Indeed, we examine with the sense of touch what we cannot judge with the rest of the senses*" (emphasis mine). Isidore, *Etymologies*, bk. 11, chap. 23; English trans. Stephen A. Barney et al., *The Etymologies of Isidore of Seville* (Cambridge: Cambridge University Press, 2006), 232. On the transmission of Isidore's text, see the translator's introduction (24–26).

11.   For more on this phrase, see Daniel Heller-Roazen, "The Matter of Language: Guilhem de Peitieus and the Platonic Tradition," *Modern Language Notes* 113 (1998): 851–80, esp. 851–60. Identifying Calcidius as a historical person has proved difficult. An eleventh-century copy of the *Timaeus* includes a dedication to Bishop Osius of Cordoba, an advisor to Constantine. This has led some scholars to assume that Calcidius wrote in fourth-century Spain. However, Calcidius's name does not appear in Isidore of Seville's list of Spanish writers, a strange omission for the writer of a text as popular as the *Timaeus*. Stephen Gersh, *Middle Platonism and Neoplatonism: The Latin Tradition* (Notre Dame: University of Notre Dame Press, 1986), 2:421–33.

12.   "Fit tamen evanida quaedam eius attrectatio sine contagio, nec ipsius mage quam eorum quae intra

ipsam sunt corporum; quae cum sentiuntur, suspicio nascitur ipsam sentiri, propterea quod ex his speciebus quas recipit formari, cum sit informis, videtur. Itaque sensus quidem specierum in silva constitutarum clarus est, ipsius autem silvae, quae speciebus subiacet, obscurus et consensus potius quam sensus est. Ergo quia silvestria quidem sentiuntur, silva vero minime sentitur natura propria, sed propter silvestria cum isdem sentiri putatur, fit huius modi sensus incertus, praeclareque dictum 'silvam sine sensu tangentium tangi' quia puro sensu minime sentiatur. . . . Sic igitur etiam silva contigua quidem est, quia contingi putatur cum ea quae principaliter continguntur sub sensus veniunt, sed contactus eius provenit ex accidenti verum hoc ipsum sine sensu, quia ipsa per se neque tactu sentitur neque ceteris sensibus." *Timaeus a Calcidio Translatus Commentarioque Instructus*, ed. Jan Hendrick Waszink (London: The Warburg Institute; Leiden: Brill, 1962), paragraph 345, on pp. 336–38; English trans. J. C. M. van Winden, *Calcidius on Matter: His Doctrine and Sources; A Chapter in the History of Platonism* (Leiden: Brill, 1959), 221–22.

13.   Of the seventeen extant copies containing both Calcidius's translation and his commentary, at least eight were produced in Germany. *Timaeus a Calcidio Translatus*, cvi–cxxxi, clxxxvii–clxxxviii.

14.   Margaret Gibson, "The Study of the *Timaeus* in the Eleventh and Twelfth Centuries," *Pensamiento* 25 (1969): 183–94; Anna Somfai, "The Eleventh-Century Shift in the Reception of Plato's *Timaeus* and Calcidius' *Commentary*," *Journal of the Warburg and Courtauld Institutes* 65 (2002): 1–21; Paul E. Dutton, "Medieval Approaches to Calcidius," in *Plato's "Timaeus" as Cultural Icon*, ed. Gretchen J. Reydams-Schils (Notre Dame: University of Notre Dame Press, 2003), 183–205.

15.   Bruce S. Eastwood, "Calcidius' Commentary on Plato's *Timaeus* in Latin Astronomy of the Ninth to Eleventh Centuries," in *Between Demonstration and Imagination: Essays in the History of Science and Philosophy Presented to John D. North*, ed. Lodi Nauta and Arjo Vanderjagt (Leiden: Brill, 1999), 171–209, and his "Invention and Reform in Latin Planetary Astronomy," in *Latin Culture in the Eleventh Century: Proceedings*

of the *Third International Conference on Medieval Latin Studies, Cambridge, September 9–12, 1998*, ed. Michael W. Herren, Christopher J. McDonough, and Ross G. Arthur (Turnhout: Brepols, 2002), 1:282–90.

16.   Gillian Evans and Alison M. Peden, "Natural Science and the Liberal Arts in Abbo of Fleury's Commentary," *Viator* 16 (1985): 109–27. See also the articles in *Gerberto: Scienza, storia et mito; Atti del Gerberti Symposium (Bobbio 25–27 luglio 1983)* (Bobbio: Archivi storici bobiensi, 1985). This is important in tracing the possible source of Bernward of Hildesheim's knowledge of Calcidius because of the bishop's close connections to the imperial court. Hans Jakob Schuffels, "Bernward Bischof von Hildesheim: Eine biographische Skizze," in *Bernward und das Zeitalter*, 1:29–46, with selected references.

17.   Fidel Rädl, "Calcidius und Paulus begründen ein Vermächtnis: Zu Bernwards Dotationsurkunde für St. Michael in Hildesheim," in Herren, McDonough, and Arthur, *Latin Culture in the Eleventh Century*, 2:328–49.

18.   Bruce S. Eastwood, "Plato and Circumsolar Planetary Motion in the Middle Ages," *Archives d'histoire doctrinale et littéraire du Moyen Âge* 60 (1993): 7–26; Eastwood, "Calcidius' Commentary"; Eastwood, "Invention and Reform."

19.   Herbert Schade, "Der 'Himmlische Mensch': Zur anthropologischen Struktur des biblischen Menschbildes in der Kunst," in *Christus und Maria: Menschensohn und Gottesmutter*, ed. Victor H. Elbern (Berlin: Mann, 1998), 18–27; Anton von Euw, "Die Majestas-Domini-Bilder der ottonischen Kölner Malerschule im Licht des platonischen Weltbildes: Codex 192 der Kölner Dombibliothek," in *Kaiserin Theophanu: Begegnung des Ostens und Westens um die Wende des ersten Jahrtausends: Gedenkschrift des Kölner Schnütgen-Museums zum 1000. Todesjahr der Kaiserin*, ed. Anton von Euw, Peter Schreiner, and Gudrun Sporbeck (Cologne: Schnütgen-Museum, 1991), 1:379–400.

20.   *Timaeus a Calcidio Translatus*, paragraph 67 on p. 114; Adam Cohen, *The Uta Codex: Art, Philosophy,*

and Reform in Eleventh-Century Germany (University Park: The Pennsylvania State University Press, 2000), fig. 34. Von Euw, "Majestas-Domini-Bilder." On the impact of cosmological diagrams on pictures of Christ Enthroned, see Bianca Kühnel, *The End of Time in the Order of Things: Science and Eschatology in Early Medieval Art* (Regensburg: Schnell & Steiner, 2003).

21. *Timaeus a Calcidio Translatus*, 32–52. The following discussion is indebted to Heller-Roazen, "Matter of Language."

22. *Timaeus a Calcidio Translatus*, paragraph 309, on p. 314.

23. Plato, *Timaeus,* in *Platonis Opera*, ed. John Burnet, vol. 4 (Oxford: Oxford University Press, 1903), lines 50d–e.

24. *Timaeus a Calcidio Translatus*, paragraph 309, on p. 314.

25. Ibid., paragraph 288, on p. 292; paragraph 309, on p. 314.

26. *Timaeus*, 52b.

27. The preface to John's gospel makes the same point. Donatien de Bruyne, *Préfaces de la Bible latine* (Namur: A. Godenne, 1920), 173. Medieval illustrations to Genesis translate the concept into pictorial form. Harry Bober, "In Principio: Creation Before Time," in *De artibus opuscula XL: Essays in Honor of Erwin Panofsky*, ed. Millard Meiss (New York: New York University Press, 1961), 1:13–28; Richard Putney, "Creatio et Redemptio: The Genesis Monogram of the St. Hubert Bible" (Ph.D. diss., University of Delaware, 1985). Frontispieces to John adopt similar strategies. Kühnel, *End of Time*, esp. 185–98 and 239–47.

28. Michael Frassetto, "Reaction and Reform: Reception of Heresy in Arras and Aquitaine in the Early Eleventh Century," *Catholic Historical Review* 83 (1997): 385–400.

29. Gregory the Great, *Moralia in Job*, in *S. Gregorii Magni Moralia in Job,* ed. Marc Adriaen, CCSL 143A (Turnhout: Brepols, 1979–85), pt. 3, bk. 14, chaps. 54–58, on pp. 739–47. Medieval commentators interpreted the same passage also as a promise of Christians' resurrection on the Day of Judgment, so that just as in the visionary pictures, the representation of the haptic perception of Christ in the Noli me tangere may relate to an underlying eschatological concern in the manuscript's pictorial program.

30. *Moralia in Job*, CCSL 143A, pt. 3, bk. 14, esp. chap. 56, on pp. 743–44. The idea of resurrection *in carne* contrasts with other ideas, circulating since late antiquity, that either dematerialized the resurrected body or believed it to be materially transformed. Caroline Walker Bynum, *The Resurrection of the Body in Western Christianity, 200–1336* (New York: Columbia University Press, 1995).

31. "Scio enim, quod Redempt[or] meu[s] [vi]vit, et in novissimo die de terra surrecturus sum, et rursum circumdabor pelle mea, et in carne mea videbo D[eu]m salvatorem meum, qu[e]m visurus sum ego ipse, et oculi mei conspecturi sunt et non ali[us]. Reposita est haec spes in sinu meo."

32. Ingrid Westerhoff, "Der moralisierte Judas: Mittelalterliche Legende, Typologie, Allegorie im Bild," *Aachener Kunstblätter* 61 (1995): 85–156; Irit Kleiman, "The Life and Times of Judas Iscariot: Form and Function," *Medievalia et humanistica*, n.s., 33 (2007): 15–40. In the roughly contemporary Quinity of Winchester (ca. 1023–65), Judas serves as an example of those who refuse the reality of Christ and the Trinity. Judith A. Kidd, "The Quinity of Winchester Reconsidered," *Studies in Iconography* 7/8 (1981): 21–33.

33. Augustine, Sermo LXXI, chap. 11. Additional critical passages on Judas in Augustine are *In Joannis Evangelium Tractatus*, bk. 50, chap. 10; both in *Opera Omnia*, ed. Cornelius Mayer (Charlottesville: InteLex, 2000), trans. as *The Works of Saint Augustine: A Translation for the Twenty-First Century*, ed. Boniface Ramsey, 2nd release (New York: New City Press, 1991–), Past Masters Database, http://library.nlx.com, © 2002.

34. This idea was already important in Carolingian debates about the Eucharist. Celia Chazelle, *The Crucified God in the Carolingian Era: Theology and Art of Christ's Passion* (Cambridge: Cambridge University Press, 2001), esp. 216–17.

35. Saint Paul equated avariciousness with idolatry, an association medieval theologians repeated with

a more literal emphasis on how being a slave to money made men idolators. William Diebold, "The Carolingian Idol: Exegetes and Idols," in *Seeing the Invisible in Late Antiquity and the Early Middle Ages*, ed. Giselle de Nie, Karl F. Morrison, and Marco Mostert (Turnhout: Brepols, 2005), 445–61. In the eleventh century, simony in general began to be characterized more frequently as a heresy, such as in Ademar of Chabannes's *Chronicon*, ed. Pascal Bourgain, Richard Landes, and Georges Pon, CCCM 129 (Turnhout: Brepols, 1999), 178–79. The idea gained stronger currency after the mid-eleventh century and was a particular concern of the twelfth century. Jean Leclercq, "Simoniaca heresis," *Studi Gregoriani* 1 (1947): 523–30.

36.   For a general overview of baptismal iconography, see Gertrud Schiller, *Ikonographie der christlichen Kunst* ([Gütersloh]: Gütersloher Verlagshaus G. Mohn, 1966), 1:137–52, esp. 148, plates 344–82.

37.   Byzantine commentary used Christ's human nature in this way as a justification for John's touch at the Baptism. Two hymnographers of the sixth century, Romanos and Sophronius of Jerusalem, emphasized how John's testimony was based on a physical, sensory experience. John feared to touch Christ and be consumed by his divinity, but Christ reassured John by recalling his human incarnation. Romanos concluded by declaring Christ's words: "For you will achieve honor from this such as did not fall to the lot of the angels; for I shall make you greater than all the prophets. No one of them saw me clearly, but rather in figures, shadows and dreams. But today you see, you touch the unapproachable light." Romanos, *Hymnes*, ed. and trans. José Grosdidier de Matons (Paris: Cerf, 1965), 2:248–50; English trans. based on Marjorie Carpenter, *Kontakia of Romanos, Byzantine Melodist* (Columbia: University of Missouri Press, 1970–72), 1:53–54, quoted in Kathleen Corrigan, "The Witness of John the Baptist on an Early Byzantine Icon in Kiev," *Dumbarton Oaks Papers* 42 (1988): 4. For Sophronius's hymns, see Sophronius of Jerusalem, "On the Holy Baptism," in *Analekta hierosolymitikes stachyologias*, ed. Athanasios Papadopoulos-Kerameus (1891; repr., Brussels: Culture et Civilisation, 1963),

5:158. It is impossible to know whether Bernward could have been familiar with these aspects of the early Byzantine construction of John's witness to Christ's dual nature, or whether the bishop developed such ideas independently. The issue of Byzantine influence on Ottonian Germany in the late tenth and early eleventh centuries is still hotly debated and tends to revolve around the question of Otto II's Greek wife, Theophanu. For a good introduction to both sides of the debate, see the collection of essays in Adelbert Davids, ed., *Empress Theophano: Byzantium and the West at the Turn of the First Millennium* (Cambridge: Cambridge University Press, 1995); Von Euw, Schreiner, and Sporbeck, *Kaiserin Theophanu: Begegnung;* and Von Euw and Schreiner, eds., *Kunst im Zeitalter der Kaiserin Theophanu: Akten des internationalen Colloquiums veranstaltet vom Schnütgen-Museum, Köln, 13.–15. Juni 1991* (Cologne: Locher, 1993).

38.   Schiller, *Ikonographie*, 1:137–52, esp. plates 344–82.

39.   Johann K. Eberlein, *Apparitio regis, revelatio veritatis: Studien zur Darstellung des Vorhangs in der bildenden Kunst von der Spätantike bis zum Ende des Mittelalters* (Wiesbaden: Reichert, 1982), 85n–86n, with further bibliography.

40.   Medieval texts frequently paired the two Johns as joint heirs in Christ. Christian iconography also consistently represented the Baptist and Evangelist together. For more on the two Johns, see Jeffrey Hamburger, *St. John the Divine: The Deified Evangelist in Medieval Art and Theology* (Berkeley: University of California Press, 2002), 65–82; Gregor Martin Lechner, "Johannes Evangelist und Johannes der Täufer," in *Lexikon der christlichen Ikonographie*, ed. Engelbrecht Kirschbaum and Günter Bandmann (Rome: Herder, 1968–76), vol. 7, cols. 191–94; Christian Heck, "Les deux saints Jean: Étude de l'iconographie jumelée de Saint Jean-Baptiste et de Saint Jean-l'Évangeliste en Occident, des origines à la fin du moyen âge" (Ph.D. diss., Université de Provence, 1979), chap. 5, and Heck, "Le portail à l'agneau de la cathédrale de Fribourg-en-Brisgau," in *Cahiers alsaciens d'archéologie, d'art et d'histoire* 32 (1989): 165–76, esp. 167.

41. The metaphor becomes so conventional in the Middle Ages that by the fourteenth century, a child's first reading primer is described in terms of a man's corpse nailed to a board. Karma Lochrie, *Margery Kempe and Translations of the Flesh* (Philadelphia: University of Pennsylvania Press, 1991), 171. Pictures also connect Christ's body to text enfleshed on the parchment page. Michael Camille, "Sensations of the Page: Imaging Technologies and Medieval Illuminated Manuscripts," in *The Iconic Page in Manuscript, Print, and Digital Culture*, ed. George Bornstein and Theresa Tinkle (Ann Arbor: University of Michigan Press, 1998), fig. 2.

42. Later medieval commentators focused on this laborious, violent process as part of explicating the book/body metaphor. In the words of a particularly vivid fifteenth-century English poem, the "Long Charter" of Christ, Christ on the cross is the stretched piece of vellum, the ink on the page is the blood running from his wounds, and the pens writing those inked letters are the tools of his torture. For more on this poem, see Mary Carruthers, "'*Ut pictura poesis*': The Rhetoric of Verbal and Visual Images," *Mentalities/Mentalités 7* (1990): 1–6. On the comparison of vellum and ink to the body and blood of Christ, see also Dieter Richter, "Die Allegorie der Pergamentbearbeitung: Beziehungen zwischen handwerklichen Vorgängen und der geistlichen Bildersprache des Mittelalters," in *Fachliteratur des Mittelalters: Festschrift für Gerhard Eis*, ed. Gundolf Keil et al. (Stuttgart: Metzler, 1968), 83–92.

43. Such as in the dedicatory text of the Carolingian Godescalc Evangeliary. Wilhelm Koehler, *Die karolingischen Miniaturen*, vol. 2, *Die Hofschule Karls des Grossen* (Berlin: Deutscher Verein für Kunstwissenschaft, 1958), 22–28; Beat Brenk, "Schriftlichkeit und Bildlichkeit in der Hofschule Karls des Grossens," in *Testo e immagine nell'alto medioevo: 15–21 aprile 1993* (Spoleto: Centro italiano di studi sull'alto medioevo, 1994), 631–82; Ulrich Ernst, "Farbe und Schrift im Mittelalter unter Berücksichtigung antiker Grundlagen und neuzeitlicher Rezeptionsformen," in *Testo e immagine*, 343–414; Bruno Reudenbach, *Das Godescalc-Evangelistar: Ein Buch für die Reformpolitik Karls des Grossen* (Frankfurt: Fischer-Taschenbuch-Verlag, 1998).

44. Jérôme Baschet, "Introduction: L'image-objet," in *L'image: Fonctions et usages des images dans l'Occident médiéval*, ed. Jérôme Baschet and Jean-Claude Schmitt (Paris: Le Léopard d'or, 1996), 7–57; Jean-Claude Bonne, "Entre l'image et la matière: La choséité du sacré en Occident," in *Les images dans les sociétés médiévales: Pour une histoire comparée; Actes du colloque international organisé par l'Institut historique belge de Rome en collaboration avec l'École française de Rome et l'Université libre de Bruxelles, Rome, Academia Belgica, 19–20 juin 1998*, ed. Jean-Michel Sansterre and Jean-Claude Schmitt (Brussels: Institut historique belge de Rome, 1999), 77–111; Herbert L. Kessler, "Matter," in *Seeing Medieval Art* (Orchard Park, N.Y.: Broadview Press, 2004), 19–44.

45. Diebold, "Carolingian Idol"; Beate Fricke, "Fallen Idols and Risen Saints: Western Attitudes Towards the Worship of Images and the 'cultura veterum deorum,'" in *Negating the Image: Case Studies in Iconoclasm*, ed. Anne McClanan and Jeffrey Johnson (Aldershot: Ashgate, 2005), 67–95; Carol Harrison, "Taking Creation for the Creator: Use and Enjoyment in Augustine's Theological Aesthetics," in *Idolatry: False Worship in the Bible, Early Judaism, and Christianity*, ed. Stephen C. Barton (London: T & T Clark, 2007), 179–97.

46. However, Cynthia Hahn argues that one consistent aspect of the Western response to relics seems to be a reluctance to touch that contrasts with the practices of the Eastern church. That reluctance can also apply to reliquaries. Hahn, "What Do Reliquaries Do for Relics?" *Numen* 57 (2010): 284–316, esp. 307–9.

47. "Res et imago duas fert ista notaque figuras / Effigiatus homo, Deus est signatus in auro"; translation taken from Herbert L. Kessler, "Image and Object: Christ's Dual Nature and the Crisis of Early Medieval Art," in *The Long Morning of Medieval Europe: New Directions in Early Medieval Studies*, ed. Jennifer R. Davis and Michael McCormick (Aldershot: Ashgate, 2008), 291–320. As Kessler points out, the seeds for the idea appear already in Carolingian art and relate to

intermittent debates about art in that period, on which see Thomas F. X. Noble, *Images, Iconoclasm, and the Carolingians* (Philadelphia: University of Pennsylvania Press, 2009), with citations to earlier bibliography. Yet on the whole, Ottonian examples of the trope are more explicit than Carolingian ones. It may relate to an Ottonian tendency to blur the careful distinctions Carolingian texts sought to draw between the matter of art and Christological bodies. Pierre-Alain Mariaux, "'Faire Dieu': Quelques remarques sur les relations entre confection eucharistique et creation d'image (IXᵉ–XIIᵉ siècles)," in *Ästhetik des Unsichtbaren: Bildtheorie und Bildgebrauch in der Vormoderne*, ed. David Ganz and Thomas Lentes (Berlin: Reimer, 2004), 95–112, and Mariaux, "The Bishop as Artist? The Eucharist and Image Theory Around the Millennium," in *The Bishop: Power and Piety at the First Millennium*, ed. Sean Gilsdorf (Münster: LIT-Verlag, 2004), 155–68.

48.   Frassetto, "Reaction and Reform."

49.   *Acta synodi Atrebatensis in Manichaeos*, chap. 13, PL 142.1304–6. Not long thereafter, Thiofrid of Echternach would insist that relics and their material containers, the reliquaries, were a single unit. Michael Camillo Ferrari, ed., *Thiofridi Abbatis Epternacensis: Flores Epytaphii Sanctorum* (Turnhout: Brepols, 1996), xxiii and xxviii; and "Gold und Asche: Reliquie und Reliquiare als Medien in Thiofrid von Echternachts 'Flores epytaphii sanctorum,'" in *Reliquiare im Mittelalter*, ed. Bruno Reudenbach and Gia Toussaint (Berlin: Akademie Verlag, 2005), 61–74.

50.   "Interim Gero, Agripinae sedis egreius provisor, obiit; de quo quia pauca prelibavi, quae tunc reservavi, paucis edicam. Hic crucifixum, quod nunc stat in media ecclesia, ubi ipse pausat, ex ligno fabricari studiose praecepit. Huius caput dum fissum videret, hoc summi artificis et ideo salubriori remedio nil de se presumens sic curavit. Dominici corporis procionem, unicum in cunctis necessitatibus solacium, et partem unam salutifere crucis coniugens pasuit in rimam et prostratus numen Domini flebiliter invocavity et surgens humilibenedictione integritatem promeruit." Thietmar of Merseburg, *Chronicon*,

ed. Robert Holtzmann, *Die Chronik des Bischofs Thietmar von Merseburg*, MGH SS rer. Germ. n.s. 9 (Berlin: Weidmann, 1935), bk. 3, chap. 2 on pp. 99–100; translation from David Warner, *Ottonian Germany: The Chronicon of Thietmar of Merseburg* (Manchester: Manchester University Press, 2001), 128. See also Annika E. Fisher, "Cross Altar and Crucifix in Ottonian Cologne," in *Decorating the Lord's Table: On the Dynamics Between Image and Altar in the Middle Ages*, ed. Søren Kaspersen and Erik Thunø (Copenhagen: Museum Tusculanum Press, University of Copenhagen, 2006), 43–62; Mariaux, "'Faire Dieu'" and "Bishop as Artist."

51.   "Bernwardus presul candelabrum hoc / puerum suum primo huius artis flore non auro non argento et tamen ut cernis conflare iubebat."

52.   Gregory the Great, *Homiliae in Hiezechihelem prophetam*, ed. Marc Adriaen, CCSL 142 (Turnhout: Brepols, 1971), Homilia 2.14, 25–26; Hrabanus Maurus, *Commentariorum in Ezechielem*, bk. 1, chap. 1, PL 110.503–4. Bruno of Segni, "Sermo I in Ascensione Dominica," *Sententiae*, bk. 4, chap. 12, PL 165.1013.

53.   Jennifer P. Kingsley, "VT CERNIS and the Materiality of Bernwardian Art," in *1000 Jahre St. Michael in Hildesheim: Kirche-Kloster-Stifter*, ed. Gerhard Lutz and Angela Weyer (Göttingen: Michael Imhof Verlag, 2012), 171–84.

54.   For Reichenau, see Walter Berschin and Johannes Staub, *Die Taten des Abtes Witigowo von der Reichenau (985–997): Eine zeitgenössische Biographie von Purchart von der Reichenau* (Sigmaringen: Thorbecke, 1992), verses 344–54; Jean-Michel Sansterre, "Vénération et utilisation apotropaïque de l'image à Reichenau vers la fin du Xᵉᵐᵉ siècle: Un témoignage des *gesta* de l'abbé Wittigowo," *Revue belge de philologie et d'histoire* 73 (1995): 281–85. On Dominic of Sora, see François Dolbeau, "Le dossier de saint Dominique de Sora, d'Albéric du Mont-Cassin à Jacques de Voragine," *Mélanges de l'École française de Rome: Moyen Âge* 102 (1990): 7–78, the miracle recounted in the eleventh-century text by Alberic on pp. 68–69; Jean-Michel Sansterre, "Un saint récent et son icône dans le Latin méridional au XIᵉ siècle: À propos d'un

miracle de Dominique de Sora," *Byzantinoslavica* 56 (1995): 447–52.

55. Paulinus of Nola, *Epistulae*, ed. William A. Hartel (Prague: Tempsky; Leipzig: Freytag, 1894), epistle 49 on p. 390; trans. Patrick Gerard Walsh, *The Letters of St. Paulinus of Nola* (Westminster, Md.: Newman Press, 1966), 2:258–75 with notes on 358–62, quotations from pp. 272–74.

56. Trans. George Englert McCracken, *Early Medieval Theology* (Philadelphia: Westminster Press, 1957), 382–99.

57. Rupert of Deutz, *De gloria et honore filii hominis. Super Mattheum*, ed. Hrabanus Haacke, CCCM 29 (Turnhout: Brepols, 1979), 382; Sara Lipton, "The Sweet Lean of His Head: Writing About Looking at the Crucifix in the High Middle Ages," *Speculum* 80 (2005): 1172–208, esp. 1175–79; Jung, "The Tactile and the Visionary."

58. Anthony Cutler first noted the wear on the ivory. Anthony Cutler, *The Hand of the Master: Craftsmanship, Ivory, and Society in Byzantium (9th–11th Centuries)* (Princeton: Princeton University Press, 1994), 34.

59. Cynthia Hahn, *Portrayed on the Heart: Narrative Effect in Pictorial Lives of Saints from the Tenth Through the Thirteenth Centuries* (Berkeley: University of California Press, 2001), 147–53.

60. Robert Deshman, *The Benedictional of Aethelwold* (Princeton: Princeton University Press, 1995), 27–30, 48–50, and 145.

61. Cynthia Hahn, "The Voices of the Saints: Speaking Reliquaries," *Gesta* 36 (1997): 20–31, esp. 27.

CONCLUSION

1. Hans Jakob Schuffels, "Bernward Bischof von Hildesheim: Eine biographische Skizze," in *Bernward und das Zeitalter*, 1:29–43, and more recently Christine Wulf, "Bernward von Hildesheim, ein Bischof auf dem Weg zur Heiligkeit," *Concilium medii aevi* 11 (2008): 1–19. On Bernward's time at court, see Heinrich Fichtenau, "Diplomatiker und Urkundenforscher," *Mitteilungen des Instituts für Österreichische Geschichtsforschung* 100 (1992): 9–49; Hans Jakob Schuffels, "*Aulicus scriba doctus*: Bernward in der Königskanzlei," in *Bernward und das Zeitalter*, 2:247–254.

2. C. Stephen Jaeger, *The Origins of Courtliness: Civilizing Trends and the Formation of Courtly Ideals, 923–1210* (Philadelphia: University of Pennsylvania Press, 1985), and Jaeger, *The Envy of Angels: Cathedral Schools and Social Ideas in Medieval Europe, 950–1200* (Philadelphia: University of Pennsylvania Press, 1994). Jaeger's conclusions suggest that Bernward's education in a cathedral school and his courtly training would have emphasized the liberal arts in intellectual discourse and thus informed his interest in the *Timaeus,* discussed in chapter 4 of this book. On the possibility that the decoration of the Bernward Gospels engages with a courtly visual vocabulary, see Stephen Wagner, "Silken Parchments: Design, Context, Patronage, and Function of Textile-Inspired Pages in Ottonian and Salian Manuscripts" (Ph.D. diss., University of Delaware, 2004), esp. 143–62; Jennifer P. Kingsley, "The Bernward Gospels: Structuring *memoria* in Eleventh-Century Germany" (Ph.D. diss., Johns Hopkins University, 2007), esp. 67–116. See also the discussion about the use of Byzantine ivories by episcopal patrons in William North and Anthony Cutler, "Ivories, Inscriptions, and Episcopal Self-Consciousness in the Ottonian Empire: Berthold of Toul and the Berlin Hodegetria," *Gesta* 42 (2003): 1–17. For a political interpretation of Bernward's bronze doors, see Adam Cohen and Anne Derbes, "Bernward and Eve at Hildesheim," *Gesta* 40 (2001): 19–38.

3. On the Gandersheim conflict, see Hans Goetting, *Das Bistum Hildesheim,* vol. 1, *Das Reichsunmittelbare Kanonissenstift Gandersheim* (Berlin: W. de Gruyter, 1973), and Knut Görich, "Der Gandersheimer Streit zur Zeit Ottos III: Ein Konflikt um die Metropolitanrechte des Erzbischofs Willigis von Mainz," *Zeitschrift der Savigny-Stiftung für Rechtsgeschichte: Kanonistische Abteilung* 79 (1993): 56–94.

4. Karl Janicke, ed., *Die Urkundenbuch des Hochstifts Hildesheim und seiner Bischöfe* (1896; repr., Osnabrück: Zeller, 1965), 1:38, no. 49 and 60, no. 64; Rudolf Pokorny, "Reichsbischof, Kirchenrecht und Diözesanverwaltung um das Jahr 1000," in *Bernward und das Zeitalter*, 1:113–119.

5.   Francis Tschan, *Saint Bernward of Hildesheim* (Notre Dame: University of Notre Dame, 1942–52), 1:151–52.

6.   Wagner, "Silken Parchments."

7.   Frauke Steenbock, *Die kirchliche Prachteinband im frühen Mittelalter: Von den Anfängen bis zum Beginn der Gotik* (Berlin: Deutscher Verlag für Kunstwissenschaft, 1965), 118–19, nos. 40–41; 121–22, no. 43; 133–36, nos. 51–52. Each of these is associated with figures with some connection to the court. In addition, the book cover on p. 138, no. 54 (Paris, Bibliothèque nationale, lat. 10514) may have been donated by one of the monks in Poussay, or by the founding bishop, Berthold of Toul; Bishop Bernward's relative Abbot Erkanbald, future bishop of Metz, may have been involved in commissioning the cover of a sacramentary, p. 151, no. 61 (Bamberg, Staatliche Bibliothek, Lit. 1 A II 52), and see other examples on 157–60, nos. 65–66; 163–67, nos. 71–74. Several ivories falling in this category were not cataloged by Steenbock. For example, Bishop Sigebert of Minden used two Byzantine ivories on book covers (ivory in private collection; and Berlin, Staatsbibliothek, MS theol. lat. qu. 3). See Anthony Cutler, "A Byzantine Triptych in Medieval Germany and Its Modern Recovery," *Gesta* 37 (1998): 3–12. Another ivory appears on the cover of the so-called Otto-Adelheid Gospels, which mentions Pope Sylvester II, Emperor Otto III, and the Abbess of Quedlinburg in a prayer at the beginning of the manuscript (Quedlinburg, St. Servatii-Domgemeinde), in Arne Effenberger, "Byzantinische Kunstwerke im Besitz deutscher Kaiser, Bishöfe und Klöster im Zeitalter der Ottonen," *Bernward und das Zeitalter,* 1:145–159.

8.   Klaus Gereon Beuckers, "Bernward und Willigis: Zu einem Aspekt der bernwardinischen Stiftungen," in *1000 Jahre St. Michael in Hildesheim: Kirche-Kloster-Stifter*, ed. Gerhard Lutz and Angela Weyer (Göttingen: Michael Imhof Verlag, 2012), 142–52.

9.   Karl A. O. Henkel, *Die Bernwardinische Kunst: Bischof Bernward und seine Werke* (Hildesheim: F. Borgmeyer, 1937); Rudolf Wesenberg, *Bernwardinische Plastik: Zur ottonischen Kunst unter Bischof Bernward von Hildesheim* (Berlin: Deutscher Verein für Kunstwissenschaft, 1955); *Bernwardinische Kunst: Bericht über ein wissenschaftliches Symposium in Hildesheim vom 10.10. bis 13.10.1984* (Göttingen: Goltze, 1988).

10.   Jaeger, *Origins of Courtliness*; Jaeger, *Envy of Angels.*

11.   Wilhelm Evers, *Grundfragen der Siedlungsgeographie und Kulturlandschaften im Hildesheimer Land* (Bremen: Dorn, 1957); Wolfgang Heinemann, *Das Bistum Hildesheim im Kräftespiel der Reichs- und Territorialpolitik* (Hildesheim: Lax, 1968); Karl Leyser, *Rule and Conflict in Early Medieval Society: Ottonian Saxony* (Bloomington: Indiana University Press, 1979); Christopher Carroll, "Bishoprics of Saxony in the First Century After Christianization," *Early Medieval Europe* 8 (1999): 219–45.

12.   Éric Palazzo, *L'évêque et son image: L'illustration du pontifical au Moyen Âge* (Turnhout: Brepols, 1999).

13.   Pierre-Alain Mariaux, *Warmond d'Ivrée et ses images: Politique et création iconographique autour de l'an mil* (Bern: Lang, 2002).

14.   Robert Deshman, *The Benedictional of Aethelwold* (Princeton: Princeton University Press, 1995).

15.   Evan A. Gatti, "Developing an Iconography of the Episcopacy: Liturgical Portraiture and Episcopal Politics in Tenth- and Eleventh-Century Manuscripts" (Ph.D. diss., University of North Carolina at Chapel Hill, 2005); Gatti, "Building the Body of the Church: A Bishop's Blessing in the Benedictional of Engilmar of Parenzo," in Ott and Jones, *Bishop Reformed,* 92–121.

16.   Evan A. Gatti, "In a Space Between: Warmund of Ivrea and the Problem of (Italian) Ottonian Art," *Peregrinations* 3 (2010): 8–48.

17.   Michel Parisse, "Princes laïques et/ou moines, les évêques du Xᵉ siècle," in *Il secolo di ferro: Mito e realtà del secolo X. 19 25 aprile 1990* (Spoleto: Centro italiano di studi sull'alto medioevo, 1991), 1:449–513; David A. Warner, "Thietmar of Merseburg: The Image of the Ottonian Bishop," in *The Year 1000: Religious and Social Response to the Turning of the First Millennium,* ed. Michael Frassetto (New York: Palgrave Macmillan, 2002), 85–110.

18.   Cynthia Hahn, *Portrayed on the Heart: Narrative Effect in Pictorial Lives of Saints from the Tenth*

Through the Thirteenth Century (Berkeley: University of California Press, 2001), 147–53.

19.   In addition to the passage from Job discussed in chapters 3 and 4, the tomb includes the inscription "servus servorum episcoporum," which, together with the tomb's eschatological iconography, helps cast Bernward as the good servant awaiting his master's return. Wesenberg, *Bernwardinische Plastik*, 159–60, 182–83, and 314–18; Ulrich Teuscher, "Das ikonologische Programm der Grabanlage Bernwards," in *Bernward und Godehard von Hildesheim: Ihr Leben und Wirken*, ed. Konrad Algermissen (Hildesheim: Lax, 1960), 202–15; Peter Lasko, "The Tomb of St. Bernward of Hildesheim," in *Romanesque and Gothic: Essays for George Zarnecki*, ed. Neil Stratford (Woodbridge: Boydell Press, 1987), 1:147–152; Rainer Kahsnitz, "Bischof Bernwards Grab," in *Bernward und das Zeitalter*, 1:383–396.

20.   A position which bishops from all over Europe cultivated in the eleventh century. Beat Brenk, "Bischöfliche und monastische *committenza* in Süditalien am Beispiel der Exultetrollen," in *Committenti e produzione artistico-letteraria nell'alto medioevo occidentale* (Spoleto: Centro italiano di studi sull'alto medioevo, 1992), 1:275–302; Gatti, "Building the Body of the Church," and Gatti, "Developing an Iconography."

21.   "Fecit et ad sollempnem processionem in praecipuis festis evangelia auro et gemmis clarissima, thimiamateria quoque precii et ponderis magnifici, calices nichilominus plures, et unum ex onichino, alterum vero cristallinum mira industria composuit." Thangmar, *Vita Bernwardi episcopi Hildesheimensis*, ed. Georg Heinrich Pertz, MGH SS 4 (Hannover, 1841), chap. 7, on p. 761, lines 43–46.

22.   *Bernward und das Zeitalter,* 2:604, IX-8.

23.   Michael Brandt, "Der Einband," in *Kostbare Evangeliar*, 56–61. On medieval book covers more generally, see Steenbock, *Der kirchliche Prachteinband*; the Bernward Gospels is cat. no. 66.

24.   Brandt, "Der Einband." For ivories on the front of medieval books, see the many examples in Steenbock, *Der kirchliche Prachteinband*; tenth- and

eleventh-century book covers include cat. nos. 22–78; for book boxes, cat. nos. 39, 44, 56, 59.

25.   On Bernward's cult, see Enno Bünz, "Der Kult des hl. Bernward von Hildesheim im Mittelalter und in der frühen Neuzeit," in *Bernward und das Zeitalter,* 1:419–30.

26.   *Bernward und das Zeitalter,* 2:554, VIII-21. The catalog's attribution of the ivory to eleventh-century Constantinople is, however, problematic.

27.   Ibid., 2:550–53, VIII-19.

28.   Ibid., 2:578–81, VIII-31.

29.   Ibid., 2:588–89, VIII-34.

30.   For the miniature, see Elizabeth C. Teviotdale, *The Stammheim Missal* (Los Angeles: Getty Museum, 2001), 79, fig. 53; Teviotdale, "The Pictorial Program of the Stammheim Missal," in *Objects, Images, and the Word: Art in the Service of the Liturgy*, ed. Colum Hourihane (Princeton: Index of Christian Art, Dept. of Art and Archaeology, Princeton University in association with Princeton University Press, 2003), 79–93. For the cross, see *Bernward und das Zeitalter,* 2:628, IX-25.

31.   *Bernward und das Zeitalter,* 2:638–9, IX-35 and IX-36.

32.   Holger Klein, *Sacred Gifts and Worldly Treasures: Medieval Masterworks from the Cleveland Museum of Art* (Cleveland: Cleveland Museum of Art, 2007), 124–25.

33.   Jan Assmann makes a useful distinction between communicative and cultural memory. According to his definition, the first consists of everyday communications about the meaning of the past that are unstable, disorganized, and non-specialized. The second involves a body of reusable texts, images, and rituals whose cultivation serves to stabilize and establish a community's self-image. Jan Assmann, *Das kulturelle Gedächtnis: Schrift, Erinnerung und politische Identität in den frühen Hochkulturen* (Munich: C. H. Beck, 1992); Jan Assmann and John Czaplicka, "Collective Memory and Cultural Identity," *New German Critique* 65 (1995): 125–33. The history of Bernward's memory at Saint Michael's suggests how medieval *memoria* used the forms of cultural memory in attempts to stabilize what was in fact a constantly recreated and unstable memory.

BIBLIOGRAPHY

PRIMARY SOURCES

Ademar of Chabannes. *Chronicon*. Edited by Pascale Bourgain, Richard Landes, and Georges Pon. CCCM 129. Turnhout: Brepols, 1999.

Albertson, Clinton, ed. and trans. *Anglo-Saxon Saints and Heroes*. New York: Fordham University Press, 1967.

Alcuin of York. *Commentariorum in Apocalypsin libri quinque*. PL 100.1085–1156. Paris: Migne, 1863.

Ambrosus Autpertus. *Ambrosii Autperti Opera*. Edited by Robert Weber. CCCM 27. Turnhout: Brepols, 1975.

Annales Hildesheimensis. Edited by Georg Waitz. MGH SS rer. Germ. 8. Hannover: Impensis Bibliopolii Aulici Hahniani, 1878.

Arens, Franz. *Der Liber Ordinarius der Essener Stifts-kirche*. Paderborn: A. Pape, 1908.

Arnold of Regensburg. *Ex Arnoldi libris de S. Emmerammo*. Edited by Georg Heinrich Pertz. MGH SS 4. Hannover: Impensis Bibliopolii Aulici Hahniani, 1841.

Augustine. *Opera Omnia*. Corpus Augustinianum Gissense. Edited by Cornelius Mayer. Basel: Schwabe, 1995. Past Masters Database, http://library.nlx .com, © 2002. Translated as *The Works of Saint Augustine*. Edited by Boniface Ramsey. Electronic edition. 2nd release. Charlottesville: Intelex, 2001.

Bede the Venerable. *Opera*. Pars 3, *Opera homiletica*. Edited by David Hurst, O.S.B. CCSL 122. Turn-hout: Brepols, 1955.

Bernard of Angers. *Liber miraculorum s. Fidis*. Edited by Luca Robertini. Spoleto: Centro Italiano di Studi sull'Alto Medioevo, 1994.

Berschin, Walter, and Johannes Staub. *Die Taten des Abtes Witigowo von der Reichenau (985–997): Eine zeitgenössische Biographie von Purchart von der Reichenau*. Reichenauer Texte und Bilder 3. Sigmaringen: Thorbecke, 1992.

Bischoff, Bernhard. *Anecdota Novissima: Texte des vierten bis sechzehnten Jahrhunderts*. Quellen und Untersuchungen zur lateinischen Philologie des Mittelalters 7. Stuttgart: Hiersemann, 1984.

Bischoff, Bernhard, and Florentine Mütherich, eds. *Mittelalterliche Schatzverzeichnisse*. Part 1, *Von der Zeit Karls des Grossen bis zur Mitte des 13. Jahrhunderts*. Munich: Prestel, 1967.

Bruno of Segni. *Sententiae*. PL 165.867–1078. Paris: Migne, 1854.

Calcidius. *Timaeus a Calcidio Translatus Commen-tarioque Instructus*. Edited by Jan Hendrick Waszink. Plato Latinus 4. London: The Warburg Institute; Leiden: Brill, 1962.

Carpenter, Marjorie. *Kontakia of Romanos, Byzantine Melodist*. 2 vols. Columbia: University of Missouri Press, 1970–72.

Chronica episcoporum Hildensheimensium. Edited by Gottfried Wilhelm Leibniz. Scriptorum Brunsvi-censia illustrantuum 2. Hannover, 1710.

Colgrave, Bertram, ed. and trans. *Two Lives of Saint Cuthbert: Texts, Translation, and Notes*. Reprint, Cambridge: Cambridge University Press, 1985.

Gerard of Arras-Cambrai. *Acta synodi Atrebatensis in Manichaeos*. PL 142.1269–1312. Paris: Migne, 1880.

Gregory the Great. *Dialogorum*. PL 77.149–430. Paris: Migne, 1896.

———. *Homiliae in Evangelia*. Edited by Raymond Étaix. CCSL 141. Turnhout: Brepols, 1999.

———. *Homiliae in Hiezechihelem prophetam.* Edited by Marc Adriaen. CCSL 142. Turnhout: Brepols, 1971.

———. *Moralia in Job.* Edited by Marc Adriaen. 3 vols. CCSL 143–143A, B. Turnhout: Brepols, 1979–85.

———. *Registrum epistularum.* Edited by Dag Norberg. 2 vols. CCSL 140–140A. Turnhout: Brepols, 1982.

Haimo of Auxerre. *Expositionis in Apocalypsin Beati Joannis.* PL 117.938–1220. Paris: Migne, 1881.

———. *Homilia II: In nativitate sancti Joannis Baptistae.* PL 118.755–59. Paris: Migne, 1880.

Honorius Augustodinensis. *Gemma anima.* PL 172.541–736. Paris: Migne, 1895.

Hrabanus Maurus. *Commentaria in Jeremiam.* PL 111.793–1272. Paris: Migne, 1852.

———. *Commentariorum in Ezechielem.* PL 110.493–1086. Paris: Migne, 1864.

———. *Commentariorum in Genesim.* PL 107.439–668. Paris: Migne, 1864.

———. *Homiliae in evangelia et epistolas.* PL 110.135–466. Paris: Migne, 1864.

Hrotsvit. *Opera omnia.* Edited by Walter Berschin. Bibliotheca scriptorum Graecorum et Romanorum Teubneriana. Munich: Saur, 2001.

Isidore of Seville. *Etymologiarum sive originum libri XX.* Edited by William M. Lindsay. 2 vols. Oxford: Oxford University Press, 1911. English translation by Stephen A. Barney et al. *The Etymologies of Isidore of Seville.* Cambridge: Cambridge University Press, 2006.

Janicke, Karl, ed. *Die Urkundenbuch des Hochstifts Hildesheim und seiner Bischöfe.* Vol. 1. 1896. Reprint, Osnabrück: Zeller, 1965.

Johansson, Ann-Katrin Andrews. *The Feasts of the Blessed Virgin Mary.* Corpus Troporum 9. Tropes for the Proper of the Mass 4. Stockholm: Almqvist and Wiksell, 1998.

John, abbot of Saint Arnulf. *Vita Iohannis abbatis Gorzienzis auctore Iohanne abate S. Arnulfi.* Edited by Georg Heinrich Pertz. MGH SS 4.335–77. Hannover: Impensis Bibliopolii Aulici Hahniani, 1841.

Lantbert. *Vita Heriberti archiepiscopi Coloniensis auctore Lantberto.* Edited by Georg Heinrich Pertz. MGH SS 4.739–43. Hannover: Impensis Bibliopolii Aulici Hahniani, 1841.

Lehmann-Brockhaus, Otto, ed. *Schriftquellen zur Kunstgeschichte des 11 und 12 Jahrhunderts für Deutschland, Lotharingen und Italien.* 2 vols. Berlin: Deutscher Verein für Kunstwissenschaft, 1938.

Leyen, Friedrich von der. *Deutsche Dichtung des Mittelalters.* Frankfurt am Main: Insel-Verlag, 1962.

Libellus de corona Virginis. PL 96.284–318. Paris: Migne, 1851.

Libri de nativitate Mariae. Edited by Jan Gijsel and Rita Beyers. Corpus Christianorum Series Apocryphorum 9–10. Turnhout: Brepols, 1997.

The New Oxford Annotated Bible: New Revised Standard Edition with the Apocrypha. Edited by Michael D. Coogan with Marc Z. Brettler, Carol A. Newsom, and Pheme Perkins. 3rd ed. Oxford: Oxford University Press, 2001.

Odo of Cluny. *De Vita sancti Geraldi Auriliacensis comitis.* PL 133.639–704. Paris: Migne, 1881.

Oldekop, Johannes. *Chronik.* Edited by Karl Euling. Bibliothek des Literarischen Vereins in Stuttgart 190. Stuttgart: Hiersemann, 1891.

Papadopoulos-Kerameus, Athanasios, ed. *Analekta hierosolymitikes stachyologias.* 5 vols. Brussels: Culture et Civilisation, 1891. Reprint, 1963.

Paulinus of Nola. *Sancti Pontii Meropii Paulini Nolani Epistulae.* Edited by William A. Hartel. Corpus Scriptorum Ecclesiasticorum Latinorum 29. Prague: Tempsky; Leipzig: Freytag, 1894. English translation by Patrick Gerard Walsh. *The Letters of St. Paulinus of Nola.* 2 vols. Westminster, Md.: Newman Press, 1966.

Peter Damian. *Vita beati Romualdi.* Edited by Giovanni Tabacco. Fonti per la storia d'Italia 94. Rome: Istituto storico italiano per il medio evo, 1957.

Plato. *Timaeus.* In *Platonis Opera,* edited by John Burnet, vol. 4, III.17–105. Oxford: Oxford University Press, 1903.

Romanos. *Hymnes.* Edited and translated by José Grosdidier de Matons. Vol. 2. Sources chrétiennes 110. Paris: Cerf, 1965.

Rupert of Deutz. *De gloria et honore filii hominis. Super Mattheum.* Edited by Hrabanus Haacke. CCCM 29. Turnhout: Brepols, 1979.

Sicard of Cremona. *Mitralis de officiis.* Edited by Gábor Sarbak and Lorenz Weinrich. CCCM 228. Turnhout: Brepols, 2008.

Sophronius of Jerusalem. "On the Holy Baptism." In *Analekta hierosolymitikes stachyologias*, edited by Athanasios Papadopoulos-Kerameus. 1891. Reprint, Brussels: Culture et Civilisation, 1963.

Talbot, Charles H., ed. and trans. *The Anglo-Saxon Missionaries in Germany: Being the Lives of SS. Willibrord, Boniface, Sturm, Leoba and Lebuin, together with the Hodoeporicon of St. Willibald and a Selection from the Correspondence of St. Boniface.* New York: Sheed and Ward, 1954.

Thangmar. *Vita Bernwardi episcopi Hildesheimensis.* Edited by Georg Heinrich Pertz. MGH SS 4.754–82. Hannover: Impensis Bibliopolii Aulici Hahniani, 1841.

Thietmar of Merseburg. *Chronicon.* Edited by Robert Holtzmann. *Die Chronik des Bischofs Thietmar von Merseburg.* MGH SS rer. Germ. n.s. 9. Berlin: Weidmann, 1935.

Thiofrid of Echternach. *Thiofridi Abbatis Epternacensis: Flores Epytaphii Sanctorum.* Edited by Michael Camillo Ferrari. CCCM 133. Turnhout: Brepols, 1996.

Vita Iohannis abbatis Gorzienzis. Edited by Georg Heinrich Pertz. MGH SS 4.335–77. Hannover: Impensis Bibliopolii Aulici Hahniani, 1841.

Vita Meinwercki episcopi Patherbrunnensis. Edited by Franz Teckhoff. MGH SS rer. Germ. 59. Hannover: Hahnsche Buchhandlung, 1921.

Vita Remigii episcopi. Edited by Bruno Krusch. MGH SS rerum Merovingicarum 3. Hannover: Impensis Bibliopolii Hahniani, 1896.

Vita Theodorici abbatis Andaginensis. Edited by W. Wattenbach. MGH SS 12.36–57. Hannover: Impensis Bibliopolii Hahniani, 1856.

Vita Willibrordi archiepiscopi Traiectensis. Edited by Bruno Krusch and Wilhelm Levison. MGH SS rerum Merovingicarum 7. Hannover: Hahnsche Buchhandlung, 1920.

Wellesz, Egon, ed. *The Akathistos Hymn.* Monumenta musicae Byzantinae: Transcripta 9. Copenhagen: Munksgaard, 1957.

SECONDARY SOURCES

Aertsen, Jan A., and Andreas Speer, eds. *Individuum und Individualität im Mittelalter.* Miscellanea Mediaevalia 24. Berlin: W. de Gruyter, 1996.

Airlie, Stuart. "The Anxiety of Sanctity: St Gerald of Aurillac and His Maker." *Journal of Ecclesiastical History* 43 (1992): 372–95.

Alexander, Jonathan J. G. "Facsimiles, Copies, and Variations: The Relationship to the Model in Medieval and Renaissance Illuminated Manuscripts." In *Retaining the Original: Multiple Originals, Copies, and Reproductions*, edited by Kathleen Preciado, 61–72. Studies in the History of Art 20. Washington, D.C.: National Gallery of Art, 1989.

Alfs, Joseph. "Die geschnitten Steine an den Kirchenschätzen in Hildesheim." *Niedersächsisches Jahrbuch für Landesgeschichte* 19 (1942): 1–39.

Algazi, Gadi, Valentin Groebner, and Bernhard Jussen, eds. *Negotiating the Gift: Pre-Modern Figurations of Exchange.* Göttingen: Vandenhoeck & Ruprecht, 2003.

Algermissen, Konrad, ed. *Bernward und Godehard von Hildesheim: Ihr Leben und Wirken.* Hildesheim: Lax, 1960.

Althoff, Gerd. *Amicitiae und Pacta: Bündnis, Einung, Politik und Gebetsgedenken im beginnenden 10. Jahrhundert.* MGH Schriften 37. Hannover: Hahnsche Buchhandlung, 1992.

Althoff, Gerd, Johannes Fried, and Patrick Geary, eds. *Medieval Concepts of the Past: Ritual, Memory, Historiography.* Washington, D.C.: German Historical Institute, 2002.

Angenendt, Arnold. "*Donationes pro anima*: Gift and Countergift in the Early Medieval Liturgy." In Davis and McCormick, *Long Morning of Medieval Europe*, 131–54.

Arnulf, Arwed. *Versus ad Picturas: Studien zur Titulusdichtung als Quellengattung der Kunstgeschichte von der Antike bis zum Hochmittelalter.* Kunstwissenschaftliche Studien Band 72. Munich: Deutscher Kunstverlag, 1997.

Ashley, Kathleen, and Pamela Sheingorn. *Writing Faith: Text, Sign, and History in the Miracles of*

Sainte Foy. Chicago: University of Chicago Press, 1999.

Assmann, Jan. *Das kulturelle Gedächtnis: Schrift, Erinnerung und politische Identität in den frühen Hochkulturen*. Munich: Beck, 1992.

Assmann, Jan, and John Czaplicka. "Collective Memory and Cultural Identity." *New German Critique* 65 (1995): 125–33.

Barasch, Moshe. "Das Bild des Unsichtbaren: Zu den frühen Christusbildern." *Visible Religion* 2 (1983): 1–13.

Barb, Alphonse A. "Krippe, Tisch und Grab." In *Mullus: Festschrift Theodor Klauser*, 17–27. Jahrbuch für Antike und Christentum, Ergänzungsband 1. Münster: Aschendorff, 1964.

Barone, Giulia. "Une hagiographie sans miracles: Observations en marge de quelques vies du Xe siècle." In *Les fonctions des saints*, 435–46.

Barral i Altet, Xavier. "Définition et fonction d'un trésor monastique autour de l'an mil: Sainte Foy de Conques." In *Haut Moyen Âge: Culture, éducation et société; Études offertes à Pierre Riché*, edited by Michel Sot, 401–8. La Garennes-Colome: Éditions européennes Erasme, 1990.

Barré, Henri. "Le sermon 'Exhortatur' est-il de Saint Ildefonse?" *Revue bénédictine* 67 (1957): 10–33.

Barrow, Julia. "The State of Research: Salian Features; 'Die Salier' at Speyer." *Journal of Medieval History* 20 (1994): 193–206.

Baschet, Jérôme. "Introduction: L'image-objet." In Baschet and Schmitt, *L'image*, 7–29.

Baschet, Jérôme, and Jean-Claude Schmitt, eds. *L'image: Fonctions et usages des images dans l'Occident médiéval*. Cahiers du Léopard d'or 5. Paris: Le Léopard d'or, 1996.

Bauch, Kurt. *Das mittelalterliche Grabbild: Figürliche Grabmäler des 11. bis 15. Jahrhunderts in Europa*. Berlin: W. de Gruyter, 1976.

Bauer, Gerd. "Corvey oder Hildesheim? Zur Ottonischen Buchmalerei in Norddeutschland." 2 vols. Ph.D. diss., Universität Hamburg, 1977.

———. "'Neue' Bernward-Handschriften." In *Bernwardinische Kunst: Bericht*, 211–25.

Bauerreiss, Romuald. *Arbor vitae: Der "Lebensbaum" und seine Verwendung in Liturgie, Kunst und Brauchtum des Abendlandes*. Munich: Neuer Filser-Verlag, 1938.

Baumstark, Anton. "Eine Antike Bildkomposition in christlich-orientalischen Umdeutungen." *Monatshefte für Kunstwissenschaft* 8 (1915): 111–23.

Becksmann, Rüdiger. "Vor- und frühromanische Glasmalerei in Deutschland: Quellen—Funde—Hypothesen." *Zeitschrift des Deutschen Vereins für Kunstwissenschaft* 52–53 (1998–99): 197–212.

Beissel, Stephan. *Das heiligen Bernward Evangelienbuch im Dome zu Hildesheim: Mit Handschriften des 10. und 11. Jahrhunderts in kunsthistorischer und liturgischer Hinsicht verglichen*. Hildesheim: Lax, 1891.

Belting, Hans. *Bild-Anthropologie: Entwurfe für eine Bildwissenschaft*. Munich: Fink, 2001.

———. *The Image and Its Public in the Middle Ages*. Translated by Mark Bartusis and Raymond Meyer. New Rochelle, N.Y.: A. D. Caratzas, 1990.

Berges, Wilhelm, and Hans Jürgen Rieckenberg. *Die älteren Hildesheimer Inschriften bis zum Tode Bischof Hezilos (†1079)*. Göttingen: Vandenhoeck & Ruprecht, 1983.

Bernwardinische Kunst: Bericht über ein wissenschaftliches Symposium in Hildesheim vom 10.10. bis 13.10.1984. Göttingen: Goltze, 1988.

Beseler, Hartwig, and Hans Roggenkamp. *Die Michaeliskirche in Hildesheim*. Berlin: Mann, 1954.

Beuckers, Klaus Gereon. "Bernward und Willigis: Zu einem Aspekt der bernwardinischen Stiftungen." In Lutz and Weyer, *1000 Jahre St. Michael in Hildesheim*, 142–52.

Bialostocki, Jan. "Das Modusproblem in den bildenden Künsten: Zur Vorgeschichte und zum Nachleben des 'Modusbriefes' von Nicholas Poussin." In *Stil und Ikonographie: Studien zur Kunstwissenschaft*, 9–35. Dresden: VEB Verlag der Kunst, 1966.

Biehn, Heinz. *Die Kronen Europas und ihre Schicksale*. Wiesbaden: Limes Verlag, 1957.

Bijsterveld, Arnoud-Jan. *Do ut des: Gift Giving, "Memoria," and Conflict Management in the Medieval Low Countries*. Hilversum: Verloren, 2007.

Binding, Günther. *Bischof Bernward als Architekt der Michaeliskirche in Hildesheim.* Cologne: Abt. Architektur des Kunsthistorischen Instituts, 1987.

———. "Bischof Bernward von Hildesheim— architectus et artifex?" In *Bernwardinische Kunst: Bericht,* 27–47.

Binski, Paul. *Medieval Death: Ritual and Representation.* Ithaca: Cornell University Press, 1996.

Bischoff, Bernhard. *Kalligraphie in Bayern 8–12 Jahrhundert.* Wiesbaden: Reichert, 1981.

———. "Literarisches und künstlerisches Leben in St. Emmeram (Regensburg) während des frühen und hohen Mittelalter." In *Mittelalterliche Studien: Ausgewählte Aufsätze zur Schriftkunde und Literaturgeschichte,* 2:77–115. Stuttgart: Hiersemann, 1966–81.

Blick, Sarah. "Exceptions to Krautheimer's Theory of Copying." *Visual Resources: An International Journal of Documentation* 20 (2004): 123–42.

Bloch, Peter. "Herrscherbild—Grabbild—Stifterbild." In *Bilder vom Menschen in der Kunst des Abendlandes,* edited by Peter Bloch, 107–20. Berlin: Mann, 1980.

———. "Zum Dedikationsbild im Lob des Kreuzes des Hrabanus Maurus." In *Das erste Jahrtausend,* edited by Victor H. Elbern, 471–94. Düsseldorf: Schwann, 1962.

Bloch, Peter, and Hermann Schnitzler. *Die ottonische Kölner Malerschule.* 2 vols. Düsseldorf: Schwann, 1967–70.

Bloch, Peter, and Erich Zimmerman. *Der Darmstädter Hitda-Codex: Bilder und Zierseiten aus der Handschrift 1640 der Hessischen Landes- und Hochschulbibliothek.* Berlin: Propyläen, 1968.

Blough, Karen. "The Princess-Abbesses of Essen and the Golden Virgin." In *De re metallica: The Uses of Metal in the Middle Ages,* edited by Robert Odell Bork with Scott Montgomery et al., 147–62. Aldershot: Ashgate, 2005.

Bober, Harry. "In Principio: Creation Before Time." In *De artibus opuscula XL: Essays in Honor of Erwin Panofsky,* edited by Millard Meiss, 1:13–28. New York: New York University Press, 1961.

Boeckler, Albert. *Abendländische Miniaturen bis zum Ausgang der romanischen Zeit.* Berlin: W. de Gruyter, 1930.

———. "Das Erhardbild im Utacodex." In *Studies in Art and Literature for Belle da Costa Greene,* edited by Dorothy Miner, 219–30. Princeton: Princeton University Press, 1954.

———. *Das Goldene Evangelienbuch Heinrichs III.* Berlin: Deutscher Verein für Kunstwissenschaft, 1933.

Boespflug, François, and Yolanta Zaluska. "Le Prologue de l'évangile selon Saint Jean dans l'art médiéval, IXe–XIIIe siècles: L'image comme commentaire." *Folia historiae atrium* 8–9 (2002): 11–45.

Bonne, Jean-Claude. "De l'ornemental dans l'art médiéval VII–XII siècle: Le modèle insulaire." In Baschet and Schmitt, *L'image,* 207–51.

———. "Entre l'image et la matière: La choséité du sacré en Occident." In *Les images dans les sociétés médiévales: Pour une histoire comparée; Actes du colloque international organisé par l'Institut historique belge de Rome en collaboration avec l'École française de Rome et l'Université libre de Bruxelles, Rome, Academia Belgica, 19–20 juin 1998,* edited by Jean-Michel Sansterre and Jean-Claude Schmitt, 77–111. Brussels: Institut historique belge de Rome, 1999.

———. "Les ornements de l'histoire: A propos de l'ivoire carolingien de Saint Rémi." *Annales: Histoire, sciences sociales* 1 (1996): 37–70.

Boulnois, Olivier. *Au delà de l'image: Une archéologie du visuel au Moyen-Âge V^e–XVIe siècle.* Paris: Seuil, 2008.

Bousquet, Jacques. "Des antependiums aux retables: Le problème du décor des autels et de son emplacement." *Cahiers de Saint-Michel de Cuxa* 13 (1982): 201–32.

Brandt, Michael. "Bau und Kult—Der Dom und seine Heiligen." In *Ego sum Hildensemensis: Bischof, Domkapitel und Dom in Hildesheim 815 bis 1810,* edited by Ulrich Knapp, 149–64. Petersberg: Michael Imhof Verlag, 2000.

———. "Bernward d'Hildesheim et ses trésors." *Cahiers de Saint-Michel de Cuxa* 41 (2010): 133–43.

———, ed. *Das kostbare Evangeliar des heiligen Bernward*. With contributions by Rainer Kahsnitz and Hans Jakob Schuffels. Munich: Prestel, 1993.

———, ed. *Der Schatz von St. Godehard*. Hildesheim: Diözesan-Museum, 1988.

———. "'. . . und geziehret mit Edelgesteinen': Zur grossen Madonna im Hildesheimer Domschatz." In *Bernwardinische Kunst: Bericht*, 195–210.

Brandt, Michael, and Arne Eggebrecht, eds. *Bernward von Hildesheim und das Zeitalter der Ottonen: Katalog der Ausstellung*. 2 vols. Hildesheim: Bernward Verlag, 1993.

Braun, Joseph. *Die liturgische Gewandung im Occident und Orient nach Ursprung und Entwicklung, Verwendung und Symbolik*. Darmstadt: Wissenschaftliche Buchgesellschaft, 1964.

———. *Meisterwerke der deutschen Goldschmiedekunst der vorgotischen Zeit*. Munich: Riehn & Reusch, 1922.

Bredt, Ernst W. *Katalog der mittelalterlichen Miniaturen des Germanischen Nationalmuseums*. Nuremberg: Verlag des Germanischen Museums. 1903.

Breeze, Andrew. "The Blessed Virgin and the Sunbeam Through Glass." *Celtica* 23 (1999): 19–29.

Bréhier, Louis. "Deux inventaires du trésor de la cathédrale de Clermont au Xᵉ siècle." *Études archéologiques: Mémoires de la Société des "Amis de l'Université de Clermont-Ferrand"* 2 (1910): 205–10.

Brenk, Beat. "Bischöfliche und monastische *committenza* in Süditalien am Beispiel der Exultetrollen." In *Committenti e produzione artistico-letteraria nell'alto medioevo occidentale*, 1:275–300. Spoleto: Centro italiano di studi sull'alto medioevo, 1992.

———. "Schriftlichkeit und Bildlichkeit in der Hofschule Karls des Grossens." In *Testo e immagine nell'alto medioevo: 15–21 aprile 1993*, 631–82. Spoleto: Centro italiano di studi sull'alto medioevo, 1994.

———. "Le texte et l'image dans la 'vie des saints' au Moyen Âge: Rôle du concepteur et rôle du peintre." In *Texte et image: Actes du colloque international de Chantilly, 13 au 15 octobre 1982*, 31–39. Paris: Les Belles Lettres, 1984.

———. *Tradition und Neuerung in der christlichen Kunst des ersten Jahrtausends*. Graz: Böhlaus in Kommission, 1963.

Bruns, Bernhard. "Das Epiphaniebild im Kostbaren Evangeliar des heiligen Bernward." *Die Diözese Hildesheim in Vergangenheit und Gegenwart* 61 (1993): 11–19.

———. "Das Widmungsbild im Kostbaren Evangeliar des heiligen Bernward." *Die Diözese Hildesheim in Vergangenheit und Gegenwart* 65 (1997): 29–55.

Bruyne, Donatien de. *Préfaces de la Bible latine*. Namur: A. Godenne, 1920.

Buc, Philippe. "Conversion of Objects." *Viator* 28 (1997): 99–142.

Büchsel, Martin. "Die Kreuzigung zwischen Antike und Christentum." *Jahrbuch der Kunsthistorischen Sammlungen in Wien* 89–90 (1993–94): 7–33.

Bynum, Caroline Walker. *The Resurrection of the Body in Western Christianity, 200–1336*. New York: Columbia University Press, 1995.

Cabié, Robert. *The Church at Prayer: An Introduction to the Liturgy*. Vol. 2, *The Eucharist*. Edited by Aimé Georges Martimort. Translated by Matthew J. O'Connell. Collegeville, Minn.: Liturgical Press, 1992.

Cahn, Walter. "Solomonic Elements in Romanesque Art." In Gutmann, *Temple of Solomon*, 45–72.

Camille, Michael. "Sensations of the Page: Imaging Technologies and Medieval Illuminated Manuscripts." In *The Iconic Page in Manuscript, Print, and Digital Culture*, edited by George Bornstein and Theresa Tinkle, 33–53. Ann Arbor: University of Michigan Press, 1998.

Carpenter, Marjorie. *Kontakia of Romanos, Byzantine Melodist*. Columbia: University of Missouri Press, 1970–72.

Carrier, Peter. "Places, Politics, and the Archiving of Contemporary Memory in Pierre Nora's *Les lieux de mémoire*." In *Memory and Methodology*, edited by Susannah Radstone, 37–57. Oxford: Berg, 2000.

Carroll, Christopher. "Bishoprics of Saxony in the First Century After Christianization." *Early Medieval Europe* 8 (1999): 219–45.

Carruthers, Mary. *The Book of Memory: A Study of Memory in Medieval Culture.* New York: Cambridge University Press, 1990.

———. *The Craft of Thought: Meditation, Rhetoric, and the Making of Images, 400–1200.* New York: Cambridge University Press, 1998.

———. "'*Ut pictura poesis*': The Rhetoric of Verbal and Visual Images." *Mentalities/Mentalités* 7 (1990): 1–6.

Carruthers, Mary, and Jan M. Ziolkowski, eds. *The Medieval Craft of Memory: An Anthology of Texts and Pictures.* Philadelphia: University of Pennsylvania Press, 2002.

Caviness, Madeline. "'De convenientia et cohaerentia antiqui et novi Operis': Medieval Conservation, Restoration, Pastiche, and Forgery." In *Intuition und Kunstwissenschaft: Festschrift für Hans Swarzenski*, edited by Peter Bloch, 205–21. Berlin: Mann, 1973.

———. "Images of Divine Order and the Third Mode of Seeing." *Gesta* 22 (1983): 99–120. Reprinted in *Art in the Medieval West and Its Audience*, 1–22. Aldershot: Ashgate, 2001.

Chavasse, Antoine. "Evangéliaire, epistolier, antiphonaire et sacramentaire: Les livres romains de la messe au VIIe et VIIIe siècles." *Ecclesia orans* 6 (1989): 177–255.

Chazelle, Celia. *The Crucified God in the Carolingian Era: Theology and Art of Christ's Passion.* Cambridge: Cambridge University Press, 2001.

Christe, Yves. *L'Apocalypse de Jean: Sens et développements de ses visions synthétiques.* Paris: Picard, 1996.

———. "Trois images carolingiennes en forme de commentaires sur l'Apocalypse." *Cahiers archéologiques: Fin de l'antiquité et Moyen Âge* 25 (1976): 77–92.

———. *La vision de Matthieu (Matth. XXIV–XXV): Origines et développement d'une image de la Seconde Parousie.* Paris: Klincksieck, 1973.

Christen, Eliana Magnani S. "Transforming Things and Persons: The Gift *pro anima* in the Eleventh and Twelfth Centuries." In Algazi, Groebner, and Jussen, *Negotiating the Gift*, 269–84.

Chroust, Anton. *Monumenta palaeographica: Denkmäler der Schreibkunst des Mittelalters: Schrifttafeln in lateinischer und deutscher Sprache.* Series 1–2, Munich: F. Bruckmann, 1902–17. Series 3, Leipzig: O. Harrassowitz, 1931–40.

Classen, Constance. *Worlds of Sense: Exploring the Senses in History and Across Cultures.* London: Routledge, 1993.

Coatsworth, Elizabeth. "The 'Robed Christ' in Pre-Conquest Sculptures of the Crucifixion." *Anglo-Saxon England* 29 (2000): 153–76.

Cohen, Adam. *The Uta Codex: Art, Philosophy, and Reform in Eleventh-Century Germany.* University Park: The Pennsylvania State University Press, 2000.

Cohen, Adam, and Anne Derbes. "Bernward and Eve at Hildesheim." *Gesta* 40 (2001): 19–38.

Collins, Kristin. "Redeemer, Mother, and Ruler: Images of the Virgin in Ottonian Germany." Ph.D. diss., University of Texas at Austin, 2006.

Collins, Mary. "Mercator Pessimus? The Medieval Judas." *Papers of the Liverpool Latin Seminar* 4 (1983): 197–213.

Constable, Giles. "The Commemoration of the Dead in the Early Middle Ages." In *Early Medieval Rome and the Christian West: Essays in Honour of Donald A. Bullough*, edited by Julia M. H. Smith, 169–96. Leiden: Brill, 2000.

Constas, Nicholas. "Weaving the Body of God: Proclus of Constantinople, the Theotokos, and the Loom of the Flesh." *Journal of Early Christian Studies* 3 (1995): 169–94.

Corbet, Patrick. *Les saints ottoniens: Sainteté dynastique, sainteté royale et sainteté féminine autour de l'an Mil.* Beihefte der Francia 15. Sigmaringen: Thorbecke, 1986.

Corrigan, Kathleen. "The Witness of John the Baptist on an Early Byzantine Icon in Kiev." *Dumbarton Oaks Papers* 42 (1988): 1–11.

Coué, Stephanie. *Hagiographie im Kontext: Schreibanlass und Funktion von Bischofsviten aus dem 11. und vom Anfang des 12. Jahrhunderts.* Berlin: W. de Gruyter, 1997.

Cramp, Rosemary. "Window Glass from the British Isles 7th–10th Century." In *Il colore nel medioevo: Arte, simbolo, tecnica; La vetrata in Occidente dal IV all'XI secolo*, edited by Francesca Dell'Acqua and Romano Silva, 67–85. Lucca: Istituto storico lucchese, 2001.

———. "Window Glass from the Monastic Site of Jarrow: Problems of Interpretation." *Journal of Glass Studies* 17 (1975): 88–96.

Cutler, Anthony. "A Byzantine Triptych and Its Modern Recovery." *Gesta* 37 (1998): 3–12.

———. *The Hand of the Master: Craftsmanship, Ivory, and Society in Byzantium (9th–11th Centuries)*. Princeton: Princeton University Press, 1994.

Dahl, Ellert. "Heavenly Images: The Statue of St. Foy of Conques and the Significance of the Medieval 'Cult-Image' in the West." *Acta ad archaeologiam et artium historiam pertinentia* 8 (1978): 175–91.

Dale, Thomas E. A. "The Individual, the Resurrected Body, and Romanesque Portraiture: The Tomb of Rudolf von Schwaben in Merseburg." *Speculum* 77 (2002): 707–43.

———. *Relics, Prayer, and Politics in Medieval Venetia: Romanesque Painting in the Crypt of Aquilea Cathedral*. Princeton: Princeton University Press, 1997.

Dam, Raymond van. *Saints and Their Miracles in Late Antique Gaul*. Princeton: Princeton University Press, 1993.

Davids, Adelbert, ed. *Empress Theophano: Byzantium and the West at the Turn of the First Millennium*. Cambridge: Cambridge University Press, 1995.

Davis, Jennifer R., and Michael McCormick. *The Long Morning of Medieval Europe: New Directions in Medieval Studies*. Aldershot: Ashgate, 2008.

Davis-Weyer, Caecilia. *Early Medieval Art, 300–1150: Sources and Documents*. Medieval Academy Reprints for Teaching 17. Toronto: University of Toronto Press, 1986.

Dell'Acqua, Francesca. *"Illuminando colorat": La vetrata tra l'età tardo imperiale e l'alto medioevo; Le fonti, l'archeologia*. Spoleto: Centro italiano di studi sull'alto medioevo, 2003.

Deshman, Robert. "Another Look at the Disappearing Christ: Corporeal and Spiritual Vision in Early Medieval Images." *Art Bulletin* 79 (1997): 518–46.

———. *The Benedictional of Aethelwold*. Princeton: Princeton University Press, 1995.

———. "The Exalted Servant: The Ruler Theology of the Prayerbook of Charles the Bald." *Viator* 11 (1980): 385–417.

———. "The Imagery of the Living Ecclesia and the English Monastic Reform." In *Sources for Anglo-Saxon Culture*, edited by Paul E. Szarmach with Virginia D. Oggins, 261–82. Studies in Medieval Culture 20. Kalamazoo: Medieval Institute Publications, Western Michigan University, 1986.

Diebold, William J. "The Carolingian Idol: Exegetes and Idols." In *Seeing the Invisible in Late Antiquity and the Early Middle Ages*, edited by Giselle de Nie, Karl F. Morrison, and Marco Mostert, 445–61. Turnhout: Brepols, 2005.

———. "'Except I shall see . . . I will not believe' (John 20:25): Typology, Theology, and Historiography in an Ottonian Diptych." In *Objects, Images, and the Word: Art in the Service of the Liturgy*, edited by Colum Hourihane, 257–73. Index of Christian Art Occasional Papers 6. Princeton: Index of Christian Art, Dept. of Art and Archaeology, Princeton University in association with Princeton University Press, 2003.

———. "The Ruler Portrait of Charles the Bald in the S. Paolo Bible." *Art Bulletin* 76 (1994): 6–18.

Dolbeau, François. "Le dossier de saint Dominique de Sora, d'Albéric du Mont-Cassin à Jacques de Voragine." *Mélanges de l'École française de Rome: Moyen Âge* 102 (1990): 7–78.

Drescher, Hans. "Einige technische Beobachtungen zur Inschrift auf der Hildesheimer Bernwardstür." In *Bernwardinische Kunst: Bericht*, 71–75.

———. "HILDENESHEM und MVNDBVRUC: Bischof Bernward als Münzherr." In Brandt and Eggebrecht, *Bernward und das Zeitalter*, 1:323–35.

Drumbl, Johann. "Stage and Players in the Early Middle Ages." *European Medieval Drama* 1 (1997): 51–75.

Dutton, Paul E. "Medieval Approaches to Calcidius." In *Plato's "Timaeus" as Cultural Icon*, edited by Gretchen J. Reydams-Schils, 183–205. Notre Dame: University of Notre Dame Press, 2003.

Dutton, Paul E., and Herbert L. Kessler. *The Poetry and Paintings of the First Bible of Charles the Bald.* Ann Arbor: University of Michigan Press, 1997.

Eastwood, Bruce S. "Calcidius' Commentary on Plato's *Timaeus* in Latin Astronomy of the Ninth to Eleventh Centuries." In *Between Demonstration and Imagination: Essays in the History of Science and Philosophy Presented to John D. North*, edited by Lodi Nauta and Arjo Vanderjagt, 171–209. Leiden: Brill, 1999.

———. "Plato and Circumsolar Planetary Motion in the Middle Ages." *Archives d'histoire doctrinale et littéraire du Moyen Âge* 60 (1993): 7–26.

Eberlein, Johann K. *Apparitio regis, revelatio veritatis: Studien zur Darstellung des Vorhangs in der bildenden Kunst von der Spätantike bis zum Ende des Mittelalters.* Wiesbaden: Reichert, 1982.

1000 Jahre Mainzer Dom 975–1975. Edited by Wilhelm Jung. Mainz: Will und Rothe, 1975.

Elbern, Victor H. *Der eucharistische Kelch im frühen Mittelalter.* Berlin: Deutscher Verein für Kunstwissenschaft, 1964.

Elbern, Victor H., and Hans Reuther, eds. *Der Hildesheimer Domschatz.* Hildesheim: Lax, 1969.

Ernst, Josef. *Johannes der Täufer: Interpretation, Geschichte, Wirkungsgeschichte.* Berlin: W. de Gruyter, 1989.

Ernst, Ulrich. "Farbe und Schrift im Mittelalter unter Berücksichtigung antiker Grundlagen und neuzeitlicher Rezeptionsformen." In *Testo e immagine nell'alto medioevo: 15–21 aprile 1993*, 343–414. Spoleto: Centro italiano di studi sull'alto medioevo, 1994.

Euw, Anton von. "Die Majestas-Domini-Bilder der ottonischen Kölner Malerschule im Licht des platonischen Weltbildes: Codex 192 der Kölner Dombibliothek." In Euw, Schreiner, and Sporbeck, *Kaiserin Theophanu: Begegnung,* 1:379–400.

Euw, Anton von, and Peter Schreiner, eds. *Kunst im Zeitalter der Kaiserin Theophanu: Akten des internationalen Colloquiums veranstaltet vom Schnütgen-Museum, Köln, 13.–15. Juni 1991.* Cologne: Locher, 1993.

Euw, Anton von, Peter Schreiner, and Gudrun Sporbeck, eds. *Kaiserin Theophanu: Begegnung des Ostens und Westens um die Wende des ersten Jahrtausends: Gedenkschrift des Kölner Schnütgen-Museums zum 1000. Todesjahr der Kaiserin.* 2 vols. Cologne: Schnütgen-Museum, 1991.

Evans, Gillian R. "Two Aspects of Memoria in Eleventh and Twelfth Century Writings." *Classica et Mediaevalia* 32 (1980): 263–78.

Evans, Gillian R., and Alison M. Peden. "Natural Science and the Liberal Arts in Abbo of Fleury's Commentary." *Viator* 16 (1985): 109–27.

Evers, Wilhelm. *Grundfragen der Siedlungsgeographie und Kulturlandschaften im Hildesheimer Land.* Bremen: Dorn, 1957.

Facciotto, Paolo. "La 'Vita Geraldi' di Oddone di Cluny, un problema aperto." *Studi Medievali,* 3rd ser., 33 (1992): 243–63.

Faust, Ulrich. *Die Benediktinerklöster in Niedersachsen, Schleswig-Holstein und Bremen.* Germania Benedictina 6. St. Ottilien: EOS Verlag, 1979.

———. "Das Hildesheimer Benediktinerkloster Sankt Michael in den monastischen Reformbewegungen." In *Bernward und das Zeitalter,* 1:397–406.

Fehrenbach, Frank. *Die Goldene Madonna in Essener Münster: Der Körper der Königin.* Ostfildern: Edition Tertium, 1996.

Fentress, James, and Chris Wickham. *Social Memory.* Cambridge: Blackwell, 1992.

Ferber, Stanley. "The Temple of Solomon in Early Christian and Byzantine Art." In Gutmann, *Temple of Solomon,* 21–43.

Ferrari, Michael Camillo. "Gold und Asche: Reliquie und Reliquiare als Medien in Thiofrid von Echternachts 'Flores epytaphii sanctorum.'" In Reudenbach and Toussaint, *Reliquiare im Mittelalter,* 61–74.

Fichtenau, Heinrich. "Diplomatiker und Urkundenforscher." *Mitteilungen des Instituts für Österreichische Geschichtsforschung* 100 (1992): 9–49.

Fisher, Annika E. "Cross Altar and Crucifix in Ottonian Cologne." In *Decorating the Lord's Table: On the Dynamics Between Image and Altar in the Middle Ages*, edited by Søren Kaspersen and Erik Thunø, 43–62. Copenhagen: Museum Tusculanum Press, University of Copenhagen, 2006.

Flanigan, C. Clifford. "Medieval Liturgy and the Arts: Visitatio Sepulchri as Paradigm." In *Liturgy and the Arts in the Middle Ages: Studies in Honour of C. Clifford Flanigan*, edited by Eva Louise Lillie and Nils Holger Petersen, 9–35. Copenhagen: Museum Tusculanum Press, University of Copenhagen, 1996.

Fleckenstein, Josef. *Die Hofkapelle der deutschen Konige*. Part 2, *Die Hofkapelle im Rahmen der ottonisch-salischen Reichskirche*. MGH Schriften 16, vol. 2. Stuttgart: Hiersemann, 1966.

———. "Problematik und Gestalt der ottonischsalischen Reichskirche." In *Reich und Kirche vor dem Investiturstreit: Vorträge beim wissenschaftlichen Kolloquium aus Anlaß des achtzigsten Geburtstages von Gerd Tellenbach*, edited by Karl Schmid, 83–98. Sigmaringen: Thorbecke, 1985.

Les fonctions des saints dans le monde occidental (IIIe–XIIIe siècle): Actes du colloque. Rome: École française de Rome, 1991.

Forsyth, Ilene H. *The Throne of Wisdom: Wood Sculptures of the Madonna in Romanesque France*. Princeton: Princeton University Press, 1972.

Fouracre, Paul, and Richard A. Gerberding, eds. *Late Merovingian France: History and Hagiography, 640–720*. Manchester: Manchester University Press, 1996.

Franz, Gunther, ed. *Der Egbert Codex: Das Leben Jesu. Ein Höhepunkt der Buchmalerei vor 1000 Jahren; Handschrift der Stadtbibliothek Trier*. Stuttgart: Theiss, 2005.

Franz, Gunther, and Franz J. Ronig, eds. *Codex Egberti Teilfaksimile-Ausgabe des Ms. 24 der Stadtbibliothek Trier*. 2 vols. Wiesbaden: Reichert, 1983.

Frassetto, Michael. "Reaction and Reform: Reception of Heresy in Arras and Aquitaine in the Early Eleventh Century." *Catholic Historical Review* 83 (1997): 385–400.

———, ed. *The Year 1000: Religious and Social Response to the Turning of the First Millennium*. New York: Palgrave, 2002.

Fricke, Beate. *Ecce Fides: Die Statue von Conques, Götzendienst und Bildkultur im Westen*. Munich: Fink, 2007.

———. "Fallen Idols and Risen Saints: Western Attitudes Towards the Worship of Images and the 'cultura veterum deorum.'" In *Negating the Image: Case Studies in Iconoclasm*, edited by Anne McClanan and Jeffrey Johnson, 67–95. Aldershot: Ashgate, 2005.

Friedrich, Annegret. "'Ich seh' dir nicht in die Augen, Kleines': Zur Rezeption der Essener Goldenen Madonna." In Klein and Prange, *Zeitenspiegelung*, 21–32.

Friend, A. M. "The Portraits of the Evangelists in Greek and Latin Manuscripts." *Art Studies* 5 (1927): 115–47.

Fulton, Rachel. *From Judgment to Passion: Devotion to Christ and the Virgin Mary, 800–1200*. New York: Columbia University Press, 2002.

Gaborit-Chopin, Danielle. "Trésors de Neustrie." In *La Neustrie: Les pays au nord de la Loire de 650 à 850*, edited by Hartmut Atsma and Karl Ferdinand Werner, 2:259–93. Sigmaringen: Thorbecke, 1989.

Gaehde, Joachim E. "La decorazione: Le miniature." In *Commentario della Bibbia di San Paolo fuori le mura*. Rome: Istituto poligrafico e Zecca dello Stato, Libreria dello Stato, 1993.

Galavaris, George. *The Illustrations of the Prefaces in Byzantine Gospels*. Vienna: Verlag der Österreichischen Akademie der Wissenschaften, 1979.

Gallistl, Bernhard. "Bernward of Hildesheim: A Case of Self-Planned Sainthood?" In *The Invention of Saintliness*, edited by Anneke B. Mulder-Bakker, 145–62. London: Routledge, 2002.

———. *Die Bernwardsäule und die Michaeliskirche zu Hildesheim*. Hildesheim: Olms, 1993.

———. "In Faciem Angelici Templi: Kultgeschichtliche Bemerkungen zu Inschrift und ursprünglicher Platzierung der Bernwardstür." *Jahrbuch für Geschichte und Kunst im Bistum Hildesheim* 75/76 (2007/2008): 59–92.

Ganz, David. *Medien der Offenbarung: Visionsdarstellungen im Mittelalter.* Berlin: Reimer, 2008.

Garrison, Eliza. "The Art Policy of Emperor Henry II (1002–1024)." Ph.D. diss., Northwestern University, 2005.

———. *Ottonian Imperial Art and Portraiture: The Art Patronage of Otto III and Henry II.* Burlington: Ashgate, 2012.

Gatti, Evan A. "Building the Body of the Church: A Bishop's Blessing in the Benedictional of Engilmar of Parenzo." In Ott and Jones, *Bishop Reformed,* 92–121.

———. "Developing an Iconography of the Episcopacy: Liturgical Portraiture and Episcopal Politics in Late Tenth- and Early Eleventh-Century Manuscripts." Ph.D. diss., University of North Carolina at Chapel Hill, 2005.

———. "In a Space Between: Warmund of Ivrea and the Problem of (Italian) Ottonian Art." *Peregrinations* 3 (2010): 8–48.

Geary, Patrick. *Phantoms of Remembrance: Memory and Oblivion at the End of the First Millennium.* Princeton: Princeton University Press, 1994.

Gerberto: Scienza, storia et mito; Atti del Gerberti Symposium (Bobbio 25–27 luglio 1983). Bobbio: Archivi storici bobiensi, 1985.

Gersh, Stephen. *Middle Platonism and Neoplatonism: The Latin Tradition.* 2 vols. Notre Dame: University of Notre Dame Press, 1986.

Geuenich, Dieter, and Otto Gerhard Oexle, eds. *Memoria in der Gesellschaft des Mittelalters.* Göttingen: Vandenhoeck & Ruprecht, 1994.

Gibson, Margaret. "The Study of the *Timaeus* in the Eleventh and Twelfth Centuries." *Pensamiento* 25 (1969): 183–94.

Gibson-Wood, Carol. "The Utrecht Psalter and the Art of Memory." *RACAR. Revue d'art canadienne* 14 (1987): 9–15.

Giese, Martina. *Die Textfassungen der Lebensbeschreibung Bischof Bernwards von Hildesheim.* MGH Studien und Texte 40. Hannover: Hahnsche Buchhandlung, 2006.

Gijsel, Jan. "Zu welcher Textfamilie des Pseudo-Matthäus gehört die Quelle von Hrotsvits Maria?" *Classica et mediaevalia* 32 (1979–80): 279–88.

Gilsdorf, Sean, ed. *The Bishop: Power and Piety at the First Millennium.* Münster: LIT-Verlag, 2004.

Godelier, Maurice. *The Enigma of the Gift.* Translated by Nora Scott. Chicago: University of Chicago Press, 1999.

Goetting, Hans. *Das Bistum Hildesheim.* Vol. 1, *Das Reichsunmittelbare Kanonissenstift Gandersheim.* Berlin: W. de Gruyter, 1973.

Goldschmidt, Adolf. "Eine sächsischer Buchdeckel aus ottonischer Zeit." In *Festschrift zur 60. Geburtstag von Paul Clemen 31. Oktober 1926,* edited by Wilhelm Worringer, Heribert Reinards, and Leopold Seligmann, 277–80. Düsseldorf: Instituts für Siedlungs- und Wohnungswesen und des Zentralinstituts für Raumplanung der Universität Münster, 1926.

Görich, Knut. "Der Gandersheimer Streit zur Zeit Ottos III: Ein Konflikt um die Metropolitanrechte des Erzbischofs Willigis von Mainz." *Zeitschrift der Savigny-Stiftung für Rechtsgeschichte: Kanonistische Abteilung* 79 (1993): 56–94.

Görich, Knut, and Hans H. Kortüm. "Otto III, Thangmar und die Vita Bernwardi." *Mitteilungen des Instituts für Österreichische Geschichtsforschung* 98 (1990): 1–57.

Gothe, August C. "St. Michael zu Hildesheim: Ergebnis der Untersuchungen 1939/40." *Alt-Hildesheim* 22 (1951): 22–28.

Goullet, Monique. "Hrotsvita de Gandersheim, *Maria.*" In Iogna-Prat, Palazzo, and Russo, *Marie: Le culte,* 441–70.

Goullet, Monique, and Dominique Iogna-Prat. "La Vierge en majesté de Clermont-Ferrand." In Iogna-Prat, Palazzo, and Russo, *Marie: Le culte,* 383–405.

Grabar, André. "Observations sur l'arc de triomphe de la croix dit arc d'Éginhard et sur d'autres bases de la croix." *Cahiers archéologiques: Fin de l'antiquité et Moyen Âge* 27 (1978): 61–83.

Grebe, Anja. *Codex Aureus: Das goldene Evangelienbuch von Echternach.* [Darmstadt]: Primus, 2007.

Green, Rosalie B. "Tenth-Century Ivory with the Response 'Aspiciens a longe.'" *Art Bulletin* 28 (1946): 112–14.

Greenblatt, Stephen. *Renaissance Self-Fashioning from More to Shakespeare.* Chicago: University of Chicago Press, 1980.

Grote, Udo. *Der Schatz von St. Viktor: Mittelalterliche Kostbarkeiten aus dem Xantener Dom.* Regensburg: Schnell & Steiner, 1998.

Guldan, Ernst. *Eva und Maria: Eine Antithese als Bildmotiv.* Graz: Böhlau, 1966.

Gutmann, Joseph, ed. *The Temple of Solomon: Archaeological Fact and Medieval Tradition in Christian, Islamic, and Jewish Art.* Missoula, Mont.: Scholars Press for American Academy of Religion, 1976.

Haarländer, Stephanie. *Vitae episcoporum: Eine Quellengattung zwischen Hagiographie und Historiographie, untersucht an Lebensbeschreibungen von Bischöfen des Regnum Teutonicum im Zeitalter der Ottonen und Salier.* Stuttgart: Hiersemann, 2000.

Hageman, Mariëlle. "Between the Imperial and the Sacred: The Gesture of Coronation in Carolingian and Ottonian Images." In *New Approaches to Medieval Communication,* edited by Marco Mostert, 127–63. Turnhout: Brepols, 1999.

Hahn, Cynthia. "The Meaning of Early Medieval Treasuries." In Reudenbach and Toussaint, *Reliquiare im Mittelalter,* 1–20.

———. *Portrayed on the Heart: Narrative Effect in Pictorial Lives of Saints from the Tenth Through the Thirteenth Century.* Berkeley: University of California Press, 2001.

———. "Relics and Reliquaries: The Construction of Imperial Memory and Meaning, with Particular Attention to Treasuries at Conques, Aachen, and Quedlinburg." In *Representing History, 900–1300: Art, Music, History,* edited by Robert A. Maxwell, 133–49. University Park: The Pennsylvania State University Press, 2010.

———. "What Do Reliquaries Do for Relics?" *Numen* 57 (2010): 284–316.

Halbwachs, Maurice. *Les cadres sociaux de la mémoire.* Paris: F. Alcan, 1925. Reprint, New York: Arno Press, 1952, 1975.

———. *La mémoire collective.* Paris: Presses universitaires de France, 1950, 1968.

———. *La topographie légendaire des Évangiles en Terre Sainte: Étude de mémoire collective.* Paris: Presses universitaires de France, 1941.

Hall, Thomas N. "The Cross as Green Tree in the *Vindicta Salvatoris* and the Green Rod of Moses in Exodus." *English Studies: A Journal of English Language and Literature* 72 (1991): 297–307.

Hallinger, Kassius. *Gorze-Kluny: Studien zu den monastischen Lebensformen und Gegensätzen im Hochmittelalter.* 2 vols. Rome: Herder, 1950–51.

Hamburger, Jeffrey. *St. John the Divine: The Deified Evangelist in Medieval Art and Theology.* Berkeley: University of California Press, 2002.

Hardison, O. B. *Christian Rite and Christian Drama in the Middle Ages.* Baltimore: Johns Hopkins University Press, 1965.

Harrison, Carol. "Taking Creation for the Creator: Use and Enjoyment in Augustine's Theological Aesthetics." In *Idolatry: False Worship in the Bible, Early Judaism, and Christianity,* edited by Stephen C. Barton, 179–97. London: T & T Clark, 2007.

Head, Thomas. "Postscript: The Ambiguous Bishop." In Ott and Jones, *Bishop Reformed,* 250–64.

Heck, Christian. "Les deux saints Jean: Étude de l'iconographie jumelée de Saint Jean-Baptiste et de Saint Jean-l'Évangeliste en Occident, des origines à la fin du moyen âge." Ph.D. diss., Université de Provence, 1979.

———. "Le portail à l'agneau de la cathédrale de Fribourg-en-Brisgau." *Cahiers alsaciens d'archéologie, d'art et d'histoire* 32 (1989): 165–76.

Heinemann, Otto von. *Die Handschriften der Herzoglichen Bibliothek zu Wolfenbüttel.* Vol. 1 (in 3 parts) and vol. 2 (in 4 parts). Wolfenbüttel: Zwissler, 1884–1903.

Heinemann, Wolfgang. *Das Bistum Hildesheim im Kräftespiel der Reichs- und Territorialpolitik.* Hildesheim: Lax, 1968.

Heller-Roazen, Daniel. "The Matter of Language: Guilhelm de Peitieus and the Platonic Tradition." *Modern Language Notes* 113 (1998): 851–80.

Henderson, George. "The John the Baptist Panel on the Ruthwell Cross." *Gesta* 24 (1985): 3–12.

Henkel, Karl A. O. *Die Bernwardinische Kunst: Bischof Bernward und seine Werke*. Hildesheim: F. Borgmeyer, 1937.

Herren, Michael W., Christopher J. McDonough, and Ross G. Arthur, eds. *Latin Culture in the Eleventh Century: Proceedings of the Third International Conference on Medieval Latin Studies, Cambridge, September 9–12, 1998*. 2 vols. Turnhout: Brepols, 2002.

Hoffmann, Konrad. "Die Evangelistenbilder des Münchener Otto-Evangeliars (Clm 4453)." *Zeitschrift des Deutschen Vereins für Kunstwissenschaft* 20 (1966): 17–46.

Honselmann, Klemens. "Eine Schenkung der Äbtissin Hitda von Meschede." *Westfälische Zeitschrift* 112 (1962): 305–7.

Houts, Elisabeth van. "Introduction: Medieval Memories." In *Medieval Memories: Men, Women, and the Past, 700–1300*, edited by Elisabeth van Houts, 1–16. New York: Longman, 2001.

———. *Memory and Gender in Medieval Europe, 900–1200*. Toronto: University of Toronto Press, 1999.

Hubert, Jean, and M.-C. Hubert. "Piété chrétienne ou paganisme? Les statues-reliquaires de l'Europe carolingienne." In *Christianizzazione ed organizzazione ecclesiastica delle campagne nell' alto medioevo: Espansione e resistenze*, 235–75. Settimane di Studio del Centro italiano di studi sull'alto medieovo 28. Spoleto: Centro italiano di Studi sull'alto medioevo, 1982.

Hughes, Andrew. *Medieval Manuscripts for Mass and Office: A Guide to Their Organization and Terminology*. Toronto: University of Toronto Press, 1982.

Hutton, Patrick H. *History as an Art of Memory*. Hanover: University Press of New England, 1993.

Iogna-Prat, Dominique. "La Madeleine du *Sermo in veneratione sanctae Mariae Magdalenae* attribué à Odon de Cluny." *Mélanges de l'École française de Rome: Moyen Âge* 104 (1992): 37–67.

Iogna-Prat, Dominique, Éric Palazzo, and Daniel Russo. *Marie: Le culte de la Vierge dans la société médiévale*. Paris: Beauchesne, 1996.

Iwanami, Atsuko. "Memoria et oblivio: Zur Entwicklungen des Begriffs memoria in den bischöflichen Urkunden des Früh- und Hochmittelalters, insbesondere im Maas-Rheingebiet." In *Urkundensprachen im germanisch-romanischen Grenzgebiet: Beiträge zum Kolloquium am 5/6 Oktober in Trier*, edited by Kurt Gärtner and Günter Holtus, 151–59. Mainz: Philipp von Zabern, 1997.

Jaeger, C. Stephen. *The Envy of Angels: Cathedral Schools and Social Ideas in Medieval Europe, 950–1200*. Philadelphia: University of Pennsylvania Press, 1994.

———. *The Origins of Courtliness: Civilizing Trends and the Formation of Courtly Ideals, 923–1210*. Philadelphia: University of Pennsylvaia Press, 1985.

Jäggi, Carola. "Stifter, Schreiber oder Heiliger? Überlegungen zum Dedikationsbild der Bernward-Bibel." In *Für irdischen Ruhm und himmlischen Lohn: Stifter und Auftraggeber in der mittelalterlichen Kunst, Festschrift für Beat Brenk*, edited by Hans-Rudolf Meier, Carola Jäggi, and Philippe Büttner, 65–75. Berlin: Reimer, 1995.

James, Liz. "Senses and Sensibility in Byzantium." *Art History* 27 (2004): 522–37.

Jestice, Phyllis G. "The Gorzian Reform and the Light Under the Bushel." *Viator* 24 (1993): 51–78.

———. "A New Fashion in Imitating Christ: Changing Spiritual Perspectives Around the Year 1000." In Frassetto, *The Year 1000*, 165–85.

Jones, Charles W. *Saints' Lives and Chronicles in Early England: Together with the First English Translations of the Oldest Life of Pope St. Gregory the Great by a Monk of Whitby and the Life of St. Guthlac of Crowland by Felix*. Ithaca: Cornell University Press, 1947.

Josten, Hans Heinz. *Neue Studien zur Evangelienhandschrift Nr. 18 des Hl. Bernward Evangelienbuch im Domschatze zur Hildesheim: Beiträge zur Geschichte der Buchmalerei im frühen Mittelalter*. Strassburg: J. H. E. Heitz, 1909.

Jung, Jacqueline. "The Tactile and the Visionary: Notes on the Place of Sculpture in the Medieval Imagination." In *Looking Beyond: Visions, Dreams, and*

Insights in Medieval Art and History, ed. Colum Hourihane, 203–40. University Park: The Pennsylvania State University Press, 2010.

Jungmann, Josef A. *The Mass of the Roman Rite: Its Origins and Development.* Translated by Francis A. Brunner. 2 vols. New York: Benziger, 1951–55. Originally published as *Missarum Sollemnia: Eine genetische Erklärung der römischen Messe.* 2 vols. Vienna: Herder, 1949.

Jussen, Bernhard. "Religious Discourses of the Gift in the Middle Ages: Semantic Evidence (Second to Twelfth Centuries)." In Algazi, Groebner, and Jussen, *Negotiating the Gift*, 173–92.

Jütte, Robert. *Geschichte der Sinne: Von der Antike bis zum Cyberspace.* Munich: Beck, 2000.

Kaestli, Jean-Daniel. "Le Protévangile de Jacques en latin: État de la question et perspectives nouvelles." *Revue d'histoire des textes* 26 (1996): 41–102.

Kahsnitz, Rainer. "Inhalt und Aufbau der Handschrift." In *Das Kostbare Evangeliar des Heiligen Bernward*, edited by Michael Brandt, 18–63. Munich: Prestel, 1993.

———. "Die Kunsthandwerk des späten Mittelalters." In *Das Germanische Nationalmuseum Nürnberg 1852–1977*, edited by Bernward Deneke and Rainer Kahsnitz, 730–60. Berlin: Deutscher Kunstverlag, 1978.

———. "'Matheus ex ore Christi scripsit': Zum Bild der Berufung und Inspiration der Evangelisten." In *Byzantine East, Latin West: Art-Historical Studies in Honor of Kurt Weitzmann*, edited by Doula Mouriki, Christopher Moss, and Katherine Kiefer, 169–80. Princeton: Princeton University Press, 1995.

Kahsnitz, Rainer, and Elisabeth Rücker, eds. *Das Goldene Evangelienbuch von Echternach: Codex Aureus Epternacensis Hs 156142 aus dem Germanischen Nationalmuseum Nürnberg.* Vol. 1 [Faksimileband]. Frankfurt am Main: S. Fischer Verlag with Verlag Müller und Schindler, 1982.

Kalavrezou-Maxeiner, Ioli. "When the Mother of God Became Meter Theou." *Dumbarton Oaks Papers* 44 (1990): 165–72.

Kallfelz, Hatto, ed. *Lebensbeschreibungen einiger Bischöfe des 10.–12. Jahrhunderts.* 2nd ed. Ausgewählte Quellen zur deutschen Geschichte des Mittelalters 22. Darmstadt: Wissenschaftliche Buchgesellschaft, 1973.

Kardong, Terrence. *Benedict's Rule: A Translation and Commentary.* Collegeville, Minn.: Liturgical Press, 1996.

Kaspersen, Søren. "Cotton-Genesis, die Toursbibeln und die Bronzetüren: Vorlage und Aktualität." In *Bernwardinische Kunst: Bericht*, 79–103.

———. "Majestas Domini, regnum et sacerdotium: Zu Entstehung und Leben des Motivs bis zum Investiturstreit." *Hafnia: Copenhagen Papers in the History of Art* 8 (1981): 83–146.

Katzenellenbogen, Adolf. *The Sculptural Programs of Chartres Cathedral.* Baltimore: Johns Hopkins University Press, 1959.

Kessler, Herbert L. "*Facies bibliothecae revelata*: Carolingian Art as Spiritual Seeing." In *Testo e immagine nell'alto medioevo: 15–21 aprile 1993*, 533–94. Spoleto: Centro italiano di studi sull'alto medioevo, 1994.

———. "'Hoc Visibile Imaginatum Figurat Illud Invisibile Verum': Imagining God in Pictures of Christ." In *Seeing the Invisible in Late Antiquity and the Early Middle Ages*, edited by Giselle de Nie, Karl F. Morrison, and Marco Mostert, 293–328. Turnhout: Brepols, 2005.

———. *The Illustrated Bibles from Tours.* Studies in Manuscript Illumination 7. Princeton: Princeton University Press, 1977.

———. "Image and Object: Christ's Dual Nature and the Crisis of Early Medieval Art." In Davis and McCormick, *Long Morning of Medieval Europe*, 291–320.

———. "Images of Christ and Communication with God." In *Comunicare et significare nell'alto Medioevo: 15–20 aprile 2004*, 1:1099–1136. Spoleto: Centro italiano di studi sull'alto medioevo, 2005.

———. "On the State of Medieval Art History." *Art Bulletin* 70 (1988): 166–87.

———. *Seeing Medieval Art.* Orchard Park, N.Y.: Broadview Press, 2004.

———. *Spiritual Seeing: Picturing God's Invisibility in Medieval Art*. Philadelphia: University of Pennsylvania Press, 2000.

Kidd, Judith A. "The Quinity of Winchester Reconsidered." *Studies in Iconography* 7/8 (1981): 21–33.

King, Norbert. *Mittelalterliche Dreikönigsspiele: Eine Grundlagenarbeit zu den lateinischen, deutschen und französischen Dreikönigsspielen und -spielszenen bis zum Ende des 16. Jahrhunderts*. Freiburg: Universitätsverlag Freiburg, 1979.

Kingsley, Jennifer P. "VT CERNIS and the Materiality of Bernwardian Art." In Lutz and Weyer, *1000 Jahre St. Michael in Hildesheim*, 171–84.

Kirmeier, Josef, Aloïs Schütz, and Evamaria Brockhoff, eds. *Schreibkunst: Mittelalterliche Buchmalerei aus dem Kloster Seeon*. Regensburg: F. Pustet, 1994.

Kirschbaum, Engelbrecht, and Günter Bandmann, eds. *Lexikon der christlichen Ikonographie*. 8 vols. Rome: Herder, 1968–76.

Klauser, Theodor. *Das Ciborium in der älteren christlichen Buchmalerei*. Nachrichten der Akademie der Wissenschaften in Göttingen, Philologisch.-Historische Klasse 7. Göttingen: Aschendorff, 1961.

———. *Das römische Capitulare evangeliorum: Texte und Untersuchungen zu seiner ältesten Geschichte*. Vol. 1, *Typen*. Münster: Aschendorff, 1935.

Kleiman, Irit. "The Life and Times of Judas Iscariot: Form and Function." *Medievalia et humanistica*, n.s., 33 (2007): 15–40.

Klein, Holger. *Sacred Gifts and Worldly Treasures: Medieval Masterworks from the Cleveland Museum of Art*. Cleveland: Cleveland Museum of Art, 2007.

Klein, Peter. "Die frühen Apocalypse-Zyklen und verwandte Denkmaler." Ph.D. diss., University of Bamberg, 1980

———. "Zur Nachfolge der karolingischen Bilderbibeln: Die touronische Vorlage des Bernward-Evangeliars in Hildesheim." In Klein and Prange, *Zeitenspiegelung*, 33–45.

Klein, Peter, and Regine Prange, eds. *Zeitenspiegelung: Zur Bedeutung von Traditionen in Kunst und Kunstwissenschaft; Festschrift für Konrad Hoffmann zum 60. Geburtstag am 8. Oktober 1998*. Berlin: Reimer, 1998.

Knapp, Ulrich. *Ego sum Hildensemensis: Bischof, Domkapitel und Dom in Hildesheim 815 bis 1810*. Petersberg: Michael Imhof Verlag, 2000.

Knapp, Ulrich, and Elisabeth Scholz, eds. *Buch und Bild im Mittelalter*. Hildesheim: Gerstenberg, 1999.

Koehler, Wilhelm. *Die karolingischen Miniaturen*. Vol. 2, *Die Hofschule Karls des Grossen*. Berlin: Deutscher Verein für Kunstwissenschaft, 1958.

Kottje, Raymond. "Monastische Reform oder Reformen?" In *Monastische Reformen im 9. und 10. Jahrhundert*, edited by Raymond Kottje and Helmut Maurer, 9–13. Sigmaringen: Thorbecke, 1989.

Krah, Adelheid. "Wo bleibt der Mensch? Das Dilemma der Typologisierungen des Sujets in hagiographischen Texten des Mittelalters." *Mitteilungen des Instituts für Österreichische Geschichtsforschung* 111 (2003): 267–85.

Kratz, Johannes M. *Der Dom zu Hildesheim: Seine Kostbarkeiten, Kunstschätze und sonstige Merkwürdigkeiten*. Hildesheim: Gerstenberg, 1840.

Krautheimer, Richard. "Introduction to an 'Iconography of Mediaeval Architecture.'" *Journal of the Warburg and Courtauld Institutes* 5 (1942): 1–33.

Krinsky, Carol Herselle. "Representations of the Temple of Jerusalem Before 1500." *Journal of the Warburg and Courtauld Institutes* 33 (1970): 1–19.

Kühnel, Bianca. *The End of Time in the Order of Things: Science and Eschatology in Early Medieval Art*. Regensburg: Schnell & Steiner, 2003.

Kupfer, Marcia. "The Cult of Images in Light of Pictorial Graffiti at Doué-la-Fontaine." *Early Medieval Europe* 19 (2011): 125–52.

Kuppers, Leonhard, and Paul Mikat. *Der Essener Münsterschatz*. Essen: Fredebeul & Koene, 1966.

Landes, Richard. "The Fear of an Apocalyptic Year 1000: Augustinian Historiography, Medieval and Modern." *Speculum* 75 (2000): 97–145.

———. *Relics, Apocalypse, and the Deceits of History: Ademar of Chabannes, 989–1034*. Cambridge, Mass.: Harvard University Press, 1995.

Lane, Barbara G. "'Ecce Panis Angelorum': The Manger as Altar in Hugo's Berlin Nativity." *Art Bulletin* 57 (1975): 476–86.

Lasko, Peter. *Ars Sacra, 800–1200.* 2nd ed. New Haven: Yale University Press, 1994.

———. "The Tomb of St. Bernward of Hildesheim." In *Romanesque and Gothic: Essays for George Zarnecki*, edited by Neil Stratford, 1:147–52. Woodbridge: Boydell Press, 1987.

Laudage, Marie-Louis. *Caritas und Memoria mittelalterlicher Bischöfe.* Cologne: Böhlau, 1993.

Lauers, Michel. "'Noli me tangere' Marie Madeleine, Marie d'Oignies et les penitentes du XIIIᵉ siècle." *Mélanges de l'École française de Rome: Moyen Âge* 104 (1992): 209–68.

Leclercq, Jean. "Simoniaca heresis." *Studi Gregoriani* 1 (1947): 523–30.

Leesti, Elizabeth. "Carolingian Crucifixion Iconography: An Elaboration of a Byzantine Theme." *RACAR: Revue d'art canadienne* 20 (1993): 3–15.

Legner, Anton, ed. *Monumenta Annonis: Köln und Siegburg, Weltbild und Kunst im hohen Mittelalter: Eine Ausstellung des Schnütgen-Museums der Stadt Köln in der Cäcilienkirche vom 30. April bis zum 27. Juli 1975.* Cologne: Das Museum, 1975.

Le Goff, Jacques. *The Birth of Purgatory.* Translated by Arthur Goldhammer. Chicago: University of Chicago Press, 1984.

Lehmann, Karl. "The Dome of Heaven." *Art Bulletin* 27 (1945): 1–27.

Lesne, Emile. *Histoire de la propriété écclesiastique en France.* 6 vols. Lille: Fac. Cath, 1910.

Lewis, Suzanne. "A Byzantine *Virgo militans* at Charlemagne's Court." *Viator* 11 (1980): 71–94.

Leyen, Friedrich von der, ed. *Deutsche Dichtung des Mittelalters.* Frankfurt am Main: Insel-Verlag, 1962.

Leyser, Karl. *Rule and Conflict in Early Medieval Society: Ottonian Saxony.* Bloomington: Indiana University Press, 1979.

Lienhard, Joseph T. "John the Baptist in Augustine's Exegesis." In *Augustine: Biblical Exegete*, edited by Frederick van Fleteren and Joseph C. Schnaubelt, 197–213. New York: Peter Lang, 2001.

Lipton, Sara. "The Sweet Lean of His Head: Writing About Looking at the Crucifix in the High Middle Ages." *Speculum* 80 (2005): 1172–208.

Lobrichon, Guy. "L'engendrement des saints: Le débat des savants et la revendication d'une sainteté exemplaire en France du Nord au XIᵉ et au début du XIIᵉ siècle." In *Les fonctions des saints*, 143–60.

Lochrie, Karma. *Margery Kempe and Translations of the Flesh.* Philadelphia: University of Pennsylvania Press, 1991.

Longo, Umberto. "Riti e agiografia: L'istituzione della commemoratio omnium fidelium defunctorum nelle Vitae di Odilone di Cluny." *Bullettino dell'Istituto italiano per il Medio Evo* 103 (2002): 163–200.

Lowden, John. "Illuminated Books and the Liturgy: Some Observations." In *Objects, Images, and the Word: Art in the Service of the Liturgy*, edited by Colum Hourihane, 17–53. Index of Christian Art Occasional Papers 6. Princeton: Index of Christian Art, Dept. of Art and Archaeology, Princeton University in association with Princeton University Press, 2003.

Lubac, Henri de. *Corpus mysticum: L'Eucharistie et l'Église au Moyen Âge; Étude historique.* Paris: Aubier, 1944.

Lutz, Gerhard, and Angela Weyer, eds. *1000 Jahre St. Michael in Hildesheim: Kirche-Kloster-Stifter.* Göttingen: Michael Imhof Verlag, 2012.

Maguire, Henry. "Disembodiment and Corporality in Byzantine Images of the Saints." In *Iconography at the Crossroads: Papers from the Colloquium Sponsored by the Index of Christian Art, Princeton University, 23–24 March 1990*, edited by Brian Cassidy, 75–90. Princeton: Index of Christian Art, Dept. of Art and Archaeology, Princeton University, 1993.

———. "Style and Ideology in Byzantine Imperial Art." *Gesta* 28 (1989): 217–31.

Maloy, Robert M. "The Sermonary of St. Ildephonsus of Toledo: A Study of the Scholarship and Manuscripts." *Classical Folia* 25 (1971): 137–99.

Mariaux, Pierre-Alain. "The Bishop as Artist? The Eucharist and Image Theory Around the

Millennium." In *The Bishop: Power and Piety at the First Millennium*, edited by Sean Gilsdorf, 155–68. Münster: LIT-Verlag, 2004.

———. "Collecting (and Display)." In *A Companion to Medieval Art: Romanesque and Gothic in Northern Europe*, edited by Conrad Rudolph, 213–32. Oxford: Blackwell, 2006.

———. "'Faire Dieu': Quelques remarques sur les relations entre confection eucharistique et création d'image (IXᵉ–XIIᵉ siècles)." In *Ästhetik des Unsichtbaren: Bildtheorie und Bildgebrauch in der Vormoderne*, edited by David Ganz and Thomas Lentes, 94–106. Berlin: Reimer, 2004.

———. *Warmond d'Ivrée et ses images: Politique et création iconographique autour de l'an mil.* Bern: Lang, 2002.

Masseron, Alexandre. *Saint Jean Baptiste dans l'art.* Paris: Arthaud, 1957.

Mathews, Thomas. "Cracks in Lehmann's 'Dome of Heaven.'" *Notes on the History of Art* 1 (1982): 12–16.

Matter, E. Ann. "Exegesis of the Apocalypse in the Early Middle Ages." In Frassetto, *The Year 1000*, 29–40.

Mauss, Marcel. "Essai sur le don: Forme et raison de l'échange dans les sociétés archaïques." *Année sociologique*, 2nd ser. (1923–24).

Mayr-Harting, Henry. *Ottonian Book Illumination: An Historical Study.* 2 vols. London: H. Miller, 1991.

Mazza, Enrico. *The Celebration of the Eucharist: The Origin of the Rite and the Development of Its Interpretation.* Collegeville, Minn.: Liturgical Press, 1999.

McCracken, George Englert. *Early Medieval Theology.* Library of Christian Classics 9. Philadelphia: Westminster Press, 1957.

Meer, Frederik van der. *Maiestas Domini: Théophanies de l'Apocalypse dans l'art chrétien.* Rome: Pontificio istituto di archeologia cristiana, 1938.

Mellinkoff, Ruth. "One Is Good, Two Are Better: The Twice-Appearing Ass in a Thirteenth-Century English Nativity." In *New Offerings,*

Ancient Treasures: Studies in Medieval Art for George Henderson, edited by Paul Binski and William Noel, 325–42. Stroud: Sutton, 2001.

Mennemeyer, Franz. "Kult und Brauchtum Johannis des Täufers in Westfalen." Ph.D. diss., University of Münster, 1940.

Micrologus: Natura, scienze e società medievali (Nature, Sciences and Medieval Societies) 10 (2002).

Miles, Margaret. "Vision: The Eye of the Body and the Eye of the Mind in Saint Augustine's 'De trinitate' and 'Confessions.'" *Journal of Religion* 63 (1983): 125–42.

Molle, Frans van. "Notes sur quelques calices funéraires du XIᵉ siècle en France et en Belgique." *Les monuments historiques de la France* 12 (1966): 113–19.

Moore, Michael E. Hoenicke. "Demons and the Battle for Souls at Cluny." *Studies in Religion* 32 (2003): 485–97.

Most, Glenn W. *Doubting Thomas.* Cambridge, Mass.: Harvard University Press, 2005.

Mouilleron, Véronique Rouchon. "Entre Orient et Occident: L'image de saint Jean du XIᵉ au XIVᵉ siècle." *Revue de l'art* 158 (2007): 35–45.

Mütherich, Florentine. *Sakramentar von Metz: Fragment: Ms. Lat. 1141, Bibliothèque nationale, Paris, vollständige Faksimile-Ausgabe.* Graz: Akademiche Druck- und Verlagsanstalt, 1972.

Mütherich, Florentine, and Karl Dachs. *Das Evangeliar Ottos III: Clm 4453 der Bayerischen Staatsbibliothek München.* Munich: Prestel, 2001.

Muthesius, Anna M. "Archbishop Hubert Walter's Tomb and Its Furnishings." In *Medieval Art and Architecture at Canterbury Before 1220*, 20–26. London: British Archaeological Association, 1982.

Nahmer, Dieter von. "Die Inschrift auf der Bernwardstür in Hildesheim im Rahmen Bernwardinischer Texte." In *Bernwardinische Kunst: Bericht*, 51–70.

Nass, Klaus. *Mittelalterliche Quellen zur Geschichte Hildesheims.* Hildesheim: Gerstenberg, 2006.

Nees, Lawrence. "Aspects of Antiquarianism in the Art of Bernward and Its Contemporary Analogues." In Lutz and Weyer, *1000 Jahre St. Michael in Hildesheim*, 153–70.

Nelson, Robert S. *The Iconography of Preface and Miniature in the Byzantine Gospel Book*. New York: New York University Press for the College Art Association of America, 1980.

Nielson, Christina. "Hoc opus eximium: Artistic Patronage in the Ottonian Empire." Ph.D. diss., University of Chicago, 2002.

Nightingale, John. "Bishop Gerard of Toul (963–94) and Attitudes to Episcopal Office." In *Warriors and Churchmen in the High Middle Ages: Essays Presented to Karl Leyser*, edited by Timothy Reuter, 41–62. London: Rio Grande, 1992.

Nilgen, Ursula. "The Epiphany and the Eucharist: On the Interpretation of Eucharistic Motifs in Mediaeval Epiphany Scenes." Translated by Renate Franciscono. *Art Bulletin* 49 (1967): 311–16.

Noble, Thomas F. X. *Images, Iconoclasm, and the Carolingians*. Philadelphia: University of Pennsylvania Press, 2009.

Noble, Thomas F. X., and Thomas Head, eds. *Soldiers of Christ: Saints and Saints' Lives from Late Antiquity and the Early Middle Ages*. University Park: The Pennsylvania State University Press, 1995.

Nolte, Josef. "Tercii Ottonis imperatoris didascalus: Die *Vita Bernwardi* von Thangmar." In *Vormoderne Lebensläufe*, edited by Rudolf W. Keck and Erhard Wiersing, 131–49. Cologne: Böhlau, 1994.

Nora, Pierre. "General Introduction: Between Memory and History." In *Realms of Memory: Rethinking the French Past*. Vol. 1. Translated by Arthur Goldhammer. New York: Columbia University Press, 1996.

———. *Les lieux de mémoire*. 3 vols. Paris: Gallimard, 1984–92.

Nordenfalk, Carl. "Les cinq sens dans l'art du moyen âge." *Revue de l'art* 34 (1976): 17–28.

———. "The Five Senses in Late Medieval and Renaissance Art." *Journal of the Warburg and Courtauld Institutes* 48 (1985): 1–22.

———. "Der inspirierte Evangelist." *Wiener Jahrbuch für Kunstgeschichte* 36 (1983): 175–90 and 249–60.

———. "Noch eine turonische Bilderbibel." In *Festschrift Bernhard Bischoff zu seinem 65. Geburtstag*, edited by Johanne Autenrieth and Franz Brunhölzl, 153–63. Stuttgart: Hiersemann, 1971.

North, William, and Anthony Cutler. "Ivories, Inscriptions, and Episcopal Self-Consciousness in the Ottonian Empire: Berthold of Toul and the Berlin Hodegetria." *Gesta* 42 (2003): 1–17.

Ó Carragáin, Éamonn. "John the Baptist and the Agnus Dei: Ruthwell (and Bewcastle) Revisited." *The Antiquaries' Journal* 81 (1999): 131–53.

———. *Ritual and the Rood: Liturgical Images and the Old English Poems of the "Dream of the Rood" Tradition*. London: British Library, 2005.

Oexle, Otto Gerhard. *Memoria als Kultur*. Göttingen: Vandenhoeck & Ruprecht, 1995.

———. "Memoria und Memorialbild." In Karl Schmid and Joachim Wollasch, *Memoria: Der geschichtliche Zeugniswert des liturgischen Gedenkens im Mittelalter*, 384–440. Munich: Fink, 1984.

———. "Memoria und Memorialüberlieferung im früheren Mittelalter." *Frühmittelalterliche Studien* 10 (1976): 70–95.

O'Reilly, Jennifer. "Patristic and Insular Traditions of the Evangelists: Exegesis and Iconography." In *Le isole britanniche e Roma in età romanobarbarica*, edited by Anna Maria Luiselli Fadda and Éamonn Ó Carragáin, 49–94. Rome: Herder, 1998.

———. "St. John as a Figure of the Contemplative Life: Text and Image in the Art of the Anglo-Saxon Benedictine Reform." In *St. Dunstan: His Life, Times, and Cult*, edited by Nigel Ramsay, Margaret Sparks, and Tim Tatton-Brown, 165–85. Woodbridge: Boydell Press, 1992.

Ott, John S. "'Both Mary and Martha': Bishop Lietbert of Cambrai and the Construction of Episcopal Sanctity in a Border Diocese Around 1100." In Ott and Jones, *Bishop Reformed*, 137–60.

Ott, John S., and Anna Trumbore Jones, eds. *The Bishop Reformed: Studies of Episcopal Power and Culture in the Central Middle Ages*. Aldershot: Ashgate, 2007.

Palazzo, Éric. *L'espace rituel et le sacré dans le Christianisme: La liturgie de l'autel portatif dans l'Antiquité et au Moyen Âge*. Turnhout: Brepols, 2008.

———. *L'évêque et son image: L'illustration du pontifical au Moyen Âge.* Turnhout: Brepols, 1999.

———. *A History of Liturgical Books from the Beginning to the Thirteenth Century.* Translated by Madeleine Beaumont. Collegeville, Minn.: Liturgical Press, 1998.

———. "Le livre dans les trésors du Moyen-Âge: Contribution à l'histoire de la *Memoria* médiévale." *Annales: Histoire, sciences sociales* 52 (1997): 93–118.

Palazzo, Éric, and Ann-Katrin Andrews Johansson. "Jalons liturgiques pour une histoire de culte de la Vierge dans l'Occident latin (Vᵉ–XIᵉ siècles)." In Iogna-Prat, Palazzo, and Russo, *Marie: Le culte,* 14–43.

Panofsky, Erwin. *Early Netherlandish Painting: Its Origins and Character.* 2 vols. Cambridge, Mass.: Harvard University Press, 1953.

Papamastorakis, Titos. "The Display of Accumulated Wealth in Luxury Icons: Gift Giving from the Byzantine Aristocracy to God in the Twelfth Century." In *Byzantines eikones: Techne, technike kai technologia,* edited by Maria Vassilaki, 35–37. Heraklion: Panepistēmiakes Ekdoseis Krētēs, 2002.

Parisse, Michel. "Princes laïques et/ou moines, les évêques du Xᵉ siècle." In *Il secolo di ferro: Mito e realtà del secolo X. 19–25 aprile 1990,* 1:449–513. Settimane di Studio del Centro italiano di studi sull'alto medioevo 38. Spoleto: Centro italiano di studi sull'alto medioevo, 1991.

Partyka, Jan Stanislaw. *La résurrection de Lazare dans les monuments funéraires des nécropoles chrétiennes à Rome: Peintures, mosaïques et décor des épitaphes; Étude archéologique, iconographique et iconologique.* Warsaw: Zakład Archeologii Śród ziemnomorskiej Polskiej Akademii Nauk, 1993.

Paterson, Mark. *Senses of Touch: Haptics, Affects, and Technologies.* Oxford: Berg, 2007.

Paz, Francisco Javier Tovar. *Tractatus, sermones atque homiliae: El cultivo del género literario del discurso homilético en la Hispania tardoantigua y visigoda.* Cáceres: Universidad de Extramadura, 1994.

Peltomaa, Leena Mari. *The Image of the Virgin Mary in the Akathistos Hymn.* Leiden: Brill, 2001.

Pentcheva, Bissera. "The Performative Icon." *Art Bulletin* 88 (2006): 631–55.

———. *The Sensual Icon: Space, Ritual, and the Senses in Byzantium.* University Park: The Pennsylvania State University Press, 2010.

Phipps, Colin. "Romuald—Model Hermit: Eremitical Theory in Peter Damian's *Vita Beati Romualdi,* Chapters 16–27." *Studies in Church History* 22 (1985): 65–77.

Picard, Jean-Charles. "Le modèle épiscopale dans deux vies du Xᵉ siècle: Saint Innocentius de Tortona et Saint Prosper de Reggio Emilia." In *Les fonctions des saints,* 371–84.

Piendl, Max. "Fontes monasterii s. Emmerami Ratisbonensis: Bau- und kunstgeschichtliche Quellen." In *Quellen und Forschungen zur Geschichte des ehemaligen Reichsstiftes St. Emmeram in Regensburg,* 17–18. Thurn und Taxis-Studien 1. Kallmünz: M. Lassleben, 1961.

Pietri, Luce. *La ville de Tours du IVᵉ au VIᵉ siècle: Naissance d'une cité chrétienne.* Rome: École française de Rome, 1983.

Pinder, Wilhelm. *Die Kunst der deutschen Kaiserzeit.* Leipzig: H. F. Menck, 1940.

Podlaha, Anton. *Die Bibliothek des Metropolitankapitels.* Prague: Verlag der Archaeologischen Commission bei der Böhmischen Kaiser-Franz-Josef-Akademie für Wissenschaften, Litteratur und Kunst, 1904.

Poilpré, Anne-Orange. *Majestas Domini: Une image de l'Église en Occident, Vᵉ–IXᵉ siècle.* Paris: Cerf, 2005.

Pomian, Krzysztof. "The Collection: Between the Visible and the Invisible." In *Interpreting Objects and Collections,* edited by Susan Pearce, 160–74. London: Routledge, 1994.

———. *Collectionneurs, amateurs et curieux.* Paris: Gallimard, 1987.

Pranger, Burcht. "Le sacrement de l'eucharistie et la prolifération de l'imaginaire aux XIᵉ et XIIᵉ siècles." In *Fête-Dieu (1246–1996),* vol. 1, *Actes du colloque de Liège, 12–14 septembre 1996*, edited by André Haquin, 97–116. Turnhout: Brepols, 1999.

Prochno, Joachim. *Das Schreiber- und Dedikationsbild in der deutschen Buchmalerei*. Part 1, *Bis zum Ende des 11. Jahrhunderts (800–1100)*. Leipzig: Teubner, 1929.

Puhle, Matthias, ed. *Otto der Grosse: Magdeburg und Europa*. 2 vols. Mainz: Philipp von Zabern, 2001.

Putney, Richard H. "Creatio et Redemptio: The Genesis Monogram of the St. Hubert Bible." Ph.D. diss., University of Delaware, 1985.

Rädl, Fidel. "Calcidius und Paulus begründen ein Vermächtnis: Zu Bernwards Dotationsurkunde für St. Michael in Hildesheim." In Herren, McDonough, and Arthur, *Latin Culture in the Eleventh Century*, 328–49.

Ramseyer, Valerie. "Pastoral Care as Military Action: The Ecclesiology of Archbishop Alfanus of Salerno (1058–1085)." In Ott and Jones, *Bishop Reformed*, 189–208.

Rasmussen, Niels Krogh, and Marcel Haverals. *Les Pontificaux du Haut Moyen Age: Gènese du livre de L'évêque*. Leuven: Spicilegium Sacrum Lovaniense, 1998.

Reallexikon zur deutschen Kunstgeschichte. Stuttgart: Metzler, 1937–.

Remensnyder, Amy G. "Legendary Treasure at Conques: Reliquaries and Imaginative Memory." *Speculum* 71 (1996): 884–906.

———. *Remembering Kings Past: Monastic Foundation Legends in Medieval Southern France*. Ithaca: Cornell University Press, 1995.

Rensing, Thomas. "Johannes der Täufer: Patron des Westwerks von Corvey und des Königtums." *Westfalen* 42 (1964): 243–328.

Reudenbach, Bruno. "Authentizitätsverheissungen im mittelalterlichen Reliquienkult und in der Gegenwartskunst." In Klein and Prange, *Zeitenspiegelung*, 375–85.

———. *Das Godescalc-Evangelistar: Ein Buch für die Reformpolitik Karls des Grossen*. Frankfurt: Fischer-Taschenbuch-Verlag, 1998.

———. "Individuum ohne Bildnis? Zum Problem künstlerischer Ausdrucksformen von Individualität im Mittelalter." In *Individuum und Individualität im Mittelalter*, edited by Jan A. Aertsen and Andreas Speer, 807–18. Berlin: W. de Gruyter, 1996.

Reudenbach, Bruno, and Gia Toussaint, eds. *Reliquiare im Mittelalter*. Hamburger Forschungen zur Kunstgeschichte 5. Berlin: Akademie Verlag, 2005.

Reuter, Timothy. "The Imperial Church System of the Ottonian and Salian Rulers: A Reconsideration." *Journal of Ecclesiastical History* 33 (1982): 347–74.

Reynolds, Roger E. "A Visual Epitome of the Eucharistic Ordo from the Era of Charles the Bald: The Ivory Mass Cover of the *Drogo Sacramentary*." In *Charles the Bald: Court and Kingdom*, edited by Margaret T. Gibson and Janet L. Nelson, 241–60. Aldershot: Ashgate, 1990.

Richter, Dieter. "Die Allegorie der Pergamentbearbeitung: Beziehungen zwischen handwerklichen Vorgängen und der geistlichen Bildersprache des Mittelalters." In *Fachliteratur des Mittelalters: Festschrift für Gerhard Eis*, edited by Gundolf Keil et al., 83–92. Stuttgart: Metzler, 1968.

Rigodon, René. "Vision de Robert, abbé de Mozat, au sujet de la basilique de la Mère de Dieu edifiée dans la Ville des Arvernes, relation par le diacre Arnaud (Ms de Clermont 145, f. 130–134)." *Bulletin historique et scientifique de l'Auvergne* 70 (1950): 22–55.

Ronig, Franz, ed. *Egbert: Erzbischof von Trier, 977–993: Gedenkschrift der Diözese Trier zum 1000. Todestag*. 2 vols. Trier: Rheinisches Landesmuseum, 1993.

Rosenau, Helen. *Vision of the Temple: The Image of the Temple of Jerusalem in Judaism and Christianity*. London: Oresko Books, 1979.

Rosenthal, Jane. "The Unique Architectural Settings of the Arenberg Evangelists." In *Sources of Anglo-Saxon Culture*, edited by Paul Szarmach with Virginia D. Oggins, 261–82. Studies in Medieval Culture 20. Kalamazoo: Medieval Institute Publications, Western Michigan University, 1986.

Rousset, Paul. "L'idéal chevaleresque dans deux Vitae clunisiennes." In *Études de civilisation médiévale*

(IXe–XIIe siècles): Mélanges offerts à Edmond-René Labande, 623–33. Poitiers: C.E.S.C.M., 1974.

Rubin, Miri. *Corpus Christi: The Eucharist in Late Medieval Culture.* Cambridge: Cambridge University Press, 1991.

Russo, Daniel. "Le Christ entre Dieu et homme dans l'art du Moyen Âge en Occident, IXe–XVe siècles: Essai d'interprétation iconographique." In *Le Moyen Âge aujourd'hui: Trois regards contemporains sur le Moyen Âge; Histoire, théologie, cinema; Actes de la Rencontre de Cerisy-la-Salle, juillet 1991,* edited by Jacques Le Goff and Guy Lobrichon, 247–79. Paris: Le Léopard d'or, 1997.

Sanderson, Warren. "Gorze Reform Architecture." In *The White Mantle of Churches: Architecture, Liturgy, and Art Around the Millennium,* edited by Nigel Hiscock, 81–90. Turnhout: Brepols, 2003.

Sansterre, Jean-Michel. "Un saint récent et son icône dans le Latin méridional au XIe siècle: À propos d'un miracle de Dominique de Sora." *Byzantinoslavica* 56 (1995): 447–52.

———. "Vénération et utilisation apotropaïque de l'image à Reichenau vers la fin du Xème siècle: Un témoignage des *gesta* de l'abbé Wittigowo." *Revue belge de philologie et d'histoire* 73 (1995): 281–85.

Santifaller, Leo. *Zur Geschichte des ottonisch-salischen Reichskirchensystems.* 2nd ed. Sitzungsberichte der Österreichischen Akademie der Wissenschaften 229. Vienna: Böhlau; Kommissionsverlag der Österreichischen Akademie der Wissenschaften, 1964.

Sauer, Christine. *Fundatio und Memoria: Stifter und Klostergründer im Bild 1100 bis 1350.* Göttingen: Vandenhoeck & Ruprecht, 1993.

Saulnier, Daniel. "La résurrection de Lazare." *Études grégoriennes* 25 (1997): 7–11.

Schade, Herbert. "Der 'Himmlische Mensch': Zur anthropologischen Struktur des biblischen Menschbildes in der Kunst." In *Christus und Maria: Menschensohn und Gottesmutter,* edited by Victor H. Elbern, 18–27. Berlin: Mann, 1980.

Schaefer, Michael. *Hitda-Codex: Evangeliar des Stifts St. Walburga in Meschede; Handschrift 1640 der Hessischen Landes- und Hochschulbibliothek in Darmstadt.* Meschede: Heimatbund der Stadt Meschede, 2003.

Schapiro, Meyer. "The Image of the Disappearing Christ: The Ascension in English Art Around the Year 1000." *Gazette des beaux-arts,* 6th ser., 23 (1943): 133–52. Reprinted in Schapiro, *Late Antique, Early Christian, and Medieval Art,* 267–87. Selected Papers 3. New York: George Braziller, 1979.

———. "Style." In *Anthropology Today: An Encyclopedic Inventory,* edited by Alfred L. Kroeber, 287–312. Chicago: University of Chicago Press, 1953. Reprinted in *Theory and Philosophy of Art: Style, Artist, and Society,* 51–102. Selected Papers 4. New York: George Braziller, 1994.

Schieffer, Rudolf. *Das Grab des Bischofs in der Kathedrale.* Munich: Verlag der Bayerischen Akademie der Wissenschaften, 2001.

Schier, Volker, and Corine Schleif. "Seeing and Singing, Touching and Tasting the Holy Lance: The Power and Politics of Embodied Religious Experiences in Nuremberg, 1424–1524." In *Signs of Change: Transformations of Christian Traditions and Their Representation in the Arts, 1000–2000,* edited by Nils Petersen, Claus Cluver, and Nicholas Bell, 401–87. New York: Rodopi, 2004.

Schiller, Gertrud. *Ikonographie der christlichen Kunst.* 5 vols in 8. [Gütersloh]: Gütersloher Verlagshaus G. Mohn, 1966–91.

Schmid, Karl, and Joachim Wollasch, eds. *Memoria: Der geschichtliche Zeugniswert des liturgischen Gedenkens im Mittelalter.* Munich: Fink, 1984.

Schmitt, Jean-Claude. "*Imago*: De l'image à l'imaginaire." In Baschet and Schmitt, *L'image,* 29–57.

Schneider, Herbert. "L'intercession des vivants pour les morts: L'exemple des synodes du haut Moyen Age." In *L'intercession du Moyen Âge à l'époque moderne: Autour d'une pratique sociale,* edited by Jean-Marie Moeglin, 41–65. Geneva: Droz, 2004.

Schneider, Wolfgang Christian. *Bernward von Hildesheim: Bischof—Politiker—Künstler—Theologe.* Hildesheim: Olms, 2010.

Schnitzler, Hermann. *Rheinische Schatzkammer: Die Romanik*. 2 vols. Düsseldorf: Schwann, 1957.

———. "Das sogenannte grosse Bernwardkreuz." In *Karolingische und ottonische kunst: Werden, Wesen, Wirkung*, edited by Friedrich Gerke, Georg von Opel, and Hermann Schnitzler, 382–94. Wiesbaden: Steiner, 1957.

Schorta, Regula. "Seidengewebe und Schliesse." In Brandt, *Kostbare Evangeliar*, 61–62.

———. "The Textiles Found in the Shrine of the Patron Saints of Hildesheim Cathedral." *Bulletin du CIETA* 77 (2000): 45–56.

Schuffels, Hans Jakob. "*Aulicus scriba doctus*: Bernward in der Königskanzlei." In Brandt and Eggebrecht, *Bernward und das Zeitalter*, 2:247–54.

Schulz-Mons, Christoph. *Das Michaeliskloster in Hildesheim: Untersuchungen zur Gründung durch Bischof Bernward 993–1022*. 2 vols. Quellen und Dokumentationen zur Stadtgeschichte Hildesheims 20. Hildesheim: Gerstenberg, 2010.

Schütz, Bernhard. "Zum ursprünglichen Anbringungsort der Bronzetür Bischof Bernwards von Hildesheim." *Zeitschrift für Kunstgeschichte* 57 (1994): 569–99.

Schwalbach, Ulrich. *Firmung und religiöse Sozialisation*. Innsbrucker theologische Studien 3. Innsbruck: Tyrolia-Verlag, 1979.

Sears, Elizabeth. "The Iconography of Auditory Perception in the Early Middle Ages: On Psalm Illustration and Psalm Exegesis." In *The Second Sense: Studies in Hearing and Musical Judgment from Antiquity to the Seventeenth Century*, edited by Charles Burnett, 19–38. London: The Warburg Institute, 1991.

Seiters, Julius. "Die Domschule zu Hildesheim im Mittelalter." *Die Diözese Hildesheim in Vergangenheit und Gegenwart* 69 (2001): 21–62.

Sheingorn, Pamela. *Book of Sainte Foy*. Philadelphia: University of Pennsylvania Press, 1995.

Shrader, Charles R. "The False Attribution of an Eucharistic Tract to Gerbert of Aurillac." *Mediaeval Studies* 35 (1973): 178–204.

Simson, Otto G. von. *Sacred Fortress: Byzantine Art and Statecraft in Ravenna*. Chicago: University of Chicago Press, 1948.

Skubiszewski, Piotr. "L'intellectuel et l'artiste face à l'oeuvre à l'époque qui peint." In *Le travail au Moyen Âge: Une approche interdisciplinaire: Actes du Colloque international de Louvain-la-Neuve, 21–23 mai 1987*, edited by Jacqueline Hamesse et Colette Muraille-Samaran, 263–321. Louvain-la-Neuve: Institut d'études médiévales de l'Université catholique de Louvain, 1990.

———. "Le titre de 'Roi de gloire' et les images du Christ: Un concept théologique, l'iconographie et les inscriptions." In *Épigraphie et iconographie: Actes du Colloque tenu à Poitiers les 5–8 octobre 1995*, edited by Robert Favreau, 229–58. Poitiers: Université de Poitiers, Centre national de la recherche scientifique, Centre d'études supérieures de civilisation médiévale, 1996.

Smith, E. Baldwin. *Architectural Symbolism of Imperial Rome and the Middle Ages*. Princeton: Princeton University Press, 1956.

Somfai, Anna. "The Eleventh-Century Shift in the Reception of Plato's *Timaeus* and Calcidius' *Commentary*." *Journal of the Warburg and Courtauld Institutes* 65 (2002): 1–21.

Sporbeck, Gudrun. "Die liturgischen Gewänder im Mittelalter: Paramente und Reliquienkult nach Ausweis kölnischer Grabornate und Textilien des 11. Jahrhunderts." In *Kunst und Liturgie im Mittelalter: Akten des internationalen Kongresses der Bibliotheca Hertziana und des Nederlands Instituut te Rome, Rom, 28.–30. September 1997*, edited by Nicolas Bock, 191–204. Munich: Hirmer, 2000.

Stähli, Marlis. *Die Handschriften im Domschatz zu Hildesheim*. Edited by Helmar Härtel. Wiesbaden: In Kommission bei O. Harrassowitz, 1984.

Stamm-Saurma, Lieselotte E. "Die 'auctoritas' des Zitates in der bernwardinischen Kunst." In *Bernwardinische Kunst: Bericht*, 137–54.

Steenbock, Frauke. *Der kirchliche Prachteinband im frühen Mittelalter: Von den Anfängen bis zum Beginn der Gotik*. Berlin: Deutscher Verlag für Kunstwissenschaft, 1965.

Stegmüller, Friedrich. *Repertorium Biblicum Medii Aevi*. Vol. 1, *Initia Biblica. Apocrypha. Prologi*.

Madrid: Consejo Superior de Investigaciones Científicas, 1950.

Steinen, Wolfram von. "Bernward von Hildesheim über sich selbst." *Deutsches Archiv für Erforschung des Mittelalters* 12 (1956): 331–62.

Stewart, Susan. *On Longing: Narratives of the Miniature, the Gigantic, the Souvenir, the Collection.* Baltimore: Johns Hopkins University Press, 1984.

Stiegemann, Christoph, and Martin Kroker, eds. *Für Königtum und Himmelreich: 1000 Jahre Bischof Meinwerk von Paderborn.* Regensburg: Schnell & Steiner, 2009.

Stratford, Neil, Pamela Tudor-Craig, and Anna M. Muthesius. "Archbishop Hubert Walter's Tomb and Its Furnishings." In *Medieval Art and Architecture at Canterbury Before 1220,* 20–26. London: British Archaeological Association, 1982.

Stumpf, Marcus. "Zum Quellenwert von Thangmars Vita Bernwardi." *Deutsches Archiv für Erforschung des Mittelalters* 53 (1997): 461–96.

Swarzenski, Georg. *Die Regensburger Buchmalerei des X. und XI. Jahrhunderts: Studien zur Geschichte der deutschen Malerei des frühen Mittelalters.* Leipzig: Hiersemann, 1900.

Swarzenski, Hans. "The Role of Copies in the Formation of the Styles of the Eleventh Century." In *Romanesque and Gothic Art,* 7–18. Studies in Western Art 1. Princeton: Princeton University Press, 1963.

Tallone, Uta Appel. *Das Arnulfziborium in der Schatzkammer der Münchener Residenz: Eine monographische Untersuchung.* Herne: Verlag für Wissenschaft und Kunst, 2003.

Teteriatnikov, Natalia. "The 'Gift Giving' Image: The Case of the Adoration of the Magi." *Visual Resources* 13 (1998): 381–91.

Teuscher, Ulrich. "Das ikonologische Programm der Grabanlage Bernwards." In *Bernward und Godehard von Hildesheim: Ihr Leben und Wirken,* edited by Konrad Algermissen, 202–15. Hildesheim: Lax, 1960.

Teviotdale, Elizabeth C. "The Pictorial Program of the Stammheim Missal." In *Objects, Images, and the Word: Art in the Service of the Liturgy,* edited by Colum Hourihane, 79–93. Princeton: Index of Christian Art, Dept. of Art and Archaeology, Princeton University in association with Princeton University Press, 2003.

———. *The Stammheim Missal.* Los Angeles: Getty Museum, 2001.

Tirot, Paul. "Histoire des prières d'offertoire dans la liturgie romaine du VIIe au XVIe siècle." *Ephemerides liturgicae* 98 (1984): 148–97.

Trilling, James. *The Medallion Style: A Study in the Origins of Byzantine Taste.* New York: Garland, 1985.

Tronzo, William. "The Hildesheim Doors: An Iconographic Source and Its Implications." *Zeitschrift für Kunstgeschichte* 46 (1983): 357–66.

Tschan, Francis, J. *Saint Bernward of Hildesheim.* 3 vols. Notre Dame: University of Notre Dame, 1942–52.

Underwood, Paul A. "The Fountain of Life in Manuscripts of the Gospels." *Dumbarton Oaks Papers* 5 (1950): 43–138.

Untermann, Matthias. "St. Michael und die Sakralarchitektur um 1000. Forschungsstand und Perspectiven." In Lutz and Weyer, *1000 Jahre St. Michael in Hildesheim,* 41–65.

Vasiliu, Anke. "Le mot et le verre: Une définition médiévale du Diaphane." *Journal des savants* 1 (1994): 135–62.

Verdier, Philippe. *Le couronnement de la Vierge: Les origines et les premiers développements d'un thème iconographique.* Paris: Vrin, 1980.

Verzar, Christine B. "Picturing Matilda of Canossa: Medieval Strategies of Representation." In *Representing History, 900–1300: Art, Music, History,* edited by Robert A. Maxwell, 73–90. University Park: The Pennsylvania State University Press, 2010.

Vikan, Gary. "Pilgrims in Magi's Clothing: The Impact of Mimesis on Early Byzantine Pilgrimage Art." In *The Blessings of Pilgrimage,* edited by Robert Ousterhout, 97–107. Urbana: University of Illinois Press, 1990.

Vogel, Cyrille. *Medieval Liturgy: An Introduction to the Sources.* Revised and translated by William G.

Storey and Niels Krogh Rasmussen, with the assistance of John K. Brooks-Leonard. Washington, D.C.: Pastoral Press, 1986.

Wagner, Stephen. "Silken Parchments: Design, Context, Patronage, and Function of Textile-Inspired Pages in Ottonian and Salian Manuscripts." Ph.D. diss., University of Delaware, 2004.

Walker, Robert M. "Illustrations to the Priscillian Prologues in the Gospel Manuscripts of the Carolingian Ada School." *Art Bulletin* 30 (1948): 1–10.

Ward, Benedicta. *Miracles and the Medieval Mind.* Revised edition. Philadelphia: University of Pennsylvania Press, 1987.

Warner, David A. *Ottonian Germany: The Chronicon of Thietmar of Merseburg.* Manchester: Manchester University Press, 2001.

———. "Thietmar of Merseburg: The Image of the Ottonian Bishop." In Frassetto, *The Year 1000,* 85–110.

Warners, Egon. "Ok Dani gaerdi kristna: Der grosse Jellingstein im Spiegel ottonischer Kunst." *Frühmittelalterliche Studien* 34 (2000): 132–58.

Webb, Chris. "Greek, Roman, Hebrew, and Byzantine Interpretations of Light and Its Origins." *Greek Orthodox Theological Review* 54 (2009): 155–67.

Weilandt, Gerhard. *Geistliche und Kunst: Ein Beitrag zur Kultur der ottonisch-salischen Reichskirche und zur Veränderung künstlerischer Traditionen im späten 11. Jahrhundert.* Cologne: Böhlau, 1992.

Weitzmann, Kurt. "*Loca Sancta* and the Representational Arts of Palestine." *Dumbarton Oaks Papers* 28 (1974): 36–39.

Weitzmann-Fiedler, Josepha. "Ein Evangelientyp mit Aposteln als Begleitfiguren." In *Adolph Goldschmidt zu seinem siebensigsten Geburtstag am 15. Januar 1933,* 30–34. Berlin: Würfel Verlag, 1935.

Wesenberg, Rudolf. *Bernwardinische Plastik: Zur ottonischen Kunst unter Bischof Bernward von Hildesheim.* Berlin: Deutscher Verein für Kunstwissenschaft, 1955.

Westerhoff, Ingrid. "Der moralisierte Judas: Mittelalterliche Legende, Typologie, Allegorie im Bild." *Aachener Kunstblätter* 61 (1995): 85–156.

Wharton, Annabel J. "Ritual and Reconstructed Meaning: The Neonian Baptistery in Ravenna." *Art Bulletin* 69 (1987): 358–75.

Wibald, abbé de Stavelot-Malmédy et de Corvey (1130–1158: Catalogue). Stavelot: Musée de l'ancienne Abbaye, 1982.

Wilmart, André. "Prières médiévales pour l'adoration de la croix." *Ephemerides liturgicae* 46 (1932): 22–65.

Wilson, Katharina M. *Hrotsvit of Gandersheim: A Florilegium of Her Works.* Library of Medieval Women 7. Rochester, N.Y.: D. S. Brewer, 1998.

Winden, J. C. M. van. *Calcidius on Matter: His Doctrine and Sources; A Chapter in the History of Platonism.* Leiden: Brill, 1959.

Wirth, Jean. *La datation de la sculpture médiévale.* Geneva: Droz, 2004.

Wirth, Karl-August. "Die Nachrichten über Begräbnis und Grab Bischof Bernwards von Hildesheim in Thangmars Vita Bernwardi." *Zeitschrift für Kunstgeschichte* 22 (1959): 305–23.

Wood, Nancy. "Memory's Remains: *Les lieux de mémoire.*" *History and Memory* 6 (1994): 123–49.

Wulf, Christine. "Bernward von Hildesheim, ein Bischof auf dem Weg zur Heiligkeit." *Concilium medii aevi* 11 (2008): 1–19. http://cma.gbv.de/dr.cma.011.2008.a.01.pdf.

Wulf, Christine, and Hans Jürgen Rieckenberg. *Die Inschriften der Stadt Hildesheim.* 2 vols. Die Deutschen Inschriften 58. Wiesbaden: Reichert, 2003.

Yates, Frances. *The Art of Memory.* Chicago: University of Chicago Press, 1966.

Young, Karl. *The Drama of the Medieval Church.* 2 vols. Oxford: Clarendon Press, 1933.

Zeh, Ernst. "Johannes Evangelist im Priestergewand: Eine ikonographische Vorstudie." *Jahrbuch für das Bistum Mainz* 6 (1951–54): 254–65.

INDEX